Rebels and Reformers
of the Airways

▶▶▶▶▶▶▶▶▶▶▶▶▶▶◀▶▶▶▶▶▶

Rebels and

Reformers

of the Airways

R. E. G. Davies

Smithsonian Institution Press
Washington, D.C.   London

Books by R.E.G. Davies

A History of the World's Airlines
Airlines of the United States since 1914
Airlines of Latin America since 1919
Continental Airlines—the First 50 Years

Library of Congress Cataloging-in-Publication Data

Davies, R. E. G. (Ronald Edward George)
Rebels and Reformers of the Airways

  Bibliography: p.
  Includes index.
  1. Aeronautics, Commercial—History, 2. Air
lines—History. 3. Aeronautics, Commercial—
Biography.
  I. Title.
HE9775.D38 1987   387.7'092'2   86-26243
ISBN 0-87474-354-0

British Library Cataloging-in-Publication Data
available

∞ The paper used in this publication meets the
minimum requirements of the American National
Standard for Performance of Paper for Printed
Library Materials Z39.48—1984.

Edited by David Howell-Jones
Designed by Linda McKnight

▶▶▶▶▶▶▶▶▶▶▶▶▶▶▶▶▶▶▶▶▶▶▶▶▶▶

Contents

Foreword   vii

Preface   xi

Acknowledgments   xv

The United States

Walter T. Varney (1888–1967): Man of Many Parts   3

Ralph O'Neill (1896–1980): Flying Down to Rio   15

Robert Six (1907–1986): The Maverick   31

Howard Hughes (1905–1976): The Phenomenon   47

James H. Carmichael (1907–1983): Coach Fares and
*   Turbine Power*   65

Stanley D. Weiss (b.1910): First with Air Coach   83

Orvis Nelson (1907–1976): Mr. Transocean   101

Edward Daly (1922–1984): Himself   119

Frank Lorenzo (b.1940): Man of Destiny   137

Donald C. Burr (b.1941): The People's Airline   153

Canada

Grant McConachie (1900–1965): A Man of His Time   169

Maxwell Ward (b.1921): Bush Service to Royal Doulton   187

The United Kingdom

Edward Hillman (1890–1934): The Cockney Sparrow   205

Captain Edmund E. Fresson (1891–1963): The Honorary
*   Orcadian*   215

Eric L. Gandar Dower (b.1895):   Actor Turned Airman   229

Sir Freddie Laker (b.1922):   The One and Only   241

Sir Adam Thomson (b.1926):   Flying Scotsman   259

Europe

*Marcel Bouilloux-Lafont (1871–1944):   The Shattered
    Dream*   283

Alfred Eliasson (b.1920):   Airline of the Sixth Happiness   299

Latin America

Lowell Yerex (1895–1968):   The Living Legend   317

C. N. Shelton (1908–1965):   The Barefoot Airline   333

Omar Fontana (b.1927):   O Cavalheiro Gigante   345

Asia

*His Highness the Prince Varanand (b.1922):   Prince to
    Pauper*   363

Australia

Ray Parer (1898–1967):   The Battler from Bulolo   383

Sir Reginald Ansett (1909–1981):   "R.M."   399

Bibliography   413

Index   417

▶▶▶▶▶▶▶▶▶▶▶▶▶▶▶▶▶▶▶▶▶▶▶▶▶▶▶

Foreword

While early birds inspired the dream of men and women actually flying through the air, the nearly infinite capacity of the airspace burst upon us only yesterday. In a couple of generations, we went from goggled visionaries and daredevils to jets, to the moon, and upward into the universe.

To fly at all was the first miracle—a miracle that had to wait for the bicyclists and eyeshade metallurgists—and it attracted a colorful following, often as not, adventurers, explorers, and wealthy sportsmen. But then flying lost its appeal as a miracle and interest shifted to what flying—aviation—might accomplish.

Military potential developed with astounding speed, thrusting along in its wake commercial use, starting with the mail. Carrying passengers was the next step, and it all happened so fast—from miracle to a search for uses to the earliest commercial application—that the kind of men who dared fly at all, who were exhilarated by the beauty and excitement of flight, who lived to fly, were those leading the way, about half a generation away from what has become the airline industry.

But the human generations would span several industry generations at the speed aviation was moving and there was always a heavy transfer of the courage, independence, vision, and dedication to the art and science of flying from the old times to the new era. Objectivity requires that mulishness be added. The early birds of the airline industry were in this way an adolescent lot, reflecting their not-so-ancient aviation heritage.

True to its past, the airline industry continued to change rapidly, and its leaders became men who could grapple successfully with the problems of their time—always weather and safety, now finance, sophisticated management, the hurdles and hazards of national and international regulation among them. Flying had become the more routine part of the business.

R. E. G. Davies has produced in *Rebels and Reformers of the Airways* a faithful and readable chronicle of what his selection of some of the leaders of the airline industry—early and modern—have contributed. In the process he relates the technical development of the industry in an engaging way. Whether the title describes best his good work is a question, though it has a nice alliterative ring to it, and perhaps it embraces many of the more inspired creators, crusaders, and culprits who forced an acceleration of growth, rather than merely the maintenance of the accepted rate. And the revolutions—large and small—continue apace as we see in Donald Burr, of People Express airline, whose revolutions per minute most recently oversped his return on investment.

Mr. Davies contributes to the airline story in another way, too. He devotes appreciative attention to what industry leaders in other than the U.S. countries, from all over the world, have contributed and from the very beginning. Parochial Americans, with our great appreciation of the Wright brothers and their first flight at Kitty Hawk in 1903, sometimes forget that aviation was just as important and perhaps even more advanced in many other countries, despite the Wrights' triumph. Certainly aviation was a long way ahead of us in Europe during World War I. European regulatory practices were ahead of ours both before and after World War I. We did not even have pilots' licenses until 1925, when demand from the industry forced issuance of the first regulations.

While it is not a popular idea, the government has contributed in many ways to the growth and success of our airline industry besides issuing pilots' licenses, and much the same can be said of the regulatory bodies in the United Kingdom, Continental Europe, Canada, and Australia.

The original demand for action by the U.S. government came in 1925, when it became clear to the barnstormers that there was no future in aviation unless people had confidence in the pilots, the airplanes, and the procedures by which they flew. Until then, much of civil aviation was regarded as sport and a matter of personal awareness, like mountain climbing. Not that the rebels and reformers saw more lift than drag in the rules. Rather, like taxes, they were to be ingeniously avoided if not blatantly evaded.

It is sometimes said that the U.S. airline industry is the most heavily regulated industry in the history of the world. Perhaps that is true—it is an enormously complex and competitive industry—but statistics make it clear that it is also one of the safest. Without that established in the public mind, there would not have been the astounding growth we have seen. The number of regulations is not a problem; it is whether they are relevant, openly and fairly established, and whether they can be changed or dropped in an orderly, responsible way. Our federal air regulations have those characteristics, I believe, and I say that having been on both sides of the table.

Success of our airlines has also depended on our air traffic control systems—often criticized but the best and most modern in the world, handling a volume and velocity of traffic unknown in any other industry. But the statistical record is phenomenally good, a record that must be borne in mind when equipment, procedures, and arrangements by management to expand its capacity are being considered.

This is not to deny the rebels and reformers their place in the scheme of things. Their spirit of individuality, sometimes even obstinacy, has been a vital element—as in our political system—which has ensured the proper ingredient of checks and balances that are the essence of democracy. These protect us from the worst excesses of bureaucracy. Those who qualify for this delicately balanced role often start as rebels, are later regarded as reformers, and occasionally end up being respected as innovative pioneers. Their stories deserve to be told, and Mr. Davies has made a notable contribution to this objective.

The airlines are certainly that part of the American aviation system with which most people are most familiar. But they are just part, just one of the users. The military and general aviation also have a place.

Besides the users—the exploiters of the airspace—there are the bureaucrats, God bless them, the regulators, the air traffic controllers, the airport people, technicians who keep the radar going, and the administrative people to support them. Altogether it is our international aviation system—totally interdependent and, despite some failures, wonderfully successful.

There have been many books about leaders of great airlines—Juan Trippe, Eddie Rickenbacker, and the Dutchman Dr. Plesman spring to mind—and many more about the great airlines themselves. They made up the upper echelon of the world's air transport industry as it moved from infancy through adolescence to maturity. Mr. Davies, who has addressed the wider subject in other books, offers us here the other, little-known side of the picture. He tells of those who, victims all too often of their own exuberant overconfidence, sometimes fell by the wayside but left something of value behind them.

It has been my privilege to be a military pilot, a test pilot, an airline executive, administrator of the Federal Aviation Administration, and now a general aviation pilot—a privilege because I have been able to fly for the last fifty-four years and a privilege to know at first hand and thereby to appreciate each of the elements in our integrated international aviation system.

The airline pioneers and later leaders—rebels and reformers as well as the pillars of the Establishment—are a vital part of the aviation success story in the United States. I know that their counterparts in other countries of the world made a contribution of equal importance. Mr. Davies's book is a fine tribute to them, and through them, to the airline industry of the world.

NAJEEB B. HALABY

Washington, D.C.
January 1987

▶▶▶▶▶▶▶▶▶▶▶▶▶▶▶▶▶▶▶▶▶▶▶▶▶▶

Preface

The most difficult decision to make in writing this book was to choose the title. In the main, the characters portrayed were and are men who have conducted their affairs against the mainstream of their chosen business environment. Many have been shamefully ignored, even ostracized, by former associates and have often been relegated to historical obscurity. But this was not the issue in searching for the *mots justes* to describe the general nature of their collective personalities.

Many evocative words suggested themselves. Were they outlaws, buccaneers, renegades? Not exactly, for although they challenged the law, they did not systematically break it, at least not much. Were they dissenters, dissidents, nonconformists perhaps? Well, yes, but in most instances these descriptions were not emphatic enough. Cavaliers, free spirits? Too mild. Pacesetters, outsiders, independents? The list went on.

The problem was to find a synthesis of the qualities of independence, individuality, vision, courage, defiance, and obstinacy, ranging from determined protest to sheer pigheadedness, which enabled these men to help change the course of an industry, in its scope and direction of influence, in its rate of growth, and most of all in its sense of purpose.

I concluded eventually that the members of this special breed were either rebels or reformers, or they were both. By a combination of intuition, intention, or circumstantial accident, they have challenged and changed the entrenched order of the airline hierarchy. Believing intensely in certain principles, they tested them in the pitiless arena of commerce. They proved that the Establishment, whether shielded internationally by a price-fixing cartel or protected domestically by a trade association or a complacent bureaucracy, was usually wrong.

In many ways they were true pioneers, but not in the same sense as the original founders of air transport. This later type of innovator, questioning the tenets of an evolving system, broke new ground or, to use a more apt metaphor, explored uncharted air.

By the late 1920s, the airlines had emerged from the embryo stage. Some had grown to become large companies, accepting government regulation as a necessary evil—necessary because they needed subsidy to remain viable, evil because those who paid the piper often ignored justice in calling the tune. But as the benefits of science, experience, and technology became more widespread, fresh minds and intellects began to question commercial practices that had been accepted as gospel. Ultimately these rebels and reformers challenged convention, and in so doing they changed the course of airline history.

This exclusive fraternity of airline leaders does not include such men as Juan Trippe of Pan American and C. R. Smith of American Airlines, fine administrators though they were. These strong personalities presided over airline empires that became synonymous with the established system. They were instrumental in creating it, they were an integral part of it, and in some instances—not entirely without self-interest—they helped to frame its laws. Represented in the corridors of power in Washington, London, or Ottawa, as were their international counterparts in Geneva, they were conditioned to preserve the status quo at the expense of progress.

Several highly independent men, however, did not agree with the dead hands of the government agencies in Washington, IATA in Geneva, or state control in other countries. From the air route across the English Channel, flown only by a privileged few, to the jungles of Central America and New Guinea, bypassed by mainline operators, these cavaliers began to snap at the heels of the chosen instruments of economic empires.

Twenty-five of these standard-bearers of free enterprise have been selected. Their airline careers are reported strictly in their historical context. This is not a book about Howard Hughes's girl friends, Bob Six's prowess with pistols, or Sir Freddie Laker's yachts and racehorses. Nevertheless, the anecdote-punctuated accounts support the familiar assertion that truth is stranger than fiction. Such anecdotes have been verified as historically accurate, illustrating the characters of the subject profiles as much as the dates and facts put them into true perspective.

Almost half the people in this book are from North America. Seven Europeans include five from the United Kingdom, two of whom were knighted by the Queen for their efforts. One Frenchman suffered grave injustice from his countrymen and country before and after his death. An Icelander did more than all the great flag carriers put together to bring transatlantic travel within the reach of the common man. Half a dozen at least ran afoul of Juan Trippe. Elsewhere, two belligerent Australians, including another Knight of the Realm, a swashbuckling Brazilian, a gallant Siamese prince, and a one-eyed New Zealander complete the list.

They did not all succeed. Some went from the traditional rags to riches. Some went from riches to more riches. Others lost their shirts. Howard Hughes sold his airline, in twenty minutes, for half a billion dollars. Prince Varanand lost a very large fortune. But rich or poor, victorious or defeated, they all passionately believed in a common cause, translated their convictions into action, and campaigned against long odds, to leave an indelible mark on the world of air transport.

Because of them, an airline passenger can cross the United States today for $99.00, or the Atlantic for $140.00, and fly to every remote corner of the world. Without them, the growth of world air traffic would have been inhibited by high tariffs imposed by rate-fixers. Routes would have been dictated by an elitist oligarchy, and the entire stature of a great industry would have been diminished by restrictive practices on the flight deck, on the shop floor, and in the boardrooms.

The course of airline development, and indeed of world history itself, has been steered at least as much by the extraordinary people whose stories are told in this book as by politicians and financiers. They broke the rules, kicked over the traces, and fought for the Freedom of the Skies. They bestowed the privilege of air travel upon peasants as well as politicians, upon coalminers as well as congressmen, upon shopgirls as well as senators. These rebels and reformers brought air travel to the Common Man.

I am deeply indebted to David Howell-Jones, who diligently and patiently subjected the manuscript to fearsome scrutiny, graciously conceded to some of my idiosyncracies, removed the worst of my clichés, and saved me from many an example of that most heinous literary crime, the hanging participle.

R. E. G. DAVIES

Washington, D.C.
December 1986

▶▶▶ ▶

Acknowledgments

In a book such as this, an author has to rely on a great variety of sources and source material. Copious reading of books, both historical and biographical; endless perusal of magazines; searching of library files: these are the normal chores that are the lot of any serious researcher. In addition to the bare bones of the life stories of the profiled personalities, however, much more was needed in the effort to flesh out the bones and add the spark of life to the skeleton of facts and figures.

I have been extremely fortunate in meeting many people who have been most generous in sharing their thoughts, their opinions, even their hearts with me. Many of these are relatives of men who are either dead or are too ill to be interviewed, and I am especially indebted to Edith Nelson, Jane O'Neill, Jessie Carmichael, and June Daly. Richard Fresson and Allan Weiss, not forgetting the Carmichael girls, spoke for their fathers, as did David Yerex for his uncle, and Guillemette de Bure for her grandfather.

Many of the subject profiles, of course, spoke for themselves, and I thank Sir Adam Thomson, Sir Freddie Laker, Frank Lorenzo, Omar Fontana, and the Prince Varanand for their patience. I must not forget the many friends—and for most of the people in this book these are legion. Sir Peter Masefield (who even knew Edward Hillman), John Stroud, Captain Eric Starling, Captain Ed Heering, Robert Beckman, and Bill Connors have been extremely helpful. I must acknowledge, too, the writings of Phil Schleit, Bob Serling, Barrett Tillman, Niels Lumholdt, and Terry Gwynn-Jones, among many others.

To make or renew the acquaintance of these fine people has

been one of the privileges granted me in writing *Rebels and Reformers of the Airways,* and I hope they will derive as much pleasure in reading the results as I have had in compiling this contribution to the annals of airline history.

R. E. G. DAVIES

▶▶▶▶▶▶▶▶▶▶▶▶▶▶▶▶▶

The United States

▶▶▶▶▶▶▶▶▶▶▶▶◀▶▶▶▶▶

Walter T. Varney

Man of Many Parts

Some of the personalities in this book would perhaps qualify more as pioneers than as rebels or reformers. The latter two epithets imply that there is something to rebel against or some institution that needs reforming. Some of the pioneers of air transport were indeed breaking new frontiers of aviation achievement, so the terminology is arguably inappropriate. Walter Varney, however, as all those who knew him would confirm, was a man out of time, for his actions were rebellious and reformative in their application and in their effect. Varney created his own imaginary Establishment against which to rebel, and in pursuing his various campaigns, he was a true free spirit in what was to become, in his time, a closely guarded and regulated industry that badly needed reform.

Walter Varney was born in San Francisco, on December 26, 1888, the son of Thomas and Ella Varney. Tom Varney was a wealthy billboard advertiser, who apparently encouraged his son both spiritually and financially, so Walter had a fair start in life. He quickly became enamored of aviation and joined the Army Air Service toward the end of the Great War, although he did not see service overseas.

When the war was over, he immediately established a flying school at San Carlos, in the Bay Area, with financial assistance from his father, then moved to San Mateo, where he obtained the northern California sales agency for Swallow Aircraft. By 1920 he was doing business in conjunction with the Checker Cab Company, with charter flights and freight haulage, and this led to his forming the Checker Air Service in 1921.

3

After a couple of years of such aviation activity, Varney made his first attempt to enter the air mail business. He dispatched his chief pilot, Leon Cuddeback, to Nicaragua in 1924, to start an airline, but after a few months, the expected contract with the government did not materialize, and Cuddeback returned.

The pilot was to have his chance to make his mark in air mail history soon afterward. With the passage of the Kelly Air Mail Act, the U.S. Post Office announced a number of routes for competitive bidding on July 15, 1925, having decided that the success of the air mail business was becoming too big to handle itself. Contract Route 5 (CAM 5) covered 460 miles of rugged territory between Pasco, Washington, and Elko, Nevada, via Boise, Idaho.

Varney was one of the few people in the entire United States who realized the potential of this route, which, to most observers of the map, seemed to link two places of small size and little significance. But Pasco was a key point for several northern transcontinental rail networks, roughly equidistant from the main cities of the Northwest, Seattle, Tacoma, Portland, and Spokane. Elko was the nearest point on the existing Post Office transcontinental trunk mail route, and any other such route was as yet only a distant prospect. The Pasco-Elko connection was thus the vital air mail link for the Pacific Northwest, and for western Canada and Alaska, not to mention transpacific shipping connections.

(An interesting commentary on Varney's decision is that he did it again in 1934, when the air mail contracts were reopened for bidding after the 1934 Air Mail Scandal, starting another route which nobody seemed to want, but which survived to become the Continental Airlines of today.)

Walter Varney was the successful bidder for CAM 5 and took the logical step of putting to use the Swallow aircraft with which he was already familiar with the Checker Air Service. Varney and Cuddeback surveyed the route and decided that the Swallows would need "high-lift" wings and 150-horsepower Curtiss K6 engines. The cities of Pasco and Boise supported the venture by providing ground installations, including hangars, while Walter's father helped purchase the six new Swallows. The Post Office had already provided all the installations needed at Elko, a stop on its old trunk route.

Varney Air Lines opened its air mail service in great style, and Leon Cuddeback—in keeping with the hero worship that most pi-

Walter Varney, with Mrs. Varney to his right, stands in front of the Swallow biplane with which Varney Air Lines began its first service from Pasco to Elko on April 6, 1926. Chief Pilot Leon Cuddeback, in flying boots, is on the right. Today's United Air Lines traces its history from this event.

lots attracted in the early days of aviation—became a local celebrity. He inaugurated the Pasco-Boise-Elko air mail service on April 6, 1926. Boise sent a sack of Idaho potatoes addressed to President Coolidge, but the prize for stylish promotion had to go to Pasco, where a number of local dignitaries attended what had become a festive occasion. The crowd at the Pasco airfield were entertained by the arrival of a stage coach from Spokane, 307 miles away, driven by one Felix Warren, described as "a colorful character of 1861."

This was not, as has been sometimes claimed, the first of the contract air mail routes to start service; that honor went to the Ford Motor Company, which already had services in operation between Chicago and Detroit. Also, Varney Air Lines came close to being stillborn. The northbound air mail on April 6 arrived by surface, with the Swallow stuck in the mud, off course, near the Idaho state line. The inadequacy of the Curtiss engines had quickly become evident, and Varney prudently asked for a sixty-day suspension, so as to re-engine the Swallows with 200-horsepower Wright Whirlwind engines. This accomplished, operations were successfully resumed on June 6, 1926.

Varney's pilots were well paid, and this was made possible by the volume of mail carried, combined with the mail rate paid, 80 percent of the maximum. It was typical of Varney that he conceived the Air-O-Gram, a regularly published advertising document that weighed exactly one ounce. It provided information about the air mail service, Varney's in particular, and was dispatched in such quantities that the post office employees at Boise were promoted because they had made record sales of air mail stamps.

There is a story that Varney employees used to send bricks to each other, neatly parceled, to provide healthy air mail payments, and the practice was only stopped when a new employee innocently left off the paper in which the brick was wrapped. The story is apocryphal, but if any of those early air mail contractors could have done it, that man was Walter Varney.

The pilots earned their keep. The flying conditions were atrocious, the mountains of northern Nevada and the cloud formations producing a phenomenon known to the pilots as "cumulo-granite," when peaks had a habit of hiding themselves behind the mists. For use in dirty weather or occasional night landings at Pasco, Varney devised portable spotlights mounted on a small trailer behind a Model T. Sadly, the conditions took their toll. Within two years, three Varney pilots had lost their lives. Such was their fame in the Northwest that one of the tragedies did not need explanation; the headline simply announced "Harold Buckner Missing."

Right from the start, however, in spite of these setbacks, Varney Air Lines did well enough. On October 1, 1926, it moved the southern terminus to the larger hub of Salt Lake City, then the transcontinental junction for routes from San Francisco and Los Angeles. After trying out a Breese biplane, Varney bought six Stearman C3B aircraft to replace the ailing Swallows. In 1928, air mail revenue amounted to $400,000, and, expecting even larger business the following year, he ordered six more Stearmans, Model M2, larger and faster than the earlier model.

On March 12, 1929, Varney Air Lines acquired a new dimension when it was incorporated under the laws of Delaware. The Corporation Commission of California authorized the sale of 100,000 shares, some of which were taken up by representatives of the Keys North American Aviation group, which already controlled Transcontinental Air Transport (T.A.T.) and Maddux Air Lines. On June 15 of the same year, the Post Office invited bids for Route 32, linking Spokane with Portland, via Pasco, and Portland with Seattle and Tacoma. Varney's contiguous operation made him in effect an incumbent, but he wisely submitted a bid that allowed for only the marginally increased cost of extending his existing route. Other bidders might have underbid him but would have had to set up a new organization. In the event, bad weather on CAM Route 32 depressed traffic during the early months after inauguration on September 15, 1929, but Varney was comforted by $700,000 in revenue in that year from CAM 5.

The injection of fresh capital permitted the upgrading of the equipment, and the first Boeing Type 40B-4 passenger-carrying biplanes entered service late in 1929. This was the first time that Varney had offered passenger service on its routes. Altogether, Varney was to acquire thirteen of the Boeing aircraft, more than any other airline.

On June 30, 1930, the United Aircraft Corporation purchased Varney Air Lines for $2,000,000, and the line became known as the Varney Division of the United Air Lines group. His former check pilot in the army, Louis H. Mueller, was on hand to advise him to raise the stakes, and United fought off a challenge from Clarence M. Keys, bidding for the North American group. Louis Mueller was later to be Varney's partner in another airline venture. On September 30, 1933, Varney lost its identity altogether, when it was absorbed completely into Boeing Air Transport, the inheritor of the Post Office Chicago–San Francisco route and the primary component of the embryo United Air Lines.

Within four short years, Varney Air Lines had epitomized the transformation of air transport in the United States, from cautious experiment, hazardous flying, and an uncertain future, to become an element of a nationwide corporation, destined to be a leader in the development of a giant air transport industry.

An interesting sidelight on Varney's sale to United and consequent affluence is that he turned down an offer from Robert Gross, of Lockheed, to buy 50 percent of Lockheed stock. Varney actually lent $20,000 to Gross but declined to accept an offer that would have changed his whole life. But Walter Varney had his heart in airline operation and had cherished the ambition to develop an airline network throughout the western United States, embracing particularly the growing affluence of California, which was showing signs of becoming a cornucopia of wealth for any reasonably successful entrepreneur.

He kept his hand in by establishing, late in 1930, an air parcel and passenger service between Oakland (Alameda Airport), Sacramento, and Marysville, using a Stinson monoplane. The connection across the Bay to San Francisco, as yet without a bridge, was made by Air Ferries, Ltd., started by Vern Gorst, a man after Varney's own heart, who had founded an airline, Pacific Air Transport, and had also, like Varney, been engulfed by the United Aircraft group.

Eager to put his capital to use on a more glamorous operation than a parcel service to Marysville, he joined forces with Franklin Rose, a former Varney pilot who had gone into business for himself in San Francisco. Armed with $100,000 of Varney's money, Rose purchased six Lockheed Orions—Varney always bought aircraft in six-packs. The full name of the company was Varney Speed Lines Air Service, Ltd., but was generally known as Varney Speed Lines. Curiously, some Orions carried the inscription Varney Speed Lanes.

Varney Speed Lines began service between Alameda, serving the Bay Area, and Glendale, serving the Los Angeles Basin, on October 15, 1931. The Sacramento route was retained, but the extension to Marysville was dropped. Varney's new venture was nothing if not stylish. The Orions were among the fastest aircraft of their day, and Varney capitalized on this fact, advertising his service as the "Fastest Airline in the World"—which it probably was.

The scheduled time from Alameda to Glendale was 1 hour, 58 minutes, and Varney offered compensation of 10 cents a minute, up to a maximum of $5.00, for late arrival. The fare was $18.95 one way, $34.11 round trip, so this publicity stunt offered a fair rebate for inconvenience. The service was very popular and became something of a status symbol, for almost every star in Hollywood trav-

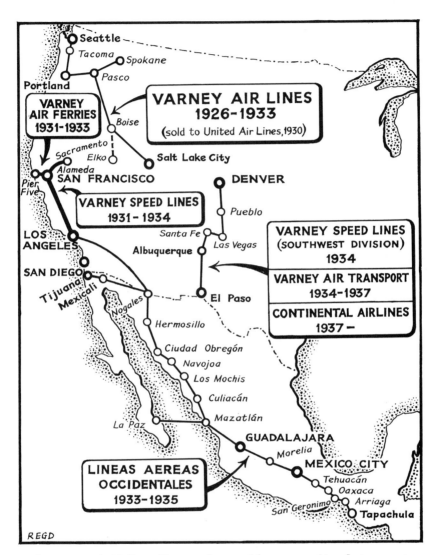

Walter Varney's Airlines. *Varney alternated between making fortunes out of running airlines and losing them. A great opportunist, he took chances with unlikely-looking prospects, only to see them taken over or usurped by others. Two important trunk airlines of today, United and Continental, trace their ancestry back to him.*

eled with Varney at one time or another. Carole Lombard, Mary Pickford, Fay Wray, Douglas Fairbanks, Constance Cummings, Maurice Chevalier, Joe E. Brown: these and many others could be seen—and often photographed—boarding a Varney Orion.

Early in March, Walter Varney purchased the Air Ferries business, doing a roaring trade across the Bay. Vern Gorst had initiated service on February 11, 1930, using Keystone-Loening seven-seat amphibious Air Yachts. He charged $1.50 for the six-minute crossing from Pier 5, at the end of Market Street, in downtown San Francisco, to Alameda Air Terminal, close to downtown Oakland. A special ten-cent taxi service connected the Air Yacht terminals with the business districts at each end. By the summer of 1930, the Air Ferries service had reached the astounding frequency of thirty daily trips each way.

By the time Varney took over in 1932, the frequency had declined, but the service was still operating hourly and connecting at Alameda with all the California Corridor air services to and from the south. Of course, Varney tailored the Air Ferry service to his own special needs. He emphasized that Varney Speed Lines was the only one of the many air services to and from Los Angeles that operated directly to the heart of San Francisco, and his timetables contained a neat pictogram comparing his Air Yacht Orion service in 2 hours 15 minutes, with the ferryboat-taxi-Fokker (no names) service from 3 hours 25 minutes, to 4 hours 15 minutes; alternatively automobile and train were also-rans at 12 hours.

Varney's Bay Area–Los Angeles Orion service was then operating four times a day, and his Sacramento service six times a day. The Air Ferries connecting service charged only $1.00 for Varney passengers, and a special limousine service charged the same price to carry customers from the Los Angeles or Hollywood business centers to the new air terminal at Burbank. The old Loening amphibians had been replaced by three Sikorsky S-39s. Orion Flight 19 made a direct connection at Burbank with the American Airways transcontinental flight to the East (American did not serve San Francisco until the 1950s), and passengers could also make easy transfers to San Diego or Agua Caliente, a resort near Tijuana, Mexico, via Gilpin Airlines.

Never has such an ideal operation been destroyed so completely or so abruptly by a single airliner crash. Other companies have had their dramatic tragedies. The infamous Knute Rockne crash ended Fokker's reputation in America for decades, but not the airline's; the early Comet crashes adversely affected de Havilland far more than they did B.O.A.C.; the DC-10 crash at Chicago hurt Douglas far more than it did American Airlines. But when a Varney Lockheed Orion crashed into a suburban neighborhood at Hayward, in the Bay Area, on March 25, 1933, killing the pilot, two passengers, and twelve residents of the houses that caught fire as a result, it was a complete disaster for Walter Varney, who saw a successful airline, if not his entire livelihood, quite literally go up in flames.

The pilot was exonerated from blame, and truth to tell, the aircraft was severely tested in conditions of low ceiling, poor visibility, and gusty conditions that probably prevailed when the Orion was trying to feel its way toward Alameda that night. But Varney was subjected to heavy damage claims, and he was hard pressed to retain possession of his aircraft. If there was any consolation in the tragedy, it was that no film celebrity happened to be on board, or Walter Varney would have been the victim of worldwide mass hatred.

There has been some suggestion that the name Varney Speed Lanes was adopted as a legal device to prevent the Varney Speed Lines fleet from being impounded by the plaintiffs' lawyers and removed from Varney's control. This is not so, as "Lanes" was already in use, and the name had appeared on literature during the preceding year. But in any event, Varney Speed Lines was finished and had closed down by the summer of 1933.

The ever resourceful Walter Varney tried again, going South of the Border in search of new pastures. Late in 1933, he negotiated a deal with the Mexican government to carry air mail between Mexico and California. Adroitly appointing the son of the president of Mexico as a vice-president, he formed Líneas Aéreas Occidentales, S.A. (L.A.O., translated as Western Air Lines, not to be confused with the U.S. airline of the same name). On April 10, 1934, this new Varney airline inaugurated an ambitious route, utilizing his fleet of one Lockheed Orion and two Lockheed Vegas all the way from Los Angeles to Tapachula, on the Mexico-Guatemala frontier, via the Mexican northwest, Guadalajara, and Mexico City.

Although Varney had a mail contract from the Mexican government, he was to discover that in aviation matters, Pan American Airways was then more powerful than any government. Early in January 1935 Mexico withdrew its twenty-year contract, and a Pan American affiliate in Mexico, Aerovías Centrales (Central Airlines) suddenly began operating in Varney's place.

The dénouement of the short-lived L.A.O. contained the elements of farce. Varney had to fly his Orions out of Mexico with indecent haste to avoid their being impounded because of outstanding gasoline bills. One aircraft got across the border only ten minutes ahead of the Mexican police. Another was caught. Walter Varney left Mexico City in his Duesenberg, cleaning out the tills and salvaging sundry office equipment at the eight L.A.O. stations along the way to San Diego.

Having operated four airlines between 1926 and 1935, each surviving for a shorter time than its predecessor, Walter Varney took one last shot at running an airline, repeating his previous performance of bidding for a U.S. air mail route that nobody else seemed to want. Ten days after the start of his Mexican adventure, he applied to the U.S. Post Office for a route from Denver, Colorado, to El Paso, Texas, via Pueblo and Albuquerque.

The route, designated Route 29, was available only because of the notorious Air Mail Scandal, which erupted toward the end of 1933 and reached its climax on February 9, 1934, when President Roosevelt cancelled all the air mail contracts because of the Postmaster General's strange interpretations of the laws that he helped to fashion. The PMG, Walter Folger Brown, had in fact, been motivated by the highest ideals, to fashion an airline and air mail system that was efficient, integrated, balanced, and potentially viable. But the viability was assisted by generous indirect subsidy through the air mail payments to the contractors, and Walter Brown had clearly favored all the large corporations at the expense of the small independents.

When Roosevelt's new Postmaster General, James A. Farley, called for new bids on April 20, 1934, Varney Speed Lines (Southwestern Division) was the successful applicant for this unlikely-looking mail route, linking what were then virtually unpopulated areas of the southern Rockies.

Bearing in mind the simultaneous activity in promoting the two ventures, the Southwestern Division and the Mexican L.A.O., Varney may possibly have had in mind the idea of an ambitious grand plan to serve the western states and Mexico, for at the time, Pan American appeared to be concentrating on the eastern ap-

proaches to Mexico. Had he been able to sustain a foothold in western Mexico and to establish the Southwestern Division to compensate for the loss of the California operation, he might have been
able to salvage something from the ashes of his former operations.
But it was not to be. Pan American's Juan Trippe had no intention
of allowing anyone to intrude into his Chosen Instrument status.

Walter Varney's association with the last airline to bear his
name was brief. In fact, the name was his main contribution, for
his astute former Varney Air Line president, Louis Mueller, provided the finance for the Southwestern Division. The partnership
was a flimsy one, but Varney did at least stay long enough to observe the inauguration of the first service, on July 15, 1934, from
Denver to El Paso, using five-seat Lockheed Vegas, advertised as
"the fastest transportation ever experienced in this territory."

Walter Varney pulled out of the Varney-Mueller Southwestern Division at the end of the year, when, on December 17, 1934, it
was reorganized as Varney Air Transport, Inc., with Mueller in sole
charge. The company retained much of Varney's flamboyant promotional flair, promoting "The Trail of the Conquistadores" as
though it were the main trunk air route of the United States. This
confident style was to be maintained by another man of ambition
and style, Robert Six, who purchased a substantial interest in
Varney Air Transport on July 5, 1936, renaming it Continental Air
Lines on July 1, 1937.

Varney must have decided finally that he and the airline business were incompatible. In 1936 he bought the Suaqui Grande Mining and Milling Company, in Cruz Roja, but this complete change
of scenery was not the answer. The venture failed, and by 1939 he
was back in the aviation business, albeit in a humble capacity. Robert Gross, the very man who had once offered Varney the chance to
acquire half of the Lockheed Corporation's stock, now gave him a
job in the personnel department.

Typically, he managed to transfer to flight operations and
worked as a copilot on the Hudson bomber program. Without
ever becoming prominent again, he stayed with Lockheed until
1954, then ran a sand-and-gravel-trucking business for a short
while. He finally retired and spent the rest of his life contentedly
playing tennis—he remained exceptionally fit for his age—passing
his last years with his daughter and grandchildren at Montecito,
California.

Walter Varney was one of those rare aviation men possessed of a fine vision, foreseeing the future of the airplane as a way of serving the public rather than as a sporting or military instrument. He came very close to becoming one of the greatest of the legendary figures in aviation. But he was never able to settle down long enough to become established. He could have retired in 1930 as a wealthy man and could have lived the rest of his life as a playboy. But that was not his style. He genuinely tried to build another kind of airline, based on the passenger business rather than air mail subsidy. The notorious crash of 1933 was a cruel blow, and to suggest he might have become one of the giants of the industry but for that single event is no idle speculation.

A happy philosopher all his life, he never regretted anything he did, and he brushed off the many disappointments with admirable equanimity. In spite of all the setbacks, which would have embittered many men and possibly deranged lesser mortals, Walter T. Varney remained happy as a clam at high tide right to the end. He died on January 25, 1967, one of the great pioneers of the air transport industry as we know it today.

▶ ◀ ▶
◀

Ralph O'Neill

Flying Down to Rio

During his time, the great leader of Pan American Airways, Juan Trippe, negotiated many a takeover bid during a career in which he built up his airline to become the so-called Chosen Instrument of the United States in its overseas air transport policy. His methods were persuasive, determined, and suave; he was ruthless and unrelenting if the opposition was strong and quite callous if the going got really tough. He fought many a pitched corporate battle with powerful rivals, invariably emerging as the winner. One of the first confrontations was with a competitor for a route system that was to become the backbone of the Pan American network for many years. The competitor was Ralph O'Neill, and the system was the New York, Rio and Buenos Aires Airline (NYRBA). Trippe's victory was achieved by methods of questionable ethical standards, and for the victim, the loss became an obsession that haunted him all the days of his life.

Ralph O'Neill was born on December 7, 1896, in San Francisco, according to the official records. To be exact, he was born in Cananea, in the state of Sonora, Mexico, the son of a banker from Arizona who had opened a branch there. But according to the custom of the times, he was registered as a U.S. citizen by the local U.S. consul.

When the Mexican bank failed during the panic of 1907, O'Neill senior went back to Nogales, Arizona, to set up another bank. He believed in the old-fashioned virtues and expected his son to start from the bottom—that is to say, the floor, literally the sweeping thereof. Those who were to come to know Ralph O'Neill in later years would probably require several sworn statements and photographic evidence to support the assertion that he had ever performed such a menial task, even for his father.

Certainly, he did not sweep floors for very long. In 1913, at the age of seventeen, he borrowed $5,000 from his father's bank and became a partner in a metallurgy company, specializing in assaying gold. After two years, he departed to Lehigh University, in Bethlehem, Pennsylvania, which held the reputation of conducting the best courses in mining engineering in the United States. In spite of his remarkable career in aviation, in the chronicles of which he wrote an imperishable chapter, his apprenticeship in mining was to outlast his involvement with airplanes by several decades.

But among his early interests, the urge to fly captured his imagination, and in 1917, when the United States entered World War I, Ralph O'Neill was already a pilot, assigned to the 147th U.S. Aero Squadron of the 1st Pursuit Group, American Expeditionary Force (A.E.F.), in France. In addition to his flying, he was the engineer in charge of the repair section and was in the flight commander of his own group. He was credited with six combat victories—was the fourth American to become an "ace"—and was thrice awarded the Distinguished Service Cross, as well as the Croix de Guerre.

Returning to civilian life after the war, he had got to know the governor of Sonora, who had learned a great deal about the effectiveness of air power from the air veteran. In 1920, the governor became the president of Mexico and sent for O'Neill, whom he charged with the responsibility of creating a Mexican air force. The contract was for $50,000 a year, which was a substantial sum in those days, and worth about $750,000 in today's money. He was exempted from combat duty and acted purely as a technical consultant, with ambassadorial privileges. He repaid his obligations in 1924 by organizing the rout of some rebel forces with the aid of twenty de Havilland DH-4s. By the end of the president's six-year term of office—and the end of O'Neill's contract—the Mexican Air Force had 2,000 trained officers and men and six fully-equipped squadrons of aircraft.

In 1927 O'Neill became the exclusive agent for the Boeing Airplane Company and the Pratt & Whitney Aircraft Company in all Latin American countries. He collected a Boeing F2B fighter and proceeded to demonstrate it in Brazil. Flying southward, he unfor-

Ralph O'Neill fought hard for the survival of his airline, the New York, Rio, and Buenos Aires Line (NYRBA) with which he pioneered the trunk air route to Brazil and Argentina in 1930. He was defeated by an alliance of Pan American Airways and the Post Office Department, which refused to grant his airline an air mail contract.

tunately crashed the aircraft in conditions of bad visibility at Minas, in Uruguay. He was extremely lucky to escape with his life, but by the time he emerged from the hospital, he found himself out of a job, the Boeing company having decided that its representative should have been selling aircraft, not crashing them.

But O'Neill was far from discouraged. His acute observations of the aviation scene in South America had revealed to him the immense potential for a direct air route between Argentina, then the most prosperous country, by a considerable margin, in the whole of Latin America, and the United States. The French company Aéropostale offered an eight-day service to Europe and in fact could offer a North American businessman a better postal service from New York to Buenos Aires or Santiago via North Atlantic shipping connections than was possible by direct sea routes from New York to Brazil and Argentina.

At the end of March 1928 O'Neill had been granted an audience with President Washington Luis of Brazil, who had arranged for him to see Victor Konder, the minister of transport. It was at this time that he made his notorious flight that ended igominiously in Uruguay, and when he was fit again he resumed his campaign.

In June 1928, he had gathered statistics to show that 60 percent of all mail traffic between the United States and South America was with Argentina, and these he presented to the Argentine au-

thorities. Receiving the nod from President Hipolito Irigoyen, he
began to negotiate on the basis of an undertaking to provide a
seven-day schedule from Buenos Aires to New York.

Returning to the United States armed with a convincing case
for starting an airline, he approached James Rand, president of the
Remington Rand Corporation, who became his main backer. Reuben Fleet, of the Consolidated Aircraft Corporation, undertook to
build a fleet of fine flying boats, based on the navy's PBY-1. Admiral William A. Moffett agreed to allow O'Neill to take delivery of
some Sikorsky S-38 amphibians ahead of the navy's standing order, as an interim fleet pending delivery of the Consolidated Commodores which were to be developed from the PBYs.

This was the period of awareness of the great potential of air
transport that had swept through the United States like a tidal
wave, following Lindbergh's dramatic flight across the Atlantic in
May 1927. Also, some ambitious moves by a German group working from Colombia through the Colombian national airline had
alerted various U.S. interests to the need to open up air services
into the Caribbean area, Central America, and South America generally. Pan American Airways had been formed, with powerful financial backing and led by a shrewd industrial tactician in the person of Juan Trippe. Trippe's tactical and strategic planning were
masterly, matched only by his negotiating expertise and remarkable ability to make secret agreements in support of his master
plan. Part of his strategy was to gain control of the U.S. mail contracts, which meant gaining special favors from the Post Office Department. This was an area neglected by O'Neill, possibly because
he thought that a U.S. mail contract would simply be granted to
the airline with the best case to offer, but partly because he underestimated the opposition, particularly Trippe's brilliance, not to
mention his questionable methods.

Nevertheless, Ralph O'Neill's campaign gained momentum,
and in February 1929 he met President Coolidge, to whom he outlined his ideas. On February 27 he received the Argentine mail contract, which gave him 25 percent of all the mail destined for the
United States and almost all points en route along the east coast,
via Brazil and the West Indies. His plans were gaining momentum.

On March 17, 1929, the New York, Rio and Buenos Aires Line
(NYRBA), registered in Delaware, was formed. Prominent among
the directors were James Rand and Reuben Fleet, together with

such leading figures of the U.S. business world as Frank C. Munson, of the Munson Steamship Line; W. B. Mayo, of the Ford Motor Company; James E. Reynolds, of International Founders; and Lewis Pierson, of Irving Trust. The president was Ralph O'Neill. The total investment amounted to $8,500,000. Reuben Fleet undertook to deliver six Commodores in time to fulfil the terms of the Argentine contract. James Rand wanted to call the airline Trimotor Safety Airways, and in fact, the name was used in tandem with NYRBA. The Ford Tri-Motor was at the time seen as the ideal transport airplane, and the idea of three engines as a safety precaution against an engine failure—not uncommon in the late 1920s—was especially appropriate for NYRBA's critical route segment, across the Andes between Buenos Aires and Santiago, where even flying precariously through the passes required an altitude of 16,000 feet. NYRBA ordered six Ford Tri-Motor 5-ATs.

One of O'Neill's justifiable claims against Pan American was that his Fords were the more powerful version of the basic type and that the Pan Am associate, PANAGRA, was handicapped. O'Neill observed pungently that PANAGRA "didn't possess a moto-railway car for transportation through the 16,000-ft high tunnels, much less an aircraft that could fly above them." Nevertheless, NYRBA's implied trimotor slogan was equally misleading, as the majority of its fleet, notably the much-publicized Commodores, were twin-engined. Earlier Commodore designs with three engines never saw the light of day.

The year 1929 was one of sustained activity by Ralph O'Neill and his team of pilots, engineers, communications specialists, and a good publicity man who later did great work for Pan Am. And of course prodigious efforts were made by O'Neill himself, especially in organizing precision scheduling, seeking the best sites for the flying-boat bases, and negotiating operating rights and mail contracts with the countries en route. O'Neill's fluency in Spanish, acquired during his Mexican experiences, also undoubtedly opened many doors. In retrospect, the one area neglected by O'Neill and his colleagues was winning friends and influencing people in the bureaucratic corridors of Washington, D.C. For even with the Commodores, the NYRBA management must have known that without a U.S. mail contract to supplement the Latin American ones, revenues would not match the considerable expenditures needed, not only to start up the airline, but to maintain and operate it.

Perhaps they innocently assumed that, by building a network of flying boat bases hitherto unmatched in the world, by launching the finest fleet of flying boats of any contemporary airline, and by assembling the best team of experienced pilots, engineers, and aviation technicians in the United States, NYRBA's clearcut superiority would guarantee a U.S. mail contract almost as a simple matter of cause and effect. Even were this not the case, the one factor needed for that kind of coup de main was a demonstration that the airline was already operating regularly and reliably over the appropriate route. And this was exactly what Ralph O'Neill set out to do in 1929.

The miscalculation that was to haunt him for the rest of his life was that he underestimated Juan Trippe, not so much for the recognizable organizational abilities of the Pan American leader, but for the manner in which Trippe would resort to Machiavellian cunning to achieve his objectives, by fair means or foul. As 1929 drew on, O'Neill was to realize that he was up against a masterful tactician who could draw upon hidden influences in government circles, through mysterious connections among his banking and business associates, and who would stop at nothing.

Contrary to the impression given by Pan American's publicity handouts in later years, it did very little pioneering of its own. Juan Trippe cynically allowed others to do the pioneering, then bought them out, secure in the knowledge that he had the coveted U.S. mail contracts metaphorically—and almost literally—in his pocket. For Walter F. Brown, the postmaster general, sincerely believed in the concept of the Chosen Instrument. In theory he was right, but his execution was wrong. During the formative years of air transport, when transoceanic flying was still only a gleam in romantic eyes, the time-honored principle of competition for international routes was not practical. Brown's misdemeanor was that he had preselected the winner: Pan American. No other airline stood a chance of obtaining an overseas or foreign mail contract, although these should have been open to competitive bidding.

Thus Juan Trippe sat in wait, like a cobra waiting to strike, and systematically bought up West Indian Aerial Express—which also had better aircraft and an existing route network—to take over the northern Caribbean in December 1928 and Compañia Mexicana de Aviación (C.M.A.) to gain routes throughout Mexico in January 1929, and formed, jointly with the W. R. Grace Corpora-

*With this flying boat, the Consolidated Commodore, Ralph O'Neill's
NYRBA was literally flying down to Rio at a time when Pan American was
only serving Central America and the fringes of the Caribbean. When Pan
American took over NYRBA, the Commodores were the flagships of the
airline until the famous Sikorsky Clipper ships took over.*

tion, Pan American–Grace Airways to monopolize the South American west coast route, in January 1930. Only NYRBA remained as
the final victim of Juan Trippe's conquest of an entire continent.

And so, while Trippe wheeled and dealt from his power base
in the United States, O'Neill, a vigorous man of action if ever there
was one, got down to the serious business of starting an airline.
And while the life of NYRBA was all too short and was easily forgotten—as its glorious story was deliberately suppressed—the drive
and energy with which a 7,000-mile airway was established within
only six months was little short of miraculous.

Consider the timetable of the inauguration of scheduled service over the arduous route: Buenos Aires–Montevideo (with the
Sikorsky S-38) on August 21, 1929; Buenos Aires–Santiago (with
Ford Tri-Motors) on September 1; Buenos Aires–Yacuiba, Bolivia
(also with Fords) on November 27; Buenos Aires–Mar del Plata
(the Argentine resort) on November 30; and Buenos Aires–Rio de

Janeiro (S-38) on December 23, 1929. The red-letter day was February 26, 1930, when, with a well-organized relay of Commodores and Sikorskys, a regular weekly service between Buenos Aires and Miami got under way, fulfilling the Argentine demand for a seven-day mail delivery to the United States. The fact that the "New York" part of the airline's title was misleading was not O'Neill's fault. The same would apply to Pan American, because the Miami–New York segment was rigorously excluded by U.S. authorities on the grounds that it was a domestic air route, with Eastern Air Transport as the incumbent carrier.

Of course, this admirable achievement was not without problems. Some, such as augmentation of the Argentine mail contract with others, were of a routine nature. Those with Uruguay, Venezuela, Chile, and Brazil were obtained between May and October of 1929 without much fuss, and on favorable terms, although the Brazilians insisted that NYRBA should operate along their extensive coastline only through a subsidiary. This was duly formed, and in authorizing NYRBA do Brasil on October 15, 1929, the Brazilian government also granted a 20 percent subsidy over the actual mail revenues received.

Much had been achieved during an historic, month-long, proving flight in the summer of that year. On June 11, 1929, O'Neill took off from the Hudson River in the Sikorsky S-38 *Washington*. This was no record-breaking headline-seeking adventure. At every point along the route, carefully selected for maximum operational efficiency in future regular service, discussions were held with the authorities to establish bases for the Commodores. These were sometimes in the form of floating docks in protected harbors, but at key points, where the Commodores were metaphorically to hand over the baton in a series of relays, substantial maintenance bases were built. One of these was at Calabouço, in Rio de Janeiro, and it is a tribute to O'Neill's perception that this site was later chosen for the construction of the famous Santos Dumont Airport, only a stone's throw from downtown Rio.

There were some jarring notes, however, which marred the otherwise systematic establishment of a magnificent long-distance air route. O'Neill and his publicity specialist, Bill Van Dusen, had arranged an elaborate christening ceremony at the Anacostia Naval Base, Washington, D.C., for the first Consolidated Commodore, the *Buenos Aires*, on October 2, 1929. Mrs. Hoover, wife of the president of the United States, the First Lady herself, was to make the traditional swipe with the champagne bottle. To O'Neill's utter chagrin he was completely upstaged, indeed usurped, by Juan Trippe, who turned up with a Secret Service escort and chaperoned Mrs. Hoover to the platform constructed by NYRBA and proceeded to take credit for the whole affair. The incident did not exactly strengthen the relationship between the rival airline principals.

Memories of the incident no doubt had something to do with the subsequent "Battle of Montenegro" in January 1930, when NYRBA ground staff were instructed to refuse to assist a Pan American crew that had made an unscheduled stop at Lake Montenegro, halfway between Cayenne and Belém, and hundreds of miles away from Paramaribo, the nearest Pan American base and at that time the terminus of Trippe's empire. The rivalry at this remote spot in the Brazilian jungle was quite unpleasant, reflecting the bitter battles at boardroom level.

This was polarized on October 29, 1929, the day of the Wall Street Crash, which plunged the entire business world of the United States into a state of siege, sent many firms hurtling toward financial ruin, and threatened many others that had extended their capital resources dangerously far. With its enormous investment in men, machines, and maintenance, NYRBA was just such a firm.

Nevertheless, Ralph O'Neill soldiered on. He was his own man, and even though Trippe's devious methods were now plain enough for all to see, it was not O'Neill's nature to try to play him at his own game. In his view—and who could have challenged the logic at the time?—NYRBA was ready to demonstrate with deeds, not words, that a seven-day air service, with luxury flying boats (not the "put-puts," as he contemptuously described the Pan Am fleet), was ready to start between the United States and Argentina.

This preinaugural flight, with Ralph O'Neill carrying the NYRBA standard throughout, took place from February 19 to February 25, 1930. True, he left Buenos Aires in grand style in the Commodore *Rio de Janeiro*, and he arrived in Miami, in equally grand style, in the Commodore *Cuba*. But throughout the entire route, from Porto Alegre in southern Brazil to Santiago de Cuba, the relays had been made by no less than six of the trusty Sikorsky S-38s. Not only that, but the S-38 *Tampa* was damaged at Santos, and the mails reached Niterói, across Guanabara Bay from Rio, only by a hair-raising dash by road and launch, with a Brazilian airline, which aspired to the Brazilian mail contract, doing its best to sabotage the entire effort.

The S-38 fleet, from then on northward, did demonstrate exactly what O'Neill had planned all along: that a well-orchestrated relay team of crews and machines could operate efficiently. The fact that the Sikorskys had to be used was unfortunate but incidental. The Commodores were coming off the Consolidated production line at Buffalo, and NYRBA was building its strength. And, as already noted, the regular scheduled service began on February 26, 1930.

The way would now seem to have been clear for NYRBA to build upon its growing reputation, skills, and resources. Indeed, only three months after beginning its weekly service, it received no less an accolade than the privilege of playing host to a National Geographic Society expedition to South America. Sadly, however, the National Geographic was not a government department, and the giant globe that Juan Trippe liked to spin in his penthouse office in New York was more influential than all the society's maps put together. While Ralph O'Neill did the front-running, Trippe bided his time and insidiously undermined the NYRBA operation as he watched it spending money at an alarming rate to keep this ambitious operation afloat, without enough revenue coming in to make ends meet.

In April 1930, William McCracken, the former assistant secretary of commerce for aeronautics, who had become chairman of NYRBA on December 4, 1929, moved over to the enemy and joined forces with Trippe. O'Neill, in one of his milder comments, described the NYRBA–Pan Am situation by this time as "the tail beginning to wag the dog." At the far end of the line, Trippe's agents were reminding Argentine postal officials that NYRBA was frequently late arriving at Miami and therefore technically in breach of contract. O'Neill was forced to deploy a small fleet of Consolidated Fleetsters at Buenos Aires. Their job was to leave the Argentine capital with the mails many hours later than the Commodores, which carried the passengers, thus cutting the time by means of a catch-up operation.

But such devices as this cost a great deal of money. The considerable investment by many financial institutions and well-heeled corporations was agonizingly slow to show any signs of profit. Despite the glamour and the attendant publicity associated with the idea of "flying down to Rio," there were, in fact, very few people who could enjoy the luxury—a privileged few rich businessmen, a few film stars, and the odd leading politician. Many of the intra-South American segments, especially out of Buenos Aires, were booked solid, with waiting lists. But the revenue from these passengers was relatively small. The various mail contracts from South America were but a drop in the ocean compared with the cost of carrying the mails.

By June 1930, Ralph O'Neill was forced to capitulate and to open discussions with the dreaded enemy, Juan Trippe. NYRBA was suffering severe losses, with little prospect of improvement during the postdepression years, when all the world's economies, particularly those in South America, were struggling to keep body and soul together and in no mood to sponsor or subsidize a luxury airline. O'Neill v. Trippe was really no contest. It was like inviting an amateur cardplayer to join a game with a champion card-sharper, with the latter holding all the high cards and with the trump ace up his sleeve—the coveted U.S. mail contract.

So heavily were the cards stacked against O'Neill that even though the valuation of the assets of the two airlines showed NYRBA's to outweigh Pan American's by a ratio of 3:2, the deal was settled, in indecent haste, on terms grossly unfavorable to NYRBA, on August 19, 1930. This was less than six months after O'Neill had triumphantly opened regular airline service between the United States and most of the major cities of the South American continent. Formal absorption, like a sprat swallowing a mackerel, was completed on September 15, 1930, by the transfer of stock. On October 17, 1930, the Brazilian subsidiary, NYRBA do Brasil, changed its name to Panair do Brasil, a change authorized by the Brazilian government on November 21.

The whole affair contained some elements of farce. Trippe had claimed, as a compensatory factor against the 3:2 assets ratio, the presence of Charles A. Lindbergh as Pan American's technical director. But Lindbergh's technical expertise was redundant, because NYRBA was a going concern. Significantly, his considerable talents were used to good effect in surveying routes across the two great oceans, the Pacific and the Atlantic, and he had made a much-publicized goodwill flight around the Caribbean perimeter. But he was never needed on the east coast of South America.

Trippe also claimed the U.S. air mail contract as an asset, an astonishing piece of impudence and arrogance, considering that he did not even have it. But the fact that he could even bring it into the discussion on these terms revealed that its award to Pan American had always been planned, by connivance between the Post Office and Pan American, and was a foregone conclusion. Indeed, it came only a few short weeks after the ruthless takeover.

Such abstract assets could not compare with the very real assets of NYRBA. In September 1930, Pan American had fifty aircraft, with a total seating capacity of 400. But many of these were old, time-expired Fokkers and Fairchilds, and only the Fords and the Sikorskys were worth very much. By comparison, NYRBA had taken delivery of eleven of its Commodores, the finest flying boats in the world at the time and indeed the largest airliners of any kind in regular operation. The Commodores could seat 22–26 people, dependent on range or mail loads, in complete comfort. NYRBA's eight-seat Sikorsky S-38s were being relegated to a second-line operation at a time when they were still the pride of Pan Am's fleet. And NYRBA's Fords could cross the Andes while Pan Am's models dared not approach the cordillera too closely.

Following Trippe's coup de grâce, Ralph O'Neill's pride would not allow him to work for Pan American, although Trippe offered him a high-level position. Most of the NYRBA staff had fewer scruples and moved over to their new employer without too much stress. O'Neill had to watch Pan American go from strength to strength, dominating the airways of the entire South American continent, using the bases that he had carefully chosen and established, as well as his fine aircraft and experienced crews. The question of loyalty did not really arise, although had it arisen he might have been disappointed. By nature, he had never suffered fools—or traitors—gladly. He was sometimes short of temper and sometimes unforgiving. But he often had reason to be, as one after another, several of his trusted lieutenants had been lured away into the Pan American camp.

One of the bitterest pills he had to swallow was to read continually the Pan American publicity about its various claims to firstliness, which, for many airlines during the pioneering days, was next to godliness. Although NYRBA's involvement in airline history was all too brief—a mere seventeen months of corporate existence and 363 days of actual operation under its own name—its achievements were out of all proportion to the length of its career. Not counting peripheral contacts around the Caribbean, NYRBA was the first airline to link the two American continents with passenger, mail, and express services. It was the first to fly passengers and mail regularly across the Andes, the first to establish air-to-ground radio communications, and the first to offer luxurious accommodations, with upholstered seats and separate cabins. It was the first to provide on-board food service and the first to put its flight personnel in uniform.

NYRBA established an eighty-hour-a-month limit for its crews (still the limit today!) with bonus payments per mile, when overtime became necessary. It prohibited the consumption of alcohol by the crews for twenty-four hours before flight duty, another first. Thus, when the popular press began to refer to the airline as "Near Beer" instead of "Nearba," as the acronym was at first and correctly pronounced, the insinuation of casual or slack company regulations was especially irritating.

Whether the misnomer was deliberately encouraged by Pan American is not known. But it was public knowledge that when the *National Geographic* published the feature article that occupied most of the contents of the January 1931, issue, pressure was applied to the publisher, Gilbert H. Grosvenor, to give all the credit to Pan American. The relationship between O'Neill and Trippe was uncompromising because it was visceral. It had started as business rivalry and developed into a personal dislike that was fanned into hatred by Juan Trippe's unrelenting determination to destroy NYRBA. The enmity was to last the rest of their lives. For O'Neill's part, he wrote a book fully thirty-five years after the demise of his beloved airline, in a style that suggested that the events had occurred the preceding year. There were passages which left absolutely no doubt that his attitude toward Trippe was one of deep hatred, although there is no evidence that Trippe reciprocated the sentiment. He had no need to. He had got his way—he almost always did—and he simply wrote off NYRBA as another chapter in the saga of his aggrandizement, which was to be his lifelong pursuit with Pan American.

Coincidentally, the two antagonists died within a few months of each other, O'Neill on October 23, 1980, Trippe on April 3, 1981.

Jane O'Neill claimed that Ralph having arrived at the Pearly Gates first, Trippe's chances of passing through must have been slender. On the other hand, O'Neill may not have thought to barricade the gates, because he would have presumed Trippe to have been languishing in the Other Place.

Ralph O'Neill remained active and energetic for the rest of his life after the NYRBA debacle. Having shrugged off for a while his personal disaster, within two years he had invested heavily in a new venture, a gold-mining company in Bolivia. The Bol-Inca Mining Corporation was incorporated in the state of New York in 1932, and it had the O'Neill stamp of confident enthusiasm written all over it. Exploring in ore-rich river valleys on the eastern slopes of the Andes, not too far from La Paz (but eight days by pack mule), the corporation drained its own resources and went into partnership agreements with others, until the U.S. entry into World War II in 1941.

Attempts to put the Bol-Inca concern on its feet dragged on for many frustrating years. The evidence was that the deposits were among the richest in South America, but their inaccessibility was a real handicap, expecially in a commercial community that had to try to maintain stability in a country where governments would change frequently, more often than not by revolution. Even as late as 1969, O'Neill was still trying to revive the fading fortunes by making an agreement with the Bolivian government. But after forty years of sometimes patient, sometimes desperate, sometimes optimistic, but all too often disillusioned effort, Ralph O'Neill finally had to retire from active business life at the age of seventy-four.

The New York, Rio, and Buenos Aires Line adventure had occupied only two and a half eventful years of Ralph O'Neill's energetic working life. The memoirs of the circumstances surrounding the shattering experience of defeat and betrayal must have stayed with him and haunted his dreams during his forty drawn-out years of mining. Ultimately, he released himself from some of the mental stress by writing his memoirs, in the book mentioned earlier, *A Dream of Eagles,* in which he exposed the political chicanery that callously thwarted his visionary pioneer work.

During his retirement, he must sometimes have wished that he had given the airline business another crack. With a fair, or even mildly unfair, chance he would have thrived on the cut and thrust of airline competition. He wrote his reminiscences and his book in an immaculate library-study, which looked out through the window onto his beloved roses, evocative of an English country garden. As Jane O'Neill was to observe later, "There was also heartbreak . . . I wondered how he could smile, and help put in some more roses."

▶▶◀ ▶▶▶▶▶▶▶▶▶▶▶▶▶▶▶▶▶▶▶▶▶

Robert Six

The Maverick

Robert Six was a big man in every way, physically—he was six feet four inches tall—and mentally—he was described accurately by Robert Serling as "one of the last of aviation's rugged individualists." His great achievement in life was to be able to express this individuality while working entirely within a strictly regulated administrative framework, in which self-expression, innovation, and competition were usually stifled by law. Six always worked within the system, yet always succeeded in doing everything, the important and the trivial, just a little better than his competitors did. Cumulatively, his actions gave his airline, Continental, the hallmark of quality, which, during a period when most travelers were businessmen, made it one of the most respected in the industry.

Robert Six dominated Continental Airlines, to whom it was said he was married all his life, although he was also married three times to members of the opposite sex. He was hot-tempered, but seldom held a grudge; he was honest to a fault, always kept his word, and demanded equal honesty from all his subordinates, placing loyalty to Continental—and to himself personally—as important as any three of the Ten Commandments put together. "The Old Man," as he was affectionately and respectfully known, was a benevolent partriarch who liked to get his own way, an amiable dictator who got things done. But the characteristic trait by which everyone with whom he came in contact remembers him is the profanity that punctuated his conversation except in the presence of women and those Washington bureaucrats whom he did not wish to of-fend. Six could deliver long tirades composed almost entirely of four-letter words without repeating himself.

Much of this ability can be attributed to his early life, before he became associated with airlines. He was born on June 25, 1907, to parents of Dutch stock who were reasonably well off. By the time he was twenty he had left home to go to sea as an ordinary seaman, in which occupation he doubtless enlarged his vocabulary. He worked briefly as a bill collector for a California Gas and Electric Company and in 1927 took flying lessons, possibly influenced by the wave of enthusiasm for flying generated by Lindbergh's epic Atlantic flight.

In 1929 he received his pilot's certificate, started the Valley Flying Service, and tried unsuccessfully to qualify as an airline pilot for Boeing Air Transport. He then went to China, where for three years he worked for Pan American's associated company. By 1932 he was expanding his education with a year in Europe, following which he drifted back to San Francisco, where he worked as driver of a delivery truck. He split his time between that occupation and an entirely different level of society, attending smart dinners with prominent citizens, and it was at the latter functions that he was introduced to influential people in the airline business and became interested in it as a career.

Robert Six joined Varney Air Transport on July 5, 1936. At this time, Varney was a little airline that had gained a precarious scheduled route franchise by sucessfully bidding for a post office mail contract that none of the well-established airlines seemed to want. It had been founded in 1934 by Walter Varney, a cavalier aviator of the early 1920s who had already operated four airlines before this one. Varney's partner was Louis Mueller, who provided the financial acumen while Varney produced the flair, and together they battled to break even while flying between Denver and El Paso. At this time, all the big airlines sought only east-west routes, which generated the lucrative coast-to-coast mail contracts. Few were interested in routes from north to south, except along the two coastlines and the Mississippi River. Along the Rocky Mountains, air mail traffic was so sparse that Mueller and Varney almost had to write their own letters, and rumor had it that the latter was not above a little machination in this field to generate traffic.

Robert Six was a confident and dynamic airline president who led a comparatively small trunk airline to a position of eminence in a tightly controlled airline environment, by innovative policies that made the name of Continental Airlines synonymous with fine service standards.

From the moment Six arrived in El Paso, his influence was evident. Although hired technically as an employee, he held 40 percent of Varney's stock. This gave him considerable authority, which he quickly exercised by negotiating the purchase of part of the Wyoming Air Service network, to consolidate Varney's precious single route to Denver. He and Mueller also mortgaged their homes to purchase, in 1937, three Lockheed 12 twin-engined airliners to replace the one Lockheed single-engined Vega remaining after two had crashed. The "Baby Electra" could carry only eight passengers, but could fly at more than 200 miles an hour and was ideal for the sparsely traveled route at that time. On July 1, 1937, Six changed the name to Continental Air Lines and invited the public to "Fly the Old Santa Fe Trail over the Route of the Conquistadores." With unabashed exaggeration, advertisements stressed the fastest and most scenic route from Denver to Los Angeles, although Continental's individual contribution to the exercise was almost hidden in the small print.

During this early pioneering period, Continental was a poor relation in the eyes of the Civil Aviation Authority, an attitude that was confirmed when the Civil Aeronautics Board (C.A.B.) was formed in 1938 and the so-called Grandfather Routes were distributed. Six had to be satisfied with only his Denver–El Paso route, but he was able to make a modest sortie into the dizzy realms of east-west traffic with a Pueblo–Wichita route in 1939.

Some measure of the stature of Six's airline before World War II can be gleaned from the fact that a small route extension from Wichita to Tulsa, the national oil capital, was regarded as a significant step. Already, under the advice of Stan Shatto, its maintenance chief, Continental had purchased the larger Lockheed Lodestar, and now it standardized on the type. Typical of Six at the time, and indeed throughout his subsequent career, he not only made the big decisions but made all the small ones as well, from the color and cut of the air hostesses' uniforms to selection of the new cutlery.

Continental struggled through World War II and by its end had added a few cities of substance to its network, including Kansas City, Oklahoma City, and San Antonio. In 1944 it had also upgraded its equipment to Douglas DC-3s, the first of these ubiquitous 21-seat twin-engined aircraft having entered service on December 22, 1944. By the end of the war, Robert Six, who had joined the U.S. Army Air Transport Command in September 1942, had little to come back to. Unlike almost every other airline in the United States, Continental received only a few small crumbs in the way of additional routes as a result of a general distribution of largesse by the C.A.B. during the immediate postwar period.

Furthermore he had problems with control of the airline. This was partly his own fault, because he liked to run everything himself and could not bring himself to delegate responsibility to his executives. An exception was Ted Haueter, in charge of operations, a small but feisty man who gave Six as good as he got. But Haueter possessed the main quality demanded by Six: loyalty, which was more than could be said for some of the other caretakers who had been running the airline while Six was in the army. Terry Drinkwater had joined Continental in 1938 and was made acting president in Six's absence. He engineered a palace revolt to confront Six when he returned, feeling that, he and Stan Shatto having preserved the airline as a going concern during very difficult times, with a flimsy network and most of its aircraft requisitioned, he was entitled to a position only a little below that of the chairman. But Six was not going to tolerate anyone leapfrogging over his old part-

ner, Louis Mueller, and Drinkwater and Shatto were gone within a
few weeks of the Old Man's return in 1944.

Trying to keep Continental alive and, more important, trying
to make it grow was an uphill task during the decade immediately
following World War II. The airlines were rigidly controlled by the
C.A.B. Not a route could be added or dropped without long litigation, and all the lucrative ones were jealously guarded by the incumbents. They were inadvertently protected by the C.A.B., which
feared unrestricted free competition in an industry where the margins of profit were slender—and almost impossible without subsidy, whether direct, indirect, or both. The board was acutely conscious of its responsibility to protect "the public convenience and
necessity," words cast in concrete in its charter. Bob Six was
caught between a geographical rock and an administrative hard
place, with a small network, serving a sparsely traveled region
very well. West of the Rockies he seemed to go nowhere in particular. In the east he did not even reach the Mississippi.

Some idea of the disparity between Continental and the
larger airlines can be gleaned by considering Six's order in 1948 for
five Convair 240s, to improve his DC-3 fleet. American Airlines ordered seventy-five of the same type during the same period, and
they were not even American's front-line fleet.

Bob Six tried everything within the limitations of the strictly
regulated industry. He tried a new slogan, calling his DC-3s
Skystreamers to fly the Blue Skyway, and he was second only to
the innovative Capital Airlines in introducing Skycoach fares, to
break the rigid first-class-only tariff structure. But this only nib-
bled at the basic problem, which was that his route network was
far too small and did not serve any major metropolis in the United
States, not even Houston.

The airline industry then came up with an ingenious idea for
a more flexible approach to route development, and Continental
Airlines was one of its leading proponents. The idea was route interchange, whereby two or more airlines would give each other reciprocal operating authority over selected routes—with the C.A.B.'s
permission, of course—and would operate their equipment on a
mutually agreeable basis. In fact, Bob Six was at last able to
glimpse the silver lining, because Continental's network, diminutive though it might be, lay athwart several important region-to-
region connections, and if any of the larger airlines wished to par-

The Gold Carpet Service was one of the measures taken by Robert Six to promote Continental Airlines as a company of quality. Passenger amenities such as this were among the few outlets for clear-cut competition during an era when almost every other device was condemned to conformity by Washington.

ticipate in the growing interregional traffic, they had to take Continental along with them.

Bob Six and his team had already, by diligent effort, improved their maintenance, operations, and commercial standards so that they were at least as good, and in some instances better, than those of their big rivals. Six now saw his chance to bring his aircraft up to the standards of the Big Four also. When the first interchange route with American Airlines opened on July 27, 1951, from several points in California to Houston, Continental started with a four-engined Douglas DC-6B. Six had to lease it from American, but he ordered two of his own within three months of the launching of the new service. At last he could show the world that anything the great American Airlines could do he could match.

Another move, in desperation to expand, was to acquire Pioneer Air Lines, one of the new breed of well-subsidized feeder airlines. It had been the first to receive the C.A.B.'s official blessing in the new Local Service category, under its old name, Essair, starting service on August 1, 1945. But when the two lines merged, on December 10, 1953, it was no more than a minimerger. Its effect did not exactly reverberate outside Pioneer's home state of Texas, and the only discernible advantage to Continental was that it consolidated its position throughout Texas, especially to Houston and Dallas. Pioneer's first-line fleet consisted of Martin 2-0-2s, which were incompatible with Six's Convairliners. Another item of note acquired with Pioneer was an aggressive vice-president named Harding Lawrence, who was to leave Six in due course to take over Braniff Airways, with spectacular results.

During the year of the Pioneer merger, Six married for the second time. His first wife, Henriette, whom he had married in 1935, could not reconcile Six's life-style with her own. An announcement from Mexico revealed that his second wife was Ethel Merman, a star of Broadway and Hollywood and very much her own person. The marriage lasted seven years, and they were divorced in 1960. Many would have predicted the break. Ethel Merman was show business personified. But Bob Six was no mean showman himself, and their interests were completely different.

Six's extroverted personality and love of showmanship were in fascinating contrast to his determined, almost harsh insistence on company discipline. His enthusiasm for extramural activities ran to a Continental basketball team that flourished during the late 1940s, the Six-Guns, a team of fast-draw shooters drawn from Continental's top echelon in the late 1950s, and Playboy Bunnies on the Los Angeles–Chicago route in the early 1970s. Yet this was the same man who would make unannounced inspections of every department in Continental, look for minuscule dust marks after an aircraft had been cleaned, and deny the office staff the right to eat sandwiches at their desks. His eagle eye ranged over menus, ashtrays, paintwork, and trash cans. It was all part of his unceasing campaign to make Continental smarter, faster, and cheaper—in short, more efficient—than any other airline in the United States.

An opportunity at last came for Bob Six to combine his flair for showmanship with his fastidious attention to detail and a disciplined approach to every aspect of airline activity. When, in 1952, the C.A.B. opened the Denver Service Case, Continental was one of the applicants for new routes east and west of that city, the airline hub of the Rocky Mountain Area. C.A.B. route cases were the regulatory machinery by which route expansion by individual airlines could be made to fit into a national pattern of growth, destructive competition could be avoided, and existing competition matched to predictable traffic volumes. There had been countless route cases to award and distribute dozens of feeder routes as that segment of the industry expanded, and, truth to tell, there was a suspicion that Continental was regarded in Washington as little more than a feeder airline. But the Denver Case was of a different order of magnitude and set the stage for a transformation of Continental Air Lines.

When the decision was announced, on November 14, 1955, the transcontinental routes of the principal trunk airlines, T.W.A., American, and United, were realigned and strengthened. But the surprise element of the list of route awards was a Continental route from Chicago to Los Angeles, via Kansas City and Denver, with nonstop authority between all pairs of cities, including Chicago–Los Angeles direct. Chicago and Los Angeles, the second and third largest cities in the country, generated more traffic than all Continental's existing network.

Some airline leaders would have taken a cautious approach, perhaps apprehensive about the prospect of challenging the might of the dominant airlines. Not Bob Six. He had proved that Continental's quality of service and strength of effort were at least as good as those of his rivals. Now he was determined to give his team the equipment with which he could demonstrate superiority. In December 1955, he ordered four 118-seat Boeing 707 jet airliners, fifteen 56-seat Viscount turboprops, and five 96-seat Douglas DC-7Bs. The total order, valued at about $64,000,000, was almost six times the book value of Continental's total fleet at the time.

A DC-7B opened the Los Angeles–Chicago service on April 28, 1957, and was promoted as the Gold Carpet Service. It featured Club Coach accommodation, in which, for the first time, coach passengers were offered some of the amenities hitherto offered only to first-class passengers. This was followed by the introduction of the Jet Power Viscount II, on May 28, 1958. Aggressive promotion, plus liberal—and marginally unethical—use of the emotive word *jet* enabled Continental to garner almost half the traffic between Chicago and Los Angeles. The final trump card in Bob Six's hand, the true jet airliner, was played on June 8, 1959, when the Boeing 707 Golden Jet—shrewdly registered as a trademark by Continental—

made its debut. Little Continental had been the third U.S. domestic carrier to order the aircraft, preceded only by American and T.W.A.

To rationalize the fleet and to come to terms with its new stature, Continental disposed of most of its old piston-engined fleet, retaining only a few DC-7Bs, DC-6Bs, and a few DC-3s. But even these last disappeared during the early 1960s as, under the provisions of two C.A.B. route cases in the Great Plains and the Southwest, most of Continental's feeder routes were transferred to the Local Service airlines, where they now truly belonged. Only ten and a half years before the 707 inaugural, Continental had been just another humble DC-3 operator. The rise to parity with the largest airlines in the United States had been truly astonishing.

During this heady period of success during the early 1960s, Bob Six was seldom out of the aviation news headlines for very long. Some occasions were in the fine American tradition of exploiting the media for his own purposes, some were ill advised, and some were tragic. On August 3, 1961, for example, Continental experienced a spectacular hijacking, long before such incidents became almost weekly occurrences in the news. On May 22, 1962, a 707 was lost because of a bomb explosion—another rare incident in those days—and Continental lost the perfect safety record that it had held at least since the early Varney days.

Undoubtedly, this safety record owed much to the standards of excellence on which Bob Six always insisted. Perhaps the precise credit cannot be allocated to him alone, but Continental's standards owed much to his example, and innovative ideas that emerged at all levels would perhaps not have germinated in a less intense airline. Continental devised the progressive maintenance system, which was copied by the entire industry. Continental managed to provide better service with fewer aircraft than other airlines because its sharply honed methods permitted more intensive use of individual aircraft. The public was drawn into Continental seats by superior publicity, and they tended to return to those seats because of superior service, on the ground and in the air. Directors of Passenger Service (D.P.S.) reduced the check-in time, and Six promoted Continental service with publicity stunts such as providing flights for popular football teams. Ground handling was superb. Aircraft were serviced at the main terminals by the most modern equipment, apparently orchestrated by an unseen ramp conductor. The ground staff wore white gloves, and this bit of showmanship sometimes appeared in unexpected places, to Continental's advantage.

Bob Six could, however, make mistakes. His biggest act of misjudgment arose out of his infatuation with the supersonic airliner. Cold-blooded analysis should have overruled his famous intuition. Possibly intoxicated by the success of the Denver Case and the new jets and turboprops, Six ordered the Franco-British Concorde supersonic airliner in July 1963, depositing $505,000 on three aircraft, only the fourth airline on the list. But, quite apart from technical considerations such as eliminating the sonic boom, he totally underestimated the initial purchase costs and, much worse, shut his eyes to the excessive operating costs. He would have had to charge about $1,000 one way between Houston and Los Angeles, and even Texas oilmen would not have filled the Concordes for long at that price, had they been allowed to fly supersonic over land.

By this time, he had married again, on August 21, 1961, to Audrey Meadows, a prominent stage and film actress though not a star. In contrast to Ethel Merman, who was determined to remain a star, Audrey Meadows lost all aspirations to stardom from the time she met Bob Six. Not only that, she took an interest in Continental's affairs in areas where her intuition was better than Bob's. When in 1963 Continental introduced a dignified new uniform for the flight attendants, for example, the finishing touch, a single string of pearls, was Audrey's idea, and later she made most of the decisions about the décor of the wide-bodied cabins and lounges of the Boeing 747.

During the mid and later 1960s, Bob Six pulled off his greatest coup in enlarging the scope of Continental's operations. Totally within the severe limits of the regulatory process, which inevitably favored the haves rather than the have-nots, he elevated his airline to intercontinental status, against all the odds and against all the predictions. This needed a measure of inspired opportunism, of which at the time even Bob Six may have been unaware. At all events, the combined result, to make Continental a transpacific operator, was a touch of genius.

Alone among all the domestic trunk airlines, Continental had no record of international operations, and this was handicap enough in the eyes of the C.A.B. Six set about getting into the Pacific by the back door. His first chance came with a contract from Military Airlift Command (MAC) in May 1964 for transpacific military charters in logistic support of the Vietnam War. This provided experience in transoceanic flying, and the contract was so lucrative that Continental was able to order a larger fleet of Boeing 707s and make enormous profits in the process. Typical of the Continental approach, the service was superb, fully up to U.S. domestic business-class standards. With the profits he bought additional equipment and, incidentally, was able to participate in the European charter market, which suited Six's temperament, although this specialized market had not yet been developed.

Continental also identified itself with the Orient forming Continental Air Services (C.A.S.) on September 1, 1965, as a wholly owned subsidiary in Laos, from which base it operated countless small aircraft types into remote airstrips in support of the War. C.A.S. was wound up on December 19, 1975, but, in combination with the transoceanic charters, it served to round off its parent company's apprenticeship in overseas operations.

The other vital element in the Pacific acclimatization process was to acquire control of Air Micronesia. The U.S. government had sponsored air service throughout the Trust Territory of the Pacific, a string of several groups of islands and atolls, formerly ruled by Japan, in the west central Pacific. Operated from July 1, 1951, by Transocean Airlines, under Orvis Nelson, a man after Bob Six's own heart, it had been taken over by Pan American when Transocean went bankrupt in 1960. The contract came up for renewal in 1968 and Continental put in a three-part bid against Pan Am. Six guaranteed to fly jet aircraft as soon as fields could be built; he undertook to train the local people in airline operation; and he pledged to revitalize the stagnant Micronesian economy by creating a tourist industry, specifically by building hotels. As a backup to these undertakings, Continental formed the United Micronesia Development Association (U.M.D.A.) in cooperation with local interests and Aloha Airlines, of Hawaii. Continental's shares in Air Micronesia would be held through U.M.D.A.

Such a combination was unassailable, and on May 16, 1968, the first "Air Mike" Boeing 707 left Saipan for Honolulu, a distance of 4,300 miles—nearly twice the distance across the United States—with seven stops. In the other direction, the airline served Okinawa.

After an extraordinary cat-and-mouse game for transpacific route rights and expansion, lasting thirteen years under different administrations, President Nixon made the final awards in 1969. Continental failed to obtain a transpacific link, but it did start service to Hawaii on September 9, 1969, and the publicity department was able to exploit this to the full, by drawing maps to show a transpacific route as far as Okinawa.

Meanwhile, it had quietly strengthened its position on the mainland, by adding Boeing 720B and Douglas DC-9 aircraft in 1962 and 1968, respectively, and "The Proud Bird with the Golden Tail" slogan in 1966.

The early 1970s witnessed the zenith of Robert Six's career, and the latter 1970s were to see his downfall. Right to the end, he did everything in a big way, and there were no halfway measures. His first priority during this period was to join the ranks of operators of wide-bodied airliners.

Less than six months after Pan American ushered in the first Jumbo-Jets, Continental introduced the 355-seat Boeing 747 on the Chicago–Los Angeles–Honolulu route on June 26, 1970. Its interiors included the Diamond Head Lounge and the Polynesian Pub, with the decor chosen by Audrey Meadows Six. To supplement the 747, which could be used only on Continental's densest routes, Six ordered the McDonnell Douglas DC-10s, in its freighter version, beginning service on June 1, 1972. The two decisions, while logical, included misjudgments: Continental's traffic density as a whole was insufficient to justify the 747s, as was the freight traffic insufficient to justify a special version of the DC-10.

Nevertheless, Six made a virtue out of necessity. He dropped the big Boeings and standardized the fleet on two types, the DC-10 and the Boeing 727-200, selling thirty-five jet aircraft in the process. But the Continental standard of service and vigorous promotion continued, with movies, disco bars, and another slogan, "We Really Move Our Tail for You." Continental still set its own pace.

During this period there was a certain restlessness among the airlines, which were straining at the bit against the restrictive reins of the C.A.B., even though that agency was relaxing some of its formerly rigid positions. Under pressure it allowed Continental to offer superior comfort on its narrow-bodied aircraft without a fare surcharge, and the airline at last obtained access to the East Coast, opening a route to Miami on February 1, 1974. But then came the Airline Deregulation Act of October 1978.

At first there was no outward sign that Continental was departing from its inexorable Sixian way to ever greater success. Deregulation permitted services to Washington, New York, and several destinations in Mexico. Denver and Houston emerged as major hubs. On October 13, 1978, a through DC-10 service was opened from Los Angeles to Taipei, so the Continental maps no longer needed to be quite so deceptive. Then, by a stroke of luck, American Airlines decided to abandon its route to Australia and New Zealand, and President Carter approved Robert Six's application to fill the breach. Continental's South Pacific service began on May 1, 1979.

But deregulation was hitting Continental hard. Severely discounted domestic fares at first generated new traffic, but the competition permitted by liberal access was ruthless and crippling. Profit margins diminished as yields declined. Some airlines, by a combination of geographic and competitive circumstances, were more vulnerable than others, none more than Continental.

Bob Six's inspired promotional efforts had been made entirely within the regulatory framework. He was frequently the first to introduce new ideas but was seldom able to turn his inventiveness to permanent advantage, simply because there was no law to keep other airlines from matching the best ideas—such as progressive maintenance—and bringing themselves up to Six's speed.

He was assailed on both fronts of the economic equation. On the revenue side, his Chickenfeed fares were no lower than those of the many competitors on the Continental gravy run between California and Texas, where three of the most aggressive of the low-cost, low-fare operators such as P.S.A., Muse Air, and Southwest almost poleaxed Continental's efforts. Some indication of Six's problems came with the withdrawal of Continental from the Chicago–Los Angeles market, the scene of so many Continental triumphs, on September 8, 1980.

Continental could not, however, lower its costs to match the new discount fares. Every avenue of cost efficiency had already been explored, and one of Six's weaknesses now came to haunt the airline. As part of his policy and general attitude toward his fellow men, he had always been generous with salaries, especially for the aircrew. Continental staff worked hard, and they were efficient. They were also among the highest paid in the industry, partly because the mutual corporate loyalty ensured long service and the consequent high salary levels, partly because Six worshiped his flying crew. Six himself was one of the highest-paid airline executives in the world.

The net effect was that Continental suddenly began to lose money at an increasing rate, a bitter pill for Six to swallow, as he had been proud of his record of turning in a profit for his airline in almost every year until the rot set in after deregulation. In 1979, Continental incurred a net loss of $13,185,000, whereas it had made a profit of $49,190,000 in 1978. In 1980, the loss was $20,700,000, but it would have been $78,000,000 without nonrecurring credits. In 1981, the net loss was $60,356,000, even after taking $40,000,000 in nonrecurring credits.

By this time, under notice from his doctors to slow down, Robert Six had begun to hand over executive control of the airline to others, and there were signs that he was losing his grip, or at least choosing to relax it. Alexander Damm, who was appointed president in May 1976, and Al Feldman, who took over in February 1980, inherited a cost structure that had got out of control.

For Bob Six to watch the airline he had built with such inspiration now collapse like a house of cards must have been an agonizing experience. Many executives in the industry remember his passionate analysis of the problems of the industry when he appeared before a Senate Aviation Subcommittee in 1971. His spirited defense at that time of the principles of free enterprise and competition and his attack on those airlines that he regarded as monopolists were of no help to him now. His views on mergers, which he claimed invariably came about when a big airline was in trouble and when a small airline was vulnerable to a takeover bid, were of no avail in 1982, when an airline which not long before had been classified as a Local Service airline now put in a bid to take over Continental. When the bell tolled, it tolled loudly and relentlessly for Bob Six. Texas International, under the direction of Frank Lorenzo, who had entered the airline arena only when Continental was introducing its DC-10s in 1972, took over control of Bob Six's airline and merged it with his own, retaining, however, the Continental name.

Bob Six never really retired in the official sense of the word. Arguably, his retirement occurred when Frank Lorenzo took over in 1982, by which time Six was seventy-five years old and had been nominally in control of Continental for forty-five years, although he had handed over the presidency to Damm in 1976. During a period when many employees were being laid off or fired under a "prosperity plan"—this was before the notorious Chapter 11 bankruptcy of 1983—Six continued to come to the office. But he no longer had any influence on the affairs of Continental. As time went on, his appearances became less frequent. The exact date of his actual retirement cannot be determined. The Old Man, rather like the proverbial Old Soldier, quietly faded away to a well-deserved retirement. The retirement was sadly short-lived. Robert Six died at his home in Los Angeles on October 6, 1986.

Howard Hughes

The Phenomenon

Almost without exception, the remarkable men who qualify for inclusion in this book would not argue with the suggestion that their careers as airline promoters represented the most important achievements of their business lives. Whether they were rich or poor, any other activity of theirs paled into insignificance beside what they did to enrich and expand the airline world. For Howard Hughes, this was not so. He was already world famous for achievements totally unconnected with the airlines when he became almost the sole owner of one of the world's largest airlines, T.W.A. He had achieved fame as a film producer, as a racing pilot, and as a round-the-world flyer. He had inherited the source of enormous wealth which contributed to, rather than drew from, T.W.A.'s finances. For other achievements in aviation he had won the Harmon Trophy and the Collier Trophy, and these successes had nothing to do with T.W.A. either.

But to assume, therefore, that Howard Hughes ran T.W.A. for more than a quarter of a century merely as a hobby would also be a mistake. Of all his work and play—and in his eventful life, there was an excess of both—he loved the airline more than anything else, more than the mighty Toolco, the oil-drilling equipment giant which was the foundation of his wealth, more than Hughes Aircraft, which built many a notable airplane, and whose name survives today, and more than the many film stars and other beautiful women with whom he enjoyed transient relationships.

Many books and thousands of feature articles for countless newspapers and magazines throughout the world have been writ-

Howard Hughes, seen here in the cockpit of his Hughes H-1 Racer, was an incredible genius whose range of talents was sometimes forgotten, especially during his later years, in the glare of the publicity generated by his unorthodox way of living.

ten about Howard Hughes. The cumulative effect of this vast outpouring of journalistic reporting and opinion shaping has been to paint Hughes as a ruthless, eccentric, philandering freak of a man. He may have been some or all of these things at some time and to some extent, but many other business moguls could have been similarly described. While it does not excuse or condone some of his subsequent actions, the fact that he was orphaned in his youth may have had something to do with his excesses. Rich orphans are handicapped during their formative years as much as poor ones, if not always in the same way.

Howard Hughes was born on Christmas Eve 1905. Howard Hughes, Sr., was a wildcat oil man who, with a partner named Walter Sharp, had drilled for oil at Goose Creek, Texas. They encountered the formidable layer of hard rock shale, whose effect on drilling bits was traditionally the scourge of oil men everywhere. Unlike others who transferred their interests elsewhere in search of oil deposits free of shale, Hughes and Sharp set about the problem of designing a new drill. Hughes came up with a brilliant design, and he and Sharp, with truly remarkable foresight, abandoned oil drilling in favor of manufacturing drills and founded the Hughes Tool Company. Sharp died in 1917, and Hughes bought out Sharp's widow. Hughes's wife, Allene, died in 1922, and Hughes himself followed her to the grave two years later. Their son, Howard Robard Hughes—in England the initials stand for "His Royal Highness"—was orphaned at the age of eighteen.

Young Howard quickly showed his mettle. Displaying a blend of the gambling instinct and the systematic manipulation of money that was to be characteristic of his business methods throughout his subsequent life, he gained sole legal ownership of the Hughes Tool Company, then worth about $650,000—not many millions, as is frequently assumed—early in 1925, when he was nineteen years old. He promptly undertook a housecleaning, replaced those whom he considered incompetent, and hired, among others, an accountant named Noah Dietrich, who was to guide the Hughes fortunes for the next thirty years.

During the latter 1920s, Hughes began to interest himself in other technical enterprises. The Tool Company, holding a virtual world monopoly of oil drilling bits, through ironclad patents, in effect ran itself and made money hand over fist, leaving the owner to pursue other interests. He had an unfortunate affair with promotion of a steam car from 1927 to 1930, abandoning it emphatically as soon as he realized that, without proper supervision, his engineers had, as the saying goes, "lost sight of their objectives, and redoubled their efforts." They had constructed a vehicle in which the driver had an excellent chance of scalding himself to death.

Hughes's other interests, however, were to lead to more fruitful developments. He learned to fly in 1927, obtained his transport rating in 1928, and earned a commercial multiengined and instrument rating shortly afterward. Putting theory into practice, he worked for three months in 1932, under the name of Charles Howard, as a Ford Tri-Motor copilot for American Airlines.

These spare-time activities, as steam car promoter and as airline pilot, helped to mold Howard Hughes's subsequent approach to his business affairs. Learning by experience, he never again delegated the policy control of a major project, and he acquired an obsession with perfection and a love affair with airplanes which, for better or worse, was to control his life.

John J. McDonald neatly expressed the former in his book about the Hercules flying boat: "Howard Hughes virtually ran the entire business operations out of his hip pocket for nearly 40 years until his mental state deteriorated." As to his qualifications as a pilot, ask the Bristol Aeroplane Company flying crew who, in 1958, took the then advanced long-range turboprop airliner, the Britannia, to Montreal, to demonstrate it to Hughes. Hughes sat up all night in the Britannia, poring over the multivolumed manuals. Next day, from the left-hand seat, without ever having flown in the aircraft before, he took this brand-new 110-seat aircraft on a series of test flights with an aplomb that astounded the hitherto skeptical British air crew.

While this review of a great man is directed toward his achievements in aviation, more particularly airline management, reference to one of his other activities during the 1920s is perhaps relevant to an assessment of Howard Hughes's career. In 1926, at only twenty years of age, he went to Hollywood and began to make films, financing them himself. Many are best erased from memory, but he produced three that will never be forgotten. *Hell's Angels*, released in 1930, revealed Hughes's perfectionism by portraying aerial combat as never before, incidentally making an unspoken commentary upon the senselessness of war. It was also the world's first multimillion-dollar talking picture. Demonstrating the way to perform an especially tricky stunt, Hughes himself crashed one of the aircraft during the shooting of the film.

Scarface was one of the classic gangster films, while *The Outlaw* was remarkable for introducing a generously endowed lady. Hughes created movie stars in all three films—Jean Harlow, Paul Muni, and Jane Russell, respectively—just as in aviation men rose to prominence in their own right while working for him.

During the 1930s Howard Hughes was always capturing headlines, pictured by the media and public alike as a dashing young extroverted playboy, enjoying his wealth. In 1934 he modified an Army Boeing P-12, won the unlimited class event in the All-American Air Meet in Miami, and received the Sportsman's Trophy for his effort. On the strength of this, he founded the Hughes Aircraft Company and set about designing a world-beating racing airplane.

The product of this enterprise was the H-1, with which he beat the world's landplane speed record, at 352 miles an hour, in 1935.

He was fairly active in 1936. In January, he broke the transcontinental speed record in a Northrop Gamma, in 9 hours 27 minutes, and broke other point-to-point records. In January 1937, he broke his own transcontinental record in the H-1, in 7 hours 28 minutes, even though his landing at New York was delayed because of congested runways. Possibly more important than the record itself was that he flew at the then high altitude of 14,000 feet, using oxygen equipment, while his engine was supercharged to cope with the more rarified air at that height. For this achievement he received the Harmon Trophy.

In July 1938, he flew around the world in less than four days in a Lockheed 14, breaking Wiley Post's 1933 record by half, averaging an amazing 202 miles an hour. Hughes made meticulous preparations for this flight, establishing a system of radio communications, weather reporting, and navigation that were in advance of the systems in use at the time. Once again he had dramatically demonstrated technical advances that would be of inestimable benefit to the progress of aviation technology. For his round-the-world achievement, the National Aeronautics Association named him Aviator of the New Year, and in December 1939, he received the prestigious Collier Trophy, presented to him personally by President Franklin D. Roosevelt.

While all this was going on—making millions from the Tool Company, producing film epics in Hollywood, building technically advanced aircraft, and breaking world air records (only partly for fun)—Howard Hughes was also embarking on another career or two. Almost simultaneously, he acquired control of an airline and laid the specifications for an airliner that was to become a landmark achievement for its builder and designer. The airline was Transcontinental and Western Air (T.W.A.); the airliner was the Lockheed Constellation.

The stories of T.W.A. and the Constellation are inextricably interwoven, with Howard Hughes as the binding thread. T.W.A. was one of the larger U.S. domestic airlines and one of the three big transcontinental companies. It was the product of a merger—the notorious shotgun marriage—between Western Express, one of the original contract mail carriers of 1926, and Transcontinental Air Transport (T.A.T.), founded as a passenger airline in 1928, with no

The Lockheed Constellation, epitomizing the best of the postwar long-range piston airliner generation, was built largely at Howard Hughes's instigation and developed to a stage of perfection largely through his persistent, often irritating, involvement with the project.

less a celebrity than Charles Lindbergh as its technical adviser. Originally in the hands of the Pennsylvania Railroad, control of T.W.A. had passed to an uneasy partnership of John Hertz, owner of Yellow Cabs, and Lehman Brothers, the financiers, following the enforced divestiture of railroad stock after the Air Mail Scandal of 1934.

Jack Frye, president of T.W.A., and his right-hand man, Paul Richter, decided that they could not work with Hertz and, at the end of 1938, discussed with Howard Hughes the possibility of his buying some other airline, which they would run for him. Hughes surprised them by suggesting that he should buy T.W.A. by the expedient of acquiring enough stock to outvote Hertz in a proxy fight, if it came to that. But Hertz was ready to sell, and Howard Hughes purchased about 25 percent of the T.W.A. stock—some 200,000 shares—for $1.6 million. By 1940 he held a controlling interest, and during the next fifteen years or so he built up his holding to 78 percent.

Jack Frye is justly credited with being the inspiration behind the famous series of Douglas twin-engined airliners, starting with the DC-1 and DC-2, which culminated in the American Airlines–sponsored DC-3. The DC-3 sold in thousands, but Frye's 1932 specifications provided the incentive for the Douglas engineers to design an airliner superior to the Boeing 247, which was claimed, with equal justification, to be the first modern airliner. The T.W.A. DC-2 started a new era when it went into service in 1934, and Jack Frye tried to repeat the performance in 1936 by ordering the Boeing Type 307 Stratoliner to introduce the world's first pressurized airliner. But partly because of T.W.A.'s financial problems and partly because of John Hertz's procrastination in making progress payments, delivery was delayed until 1940. Then, with the onset of war and the requisitioning of all the best commercial aircraft by the U.S. government, most of the Stratoliner's work was performed for the armed forces, and it saw little commercial service.

Before the Stratoliner went into service in 1940, however, Howard Hughes and Jack Frye had crystallized their thoughts on the Constellation, as the great Lockheed airliner was later to be called. In June 1939, at an historic meeting of T.W.A.'s top men with Lockheed's President Robert Gross and designers Hal Hibbard and Kelly Johnson, the specifications were set. Drawing on the conviction that, like the Stratoliner, it had to be pressurized, they set its size at sixty seats, its range at 3,500 miles, and its speed at almost 300 miles an hour. This was not only about 100 percent better in all respects than anything flying at the time, even the Stratoliner, it was about 50 percent better than anything else on the drawing boards, including the Douglas DC-4. Hughes's predictable insistence upon secrecy was readily accepted and carefully put into practice.

At this time, T.W.A. had no ready cash, at least not enough to place an order for a number of airliners costing $450,000 each. Howard Hughes came to the rescue. In a decision that was as historic as the creation of the aircraft itself, to finance the order he came up with a plan that was bold and simple. The Hughes Tool Company would purchase the aircraft—which it could almost manage to do from petty cash—and then pass them on to T.W.A. under terms that could be worked out later. Because Hughes owned the

Tool Company outright and about 70 percent of T.W.A., such terms were hardly worth discussing. In practice, it was the enabling act that permitted Kelly Johnson and his crew to go ahead, with all speed and without hindrance—except from Hughes's irritating insistence on perfection—to design and build one of the greatest commercial airliners in world aviation history.

Within two years the secrecy had to be broken, as war clouds gathered and aircraft production was geared exclusively toward the military. Thus, the Constellation became the Army's C-69 and the Navy's R70/R7V, while Hughes persuaded Gross to agree not to sell the aircraft to a direct transcontinental competitor. This was a neat turn of the tables, for in 1933 the refusal of the Boeing Company, then in control of United Air Lines, to sell the Model 247 to T.W.A. had been the inspiration for Jack Frye's historic letter leading to the development of the DC-2. Now, United would be tied to the unpressurized, slower, and smaller DC-4 when it resumed normal operations after the end of World War II.

Howard Hughes and Jack Frye shared the honor of delivering the first Lockheed Constellation to the Air Corps; they did it in as dramatic a fashion as Hughes could have devised for one of his Hollywood spectaculars. On April 17, 1944, they delivered the aircraft to Washington, having left Burbank only 6 hours 58 minutes earlier, shattering the transcontinental speed record, an all the more impressive achievement because this was a commercial airliner, not a racing airplane. Provocatively, the Constellation was painted in T.W.A.'s colors, although legally it was an army aircraft. Hughes also managed to make a few demonstration flights for government officials, and he cut two engines on the occasion when the entire Civil Aeronautics Board was aloft, just to emphasize the superior performance of this fine aircraft.

By this time, Howard Hughes had associated himself with another mighty project, by comparison with which even the Constellation was dwarfed. In 1942 the shipbuilder Henry J. Kaiser, who had achieved fame and fortune with his ingenious application of mass-production methods to merchant shipping, was promoting the idea of building giant flying boats as a means of evading the ravages of German submarines on the North Atlantic supply lines to Great Britain. Kaiser cherished the dream of turning out huge transoceanic aircraft at the rate of 500 a year, each of which could carry about sixty tons of cargo. Formidable though such a revolutionary idea was at the time—such aircraft have been feasible only during the last few years—there were some who judged that, in the face of the looming prospect of a complete U-Boat victory, which would bring Atlantic shipping convoys to a standstill, this imaginative solution was not entirely a pipe dream.

Nevertheless, Kaiser could not find an aircraft manufacturer to join him in his ambitious venture until he met Howard Hughes. Hughes cared less for patriotism and profits than for the technical challenge and the opportunity to show that he could undertake a vast project that rival manufacturers would not. And what a challenge! The Hughes Hercules—for this was the aircraft that emerged from his fertile imagination—remains today the largest, if not the heaviest aircraft ever built. It was designed to carry a sixty-ton Sherman tank or 750 troops and was built almost entirely of wood—laminated birch veneer—during a metal-starved era. No less an aviation authority than Grover Loening, consultant to the War Production Board, gave the Hercules his enthusiastic stamp of approval in 1943.

The story of the Spruce Goose, as the headline-hungry press dubbed it—Hughes hated them for it—is well known. After much delay, it made its historic single short flight at Long Beach on November 2, 1947. By this time, large landplanes, including Lockheed's pace-setting Constellation—ironically with Hughes's own T.W.A. as the launching customer—had taken over the U.S. commercial airways from the now obsolete flying boats. The Hughes Hercules was a museum piece before it was finished.

There had been much delay before the boat finally became airborne as development work continued, even after the war had ended. Some of the delay was because of Hughes's constant and unremitting perfectionism. But there were other problems beyond his control, such as the flooding of the dock site, leading to a lawsuit that lasted nearly ten years, by which time Hughes had lost all practical interest. Although there was only one Hercules, ultimately a flying white elephant, it was nevertheless a thing of incredible beauty, built with precision and loving care, and is fittingly preserved as a memorial to Hughes's genius in Long Beach, California.

The development of the Constellation and the Hercules were not enough to keep Hughes's alert mind fully occupied, possibly because Noah Dietrich was looking after the principal source of income, the Tool Company. In the prime of life, Hughes was taking various romances in his stride, but his first love, plainly and simply, was flying. Like the illustrious Lindbergh, he flew as much with an instinct for testing innovations and improvements in the science of aeronautics as he did for the sheer enjoyment. Hughes's great flights usually proved the efficiency of new instruments or techniques, just as Lindbergh's did. Indeed, his round-the-world Lockheed 14 was dubbed the Flying Laboratory. The difference— and this is often forgotten—is that Hughes was, in his way, just as good as the revered Lindbergh, and his achievements were executed in a more complex technical environment.

His success with speed and his pride in the high-altitude Hughes H-1 racing airplane had persuaded him to embark on the Hughes XF-11 project, a twin-engined high-altitude photo-reconnaissance aircraft for the army. Work began in 1943, but the sleek new airplane was not ready for its test flight until July 7, 1946. Howard Hughes himself—who else?—made the taxi tests and took off, only to crash spectacularly because the landing gear did not fully retract and the contrarotating propeller system failed. Miraculously, although seriously injured, Hughes survived the fiery crash and test-flew the second prototype—without contrarotating propellers—only six months later.

While this account is mainly to assess Howard Hughes as an airline leader, the apparent digressions are necessary to place his actions with T.W.A. in their proper context. By the time he was forty-two years old, in 1947, he had, at one time or another, flown faster, or farther, or with a larger aircraft than anyone else in the world. As Hughes Aircraft he built airplanes, and as T.W.A. he operated them. In both activities, he enjoyed success and suffered failure. But while the failures in aircraft construction were outweighed by successes— Hughes Aircraft survives today, albeit under a new owner—his dream of leading T.W.A. to greatness was to become a nightmare.

There was a glorious postwar period when it seemed that T.W.A. could do no wrong. As one of the contributors to the war effort, by its supply of aircraft such as the Stratoliner, and by providing pilot training to thousands at its Eagle Nest flying school at Albuquerque, the airline was rewarded with a share of the coveted transatlantic air route, awarded in 1944. With the Constellations, T.W.A. had the best flying equipment for this operation, but Hughes must have regretted his magnanimity back in 1941 in allowing Pan American to purchase this aircraft as well. At that time, he did not imagine T.W.A. as a potential overseas operator, with Juan Trippe firmly in control of the U.S. Chosen Instrument for foreign air commerce.

But when opportunity knocked he was quick to answer. T.W.A. eventually overtook Pan Am to become the leading transatlantic airline, and the time would come when its international operations became T.W.A.'s dominant segment. During the early postwar years, as T.W.A. sought to extend the Atlantic service and to encircle the globe with a round-the-world route, Hughes's team explored every avenue in support of this goal. Frustrated by a strictly regulated system of route allocation by the Civil Aeronautics Board (C.A.B.), he was barred from flying the Pacific Ocean. T.W.A. tried to forge a link with Northwest Orient Airlines, one of the Pacific incumbents, and Hughes changed the lengthy name of his airline to Trans World, at the same time reflecting his global aspirations.

T.W.A. also made arrangements with selected overseas airlines, in a praiseworthy effort to organize supporting sources of traffic. It invested in airlines in Italy, Iran, Ethiopia, Saudi Arabia, and the Philippines. T.W.A. also bought into Transportes Aéreos Centro-Americanos (TACA), a colorful airline with headquarters in Panama, a move that in theory, if not in practice, could fashion a network throughout Latin America. Jack Frye, president of T.W.A., was as much responsible for such expansion as Howard Hughes, and even though Frye left T.W.A. in 1947, this was because of Dietrich, not Hughes. Of all the experiments with overseas route expansion and airline affiliation, only the TACA experiment was clearly disastrous, and this was primarily Frye's project. But they all had one thing in common: they were all aimed at the erosion of the dominance of U.S. air routes overseas by Pan American Airways. More than any other single airline, T.W.A. destroyed Pan Am's Chosen Instrument status, and more than any other single man, Howard Hughes curtailed the dominance and influence of Pan Am's dictator, Juan Trippe.

Strangely, historians often forget that Howard Hughes was ultimately responsible for T.W.A. policy during the critical postwar period of development. He and his president steered T.W.A. to a position in which it was one of the technical and commercial leaders of a great industry. Pan American owed its tremendous success to a whole army of great administrators, pilots, engineers, and marketing men, but Juan Trippe has always been granted most of the credit. Equally, however, Howard Hughes is entitled to much of the credit in taking over a great airline and turning it into an even greater one. And this is not to diminish recognition of the acknowledged work of the presidents who succeeded Jack Frye, especially the impressive Ralph Damon, whose death, in 1956, was almost a mortal blow both to the airline and to Howard Hughes himself.

True, Trippe did not commandeer aircraft at short notice to go and visit a girl friend, leaving an irate group of passengers stranded at the airport. Neither did he keep executives awake half the night with telephone calls to their homes. But in other ways Trippe was just as mindless of other people's feelings. Few employees of Pan American had much better access to the corporate records and files than did those of T.W.A. Howard Hughes's inaccessibility was simply more erratic and therefore more widely publicized than Trippe's, and in later years it was retrospectively exaggerated.

Also forgotten is the fact that United Air Lines was offered a selection of postwar North Atlantic routes; yet Pat Patterson, the methodical leader who had guided that airline to its leading position as the largest airline in the Western world, turned down the offer on the grounds that his analysis showed that the total traffic would be insufficient to sustain more than about twenty aircraft for the foreseeable future and that United's share would not be worth the investment. Howard Hughes did not miss a golden opportunity. Hughes was right and Patterson was wrong. Yet Patterson was never castigated for a monumental misjudgment.

If T.W.A.'s record in route expansion was wholly satisfactory and if the Constellation and its progeny reigned supreme during the decade following the end of World War II, Howard Hughes had an Achilles' heel, which began to reveal itself with the advent of the Jet Age. With hindsight, it is intriguing to speculate that the excellent qualities of the Constellation, with whose development Hughes had been intimately concerned, were indirectly the cause of T.W.A.'s losing its grip. The Constellation was developed into the Super-Constellation, then into the ultimate piston-engined airliner, the Model L.1649A Starliner. Kelly Johnson's design team at the Lockheed "skunk works" kept the Connie's nose in front of the Douglas series of DC-4, 6, 6B, 7, 7B, and 7C. Possibly the Constellation just went on too long.

Extracting the ultimate performance from the Constellation

stable began to acquire the onus of misjudgment after Juan Trippe and Pan American announced its epoch-making order for forty-five big jet aircraft in 1955. The L.1649A did not enter service, on the New York–Paris nonstop route, until June 1, 1957, and during the intervening period there was still no unamimity about the fate of propeller-driven aircraft, which many thought might be more economical to operate, if slower, than the jets. Hughes came close to ordering the British Bristol Britannia, the Whispering Giant, which had gone into service with the British national airline, B.O.A.C., in February 1957.

But at the very time that Hughes and T.W.A., on the threshold of the jet age, needed cash as never before, their fairy godmother, the Hughes Tool Company, suffered a sharp decline in earnings. Under the arrangements that Hughes first instigated when T.W.A. needed ready cash to launch the Constellation, T.W.A.'s first aircraft were financed by the Hughes Tool Company, not from traditional sources such as banks and other financial institutions. An alternative source of internal Hughes financing, Hughes Aircraft, was unavailable because Hughes himself had transferred ownership to the Howard Hughes Medical Institute, a nonprofit research foundation, whose inheritance included the profits of the aircraft company.

In short, T.W.A. was desperate to obtain quick delivery of a big fleet of jet aircraft but lacked the means to buy them. It could not make the progress payments to Boeing, from which it had ordered thirty-three Boeing 707s, nor to Convair, for thirty Convair 880s.

Years before, when in 1946 Hughes Tool (Toolco) had put $10 million cash into a trouble-torn T.W.A., then handicapped by crashes, a pilots' strike, and the grounding of the Constellation, it had taken back convertible notes and the power to name the majority of T.W.A.'s directors. Equitable Life, holding $40 million in loan debentures, agreed on the condition that if T.W.A. defaulted, Toolco's stock could be put into an Equitable-controlled voting trust. After lying dormant for twelve years, this clause now emerged as a weapon with which to attack Hughes.

In 1958, Hughes had to raise $12 million for T.W.A. on a ninety-day guarantee by Toolco. Living an apparent hand-to-mouth existence, Equitable insisted that long-term financing must be arranged quickly. Otherwise it would invoke the voting-trust clause of the 1946 agreement. During the next two years, Hughes maneuvered ingeniously but desperately, like a chess grand master who had lost his queen. That T.W.A. kept going during this period, even maintaining its competitive edge, was a minor miracle, thanks in part to a fine management team and a disciplined staff, but in part, let it be added, to Hughes's shrewd manipulation of T.W.A.'s money.

The end came when, in May 1960, as a condition of a $300 million long-term financing plan from Irving Trust, Hughes had to agree that Equitable's old long-term loan should be converted to a short-term loan. The critical clause in the agreement was that if any change of management was thought to be adverse, Equitable could demand that Hughes's stock—some 77 percent of the total—be put under the control of a voting trust.

When on July 27, 1960, T.W.A. president Charlie Thomas resigned because of prolonged differences with Hughes over the purchasing program, the potential lenders suddenly became as hard to get in financial negotiation as Hughes had been in his withdrawal from public life. For by this time the trials of the protracted business battles in which he was involved were beginning to take their toll, and Hughes had sought refuge from the stress by becoming a recluse. He avoided public appearance, refused to be photographed, and in effect disappeared from human ken. He was out of reach of all but his most intimate associates, and as often as not he was not even available to them. He became notorious for making telephone calls in the middle of the night, or from telephone booths, and even of meeting people in public lavatories, so intense was his obsession with privacy. This kind of conduct led inevitably to the conclusion that Hughes was becoming a bit eccentric.

On December 31, 1960, Hughes capitulated. Equitable took control and placed his stock in the hands of a voting trust, which promptly appointed a new board and management. One of their first actions was to file an antitrust suit against the Hughes Tool Company, on the grounds that, as both supplier and financier of aircraft for T.W.A., it had excluded other suppliers. This was a harsh irony in a harsh business world where normally no quarter was asked or given. In this case, the history of the Constellation, which Hughes had specified and financed and which had led T.W.A. to great heights, was being totally ignored. Without Hughes there might have been no airline and no Constellation.

There were more legal battles, in which the Civil Aeronautics Board became involved. There were suits and countersuits. Astonishingly, amid all the labyrinthine legal arguments, the C.A.B. granted Hughes permission to control Northeast Airlines and even, in July 1964, declared that he could resume control of T.W.A., provided that he disposed of his interest in Northeast. But the opposition lawyers soon put a stop to that promising escape route. Ultimately, in September 1968, the Hughes Tool Company had to pay $138 million in treble damages. Howard Hughes had, after a ten-year struggle, lost more than a battle. He had lost a war.

The most extraordinary outcome of the whole affair was that, in the midst of all this litigation, T.W.A., under a steady management, was sharing in the fantastic airline boom of the 1960s precipitated by the advent of the jet age. It had been making a great deal of money, and its reputation had never been better. By the time the Hughes Tool Company had had to cough up the treble damages, it had, in May 1966, sold its entire trustee-held stock through a secondary offering to the general public. A total of 6,584,937 shares, valued at $86 each, changed hands—in twenty minutes—for $566,304,582.

Materially, Howard Hughes was suddenly half a billion dollars richer. Spiritually, having lost T.W.A., he was a pauper.

Fortune magazine commented that "this is the largest sum to come into the hands of one man at one time." It also published a penetrating analysis of the whole affair, which, it said, raised some important questions. Why should the owner of 77 percent of the stock of a company, however unorthodox he may be, be prevented from voting that stock? How much power should large-scale lenders be allowed, so as to protect their loans? And what is the public interest in the case of an airline, which is a quasi-public utility? *Fortune's* implication was that Hughes had perhaps been manipulated.

Possibly. It was rough justice. In the past he had been the manipulator, par excellence. And he still was.

When, in September 1968, the protracted litigation over the T.W.A. affair finally went against Hughes, he was sixty-three years old. With net assets that made him one of the richest men in the world and with a lifetime record of achievement that would have satisfied the collective aspirations of any dozen normally ambitious men, he could have enjoyed a withdrawal from the rat race of high finance. Not Hughes. He had aviation in his blood, and if he was too old and infirm to be an active pilot, his mind was still sharp enough that he could wheel and deal within the airline world. He would dearly have liked to wriggle his way back into T.W.A., but he must have known that he would never be able to control that airline again. So he looked elsewhere.

Over on the West Coast a three-way merger had been forged from three local service airlines, West Coast, Pacific, and Bonanza. The resultant airline was far from local, ranging as it did over eight large western states, with branches flying to Canada and Mexico. The driving force behind the merger was ostensibly Nick Bez from Seattle, head of West Coast Airlines, and he became chairman of the new airline, which began combined operations on July 1, 1968. Six weeks later, on August 12, Bez announced that the Hughes Tool Company had agreed to buy the airline for $90 million. Other directors of Air West were said to express disfavor with the idea, probably the understatement of the decade.

There followed a series of events that no writer of fiction or soap opera script would have dared to invent. On December 27, 1968, after much maneuvering, the Bez group carried the shareholders' vote by a narrow margin; next day, the directors reversed the decision because of a last-minute counteroffer from another airline. On December 31, six of the thirteen anti-Hughes directors changed their minds in Hughes's favor. They were believed to have been under severe pressure, to put it mildly. The C.A.B. and President Nixon eventually, in July 1969, approved the acquisition by Hughes Tool. After further Machiavellian financial manipulations, the sale was completed on March 31, 1970, to a new company, Hughes Air Corporation.

Seventy-eight percent of Hughes Air was owned by the Hughes Tool Company, 100 percent of which was owned by Howard Hughes. The remaining 22 percent was held directly by Hughes himself. One former shareholder was quoted, "I can't believe that awful record . . . was a series of coincidences. It's been such a colossal series of errors that it seems it must have been masterminded by someone."

History repeated itself in a familiar pattern, and the old manipulator seemed to be shaping that history once again, according to a T.W.A.-inspired precedent. Money was injected into the ailing airline, which in July 1970 was renamed Hughes Air West and given a trendy new image as well as a streamlined new management. Then the trouble broke out again. In December 1972, a Federal Grand Jury indicted Howard Hughes for conspiracy, and half the lawyers west of the Rocky Mountains went to work again. A seesaw battle then ensued as Federal Judge Bruce Thompson sided with Hughes, and the case went backward and forward several times until January 1979, when the Summa Corporation, inheritors of the relevant Hughes liability, agreed to pay $37 million to the former shareholders of Air West, who had been deprived of their business lives back in 1968.

The whole affair sometimes had the elements of farce. Key witnesses would disappear; even Jimmie the Greek, of Las Vegas gambling fame, became involved; and in the middle of it all, on April 5, 1976, as if to have the very last word, Howard Hughes died.

During the last decade of his life, Hughes's health had deteriorated rapidly. He was ailing physically, and while he was still sharp as a tack in business matters, even if he made occasional mistakes, his mental attitudes were curiously warped in several directions. His habitual love of privacy developed into an obsession, and he became a hermit. Hughes's idea of a hermit's cave, however, was a whole floor, or even two, of a luxury hotel, whether this was in one that he owned in Las Vegas, or one that he visited occasionally in the Bahamas, or London, or elsewhere. He mistrusted everybody, including the doctors he really needed, and in his declining years surrounded himself with only a handful of confidants, drawn mainly from the Mormon Church. His eccentricity in this respect led to wild exaggeration by a frustrated press, which, like many a politician or administrator, had never forgiven him for past insults. The more desperately Hughes sought the privacy he yearned for, the more his pursuers tried to deprive him of it. In this particular conflict, Hughes may be said to have won, for few people ever set eyes on him during the last five years of his life; if they did, they knew not whom they saw.

Throughout his career, to a greater or lesser degree, Hughes's main vice was his complete contempt for the feelings of his fellow men, although he respected many opinions without necessarily making any concessions graciously. He seemed incapable of realizing that, because he kept unearthly hours, others wished to sleep. He coarsely believed that money would buy anything or anybody—and this belief was supported by experience. He was a philanderer, and he treated most women as chattel, paying for them, whether in cash or in kind. In this respect he was not alone among great men, from presidents to prime ministers, kings to emperors.

Those who knew him well can always recall times when Hughes was charming, considerate, thoughtful, even kindly—such adjectives spring to mind. Unfortunately, such references are invariably made defensively and quoted as exceptions to the general rule. Hughes was a loner, and because of his immense wealth he could indulge himself in whatever whim took his fancy: buying an airplane, an airline, a management team, or a woman, without giving a second thought to the effect of his actions on anyone else.

Howard Hughes was an enigma. His ethics apart, however, he was far from being the half-crazed eccentric that the media chose to adopt as their stereotype Hughes. For most of his life, he was no recluse. He was highly visible, yet displayed a modest bearing that contrasted with the egotism of lesser aviation celebrities. He created much talent, and some of his virtues, his perfectionism, his determination, and his sheer love of aviation rubbed off on others. Above all, as a record-breaking pilot, as an inspiration to airplane designers, as an imaginative financier, and as an inspired airline promoter, he was in a class all his own.

At one period of his career, which might be called its zenith, he simultaneously owned one of the biggest airlines in the world, created its flagship—which was also the best airliner in the world—and was able to fly it as well as any four-ringed captain. There has never been anyone who instinctively possessed so many varied aeronautical talents as Howard Hughes, and there probably never will be. He was truly phenomenal.

▶▶▶▶ ◀ ▶▶▶▶▶▶▶▶▶▶▶▶▶▶▶▶▶▶▶

James H. Carmichael

Coach Fares and Turbine Power

Some indication of the importance of Slim Carmichael's contribution to the U.S. airline industry can be gathered from the knowledge that every year Carmichael is toasted by the veteran retirees of the airline which he led from near obscurity almost to greatness. Although Capital Airlines disappeared from the records a quarter of a century ago, it is remembered with affection, and its demise is regretted more as an accident of circumstances than as a deserving sequel to bad management. Capital was a pioneer in the advocacy of low fares, which were to extend the accessibility of airline travel to a wider public, and the innovator of turbine power in the United States. For these two remarkable steps across the thresholds of orthodoxy, Slim Carmichael's place in airline history is guaranteed.

James H. Carmichael, or Slim, as he became known to one and all, was born on April 2, 1907, in Newark, New Jersey. His father, James H., Sr., was a devil-may-care Irishman, and he shuttled the family backward and forward across America, once even going to Europe, as he sought the formula for success. But, as the *Saturday Evening Post* once reported, "his talent for making money was often overmatched by his genius for getting rid of it." Nevertheless, young James was able to attend Suffield Military Academy, in Suffield, Connecticut, and was graduated in 1924 at the age of seventeen.

65

During his stay at Suffield, Slim showed a talent for sports, and he did the usual moonlighting jobs to work his way through school in the traditional American way. Perhaps his most notable achievement during this period was to earn a $300 credit for tutoring an Armenian who spoke nine languages, none of them English. He worked in an amusement park for a while, and then, when his family split up, he worked for his father on an eighty-acre truck farm in Michigan, to accumulate an interest in it. But he felt there must be easier ways to make a living, so he left after two years, still not yet twenty years old.

He had always been interested in flying, so he left Michigan in December 1925 and went to Chicago to learn to fly. At first he pursued the familiar round of washing, oiling, and greasing airplanes in Chicago, so as to get to know aviation people and to fulfill his ambition of learning to fly. After only six hours of flying experience, he soloed in a Jenny in 1926, and the next year he landed his first contract. He was once hired to take a small party of men to Louisville in a Ryan Brougham; although he observed them swapping briefcases, only later did he discover that his customers were Chicago gangsters and that, as a novice, he had been given the assignment because no one else wanted it. Young Slim must have grown up very quickly in the tough environment of Chicago in the late 1920s, but there were compensations. He became acquainted with many of the famous jazz musicians of the Windy City, including the legendary Bix Beiderbecke.

Slim Carmichael barnstormed the Midwest for a couple of years, offering, as was customary at the time, joyrides for $5.00 a trip. He recalled that on one occasion, at Rockford, Illinois, he was temporarily grounded because his airplane needed minor repairs, and the resourceful Roscoe Turner turned up and took all his business for the day. Elevating himself from this particular School of Hard Knocks, he went back to New York and became an instructor-pilot for the Newark Air Service, close to where he was born. This was in October 1929, and very soon, after selling an airplane on commission and receiving the princely sum of $700, he was married on July 4, 1930, to Jessie Northrop (no relation to the famous aircraft designer), whom he had first met in Michigan. They were to have two children—Joan, born in 1934, and Judith, born in 1937—and were always a close-knit family thereafter.

Carmichael gained a great reputation among his peers as a pi-

Slim Carmichael, seen here in front of the Vickers Viscount, the British airliner with which he introduced turbine power to the U.S. airline industry, steered Capital Airlines from regional status to become the fifth largest passenger carrier in the Western world.

lot, and he participated in a few airplane events that drew attention. In November 1932, for example, he flew mail, newspapers, and movie film in a floatplane to an ocean liner headed for Europe to announce the news of Franklin Roosevelt's election before anyone else. He flew Amelia Earhart's Lockheed Vega, with a broken stabilizer, from Hartford to Newark, just before her Atlantic flight. He worked semipermanently flying John Kluge, who manufactured labels for clothing on a near-monopoly basis, in a Loening amphibian, which must have been one of the earlier examples of the use of aircraft for executive flying. He piloted Stinson trimotors for Ludington Airlines, between Newark and Washington, and from then on he was an airline man.

In 1933 Slim Carmichael moved west to work for Pittsburgh Airways, also flying Stinson trimotors, as second pilot to the veteran Merle Moltrop, who had previously been with Pennsylvania Airlines. The latter company, controlled by a group of Pittsburgh businessmen, operated from Pittsburgh to Washington. It had originally flown across the Allegheny Mountains, on one of the air mail routes to be contracted by the U.S. Post Office in 1926. Clifford Ball had won the contract, advertising the service as "The Path of the Eagle," and sold it to the Pittsburgh group which was headed by C. Bedell Monro, in association with his brother-in-law, Frederick R. Crawford, and a prominent attorney, George R. Hann. Carmichael's position with the rival Pittsburgh Airways was simply that of a pilot, but he was to play an important part in both airlines' affairs as time went on.

The entire airline industry in the United States went through a metamorphosis during the early months of 1934, in the notorious Air Mail Scandal, in which all the major air mail contractors were the subject of investigation by a special congressional committee. A great deal of public money had been distributed to the airlines as mail payments, on a rather liberal scale, and the postmaster general was accused of connivance with certain airlines that he favored. On February 19, 1934, all contract air mail operations were canceled by the Roosevelt administration, and the U.S. Army Air Force took over during a dramatic few weeks, in which exaggerated publicity was given to several tragic accidents, caused mainly by the lack of experience by the army pilots, flying aircraft unsuited for the task.

The government quickly admitted its error, and the post office readvertised the mail routes on May 5. In general, most of the routes were awarded to the old contractors, who made their bids under slightly different names, to comply with the small print of the new regulations. Thus, Pennsylvania Airlines was reorganized as Pennsylvania Airlines and Transport Company, but it was outbid by a new company, Central Airlines, which was, in fact, Pittsburgh Airways under another name.

Central Airlines, owned by two heirs to a coal fortune, John and Richard Coulter, won the mail contract against Pennsylvania and began service on May 17, 1934, on a Detroit–Cleveland–Pittsburgh–Washington route, with Stinson trimotors, at a frequency of three flights a day each way. Pennsylvania continued to operate without the mail contract, but had Ford Tri-Motors and gave Central such stiff competition for the passenger traffic that Central was forced to acquire Fords as well. Slim Carmichael was indirectly mentioned in the publicity for the Fords: "Two Pilots—Two-way Radio."

During the following year, Carmichael managed to find himself in the newspaper headlines on a number of occasions. He made two fairly harmless emergency landings and one spectacular one in the capital, where any incident was bound to attract attention. On April 22, 1935, he had left Washington's Hoover Field at night en route for Pittsburgh in a Ford Tri-Motor. Eighty miles out, at 5,000 feet, an outboard engine parted company from the airplane, taking with it sundry electrical circuits, damaging the center engine controls, and worst of all, taking with it one of the two landing wheels. Slim Carmichael found himself with a twin-engined, one-wheeled Ford, at night, without lights. Broadcasting the airman's SOS, "Mayday, Mayday," he wisely selected the army's Bolling Field at Washington, where he knew that the emergency equipment was probably the best in the country.

Carmichael landed the Ford on one wheel, and the passengers were escorted into taxicabs without a scratch. For this unusual demonstration of the skills demanded of an airline pilot during a typical day's work, he was one of the group of deserving airmen to receive the Air Mail Flyer's Congressional Medal of Honor, presented by President Roosevelt for distinguished service as an air mail pilot. This was on October 29, 1935, and he demonstrated his versatility two weeks later when, on November 16, he made another unorthodox landing at Pittsburgh, attracting the headline in the local newspaper, "Carmichael slithers on his belly thirty feet." This, if anything, was an understatement. He had tried to take off but there was water in the gas tank. His slither brought him to the end of the field, which was at the edge of a precipice.

By this time, the duel for supremacy on the route from the Great Lakes to the capital, via the industrial region of Cleveland–Akron–Youngstown–Pittsburgh, was intensifying. On January 8, 1935, Pennsylvania had introduced the Boeing 247-D, recognized as the first modern airliner and capable of cruising at 160 miles an hour—about 70 miles an hour faster than the Ford. Central Airlines retaliated by introducing the so-called high-speed Stinson Model A and also entered into a desperate, fare-cutting price war.

After much acrimony, both airlines decided to bury the hatchet and came to the only sensible solution. They merged on September 21, 1936, to establish Pennsylvania-Central Airlines, later to become known familiarly by its initials, P.C.A., and still remembered affectionately by many people from that era, both within the airline and among the general public in the area it served. C. Bedell Monro, of Pennsylvania, became president of the new airline, and James H. Carmichael, of Central, was named operations manager. The operations of the two airlines were consolidated on November 1, 1936.

During the next few years, Pennsylvania-Central tried steadily, if not spectacularly, to establish itself as an airline of respectable stature. It expanded its single Washington–Great Lakes route in 1937 by adding a second, from Washington to Buffalo, via Baltimore and eastern Pennsylvania, and by a sortie into West Virginia, which, however, was not sustained. After the passage of the Civil Aeronautics Act in 1938, however, the network spread to include Norfolk, Virginia; Chicago, as a branch line from Grand Rapids; a direct link from Pittsburgh to Buffalo; and a feeder line into northern Michigan as far as Sault Sainte Marie.

These "grandfather certificates" of route authority issued by the Civil Aeronautics Board established P.C.A.'s permanent presence as an important airline serving the Great Lakes and the national capital region. The area was not extensive geographically, compared with the coast-to-coast empires of the large domestic trunks such as United and American, but the importance of the many large cities served guaranteed a solid traffic base. Thus, although on the last day of 1937 Pennsylvania-Central had purchased a fleet of Boeing 247-Ds from United Air Lines to replace the older 247s and the one remaining Stinson A, these were soon due for replacement.

In December 1939, Slim Carmichael went to the Douglas factory in California and flew the first DC-3 to Pittsburgh; this acknowledged breadwinner went into service on the Washington–Detroit main line route on January 2, 1940. Fitted with twenty-one seats, a fleet of six DC-3s supplemented thirteen Boeing 247s, and Pennsylvania-Central introduced its first stewardesses and food service to go along with the upgrading of its fleet.

The next two years brought further success in consolidating and extending its routes. Pennsylvania-Central established its presence in the South, with extensions from Norfolk to Knoxville, in November 1939, followed by a link to the same east Tennessee city from Pittsburgh, and on to Birmingham, Alabama. Equally important to the additional route mileage, the C.A.B. authorized nonstop authority between some of the big cities, such as Detroit–Milwaukee, Detroit–Washington, and Detroit–Pittsburgh. In those days, every route had to be operated exactly according to the wording on the C.A.B. certificate, and any deviation had to be covered by an amendment or an exemption, so strict were the conditions of the regulatory system.

Aside from the route expansion, two events late in 1941 were to change the course of Pennsylvania-Central's growth. Late in 1941, the airline moved its headquarters from Pittsburgh to Washington, a move that coincided with that momentous day, December 7, of the year that the United States was plunged into World War II.

The four years of wartime activity had a profound effect on Pennsylvania-Central's progress. There were handicaps and benefits, and as head of operations, Slim Carmichael was in the thick of things throughout. On the one hand, he had to try to keep an airline going with only a third of its fleet available. The government requisitioned eleven of the airline's eighteen DC-3s and its four remaining B-247s, leaving Carmichael to juggle with "The Seven Planes That Stayed Home"—as a press advertisement described the precarious position. For the operation of the scheduled network this was little short of disastrous, and several routes were suspended for the duration of the conflict.

On the other side of the coin, however, valuable experience was gained. On April 1, 1942, for instance, Pennsylvania-Central Airlines began the first domestic scheduled military air cargo in the United States, thus chalking up a first, a privilege normally confined to the dominant Big Four airlines. Carmichael's team flew twenty special missions, as far as Alaska and Greenland, and set up training programs for the military in Washington and Roanoke. By 1943 Pennsylvania's military operations were twice as big as its commercial ones, when it took over the responsibility of flying the twenty-three aircraft of the 10th Ferrying Command.

But there were some compensations. Traffic on the few intercity routes that Pennsylvania-Central had retained was intensive, for they linked many of the wartime production centers with the seat of government. The seven DC-3s were always full, with long waiting lists, so the scheduled operations, though curtailed, were profitable. The situation began to ease in 1944, when some of the DC-3s returned from war duty, increasing the fleet to fourteen.

During the summer, the somewhat cumbersome name Pennsylvania-Central Airlines was accompanied by the abbreviation P.C.A., which, in December, superseded the old name entirely.

This move toward the creation of a sharper image was just in time for some long-awaited improvements to the route structure. On December 16, 1944, the C.A.B. awarded P.C.A. a new route from Pittsburgh to New York, permitting through flights from Chicago, via Detroit, and during the first six months or so of 1945, as the war drew to its close, P.C.A. started direct service from Chicago to the East Coast cities, culminating in a Chicago–New York two-stop service on July 2.

By this time, Slim Carmichael had moved up to become executive vice president of P.C.A. and was taking the lead in shaping the fortunes of the airline. Even though traffic was healthy and the loads were good, especially during the boom that followed the end of hostilities, P.C.A.'s route network consisted entirely of short segments. These are always costly to operate, because only a small percentage of the total operation is flown at the most economical cruising speed and altitude. The time-wasting and expensive procedures preceding and following the flight itself are the same for a 100-mile segment as for, say, an 850-mile New York–Chicago journey. On the other hand, the traffic density between P.C.A.'s principal cities demanded additional capacity.

In September 1945, all the airlines, by agreement with the C.A.B., cut their fares by 25 percent, a move with which Carmichael was not in accord, but he had to go along. To reduce fares at a time when the public was prepared to pay higher fares, during the postwar period when the popularity of air travel was intensifying, seemed illogical. Nevertheless, P.C.A. did what it had to do, which was to provide adequate service to the public, and, with Slim Carmichael heavily involved, it registered another modest first. On January 15, 1946, the little eastern trunk airline inaugurated the first scheduled Douglas DC-4 service in the United States. This was not the first four-engined service, that honor having gone to T.W.A. in 1940, with the Boeing Stratoliner, but the DC-4 was the first successful postwar airliner capable of transoceanic flight and able to carry as many as sixty people on short hauls.

As it turned out, P.C.A. soon found that the basic short-haul economics worked even more heavily against the DC-4 than they did against the DC-3, and, finding itself in a deteriorating financial situation, it was compelled to sell three aircraft to Northeast Airlines, of Boston. Carmichael and his colleagues recognized Northeast as a small so-called trunk airline with difficulties similar to their own, having a network composed of very short routes, but including a very dense one, Boston–New York, for which the four-engined DC-4 was absolutely necessary, because of ruthless competition from competing airlines such as American and Eastern. In fact, in 1945, preliminary talks had taken place between P.C.A. and Northeast with a view to a merger. The idea fell through, but to envisage the effect of such an amalgamation is an interesting speculation, especially as Carmichael was subsequently to attempt other mergers.

During 1946 and 1947 the C.A.B. did offer some relief in the way of route extensions and nonstop authority. But collectively they were only a panacea. The fact that Washington–Chicago nonstop service was finally authorized in September and was inaugurated on October 17, 1947, was an ironic commentary on the depth of restriction that the C.A.B.'s mandate could impose. P.C.A. and its predecessors had operated the route for twenty-one years yet had to plead to be able to take advantage of the air travel market it had created.

There were other minor route extensions, to Memphis and to Minneapolis, but these did nothing for an airline which even its competitors described, with implicit sympathy, as the largest feeder airline in the country. It was losing money hand over fist, almost entirely because of its inability to obtain the rights to operate long routes to compensate for, or cross-subsidize, its plethora of short stages. In less than two years, P.C.A. lost more than $3,500,000, which was a lot of money for a quasi-feeder airline in those days. The airline was clearly heading for bankruptcy, and it was at this inauspicious moment, on October 1, 1947, that the directors of P.C.A. called upon Slim Carmichael to rescue their company from almost certain extinction.

On that day he became president, C. Bedell Monro moving over as chairman, and things began to happen, quickly and drastically. Many of the policies hurt, especially the economy measures aimed at cutting costs. These were absolutely necessary, because, with the C.A.B. continuing to turn a blind eye to the obvious need for route-strengthening and with no hope of increasing revenues, the expenditure side of the economic equation was the only possible target for positive action.

In its shrewd commentary on Carmichael in 1949, *The Saturday Evening Post* reported that, with P.C.A. owing more money than it was worth, "some of Carmichael's friends felt sorry for him. It appeared that he was just a nice guy who chanced to stroll by," and "Skeptics hinted that he was a stand-in, soon to be dislodged by a hard-boiled money man." The *Post* then went on to remark that the nice-guy theory soon evaporated, and that "he is one of the toughest cookies who ever read a balance sheet, roared in pain, and started firing brass hats. He cuts costs to the bone; then he polishes the bone." The statistics showed that he trimmed the staff of P.C.A. from 4,800 to 3,000, eliminating whole departments and removing sinecures. Every item of expenditure was cut: office rentals, telephone calls, ground services, everything.

Frustrated by the powers in Washington, he shopped around for supplementary business, for charters of every kind—flying football teams, offering sight-seeing flights, and ensuring that every cent of mail pay due to P.C.A. was paid. With disarming honesty, he did not describe the last source of income as mail pay, or even subsidy. He said "It's a damned dole. We're going to get off it some day."

The year 1948 was one in which Slim Carmichael and P.C.A. made it quite clear to the U.S. domestic airline industry as a whole that, in spite of the obvious handicaps, the company that had been forced to struggle for survival on the crumbs from the master's table was about to discover sources of nutrition of its own. In a little more than six months, P.C.A. suddenly became the talking point of aviation commentators and drew headlines from the media as Carmichael began to make his presence felt.

He made three important moves in 1948. The first was orthodox, simply a couple of route extensions in the south. But these were not to medium-sized cities such as Knoxville and Birmingham; they were to the southern port and tourist destination, New Orleans, and to booming Atlanta. True, Slim would have preferred Miami, but the route pattern was substantially strengthened in a direction that held out hope of long-haul routes in the future. Philadelphia also joined the network, completing the chain of major East Coast cities from New York to Norfolk.

On May 12, 1948, Carmichael changed the name of his airline from P.C.A., which few could identify correctly with its full name, to Capital Airlines, a title that was immediately popular and carried with it a certain flair, not to mention the opportunity for some promotional punning, which did more than link the airline with the national capital. Such was the impact of this important change that the name is still remembered with affection today.

Then, on November 4, 1948, Capital Airlines claimed another first. This time it was not just a scoop in the United States. It was an innovation that changed the course of air transport all across the globe. For on this date, Capital introduced the first coach-class scheduled air service in the world, by inaugurating the Nighthawk flights, also referred to as Skycoach, between New York and Chicago. The service was offered only at night. It was thus inconvenient for passengers, but it was economical to operate, for the aircraft would otherwise have been on the ground. The standard of service was strictly austere, with only one stewardess for the DC-4, no meals, no giveaways, and no reservations. But in compensation, the fare was cheap, $29.60 one way, instead of the normal $44.10, which also happened to be the same as the Pullman-class rail fare. Rail coach was slightly cheaper, at $27.30, but Capital's four-hour, ten-minute flight was worth the extra $2.30 when the New York Central or the Pennsylvania Railroad took sixteen or seventeen hours.

The inspiration for this revolutionary experiment in low fares was undoubtedly shared by several of the top executives of Capital, notably James B. Franklin, vice-president for operations. But most of the credit should go to Slim Carmichael, who recognized a good idea when he saw one and provided the leadership and drive to carry it through.

Soon, coach-class services were introduced on other Capital routes. But sadly, although the C.A.B. removed many restrictions, allowing more nonstop segments between many major cities, Carmichael and his team had to watch their advantage evaporate. Other airlines, observing the success of Nighthawk, some of whose frequencies ran in several sections, initiated their own coach services, to such an extent that Capital's revolutionary idea was copied the length and breadth of the U.S. by every domestic trunk airline, each proclaiming the joys of cheap air travel and claiming a share of the credit. There seemed to be some injustice about the fact that an airline could not sustain a tariff innovation within a regulated framework and enjoy some protection, in the same way that the grandfather routes were almost sacrosanct, strongly protected by the C.A.B. against incursions from competitors.

The early and mid 1950s found Capital Airlines firmly on the airline map and in the public eye, attracting as much attention as the big airlines, with aviation reporters constantly alert to see what Carmichael and Capital might do next. They were seldom disappointed. In 1950, supported at last with some routes of reasonable length, Capital introduced Lockheed Constellations—no revolution, but upgrading its equipment to the likes of T.W.A. and Eastern— and deploying them, for instance, on a nonstop service from New York to Atlanta.

On March 16, 1951, vicarious access to the affluent Florida market was achieved through an interchange agreement with George Baker's National Airlines. Aircraft of the two companies alternated in flying a Detroit–Cleveland–Pittsburgh–Washington– Miami route, and the arrangement lasted for more than seven years, until Capital finally received the coveted route authority itself.

Then, on May 19, 1952, Carmichael came very close to pulling off the biggest merger in U.S. domestic airline history up to that time. At a Northwest Airlines stockholders' meeting, a proposed merger with Capital narrowly failed. Capital had already agreed, but the Northwest vote fell short of the statutory two-thirds majority. As with the effort in 1945 to merge with Northeast, the action probably stemmed from Carmichael's conviction that, with the C.A.B. implacably determined to block Capital's need for natural expansion, a sympathetic merger with another airline was the only solution.

Two years later, in May 1954, Slim Carmichael was once again in the news, in banner headlines this time. After visiting England, where great strides were being made in the technical development of airliners and turbine engines alike, he placed an order for three forty-seat Vickers Viscount four-engined airliners. The difference between this aircraft and others was that it was powered by four Rolls-Royce Dart turboprop (or propjet) engines of revolutionary design, at least for commercial application. Such was the reliability demonstrated by the Viscount in service, not to mention its economy of operation, by the launching carrier in Europe, British European Airways, that Carmichael augmented the order to forty in August 1954 and raised it again to sixty in November.

The action was revolutionary in that, for the first time, a U.S. airline had placed a substantial order for a foreign-built aircraft. In fact, an intensive search of official records would be required to locate *any* order for a foreign airliner. By ordering sixty, Slim Carmichael made a clear-cut statement that he had found a solution to one of the problems that confront all airlines: to introduce an airliner that is demonstrably superior by a comfortable margin to all the competition. To patriotic Americans, it was unfortunate that, to do this in the 1950s, the shopping had to be in Europe. But there was no gainsaying the commercial wisdom of the decision, and several other airlines followed Capital's lead and purchased Viscounts.

On June 16, 1955, Slim Carmichael and a special crew delivered the first Viscount from Weybridge, England, crossing the Atlantic to New York via Prestwick, Reykjavik, a wartime transatlantic staging airfield located at Narsarsuaq, and Montreal. The story goes that, final touches to the Viscount having only been completed at the end of the day, slightly behind schedule, Vickers wished to dispatch the airliner the next morning. Carmichael announced "We are leaving" and with the help of a battery of volunteer car headlights, he took off into the night—doubtless feeling a little more secure than the time twenty years earlier when he had coped with a twin-engined, one-wheeled Ford Tri-Motor.

Viscount services opened on July 26, 1955, in a blaze of glory and publicity. The correct description of the Dart engine as a turboprop was quickly, if inaccurately, simplified in the public mind to jet, while the Viscounts were often advertised as Rolls-Royce Jets, to take advantage of the Name. For a few frantic, breathless months, Carmichael had the airline world at his feet and made Capital the most talked-about airline in the whole world, even though this was the year when Pan American placed its order for the big jets, the DC-8s and the 707s. The Washington–Chicago flights were named, impressively, Diplomat, President, Independence, and other emotive titles. As more Viscounts were delivered, there was a general intensification of services throughout the Capital system, for wherever the new airliner made its appearance, Capital's share of the market leaped upward, at the expense of the competing carriers that still operated piston-engined equipment.

Even the C.A.B. relented and granted Capital the previously un-imaginable luxury of being able to fly nonstop from New York to Chicago and to add nonstop segments, such as Pittsburgh–Atlanta and Pittsburgh–Birmingham. By February 20, 1956, the frequency on Capital's own traditional route, from Washington to Chicago, was up to six a day.

Continuing the headlong race, and with success following the Viscount wherever the unfamiliar sound of the Dart engine's whine was heard, Slim Carmichael did not rest on his laurels. The C.A.B. had always maintained that if an airline wanted new routes, it must demonstrate the ability to serve them. Accordingly, Slim in-creased Capital's potential seating capacity by another quantum leap. On July 24, 1956, he ordered fifteen more Viscounts, bringing the total order to seventy-five, and placed a new order for fourteen de Havilland Comet IV jet aircraft from England. He had made an extensive and thorough survey of the turbine equipment then avail-able, judged that both the 130-seat DC-8 and the Boeing 707 were too big for Capital's route structure, and chose the smaller 90-seat Comet. He had also evaluated and flown the French Caravelle jet and the British Bristol Britannia turboprop, so the selection was very much Carmichael's personal effort.

For personal reasons, he went through a procedure to have his license downgraded to that of an F.A.A. Instructor in September of the same year. This was so that he could take his daughter on a se-vere check flight before she obtained her pilot's license. From that time on, Capital Airlines ran into trouble. The financial situation deteriorated steadily, not because the Viscounts were failing to do the job that was asked of them, but simply because the route struc-ture was inadequate for the fast, smooth-riding machine to derive maximum benefit from its overall performance. The C.A.B.'s mea-sures were only a palliative. However many nonstop routes were authorized on the existing network, the Capital system was geo-graphically incapable of providing greater opportunities. The aver-age stage distance remained about 250 miles, and Carmichael de-scribed the route pattern as "the curse of Capital Airlines." Also, the competing airlines were beginning to hit back with vigorous competition in frequency and capacity.

In a Catch-22 situation, Capital had to defer the Comet order because of deteriorating cash flow, and the C.A.B. refused to award some good routes, citing inadequate equipment. New York–Chicago and Washington–Chicago nonstop were welcome improvements, appreciated by Capital. But for the transcontinental air lines, these were merely segments of their stopping services, which supplemented long-haul routes. Even Eastern, a nontranscontinental operator, was able to fly nonstop from the northeast cities to Florida, the southern states, and Texas. What Capital needed was routes of equal stature, such as Chicago and the Great Lakes cities to Florida, and these the board resolutely refused to grant.

At a time when teamwork and stability were needed at the top, Slim Carmichael suddenly found himself short of real friends and strong supporters. In an all-too-familiar move, on July 24, 1957, he was appointed chairman of the board, and Major General David H. Baker became president and chief executive officer. George H. Hann was elected chairman of the executive committee, replacing Charles Murchison, an attorney who, however, remained a member of the board and its legal counsel and a force to be reckoned with.

As Carmichael's influence declined and Baker took over the direction of the airline's affairs, things went from bad to worse, even though—too late to have been of any use—the C.A.B. finally, in March 1958, awarded routes to Florida. By this time, Jim Austin, one of Carmichael's closest associates, had resigned to take over the presidency of Northeast. Vickers was pressing hard for progress payments on the Viscounts. The Comet order was definitely canceled, and Capital asked permission of the C.A.B. to go back on subsidy. On successive days, on January 24–25, 1958, the C.A.B. approved an increase in fares, and Capital ordered nine Convair 880s, at the same time asking for a subsidy of $12 million, to be spread over two years.

Why Capital should have canceled the Comet order, only to order Convair 880s, which were larger and less suitable aircraft, is not quite clear, although a better financial package from the manufacturers might have been a short-term temptation. But it is reasonably certain that Slim Carmichael had nothing to do with it. He had been convinced for several years that without long-haul routes Capital could not survive. And history has proved him right, for no trunk airline deprived of such an asset has survived. "If you can't beat 'em, join 'em" was, he felt, the only possible survival plan. Besides earlier flirtations with Northeast and Northwest, he had had serious discussions in September 1957 with Robert Six, of Continental Airlines, also a Viscount customer, about a possible merger. The idea made a great deal of sense, although it is interesting to speculate who might have emerged as the head of the combined transcontinental airline. At all events, the promising idea collapsed.

On July 23, 1958, Slim Carmichael resigned from Capital Airlines, mainly over a furore concerning a proposed merger with United Air Lines that he was trying to promote behind the scenes. Even though Capital had been through troubled times, the new Florida route awards and the demonstrable success of the Viscounts would have enabled it to bargain, if not from strength, at least with firmness and dignity. Furthermore, such was the long-term relationship between the two airline heads, William Patterson of United and Slim Carmichael of Capital, that Patterson was to have been chairman and Carmichael president of the merged company, thus assuring Capital employees of a fair shake. But it was not to be. In a palace revolt at Capital, with Patterson opposed to certain personalities on the Capital board, Slim Carmichael was placed in an untenable position.

He left behind an airline that quickly became a shadow of its former self. In October 1958, services were suspended through strike action, and although the vital Florida routes finally got under way in January 1959, much of the promotional value was negated on May 2 of that year when Capital sustained two crashes on the same day. Desperate measures were taken to obtain aircraft for the Florida routes. While Lockheed Electra turboprops were ordered in October 1959, Douglas DC-6Bs—good old thoroughbred piston-engined airliners—were leased from Pan American. By the spring of 1960, with Vickers pressing even harder for payment for its Viscounts, to the extent that it initiated a foreclosure suit, Capital Airlines, now in a position of weakness, proceeded toward a merger with United. In truth, it was no merger; it was a takeover by the big airline, announced on July 28, 1960, approved by the C.A.B. on January 31, 1961, and formally put into effect by United on June 1, 1961. One month later the schedules of the two airlines were amalgamated, and the only visible signs of Capital were the forty-one remaining Viscounts, the sole aircraft judged by United to be worthy of retention. These Viscounts, introduced into the United States by Slim Carmichael as the harbinger of a new era, were to serve United well for many more years.

Carmichael joined the Fairchild Aircraft Corporation as vice-president on September 9, 1958, and was made president later that year. But he left after two years to form his own consulting firm in Washington. He went on to join the Federal Aviation Administration (F.A.A.) in its International Division and eventually retired to Florida in 1978. During the postwar years, he also headed a task force in Germany to study the state of the industry in that country after World War II. He had received the Horatio Alger Award in 1958 and had been a vice-president and director of the U.S. Chamber of Commerce.

Although the event that precipitated his retirement was his wife's illness, he was ready, at the age of seventy-two, to retire from the aviation scene anyway. Five years later, on December 1, 1983, he died of cancer, after several months of severe and painful illness.

Slim Carmichael came near to true greatness. With a smile or two from Lady Luck, or, more to the point, a vote or two from short-sighted members of the Civil Aeronautics Board, he could have built Capital into a solid and impregnable airline. With his daring Viscount deal, he came out fighting and had his opponents on the retreat. But the bureaucratic umpires in Washington held him back, gave his opponents time to get their second wind, then pinned one hand behind his back. More than one airline breathed a sigh of relief when Capital, under subsequent inexperienced management, went under.

In Washington, D.C., there is an annual event at which many former Capital employees gather to eat and drink and talk about old times. The Capital Airlines Association, as it is called, is a full-fledged dues-paying club with more than 2,000 members. They talk a lot about old acquaintances, but no single person is talked about more, or with greater animation, than the man who very nearly turned a struggling feeder airline into a major trunk carrier. He was the United States scheduled-airline standard-bearer for coach fares and turbine power, two giant innovative steps for which the name of Capital Airlines will always be enshrined in airline history. For these two achievements alone, Slim Carmichael will also be remembered by his peers with honor, respect, and affection.

▶▶▶▶▶ ◀ ▶▶▶▶▶▶▶▶▶▶▶▶▶▶▶▶▶▶

Stanley D. Weiss
First with Air Coach

During the 1950s, Stan Weiss, operator of a nonscheduled airline, contrived to fashion an organization that came very close to revolutionizing the entire U.S. airline industry. The government agency of the time, the Civil Aeronautics Board, the powerful lobbies of the established airlines, and even the Supreme Court itself, all combined to deny North American Airlines—Trans American Airlines at the time of its demise—the right to offer the American public the benefits of cheap air travel. As the first operator of cheap air services to the American public, Stan Weiss has a just claim to being called the innovator of coach fares, and as such he deserves an honorable place in airline history.

Thirty years after Stan Weiss and his partners had been regulated and legislated out of business, the principles for which they battled endlessly through the machinery of the regulatory agency and the courts were finally recognized as an essential feature of the American way of life, as legitimate principles that should be encouraged, not condemned. But Weiss was three decades ahead of his time and was pilloried for his actions. His was the last of the nonscheduled airlines to do any substantial business for a decade.

But his influence on the course of air transport was considerable. Although many years were to pass before this become evident, Stan Weiss and his associates had forced the authorities to review the basic purposes for which the original air transport regulations had been framed in 1938. This influence was particularly applicable to the manner in which passenger fares should be set. North Ameri-

Stan Weiss was one of the happy band of former airmen who sought to enter the airline business after World War II. He introduced coach fares to the American flying public, but his North American Airlines was thwarted by bureaucratic machinations that would seem ludicrous in the deregulated airline world of today.

can devised a system that was clearly superior to the out-of-date methods of the scheduled airlines. No one who was connected with the airline industry in the United States during the critical period of the mid 1950s has ever forgotten it, and many believe to this day that both the company and the man did more than any other to pioneer low fares. Neither has been given full credit for the remarkable achievement.

Stanley D. Weiss (pronounced Weese) was born on June 8, 1910, in Gotebo, Oklahoma, the son of the only pharmacist in town. He attended high school in Gotebo but then went to live with his mother in New York, where he received a degree in pharmacology at Columbia University and worked as a pharmacist, among other occupations, during the 1930s. He became interested in aviation, learned to fly in 1937, and by the outbreak of World War II had amassed several hundred hours of flying time.

Immediately after the Pearl Harbor incident in 1941, he joined the Army Air Corps, which became the U.S. Air Force, and had a varied career. He was successively a flight instructor, a ferry pilot, and a member of that exclusive breed of "hump" pilots in the China-Burma-India (C.B.I.) theater, where he flew Curtiss C-46s,

Douglas C-54s, and Consolidated B-24s across the treacherous terrain of the southwest China frontier.

Already married, with two children, when the war ended, he vowed that he would never go back to rolling pills again. He and his family established their home at Long Beach, California, where he had last been stationed, and it was here that Stan Weiss began to think seriously about forming an airline. By this time he was not obliged, as some of the postwar aspiring airline promoters were, to depend heavily as a source of finance on the gratuity granted by the armed forces on discharge. He had been thrifty during his war service and had enhanced his bank balance with winnings at poker, a favorite pastime in the China theater and one at which he apparently excelled.

For his first venture he went into a precarious partnership with Colonel Charles Sherman, another airline entrepreneur who flitted across the nonscheduled airline scene, in one company or another, for several years after World War II. Together they founded a company rejoicing in the name of the Fireball Air Express, which, because they intended to carry air freight, seemed appropriate at the time. But before the company began to operate, they realized that many returning veterans were loitering around Long Beach Airport, seeking a ride eastward, and to carry them seemed only natural. Thus, on January 17, 1946, Stan Weiss operated his first DC-3— more precisely, a war-surplus C-47, converted for civilian use—from Long Beach to New York via Kansas City and Chicago. This date can, with some justification, be claimed as the inauguration day of air coach service in the United States, or, for that matter, anywhere in the world—although some British operators had undercut Imperial Airways during the 1930s.

Fireball Air Express may be said to have been born on December 4, 1945, when Weiss and Sherman made a down payment of $3,000 each to the Reconstruction Finance Corporation for two Douglas C-47s. On December 17 they signed a Certificate of Fictitious Firm Name—as the official jargon insisted—and on the following day borrowed $18,000 from the Bank of America in Long Beach, at the same time applying to the Civil Aeronautics Authority (C.A.A.) for registration as an air carrier. A month later, they borrowed a further $32,000 from the Cherry/Anaheim Branch of the Bank, mainly because the manager "liked the cut of Stan's uni-

This rare picture of a Standard Air Lines Douglas C-47 is illustrative of the way in which the nonscheduled industry started—with war-surplus aircraft, purchased cheaply and operated economically, without frills. Only after decades of struggle against the established hierarchy were the nonskeds able to demonstrate their value in a competitive environment.

form." He must also have liked the cut of Stan's proposition, which was to make airline history.

In 1946 the fate-tempting name of the airline had been changed to the more demure Standard Air Lines, in keeping with the unplanned change from air freight to passenger service, and it was under this name that Weiss and James Fischgrund (Sherman was no longer a partner) obtained a Letter of Registration from the Civil Aeronautics Board (C.A.B) as a Large Irregular Carrier.

Standard was not the only company in the transcontinental nonscheduled airline business. There were several others, most of which quickly ceased operations as soon as something went wrong—normally the inability to attract a steady flow of passengers or to keep the aircraft flying by a proper maintenance schedule. One of them, however, Viking Air Lines, was a formidable competitor, flying DC-3s on the same transcontinental route and with

connections to Miami. Viking had also been founded in 1945, by
Ross R. Hart and Jack B. Lewin, and was based at the Lockheed Air
Terminal at Burbank. Charging a transcontinental fare of only
$99.00, both airlines were beginning to tap a new passenger mar-
ket—the nonbusiness people who could not normally afford the
fares being charged by all the scheduled airlines. Fares were rigidly set by the C.A.B. according to a mileage formula, which did
not vary among the domestic trunk carriers that were the fortunate
possessors of the grandfather certificates handed out in 1938. Competition in fares did not exist, in spite of the fact that the C.A.B. was
specifically charged with promoting it.

   Then in 1948 the board took its first action to limit the activities of the precocious newcomers and applied what became known
as the 3 and 8 Rule. This meant that a nonscheduled Large Irregular
airline was permitted to fly only eight round-trip flights a month between any pair of cities in the U.S. and only three on certain high-
density routes—that is, all the best routes coveted by the scheduled
operators, some of them monopolies or near monopolies.

   Neither Standard nor Viking flew strictly within the 3 and 8
Rule, and in 1949 the two companies merged to form a stronger airline, with more equipment and greater financial resources. Stan
Weiss and his then partners devised an ingenious stratagem to
evade the intentions of the C.A.B. restrictions without actually
breaking the law.

   Early in 1949, Standard and Viking formed the North American Airlines agency. This was a ticketing organization that sold the
transcontinental air coach service to the public, although it was
not registered as an airline. The operating certificates, as Irregular
Carriers, were still held by the original two companies. Weiss,
Fischgrund, Lewin, and Hart then acquired other Irregular Carrier
certificates: those of Twentieth Century Airlines, formed by Edward McAndrews; Trans-American Airways, formed by Mauri
Swidler; Trans-National Airlines; and Hemisphere Air Transport.

   The combined fleet grew to a total of fourteen Douglas DC-3s
and a DC-4, initially leased late in 1949 from Stan Weiss's good
friend and fellow pioneer Robert W. Prescott, founder of the Flying
Tiger Line, until 1986 the preeminent all-cargo airline. Flying resumed, accompanied by some organized promotion, on a route from
Los Angeles to New York via Alburquerque, Kansas City, and Chicago. The DC-3s, fitted with twenty-eight austere seats, could not

compete in comfort or speed with the pressurized Constellations and DC-6s of the scheduled trunk lines such as American and T.W.A., but the North American fare was only $99.00 one way, substantially lower than those of the trunk carriers. The public had a choice: higher fares and comparative luxury or lower fares without the frills. To the chagrin of the established airlines, railroads, and long-distance bus lines, the public flocked to North American Airlines.

The essential feature of the service was that it combined the individual authorities of the member companies in the North American group, so that, by simple arithmetic, even under the 3 and 8 Rule, they could offer a daily service. Eight round-trip flights a month need be multiplied only by four to produce thirty-two, ample for even the longer months. By cutting out the costly amenities and carefully matching schedules to demand, North American was able to sustain its bargain fares and still make a profit—at a time when the scheduled airlines were charging much higher fares but wasting half their product; that is, by flying with only about 55 percent of the seats actually occupied. At that time, moreover, the airlines were still receiving federal subsidies, in addition to air mail payments, which cushioned their losses.

The curious paradox was that the C.A.B. was party to a subsidy to the privileged air travelers, most of them businessmen and the wealthy, who could afford to fly. Those in the lower-income groups, on the other hand, seemed well pleased with North American's style and began to patronize the new service. Because of the tight scheduling and the limited capacity, customers could not always be accommodated on the days they preferred to fly, but at $99.00 from the West Coast to New York, they did not mind waiting a day or two. The alternative was to pay $159.00 standard fare by the scheduled airlines, or $110.00 by their night coach—the Red-Eye Specials as they became known.

North American could guarantee that its aircraft were maintained and flown as skillfully and professionally as those of its richer rivals. Indeed, throughout the history of the bitter litigation that was to follow, no criticism was ever leveled at North American on the grounds of poor maintenance or operating procedures or of not keeping to the strictest safety standards. Nevertheless, this did not prevent the appearance of certain scurrilous articles in the press, possibly influenced by the weight of Establishment pressure.

Stan Weiss and his partners were so successful that they had to obtain larger aircraft. By the mid 1950s, North American was a predominantly four-engined airline. Later, in 1955, Weiss established rewarding business relations with Captain Eddie Rickenbacker, of World War I fame, then the feisty president of Eastern Air Lines, to purchase the entire fleet of DC-4s owned by Eastern. Rickenbacker, a businessman through and through, insisted that if Weiss purchased the aircraft, he would also have to buy $1 million worth of spare parts. Weiss agreed, figuring that the full value of the fleet far exceeded whatever the spares would cost.

No sooner had the deal been signed when Eastern realized that it needed some of the DC-4s back because of late delivery of the replacement aircraft. It therefore needed the spare parts back as well, and, to the accompaniment of much profanity, Rickenbacker had to purchase back the exact same spare parts that he had just unloaded. Much to Rickenbacker's surprise, Weiss sold the spare parts back for exactly what he had paid for them, saying "I didn't need them in the first place and was happy with the deal as it stood."

Rickenbacker never forgot Weiss's business acumen or his honesty. Many years later he offered Weiss the opportunity to succeed him as president of Eastern Air Lines. Weiss did not elect to accept this most flattering offer because of conflicting demands on his time and energy. But to imagine Eastern under the direction of Stan Weiss makes an interesting speculation.

As the four-engined DC-4s were added, North American disposed of its DC-3s. Two of these were sold in 1951 to Ken Friedkin, who had founded Friedkin Aeronautics, which became Pacific Southwest Airlines (P.S.A.). This later developed into the famous California intrastate airline that proved, in a different operating environment, that low fares could still yield profits if the airline was operated efficiently. Weiss sold the DC-3s for $90,000 each on a handshake. Shortly thereafter, the Korean War started and the market price for the DC-3s shot up to $400,000 each. Friedkin became worried about the validity of a contract based on a handshake and was mightily relieved when Stan Weiss never wavered from their oral agreement, delivering the aircraft as and when promised.

Turning from matters of equipment to matters of public policy and concern, the period from about 1949, when North American introduced its first DC-4, until its eventual demise was stormy, to put it mildly. In 1949, faced with what they believed to be a determined effort by the C.A.B. to eliminate them entirely from the air transport field, the nonscheduled carriers appealed for justice, and hearings were held before the Senate Interstate and Foreign Commerce Committee, under the chairmanship of Senator Edwin Johnson. This led to a further review by the Select Committee on Small Business, under the chairmanship of Senator John Sparkman.

In its report issued on July 10, 1951, the committee noted that the nonskeds had managed to survive "in spite of constant harassment: the C.A.B.'s ever-narrowing interpretation of its regulations designed to limit them almost entirely to noncommon carrier operations; vigorous enforcement activities and regulatory actions which will, if unchecked, inevitably eliminate them within a year or two; and a campaign possibly inspired by major airlines to discredit them in the public mind."

Such testimony, from such an impeccable source, hushed criticism, and the C.A.B. retreated into its shell for a while. Temporarily unleashed, North American Airlines did so well that, in 1953, in the famous Denver Service Case—the statutory machinery under which the C.A.B. distributed scheduled airspace—it applied to operate a Los Angeles–Denver–Kansas City–Chicago route at three cents a mile plus $2.00 a ticket. This would have worked out to less than $60.00 one way from Los Angeles to Chicago. When the C.A.B. decision was handed down, all the big transcontinental airlines were granted aditional routes, and both Continental Airlines and Western Air Lines were given a share of this lucrative pie. But the board found that North American was "unfit, unwilling, and unable" to perform the services, because of "knowing and wilful" violations of the board's Economic Regulations. This is particularly noteworthy, for by this time North American had surpassed some of the principal trunk airlines in size, measured in annual revenue passenger-miles flown.

The decision caused controversy among the nonscheduled airlines and, indeed, among many sections of an interested public as well. North American Airlines had proved beyond any shadow of doubt that it was fit, willing, and able to operate. It was also prepared to do so with its own money, without subsidy or support of any kind. And it offered to lower its fares so that many more people could afford to fly. In retrospect, the C.A.B.'s decision seems to have been extraordinary.

The reason for such violations seemed to be more that the C.A.B. had been affronted by someone exposing an injustice, even possibly an infringement of its own mandate. The terms of the original Civil Aeronautics Act did not specifically preclude the entry of additional airlines into the U.S. airline industry. Yet by mutual agreement, the C.A.B., with vigorous support from the Air Transport Association, representing the certificated airlines, and tacit approval from other government departments, appeared to follow an unwritten law that the only organizations which could operate airlines were those nominated in 1938 under the grandfather rights certificates. Many years later, the Freedom of Entry issue was to be a cornerstone of the principles that shaped the Airline Deregulation Act of 1978.

Nevertheless, North American continued to operate under its ingenious system. It cheekily applied for further route extensions under existing rules, thus adding to the growing confusion in the C.A.B., which must have been conscious of the question of ethics, when the Select Committee on Small Business in the Senate recommended that the 3 and 8 rule be changed to one permitting fourteen flights a month.

There now seemed to be no stopping North American. In 1954, with a fleet of two DC-3s and seven DC-4s, it flew almost 330 million passenger-miles, carrying almost 200,000 passengers. The passenger-mile figure was larger than that of any of the three smallest domestic trunk airlines—Western, Continental, and Northeast—owing entirely to the $99.00 fare. Profits were realized because North American was able to fill 85 percent of its seats, an unprecedented percentage in the stereotyped world of the scheduled carriers.

In December 1954, North American took the plunge and ordered seven new Douglas DC-6B pressurized aircraft, each fitted with 102 seats, so as to compete on equal terms with the big airlines. Once again, a loan was obtained from the Bank of America, which must have felt that in Stan Weiss it was investing well. The marketing department at Douglas was in a quandary, for it was under pressure from certain quarters not to sell airplanes to this upstart airline. Donald Douglas, Sr., gave strict instructions: "If Stan Weiss has the money, you sell him the airplanes."

On May 1, 1955, to the consternation of United, T.W.A., and American, North American Airlines inaugurated DC-6B transcontinental service, charging $160.00 round trip as before, but reducing the one-way fare to $88.00. Flight times were 7 hours 55 minutes eastbound, and 8 hours 55 minutes westbound. North American utilized its aircraft at the rate of thirteen flying hours a day, whereas the scheduled airlines felt they were doing well to achieve eight. At the time, this was a daily utilization record for any airline operating with Douglas equipment.

North American's literature contained an interesting comparison of travel costs coast to coast, taking into account the extra costs of tax on the tickets, the cost of food and tips, and the cost of time at $10.00 a day. This made a valid argument to support the claim that it provided substantial savings over first-class air fares and pullman trains and also offered comfortable savings over air coach, rail coach, and even bus travel.

The scheduled airlines were forced to take drastic steps, and the three transcontinental airlines suddenly found ways and means to reduce fares. Their excursion packages, however, contained certain irritating restrictions, in that they were valid for only thirty days and could be used only on certain flights. (Exactly the same situation arose almost thirty years later when, after deregulation, Continental Airlines set new lower fares, on an unrestricted basis, against those of its competitors, which were complicated by various kinds of ifs and buts.)

Within two months, the C.A.B. came to the rescue of the desperate airlines, which visualized the erosion of their cherished heritage. On July 1, 1955, the board revoked N.A.A.'s various certificates for what it called "serious and wilful violations" of the economic regulations and ordered Stan Weiss and his partners in effrontery to cease "unlawful operations" from September 1 of that year. The scheduled airlines, of course, applauded this action, and R. A. Fitzgerald, of National Airlines, expressed the consensus by describing N.A.A. as "professional violators."

In making its judgment, the C.A.B. appears to have forgotten—or deliberately ignored—one of the most important goals of the act of 1938, which was to promote air travel. It could have met the new situation by other means. It could have increased payments to the scheduled airlines, for example, if it could have been proved that their operations were efficient yet unprofitable, or it could have relieved the scheduled airlines from having to operate unprofitable routes, a course which it adopted with respect to Local Service operations some years later. The C.A.B. seemed, in fact, by choosing the most drastic course, to be advocating the cause of those it was only supposed to regulate. Indeed, a member of the board, Joseph P. Adams, in a minority opinion, condemned the majority for refusing even to meet the carrier's (N.A.A.'s) officers or to consider some penalty other than the most drastic, the revocation of its Letter of Registration.

The legal battle intensified. On July 29, the C.A.B. stayed its revocation of the N.A.A. license, pending review by a U.S. Court of Appeals. Meanwhile, the unrepentant airline reported a gain in traffic for the month of June of 47 percent over traffic in June of the previous year. On August 24, N.A.A. formally appealed to the U.S. Court of Appeals, D.C. Circuit, to stay the cease-and-desist portion of the C.A.B. order and revealed its position when James Fischgrund stated at the hearing that N.A.A. would be forced to disband if the stay was not granted. On September 5, the C.A.B. denied North American's application to enter the New York–Chicago market, although, by any criterion, there seemed to be plenty of room for another competitor on this much-traveled segment. On October 4, the U.S. Court of Appeals, 9th Circuit, upheld North American Aviation's claim that North American Airlines should not be allowed to trade under a name that was almost indistinguishable from the manufacturer's.

Throwing caution to the winds, and with some justification, believing that the weight of public opinion, reflected through its legislators, would eventually see that justice was done, North American played another card. On December 8, 1955, it asked the C.A.B. for a three-year exemption to operate low-cost transatlantic coach services, proposing two daily round-trip services at fares of $125.00 from New York to Shannon, Ireland, and $140.00 to London. These were 43 percent less than the tourist fares then in force.

In its application, N.A.A. stated that DC-6Bs would be used and quoted its U.S. transcontinental experience. There could be absolutely no doubt that it was "fit, willing, and able." As to the legality, it admitted that its operating authority had been revoked but that it was appealing to the courts and was continuing to operate until a final decision was handed down. The C.A.B. could hardly claim that there was insufficient traffic to justify another U.S. operator, although admitting another operator may have led to some problems with bilateral traffic rights with the countries of Europe. The North Atlantic market was booming, for even the schedule of tourist fares, introduced in 1952 and 43 percent higher than that proposed by N.A.A., had sounded the death knell for transatlantic passenger shipping. Years later, after passage of the 1978 Airline Deregulation Act—and even earlier—the number of U.S. airlines plying the route had multiplied considerably, with almost every trunk airline participating.

But predictably, in January 1956—within a month after its submission—the C.A.B. turned down North American's application on the grounds that the issues were too complex to be decided by the exemption process. This, in retrospect, was an extraordinary claim, for many complex issues and extremely complicated route cases were continually resolved by the hard-working staff of the C.A.B. The board also stated that "a very serious question remains unresolved" as to N.A.A.'s qualifications, in view of the fact that the airline had been found guilty of violations and its operating authority had been revoked. Stan Weiss and his partners had heard that old tune before.

This was far from being a case of protecting the unsuspecting public against some entrepreneur who was trying to make a quick buck. Stan Weiss had a genuine desire to become a legitimate scheduled operator, accepting the risks and the obligations which that status would confer. As to the public interest, a virtue so often quoted by the C.A.B. in other contexts, the public had given its blessing to North American Airlines. In 1955 N.A.A. carried almost 275,000 passengers, an increase of 40 percent over the previous year. Its fleet consisted of seven DC-4s and two DC-6Bs, and five more of the latter were on order.

In 1955 North American had made about $1 million profit on $15 million revenue, a better return on investment than was realized by most of the certificated airlines. Yet North American's success had been built on substantially lower fares than the C.A.B.'s, and there was a clear message implicit in these facts, which was obvious to all but closed minds. As North American stressed, its clientele consisted almost entirely of first-time air travelers, and it was drawing traffic, not from other airlines, but from the bus lines and the railroads.

In February 1956, when N.A.A. was gambling on its future existence and still awaiting delivery of additional new DC-6Bs from Douglas, the chairman of the House Commerce Transportation Sub-Committee commented that he was "impressed by the objectives, but not with the methods" of North American, which, on March 12, said it was prepared to back up charges that the C.A.B. had been "a willing party to a callous, calculated conspiracy" to ostracize new trunk-line carriers. Stan Weiss carefully pointed out that his charges were nonpolitical, aimed at Republican and Democrat alike, and that both had hatched their conspiracy under "constant prodding and behind-the-scenes pressures" from "monopoly-minded trunk airlines."

He claimed that "the C.A.B. has sought to regulate us out of business" and that "the more the public welcomed and accepted our original concept of efficient, reliable, low-cost air transportation, the greater were the regulatory handicaps imposed upon our growth." He told the subcommittee that C.A.B. Chairman Ross Rizley had admitted that the board approved rates and other "monopoly agreements" made by the scheduled airlines and that it had "no standard yardstick" for measuring these agreements. Furthermore, it did not regularly consult with the Justice Department on the antitrust aspects of the agreement. Weiss's counsel, Hardy Maclay, observed that the efforts of the C.A.B. to increase competition had never been responsible for lower rates and that, as the chairman of the subcommittee recognized, such competition had been limited to service factors.

While the public was clamoring for lower fares—which North American Airlines had demonstrated were perfectly feasible—the C.A.B. would argue interminably about a minor modification to a multisegment route, or the seat pitch allowed, or the standard of meal service permitted, wading through enormous stacks of testimony in the process. Reminiscent of debate by the International Air Transport Association (IATA) on the permissible ingredients of a sandwich, the prognostications of the C.A.B. were often reminiscent of the mediaeval philosophers' arguments about the number of angels that could dance on the head of a pin.

The C.A.B. also alleged that in international route decisions it had to capitulate to IATA rate agreements because of "tremendous pressures from our own carriers and foreign airlines and governments." IATA was quite blatantly a cartel, setting air fares at rates decided by the member airlines, including the flag carriers of the United States. North American countered this excuse by applying, on April 30, 1956, for exemption to fly to Luxembourg, a small country in Europe whose air policy did not include IATA membership, which welcomed foreign airlines, and which was geographically situated to tap the entire northwest European market. In fact, the Icelandic airline, the pioneer of low fares across the North Atlantic, has successfully used the Luxembourg hub-gateway for more than two decades in recent times.

Both the C.A.B. and the U.S. State Department criticized North American for conducting unilateral negotiations. This seemed to have been a bizarre commentary, as there were many precedents for airlines to open discussions without prior consultation with Washington. Of course, by these protracted wranglings the issue of low fares was continually obscured and evaded.

The harassment of North American continued. Also on April 30, the Supreme Court denied the petition of North American to reverse the lower court's decision on the name issue, and N.A.A. promptly changed its name, on May 12, 1956, to Trans American Airlines (T.A.A.). Shortly thereafter, on July 12, the use of the word *American* was upheld by the U.S. Court of Appeals. For any one company to claim exclusively for the use of that evocative word would have been preposterous.

On June 11, Trans American amended its still-pending application for exemption. It offered to discontinue its proposed service if the C.A.B. could find that any competitor was injured thereby. Furthermore, it agreed to charge "such rates as the Board found proper." This put the C.A.B. in an extremely delicate position. To quote Stan Weiss, "How could they say that we should charge more when we were making money on what we were doing?"

But the sands were running out. Casting logic aside, the C.A.B. rejected T.A.A.'s application on July 29, and its Office of Compliance opened enforcement proceedings. In December 1956, the U.S. Court of Appeals upheld the C.A.B. order to ground Stan Weiss and his recalcitrant and unrepentant airline. After repeated stays of execution, through the T.A.A. lawyers' use of every possible legal maneuver, amounting almost to a filibuster, the last of the Large Irregular Carriers closed up shop on January 19, 1957, the last day of the term of the C.A.B.'s authorization.

In one last desperate appeal for justice, on March 12, 1957, Trans American Airlines asked the Supreme Court to review the decision of the U.S. Court of Appeals to uphold the C.A.B.'s revocation action against it. On April 23 of the same year the Supreme Court denied the appeal.

North American/Trans American was finished. Because, under the law, the decision of the Supreme Court left it only forty-five days to liquidate its assets, it leased its fleet of seven DC-6Bs to Eastern Air Lines (five were already on hand, and two more were about to be delivered). By this action, the four partners, Weiss, Fischgrund, Lewin, and Hart, all made a great deal of money over and above their earnings while the airline was operating.

The sighs of relief in Washington, particularly at the headquarters of the Air Transport Association and at the C.A.B., could have been heard in Baltimore. But the issues remained and were to haunt the regulatory body and the trade association for decades to follow. Were the regulations adopted without fair hearings? Were the regulations deliberately framed so as to make nonscheduled airline operations impossible? Was the public interest protected? By subsequent legislation, through the gradual liberalization of what became the Supplemental Airlines and culminating in the Airline Deregulation Act of 1978, the answers to these fundamental questions have come down emphatically on the side of Stan Weiss and his partners. The influence of the A.T.A. on the course of airline affairs has diminished almost to insignificance, and the airlines are no longer subject to the whims of the Gang of Five who used to preside at the C.A.B.

Unlike some of the visionaries of airline progress whose efforts ended in complete failure and disillusionment, not to mention financial hardship, Stanley Weiss was not a man to cry over spilt milk. He didn't need to. During the ascendancy of North American Airlines he and his partners had been in the 90 percent tax bracket, all earned, in the real sense of that often misused word, by bringing the benefits of air travel to a public that had been deprived of them. And so, denied the right to operate aircraft, he turned to an occupation that had until then only been a supplementary activity: he went into the business of trading and leasing aircraft.

As Twentieth Century Aircraft, Stan Weiss bought, sold, and leased many aircraft during the late 1950s and into the 1970s. Having first taken advantage during the mid 1950s of a law that did not allow banks to go into leasing, Weiss and other associates bought Super Constellations from Lockheed and leased them to Seaboard World Airlines, then one of the largest air freight airlines in the world. Additionally, through other associated leasing companies in New York, he and his partners completed what is believed to have been the first sale-leaseback of airline equipment in the history of air transport, the aforementioned DC-4 deal.

Between 1958 and 1960, Twentieth Century Airlines, like a determined terrier that would not let go of the bulldog, fulfilled its destiny as a contract carrier on assignments that were free of C.A.B., A.T.A., or other encroachment. It carried military personnel all over the world, with DC-6Bs purchased from American Airlines and the Dutch airline, K.L.M., together with Super Constellations purchased from Lockheed and the Australian airline, QANTAS. In a wave of misplaced optimism, it petitioned for a Supplementary Certificate when Public Law 87-528, enacted July 10, 1962, conferred the status of legitimacy on those airlines that had until then been the pariahs and outcasts of the industry. But Stan Weiss was persona non grata in the corridors of airline power in Washington, and his was a lost cause.

Stan Weiss's semiretirement began at the age of forty-seven, as a direct result of the cease-and-desist order issued against his airline. The order might well have been termed a cease-and-desist order against the American public for having the effrontery to recognize a real bargain when they saw one. Eventually the public, through its legislators, rebelled. The C.A.B. was itself destroyed, mourned by some but certainly not by the old-timers of the nonscheduled airlines, who were, without stretching the analogy too far, martyrs to a cause.

Stan now lives quietly at home in Long Beach. In the material sense he is comfortable, with many investments and considerable assets. He has remained active in aviation and in his personal leisure pursuits, among which is serving as voluntary consultant to a host of friends. Many would never have recovered from the understandable disillusionment and disenchantment, together with the complex emotions generated by the loss of the airline of which its creator was justly proud. But he did not brood over the injustice that he felt had been enacted through manipulation in high places. Neither did he allow the C.A.B.'s implication that what he had done was dishonorable to interfere with his unending love affair with aviation. This continued in his active life as broker, investor, and financier and in recreational and business flying well into the 1970s.

All the activity that was self-righteously regarded as dastardly practice in the 1950s is now perfectly legal, and no one would dream of questioning it. Stan Weiss had had to live with a sense of injustice for thirty years. But by an odd twist of fate, Twentieth Century Aircraft, legitimate descendant of a much-maligned Irregular Carrier, still exists. The sun had, however, irrevocably set on the Civil Aeronautics Board, which ceased to exist on December 31, 1984.

Orvis Nelson

Mr. Transocean

If ever an airline promoter was the victim of a subtle form of aviation apartheid that permeated the minds of those in control of commercial aviation in the United States during the first two decades following World War II, that man was Orvis Nelson. In the face of constant opposition—sometimes practiced by unethical methods, both from his rival airlines and from the bureaucrats in Washington—he built an airline that was among the fifteen largest in the country. He was cynically excluded from the honored place in the scheme of things that his prodigious efforts had truly earned him. Sadly, he did not live to witness the demise of the government agency that opposed his every attempt to consolidate on the firm organizational base he had worked so hard to fashion. And his family will maintain to this day that the stresses and strains of the relentless battle were a contributory cause of his death.

Orvis Marcus Nelson was born in Tamarack, Minnesota, on March 18, 1907, into a Norwegian-American family. His early schooling was sporadic, and he spent most of his adolescent years working in lumbering. When Lindbergh made his classic flight across the Atlantic in May 1927, twenty-year-old Orvis was particularly influenced, not only by the wave of enthusiasm that swept through the whole country, but also by the Nelson family's acquaintance with the Lindberghs, who lived at Little Falls, only about sixty miles away. Orvis promptly joined the Army Air Corps. He was assigned as a technician to a large-scale aerial survey of the Philippines, work that he found totally absorbing, even though this was not exactly the flying career he had wished. In 1929 he bought

101

his way out of the army, attended Franklin College of Indiana, and obtained his B.A. degree in mathematics in three years.

He worked his way through college partly by doing some aerial photography for local farmers. He then reenlisted at Randolph Field, San Antonio, Texas, and completed his flight training, mainly under the care of an instructor who believed that flying under power lines was good for an aviator's soul. Nelson passed with a high grade as a cadet captain, good enough to be able to move on to multiengined aircraft and to graduate from Kelly Field in October 1933. Shortly thereafter he was assigned to fly the air mail in a B-7 bomber on the difficult Oakland–Salt Lake City segment of the transcontinental route. This was during the ill-fated episode of 1934, when the commercial air mail contracts were canceled and the army was asked to fly the mail, during the worst Februrary weather on record, with pilots who had had no experience in that type of flying. Nelson lost several good friends in accidents, and it taught him a sharp lesson in the value of the right training and the right equipment.

In 1935, with flying cut down to four hours a month, Orvis Nelson resigned from the Air Corps and joined United Air Lines as a copilot. He gained experience on almost all its routes and checked out as a captain in 1937. Continuing to work steadily in his profession, he was assigned to Alaska in 1943, when United received a contract for support operations in that theater for the Air Transport Command. When Northwest Airlines took over the contract in 1944, he transferred to the California–Hawaii segment and to the islands beyond, a part of the world to which he would return in a different role after the war.

During the war Nelson displayed his versatility and latent leadership qualities when he became first vice-president of the Air Line Pilots' Association (ALPA) in 1942 and subsequently became its leading negotiator with the government in deciding whether commercially contracted pilots should fly as civilians or as commissioned air force officers. Although he favored taking commissions, the pilots remained as airline employees, and Nelson kept his United uniform on until the end of the war.

Assigned as he was to the Pacific, Nelson was one of the group of airmen chosen to land the first wave of occupation troops in Japan, and it was while he was in Okinawa, in August 1945, that the idea of forming an independent airline was first broached by Nel-

Orvis Nelson was a free-ranging airline cavalier who earned the right to become a certificated transpacific operator. His company, Transocean, was the international equivalent of Stan Weiss's North American in that it was cynically suppressed by a collusion between the regulating authority and the incumbent airlines.

son to some of his fellow pilots. At this time he had chalked up 12,000 hours in his log book and was without question one of the finest and most highly respected pilots in a critical and discerning fraternity. His ALPA activities had given him experience in organization, he had shown ambition and initiative with his photographic ventures, and he had even taken a master's degree in creative writing in his spare time at Seattle during his Alaska flying days. Temperamentally he was self-disciplined, he neither smoked nor drank, he held strong ethical standards, and he had the kind of personality—often described as charisma—that made him immensely popular. He was destined to form an airline.

After the war had ended, Nelson was back flying domestic runs for United, but he heard through his private grapevine of pilot friends that substantial reinforcement of air transport operations was needed in Japan and the western Pacific. United Air Lines was ideally placed to claim this market, but the cautious William Patterson, president of United, turned down the opportunity to become a transpacific operator. When Nelson explored ideas of starting an airline in Japan, Patterson pledged his support, but General MacArthur declined to give permission before a peace treaty had been signed. The general was dissatisfied with the service he was

getting from a seriously overextended Air Transport Command
(A.T.C.), however, and the wartime pattern of subcontracted flying
was put forward, the government supplying the aircraft and the private operator supplying the crews, support, and maintenance.

On March 9, 1946, Orvis Nelson received a telephone call
from Jack Herlihy, vice-president of operations at United, asking
him whether he could set up a subcontracted flying operation between Oakland and Honolulu within ten days. Nelson immediately
placed advertisements for crews in newspapers in San Francisco
and Los Angeles. He received 5,000 telephone calls during the first
twenty-four hours. He gathered together some friends from his
Okinawa days and picked up twelve war-surplus Douglas C-54s
(DC-4s). On Sunday, March 18, the first aircraft took off from Oakland to Honolulu—on Orvis Nelson's thirty-ninth birthday. Ten
days later he married Edith Frohboese, a United Air Lines flight attendant, who immediately identified herself with her husband's future career.

At first the Nelson enterprise was organized as ONAT—Orvis
Nelson Air Transport—and was somewhat precariously financed
by a friendly bank. The only money that Nelson had to put up was
a down payment of $1,000 on $25,000 worth of life insurance. The
aircraft were supplied without payment, as war surplus; the pilots
were all fully trained, courtesy of Uncle Sam; and the contracts
were underwritten by the government. ONAT was, however, a one-man project, formed only to put the enterprise on some kind of legal footing, and Nelson quickly moved to bring his old pilot friends
into the business by forming Transocean Air Lines (T.A.L.). This
was also to satisfy the government stipulation that to qualify for
government contracts 50 percent of the shares must be held by veterans. Transocean became a reality on June 1, 1946, with Orvis Nelson holding 27 percent of the stock.

At first Transocean and its fellow contractor, Pacific Overseas
Airways, made handsome profits—about $2,000 a day—but United
Air Lines soon persuaded A.T.C. to reduce the rates. Nevertheless,
ONAT/Transocean soon had enough cash to buy its own aircraft:
two C-54s, on which it made a down payment of $27,000 and on
which $150,000 was spent on modification to meet certification
standards of the Civil Aeronautics Administration (C.A.A.).

Scouting for business, Nelson agreed to furnish air transportation to a Filipino newspaper publisher to take a group of his countrymen to Manila for their July 4 independence celebrations. Although he lost the job on the outbound leg, because the DC-4s had not been modified in time, he sent one out for the return load. There was a good market for transpacific air travel, and an unprecedented opportunity arose. Colonel Andres Soriano, owner of Philippine Air Lines (P.A.L.), until then a small domestic operator, had observed Transocean's DC-4 takeoff from Manila en route to the United States. He telephoned Nelson and arranged for a DC-4 charter between Manila and San Francisco. The first flight took off from Oakland on July 23, 1946, in the Transocean DC-4 *Taloa–Manila Bay*—Taloa being the cable code for the airline's base in Oakland. On this flight, Edith Nelson was the stewardess and was probably the first to perform these duties west of Honolulu, for Pan American, the monopoly operator of the commercial route, employed only male stewards at that time.

These were hair-raising times for Transocean, because the air bases throughout the Pacific islands were staffed by men suffering from—or enjoying—a spell of postwar irresponsibility. Indeed, stopovers were hazardous, especially for the stewardesses, who were forced to sleep in the aircraft to avoid the attentions of amorous men. In Manila, the lawlessness was such that armed guards were always present to protect the compound in which the Transocean crews spent their layovers. Making a virtue out of necessity, Nelson decided to fly the DC-4s straight through with a double crew. This not only avoided unpleasantness in such places as Kwajalein and Johnston Island, but Transocean's airplanes made the transpacific flight faster than did Pan American. The *Taloa–Manila Bay*—Old 635 as it was affectionately called—operated the P.A.L. charter alone for six weeks, until the second DC-4 was delivered, a testimony to the fledgling airline's operational and technical efficiency.

Toward the end of 1946, United Air Lines decided to relinquish its transpacific contract operations for the A.T.C., and Transocean and Pacific Overseas made independent bids for the privilege. But both were underbid by Flying Tigers, aggressively promoted by Bob Prescott, a veteran of the China theater, and Nelson was forced to take some swift steps to survive. He shrewdly sold his two DC-4s to Philippine Air Lines in exchange for about 14 percent of the airline's stock. Transocean also took over the contract for running the Philippine domestic operations formerly held by T.W.A.

In addition to the transpacific schedule, P.A.L.-Transocean flew a number of charters in Southeast Asia, flying into Hong Kong, Singapore, and Batavia (the Dutch name for Jakarta), but the political climate in those regions was far too unsettled to risk setting up a permanent network. However, the partnership did succeed in inaugurating a scheduled P.A.L. service to Europe, terminating in Madrid. Nelson used the double-crew technique, and on one occasion, in the spring of 1947, one of the aircraft made a transatlantic charter flight from Rome to the U.S. West Coast, completing what was probably the first commercial circumnavigation of the globe by a passenger-carrying airliner.

While the Transocean-P.A.L. relationship was an amicable and upright business affair and Transocean was able to acquire four more DC-4s to service the operation, Orvis Nelson was well aware that, like all such contracts, it was to last only until P.A.L. could stand on its own feet, or more aptly, could fly with its own wings. Accordingly, he looked for other business, and he found it on the transatlantic market. Transocean did a roaring trade in the postwar immigration movement, beginning with a contract with Trans-Canada Air Lines to bring 7,000 English immigrants to Canada. The first flight left England August 2, 1947, and the three DC-4s allocated to the task had completed the contract by April 1948. Then the International Refugee Organization (I.R.O.) signed a contract with Transocean to move 25,000 displaced persons and refugees from Europe to South America. This contract occupied seven DC-4s throughout the rest of 1948 and most of 1949. Although its fulfillment was virtually without incident, there was a moment of uncertainty when an overzealous British antiaircraft unit used one of the Transocean aircraft for target practice, and there was an episode of tragedy when a DC-4 ditched in the ocean and seven of the sixty-four passengers and

Transocean's Worldwide Influence. *One of the biggest injustices of the C.A.B.–controlled era of U.S. air transport was the cynical rejection of the legitimate claims of Orvis Nelson's Transocean Air Lines, the result of inspired free enterprise in the American tradition.*

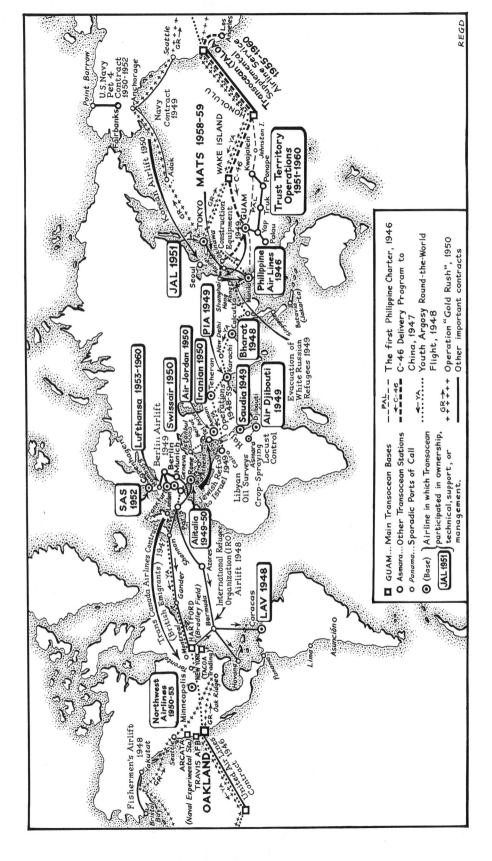

one of the crew died before they could be picked up by a fishing trawler.

Nevertheless, Transocean's reputation was growing as the news got around that here was an airline which fulfilled its promises to "carry anything, anywhere, anytime." As a result of the South American refugee service, the Venezuelan government asked Transocean to set up a scheduled service to Italy, in collaboration with the national airline. This continued for two years, but Nelson was eventually ousted from this sphere of operations by another U.S. group.

During this time, in the fall of 1947, there was a problem in the Pacific. The military wished to evacuate all civilian operations from the islands between Honolulu and Guam, and Transocean was obliged to seek quarters at Wake. There was an unsavory episode when, after unsuccessful attempts to negotiate a reasonable installations-sharing deal with Pan American, Transocean attempted to establish its own base at an old Seabee camp at the opposite end of the island from the Pan Am base. During the absence of Transocean staff in the United States to arrange for supplies, the camp was completely vandalized, with a bulldozer hooked up to pull down the water tower, all the toilets destroyed with sledgehammers, and refrigerators and other equipment ruined with cutting torches. When the dust had settled, Transocean and Pan American subsequently shared the available space and equipment in maintaining transpacific commercial and Korean airlift operations and providing full servicing for the many airlines engaged in that work.

Some idea of the extent of Transocean's worldwide activities and an indication of Orvis Nelson's flair for imaginative marketing of the skills and talents of his Transocean team can be gleaned from the Pakistan story. After selling some of P.A.L.'s old aircraft to Orient Airways, Nelson learned that the international air routes were almost certain to go to another group, which formed the airline now known as Pakistan International Airlines (P.I.A.). Unfortunately, although P.I.A. purchased five aircraft from Transocean—two DC-4s and three DC-3s—it insisted on doing its own maintenance. In February 1949, after a DC-3 had crashed, Transocean received a management contract. The next problem was that the Pakistani pilots, who had been trained at Oakland by Transocean's Taloa Academy of Aeronautics (established in 1946), insisted on being given the rank of

flight captains, even though most of them were clearly not yet qualified except as copilots. There was another DC-3 crash, and
Transocean pulled out, as did the family that had started the airline.
Nelson had to buy his DC-4s back, using money owed to him as the
down payment.

Anything, anywhere. During 1947 and 1948, Transocean transported 2,000 fishermen from Yakutat to Bristol Bay in Alaska for
seasonal fishing. This was followed by a contract with the Navy Bureau of Yards and Docks to move labor and equipment from Seattle to Anchorage and Adak, and fulfillment of this contract led to
the Pet 4 operation, which was successfully bid under a Navy contract to transport personnel and equipment from Fairbanks (Navy
Petroleum District Number 4 headquarters) to Point Barrow, site
of the embryo Alaskan oil industry, from 1950 to 1952. This was an
unusual operation, demanding twin-engined C-46s and DC-3s fitted with skis, together with the rugged little Norseman bush aircraft, built in Canada specifically to cope with the severe climate of
the far north of the American continent. While Point Barrow is now
firmly on the airline map, with scheduled service to the rest of civilization, Transocean, as usual, was there at the beginning, a pioneer in this difficult assignment.

Also in 1948, Transocean undertook a project to which many
experts gave little chance of success. The Chinese Nationalist government had purchased 150 C-46s from the U.S. government during the latter part of 1947. Transocean was unsuccessful in bidding
for the necessary overhaul contract but did persuade the authorities to allow it to fly the aircraft to Shanghai, by fitting them with
long-range tanks, instead of dismantling them and sending them
by ship. The mission was completed between April 20 and September 16, 1948, without loss or damage.

As a sequel to the China operation, the I.R.O. asked Orvis Nelson to arrange for the evacuation of a colony of 5,000 White Russians who had settled in Shanghai after the mass exodus from Rus-
sia in 1919–20. This was accomplished despite some obstructions
put in the way by the Chinese government, which had been solic-
ited by C.N.A.C., the Pan American associated airline in China at
the time, to carry the refugees. Also the Philippine airline, then controlled by other influential groups, persuaded its government to
deny landing rights to Transocean. These difficulties were overcome, partly through a compromise with C.N.A.C., and partly

through Colonel Soriano's personal intervention on behalf of Transocean.

One of the Chinese flights, this time for Chinese refugees from the Communists who had made their way to Hong Kong, provides a perfect example of the complexities of flying charter and contract flights during the postwar period, when half the population of the world seemed to be on the move for one reason or another. This flight was destined for South America, but the United States refused transit visas to the passengers. Transocean arranged for the aircraft to fly the other way around the world, with assistance from the British authorities, to Panama, by way of a transatlantic crossing. This aircraft then picked up a load of stranded seamen and flew them to India, shuttled a load of Jewish immigrants from India to Israel, then headed for Germany to pick up for the I.R.O. some displaced persons bound for South America.

The breadth and variety of Transocean's activities during the postwar years were truly astonishing. By December 1947, Nelson had negotiated the purchase of a complete overhaul base at Oakland, which became AEMCO, the Aircraft Engineering and Maintenance Company, at which Transocean not only handled its own aircraft but also undertook overhauls and other work for many other airlines. It was the nucleus of the considerable installations that exist at Oakland International Airport today, under the control of other airlines that survived Transocean after its demise. One of AEMCO's first contracts was to put a large number of decommissioned DC-4s back into working order and to overhaul the aircraft that participated in the Berlin airlift. One of these aircraft was *Workhorse Harry*, which had flown 1943 airlift flights—including 194 during February 1949 alone—from Frankfurt to Berlin, carrying coal. One of the aerial coal trucks yielded 243 pounds of dust at Oakland, and it was typical of Transocean that this was packed in jars and given to employees as prizes to stimulate production.

In August 1949, Orvis Nelson set up Air Djibouti in what was then French Somaliland, on the Red Sea, and used this foothold in the Middle East to conduct all kinds of charter operations, including many pilgrimage flights to Mecca during the Hajj season. He also organized the transfer of the entire entourage of King Ibn Saud of Saudi Arabia from Riyadh to the summer residence at Taif, 4,500 feet above sea level. This movement demanded the use of about twenty-five aircraft, from Air Djibouti and from the Saudi airline, and took five days to complete. Several months later the whole process was reversed.

Fortunately Transocean was completely neutral in serving the opposing sides of the religious confrontation in the Middle East. It operated a scheduled service from Geneva to Lydda, Israel, for almost a year, simultaneously ferrying refugees to South America for the I.R.O. Altogether Nelson's team carried about 50,000 refugees from Europe to Israel, curiously enough during the same period that it was participating in the Moslem Hajj operations and was serving the Saudi Arabian royalty. That all the Transocean aircraft and crews survived is a measure of the law-abiding habits of all concerned in an era before hijacking or terrorism on aircraft had been thought of.

While the pressures on airlines, such as Transocean, that conducted airlifts of refugees were considerable, Orvis Nelson never allowed his people to lower their standards, even in the face of unethical and unsafe competition. While Transocean managed to seat seventy passengers quite legally in a DC-4 by removing all the amenities except the toilet and reducing the pitch of the seats, one competitor set the unenviable record of carrying 153 people in the same type of aircraft. Five died en route and the rest were half dead on arrival.

Transocean was ready to take on any challenge. During the winter of 1948–49, for example, it carried a 6,000-pound load from the Atomic Energy Plant at Hanford, Washington, to Oak Ridge, Tennessee. The operation had to be planned with great precision because of the severely limited time during which the precious consignment could be allowed out of captivity. It arrived at Richland Airport escorted by armed cars. It was then loaded in record time, and the Transocean aircraft made the journey in the planned thirteen hours, the maximum permissible for this radioactive consignment, without incident.

No less valuable, though slightly less hazardous, was the movement, in the spring of 1950, of forty-five tons of gold from Tokyo to New York. Owned by the Bank of Thailand, it had to be shipped to the United States, all $46,374,000 worth, and Transocean completed Operation Gold Rush in nine days, using seven aircraft to do the job.

Transocean was one of the first airlines to discover the cost benefits that could be passed on to the customer through group travel arrangments. In a special charter for college students in the summer of 1948, Nelson contracted with an organization called Youth Argosy to transport groups of young people all the way around the world, on a combined educational and goodwill tour. Because the students stopped for a few days at various points and the aircraft had to wait for them, this was not the most economical way to utilize the fleet. Transocean invested in the program, however, charging only $1,000 each for the complete round-the-world trip and consciously losing money as a way of gaining experience in this new application of cheap fares. It was not able to develop an efficient series of such programs because the Civil Aeronautics Board would not, at that time, permit such a revolutionary way of bringing the benefits of air travel to a deserving public.

The C.A.B., of course, had fewer qualms when the time came for a national emergency. In June 1950, when danger threatened in Korea, the call came to provide aircraft for a transpacific movement of passengers. Eventually deploying seven aircraft on the Korean airlift, Transocean had already made two round trips, on twenty-four hours' notice, before any other airline or contract carrier had even departed from the United States and subsequently accounted for 14 percent of all Korean airlift flights.

Shortly after the beginning of the Korean flights, Transocean won the contract for a vastly different kind of operation. The United States had inherited about 3 million square miles of the western Pacific, formerly administered under a League of Nations mandate by the Japanese and redesignated the Trust Territory of the Pacific Islands under the United Nations. Most of this territory is now the Federated States of Micronesia, Palau, the Marianas, and the Marshall Islands having become independent. The territory includes about 2,000 islands, of which fewer than 100 are inhabited. During the summer of 1950, several airline operators, including Transocean, were invited to join a survey party, which included representatives of the C.A.B. and the Departments of the Interior and the Navy. The outcome was that Transocean was the successful bidder to provide the vital air link among all the main islands of the Trust Territory. Four twin-engined PBY-5A amphibious aircraft were supplied by the navy, and Transocean maintained the weekly scheduled service from its base in Guam until the airline was forced to terminate all its activities in 1960.

Always ready to seize an opportunity whenever one appeared, Orvis Nelson quickly perceived one in Japan during the summer of 1951. The Japanese had been forbidden to operate an airline at all, since the *Green Cross* medical supply flights were banned on October 10, 1945. But then the Allied Command permitted the gradual resumption of air service in Japan, at first with the stipulation that no Japanese crews should be used until the signing of the peace treaty. Japanese Air Lines (J.A.L.) was formed on August 1, 1951, and began operations in October of that year, ostensibly under contract with Northwest Airlines but actually with aircraft and crews of Transocean Airlines, at first using four Martin 2-0-2 twin-engined airliners. The enormous potential of the Japanese domestic air travel market quickly became evident, and although Transocean brought in additional aircraft, its venture in a foreign domain was short-lived, for Japan Air Lines, a full-fledged Japanese airline, was formed in October 1953 and took over from the Transocean-Northwest temporary arrangement.

The foregoing account is a drastic condensation of Transocean's widespread airline activity during the critical post-war period, when the entire air transport industry was responding to new challenges of commercial opportunity and adapting its efforts to keep pace with the rapid technological progress being made by the aircraft manufacturers. A third element in the complex equation that needed to be solved satisfactorily if a viable, solid airline base was to be created was sympathetic government regulation. With the last element Transocean was conspicuously unsuccessful, in spite of the clear evidence that, in a phrase often employed by the Civil Aeronautics Board, it was "fit, willing, and able" to perform any task assigned to it.

The treatment of Transocean by the government agency was a travesty of justice. The C.A.B. seems to have carried out a policy of deliberate extermination by procrastination, following the blueprint supplied in a memorandum dated September 16, 1948, written by its chief of the Bureau of Economic Regulations, Louis W. Goodkind, who was far from being either good or kind to the non-scheduled airlines. He outlined ways in which their attempts to attain legitimacy in the eyes of the board could be thwarted, and the board's treatment of Transocean was a textbook case.

On September 21, 1951, the C.A.B. did make an attempt to clarify the status of the nonscheduled operations by instituting the

Large Irregular Carrier Investigation. Meanwhile, it limited the scope of their operations and concentrated on endless hearings of the certificated airlines, which, while jointly protecting what they considered their birthright, squabbled among themselves for extensions of the grandfather rights bequeathed to them under the original Civil Aeronautics Act of 1938.

The problem with the Irregulars was that there were many whose operations were highly irregular. Desperate to survive, many resorted to practices which, if not actually illegal—and some of them were—were quite unethical. A few rotten apples affected the healthy ones, but the public was unable to distinguish the good from the bad. Worse, the financial institutions seemed similarly unable, and sound airlines such as Transocean could not obtain adequate financial support from traditional sources. The irony was that—in a real Catch 22 situation—without the blessing of the C.A.B. an airline lacked respectability in the eyes of the financiers, but the C.A.B. would not provide the respectability unless the airline was well financed.

The 1950s were difficult years for Transocean, for its aircraft were beginning to look old, as indeed they were. Orvis Nelson needed pressurized equipment but did not have the resources to purchase a fleet of modern four-engined aircraft and could not obtain outside financing. There was an unhappy experience when R. Stanley Dollar, of the Dollar Steamship Line, lent $500,000 to Transocean and agreed to finance a fleet of aircraft in exchange for a large block of stock. This almost led to the purchase of Model 749 Constellations from the British airline B.O.A.C., but early in 1957 Dollar backed out.

Shortly thereafter Orvis Nelson's own lawyer disclosed that the Atlas Corporation, a New York investment corporation headed by Floyd Odlum, had acquired 40 percent of Transocean's stock. On July 1, 1957, an agreement was signed between the Transocean Corporation of California, the parent company of T.A.L., and the Atlas Corporation. From that time on, Orvis Nelson steadily lost control of the airline that he had worked strenuously to build. His experience was akin to that of a man whose house is on fire but who is forced to watch the firemen either looking the other way or actually pouring gasoline on the flames.

The Civil Aeronautics Board were the firemen looking the other way. Late in 1954, in the Transpacific Renewal Case, the

C.A.B. Examiner had recommended that Transocean should receive a temporary certificate, but the board rejected this by a 3:2 vote. Subsequently, when petitioned by Transocean for reconsideration, one of the opposing voters had been replaced by a new member known to favor Nelson's case, but he was absent from Washington. A vote was hurriedly taken, and the 2:2 vote sustained the original decision, placing on record a rather unsavory episode in the annals of the C.A.B.

On November 15, 1955, the board concluded that the Large Irregular Carriers had a place in the airline world, and should thereafter be known as Supplemental Carriers, a term that more closely described their function. The terms of operation were, however, still restrictive, limiting to ten the number of flights per month between any two points. By April 1957, Transocean was using the word *Supplemental* in its published timetable for its transpacific service and is believed to have been the first airline to use it in its promotional documentation.

By this time the Atlas Corporation was in complete control of Transocean and was making some curious decisions, not least of which was to lease two badly needed Constellations at twice the going rate. Interference with management and the consequent loss of some good executives forced Nelson to ask for a new agreement with Atlas, which, on November 20, 1958, turned over to Odlum's corporation almost all the Transocean organization except the airline itself.

The bitterest pill of all for Nelson to swallow was the knowledge that his airline was at a level of efficiency and performance equal to those of many of the certificated domestic trunk carriers. It employed an experienced staff of 6,500, including many veterans in the business. It had an impressive record of operating success behind it. Its gross income in 1957 had exceeded $50 million, and the net profit had topped $1 million. It operated all the charter flights it could handle within the C.A.B.'s law from the mainland to Hawaii and across the Pacific and the Atlantic and was poised to reap the rewards of its labors. Its Constellations were supplemented by Boeing Stratocruisers in 1959, although astonishingly the Atlas Corporation blocked the supply of spares.

By the time the C.A.B. approved the amended Atlas Agreement, Transocean was only a shadow of its former self. Under the insidious influence of Atlas, which was aided, consciously or unconsciously, by the C.A.B.'s agonizing delay in making decisions, Transocean just fell apart, deprived as it was of its affiliated maintenance, manufacturing, and construction companies through the Atlas deal. In effect Orvis Nelson's proud airline ceased to exist in January 1960, maintaining only the Trust Territory operation until Pan American took over in the summer of that year. By then, Transocean was bankrupt, and on July 11, United States Overseas Airlines (U.S.O.A.) took over the remnants of the route network.

The supreme irony during this bitter period was that, at last, under severe pressure from Congress, the C.A.B. was relenting on its rigid policy against any form of air transport that did not conform to the wishes of the holders of the grandfather rights. On January 29, 1959, it had issued interstate certificates to twenty-three Supplemental airlines that it found to be qualified and later issued similar certificates for overseas and foreign routes. Although on April 7, 1960, the action of the Board was found to be legally defective, this was straightened out, and a compromise proposal, validating existing certificates, was adopted on June 27, 1960.

Orvis Nelson, creator of the biggest Supplemental of them all, had to watch all this from the wings, rather like an actor who has lost his voice on opening night. Others reaped the benefit of his labors, though in fairness it must be said that their luck in picking up the slack as Transocean departed the scene was not born of malice toward Nelson, who had no enemies, except possibly in certain corridors of power in Washington or Wall Street. When the Transpacific Route Case was reopened on July 27, 1961, Orvis Nelson, who had had as much Pacific experience as any single participant in those long-drawn-out hearings and arguments, was a mere onlooker.

And so it went. Public Law 87-528, passed on July 10, 1962, established the permanent legitimacy of the Supplementals, and the C.A.B. assigned specific spheres of influence to all those who had survived. Perhaps significantly, the two biggest were World Airways and Trans International Airlines (T.I.A.), which shared the biggest slice of the nonscheduled cake from the vantage point of the Oakland base, which had formerly been Transocean's. On April 18, 1964, only four years after Orvis Nelson had been ruthlessly disposed of by a combination of C.A.B. intransigence and corporate greed, both World and T.I.A. were granted five-year transatlantic certificates.

During the 1960s, Orvis and Edie Nelson tried to salvage

something out of the personal disaster that had descended upon them. Putting aside the sense of betrayal and acute disillusionment with the entrenched U.S. Establishment, they went to Europe, trying to find the special niche into which Nelson's abundant talents could find a secure hold. There was a venture in Italy, but this never matured. In 1966 Nelson, flying as a copilot in Africa, was involved in a crash. Five months in a hospital in the middle of that continent completed his disenchantment.

The Nelsons returned to Minnesota in 1966, but after a few years the old urge returned. Aviation was in Orvis's blood, bones, and nervous system. He was an active aviation consultant for a few years and participated in some promotion, including an effort to tap the Indonesian tourist market—an effort in which he was perhaps a few years ahead of his time.

On October 6, 1976, Orvis Nelson made a statement before the Senate Small Business Committee. He outlined the history of Transocean, listed its many achievements, documented the machiavellian maneuvers of the C.A.B. and the Atlas Corporation, and made an impassioned appeal for justice. In closing, he recommended that Congress "take the necessary steps to force deregulation by the Board to the greatest extent possible. Start with cancelling control over air fares, give unlimited right of entry into the airline business domestically and right of entry and departure from points served." And he elaborated in greater detail.

Orvis Nelson died of a heart attack on December 2, 1976. President Carter signed the Airline Deregulation Act on October 24, 1978.

Edward Daly

Himself

When Edward Joseph Daly purchased World Airways in 1950, he bought little more than permission to fly commercial airplanes, on a perilously uncertain basis, using a Letter of Registration from the Civil Aeronautics Board (C.A.B.) under a general category curiously called Large Irregular Carrier. The assets, in aircraft and supporting equipment, did not amount to much, although they were typical of the equipment owned by the happy band of cavalier operators who had started charter airlines at the end of World War II, financed largely by the pensions and gratuities they had earned as pilots in the air forces. None of the carriers was large, but all were certainly irregular. Indeed, most were erratic and unreliable.

In truth, World Airways was a little different, mainly in that it started with a small fleet of flying boats, rather than with the familiar Douglas C-47s (military DC-3s) or Curtiss C-46s, which could be picked up for a few thousand dollars from war surplus stocks. World was incorporated in the state of Delaware on March 29, 1948, by Benjamin Pepper. Ed Daly purchased the airline from the Berkoviche Steamship Company, which was the owner of record in 1950.

World had acquired the three remaining Boeing 314 clippers and could thus claim to be the only operator of the world's finest flying boats, other than Pan American Airways and the British Overseas Airways Corporation. Not that the business-minded Berkoviche would have worried about records; he was interested in putting the boats to work, operating on a fairly regular, if not scheduled, basis between San Juan and New York. This was at the

119

Ed Daly built the largest supplemental airline in the world, without a single scheduled route, in less than two decades. World Airways survives today as the legacy of a fearless and feisty Irishman who thrived on doing the unpredictable. His Da Nang adventure lives in the elite annals of transport aviation.

height of the Puerto Rican immigration boom, and in their dying years the 314s were kept busy.

World Airways also used the flying boats on the route for which they were originally designed, the North Atlantic. They made occasional flights from the old Marine Air Terminal at La Guardia, New York, to Foynes, Ireland, still in use as a flying-boat base while the new airport at nearby Shannon was under construction. One of the Boeings had to make an emergency alighting in the Atlantic, fortunately close to one of the Coast Guard vessels that were stationed permanently in fixed positions on the main air route as weather-reporting stations and for navigational aid and emergencies just as this. All the passengers were taken safely on board the vessel, but the Boeing 314 had to be sunk by gunfire.

In the early weeks of January 1949, World suspended operations and the Berkoviche Steamship Company acquired the flying boats, subletting its Irregular Carrier Letter of Registration to Marvin Stadden, who did not want the flying boats either. He chose instead to lease a Curtiss C-46 from the War Assets Administration, through the Reconstruction Finance Corporation, and substituted it on the Puerto Rican route. He also bought another C-46 but used it only for spare parts.

This was the rather flimsy foundation on which, one year later, Ed Daly built the largest nonscheduled airline in the world. Of the 150 Large Irregular Carriers that survived until 1986, World was one, and the Small Irregulars are long gone. World became for a while one of the reputable transatlantic airlines of the United States, operating both scheduled services—after airline deregulation—and charter services, until it was overcome by the sheer force of about forty or fifty competitors, many of whom could cross-subsidize their loss-sustaining routes from other sources. By any criterion, the man who did all this was a remarkable person.

Edward J. Daly was born in Chicago on November 20, 1922. His father was a fireman who had four children, two boys and two girls, and the family just about made its way during the hard times of that era. But in 1937, Daly Senior died and Ed was forced to fend for himself. He even became a Golden Gloves boxer, and his accomplishments in this field of endeavor were to emerge occasionally in his subsequent career.

In December 1941, Daly was drafted into the army and sent to Hickam Air Force Base, Honolulu, moving on later to Saipan and Tinian in the western Pacific. After the war, he gained his first experience with commercial aviation while working as a passenger agent for Scotty O'Carroll, in a small office at Midway Airport, Chicago. He handled bookings for all the nonscheduled airlines, which were picking up business where they could as crumbs from the table of the scheduled airline masters. These were the days when even coach class fares—now rated on the high side since discounting became a way of deregulated life—had not been thought of. The scheduled airlines had only one fare level, first class, and this suited business travelers. The general public was, as yet, only dimly aware of the potential for air travel, particularly for vacations, and the charter operators had a tough time trying to break through the web of regulations that prevented them from offering cheap fares to an unsuspecting public.

One of many visionaries who foresaw the inevitability of a massive low-fare air travel market was this ticket agent at Midway Airport, Ed Daly. Early in July 1950 he borrowed $50,000 from a small trucking company to buy the World Airways certificate. He also assumed about $250,000 of debts, but the story that he won the money to do all this in a poker game is apocryphal, doubtless based on the assumption that this was the kind of thing Ed Daly might easily have done. Actually, Daly's favorite card game was gin rummy. Although he was never a master at it, he would play the game with his friends for more than twenty-four hours at a time.

In October 1949 he had married June Chandler, a Pan American Airways stewardess. June had flown with Pan Am throughout Latin America and was well versed in airline knowledge and folklore. She was to be Ed's partner and adviser through many stormy and eventful years, playing an active part in World Airways administration and surviving him as deputy chairman of the airline today.

Daly continued the Puerto Rican airlift, fitting out his entire staff with new uniforms and, in the summer of 1951, moving the headquarters of World Airways from La Guardia to Teterboro, New Jersey, where the overhead was much less. He then set about the task of acquiring better equipment at minimum cost. First, he leased a DC-4 from Braniff, but this was no ordinary transaction. Before taking delivery, Daly had to repair and recertificate the aircraft, which had been badly damaged in a wheels-up landing at Brownsville, Texas. The old C-46, meanwhile, continued to earn its keep, notably on a three-month DEW-line (Distant Early Warning line) contract in Canada.

In 1953, during a lean period when World Airways was living from day to day, Ed Daly hired Augustine Martin, who may have been the first black man to be hired as an airline pilot. In those days, blacks were typically employed as janitors, porters, or bellhops, but Augie had prepared himself well, and the outcome was that, in the face of protest, Daly offered him a job. The instructions to the staff were succinct: "If he can fly, you put him to work." One Caucasian pilot from the deep South resigned rather than risk contamination from a black man on the flight deck. Augie was later shot down while flying a Constellation (but not for Daly) airlifting supplies during the Biafran campaign in West Africa.

For the struggling nonscheduled survivors of the band of Large Irregular Carriers that had mushroomed into existence in 1946 and 1947, a glimmer of hope appeared in 1955. On November 15 of that year, the C.A.B. concluded that their authority should be enlarged and that they should be known thereafter as Supplemental Air Carriers, a term that more closely described their function and gave them a semblance of legitimacy.

By this time Daly had identified another suitable candidate for his fleet, one that he could call his own. A U.S. government–owned C-54 (the military DC-4) was languishing at Northolt Airport, near London, having been damaged by fire. Daly undertook to restore the wreckage, at a cost of $35,000, which presumably included the rental of the limousine in which he slept at Northolt while a team of aircraft miracle workers from Eagle Aviation worked under pressure to meet the time limit so as to avoid British taxation. Daly flew out on the day before the time limit expired. It was a close call, one of many that his career would encompass.

The DC-4 augmented the World Airways fleet to two airplanes, one of which was four-engined, albeit still unpressurized; but at least it could theoretically fly across the Atlantic or the Pacific, a capability that Daly correctly judged to be an absolute minimum qualification for any government contract that was worth a candle. On the other hand, as one writer put it, his position was similar to that of a taxi operator who owned only one cab and was dependent on chance pickups before the meter would begin running.

In retrospect, Daly's intuition and instincts during this period were uncanny. During the previous year, on May 7, 1954, the French had undergone the humiliation of the military defeat at Dien Bien Phu, in Tonkin province of French Indochina, now northern Vietnam, and on July 21 of the same year, the Geneva agreement had divided Vietnam into two parts at the 17th parallel. In 1955, he had, by salvaging the DC-4, acquired an aircraft that qualified him—by a hair's breadth—to bid for transocean contracts. During March 1955 he began operation on a DEW-line contract that lasted eighty-six days, using his two C-46s. In March 1956 he moved his base once again, from Teterboro to Oakland, California, where he was geographically well placed for future transpacific work. On September 16 of that year, the Military Air Transport Service (MATS) contracted with commercial operators, including World, for transpacific support work.

Daly was not yet ready for the long-haul transpacific work, for one DC-4 was insufficient and uncompetitive. But he found work for his sole four-engined aircraft and another one besides, which he quickly leased. This was really fortuitous. On October 23, 1956, the Hungarian people began a spontaneous uprising against the Communist government and were so harshly suppressed that 180,000 refugees fled into neighboring countries, principally Austria. The United States accepted 38,000 of these people, and Ed Daly's World Airways was one of the companies with which the International Commission for European Migration contracted to provide an airlift to the United States. The two DC-4s made fourteen transatlantic trips, and Daly was on hand in Vienna to visit the refugee camps and become personally involved. This was a habit that was characteristic of his day-to-day activities throughout his career. He was to be found wherever there was action of this nature, and World Airways was always to be found in the front line.

No sooner had the Hungarian airlift ended than World Airways was committed to an operation on the opposite side of the globe. On December 16, 1956, Daly won a MATS contract to provide an interisland service from Tokyo to Okinawa, Taiwan, and Manila, in general support of U.S. forces based in the western Pacific. Forty-eight hours before the contractual date, his two DC-4s were still at their base in Oakland, California. But they were transferred to Tokyo, along with a staff of 100 and their families in support, in time to begin a daily scheduled service, as contracted, on January 1, 1957.

In the United States at this time, changes in commercial airline regulations were being made that were to have far-reaching effects. On January 29, 1959, the C.A.B. issued a Supplemental Air Carrier certificate to World Airways, among others, to operate domestic nonscheduled services for five years. This piece of paper did not change things very much at first. World Airways, like all the Supplementals, was hampered by a bewildering maze of regulations that were designed to prevent them from encroaching on the fortified preserves of the scheduled airlines. But possession of such a certificate gave World a degree of respectability during a period when many of the old Large Irregulars were gradually disappearing by a process of attrition.

Without such a certificate, Ed Daly could never have won, on June 15, 1960, a vitally important Logistics Air Lift (LOGAIR) contract from the U.S. government to operate transcontinental air routes, carrying military personnel and matériel. The losing bidder was Resort Airways, another enterprising airline that had pioneered the inclusive air tour industry and was itself to become a victim of crippling and restrictive legislation that appears ludicrous in today's liberated regulatory climate. For World Airways it was like winning a lucrative lottery, or like hitting the jackpot numbers in a high-stakes game at Las Vegas. Nothing was ever the same again.

Ed Daly promptly leased a fleet of seven Douglas DC-6s—pressurized aircraft for the first time—from the losing bidder, Resort, which retired from the airline business with about $3 million in the bank. From this moment on, World Airways grew rapidly, thanks to a succession of government contracts. In 1961, it introduced eight DC-6As and four Lockheed Super-Constellations and in the following year added three Lockheed L-1649A Starliners. By the summer of 1962 Ed Daly could boast a fleet of fifteen modern airliners, in striking contrast to the two unpressurized aircraft of only two years earlier.

The new fleet was used on transpacific airlift contracts, mainly to and from the western Pacific atomic proving grounds in the Marshall Islands. World's operation from Hawaii to Kwajalein and Eniwetok was intensive, efficient, and profitable. Its service record of regularity and punctuality was observed by an important government contractor, who also obtained the services of World Airways over the same routes. This was to be a lucrative contract, which lasted several years.

But there was another side to the business, sometimes forgotten by commentators who were later to record Daly's amazing success. To quote Mrs. Daly, who shared the triumphs and the risks: "When you bid on a military contract, you had everything on the line, your home, the clothes on your back, everything."

Fortunately, the risks were justified. World Airways made a profit of $5.5 million in two years and on June 7, 1962, ordered three Boeing 707-320s, the long-range version of this epoch-making jet airliner. World was the first airline to order this series of the 707—first called the 707-350C—even before the orders that were customarily placed by the leaders of the scheduled industry, such as United or Pan American. The decision was a reflection of Daly's instinct that World's future lay with commercial markets, in spite of its extensive preoccupation with military contracts in the past. It also served notice on the aircraft manufacturing industry that the Supplemental airlines were now a force to be reckoned with, to be included in their market forecasts as customers of integrity, and no longer temporary users of handed-down used equipment.

The mid 1960s saw World Airways consolidating its now prominent position as an industry leader. Public Law 37-528, enacted by Congress on July 10, 1962, confined the Supplementals to charter services—several of them had tried to operate quasi-scheduled routes—but this was a further confirmation of legitimacy from the administration. Under section 401 of the Civil Aeronautics Act Supplemental airlines were permitted to apply for certification within designated geographic areas. Instead of being denied their inheritance, World Airways and its fellow pioneers could now lay claim to a portion of the airline estate. Ed Daly continued to be one of the most effective—and certainly one of the most forceful—of the campaigners for the rights of the Supplemental underdogs.

In the late summer of 1963, World Airways introduced the first of its Boeing 707-320C jet fleet, placing it immediately on the Pacific MATS contracts, and replacing the piston-engined fleet. On August 10 it made the first commercial nonstop flight from California to Japan, covering the 6,600 miles in 9 hours 52 minutes. Maintaining the reputation for impeccable fulfilment of its obligations that had been set with the DC-4s and DC-6s, the Boeings attained, in the month of February 1964, a reliability rate of 100 percent during a program of ninety-one trips in a month without a single deviation from the schedule.

The year 1966 was one of concentrated, almost frenzied activity for the Supplemental Air Carriers. On March 14, World was one of ten airlines that were granted permanent domestic operating authority for charter traffic and inclusive air tours and also worldwide charter authority. A month later, World Airways made a public stock offering, when on April 18, Ed Daly sold 19.5 percent of his 100 percent ownership for $22.9 million, which, even after taxes, was worth about $17 million. By any stretch of the imagination, this was not bad for a man who, a bare sixteen years earlier, had borrowed money to purchase a precarious operating certificate and an old C-46.

On June 30, 1966, Daly made one of his rare misjudgments. Swept along by the then current euphoria generated by the promoters of the supersonic airliner, World Airways reserved delivery positions with the Federal Aviation Agency for three Boeing 2707 Mach 3 airliners. Daly was not alone among the leaders of the airline industry who were deceived by unsupported political rhetoric. But the fact that a Supplemental airline could join the leaders of the scheduled industry in such a venture was itself significant. A former poor relation had come of age. Fortunately for Daly, as for everyone else when Congress wisely rejected the SST, he got his money back, with interest.

On September 30, 1966, the C.A.B. granted World Airways international authority for general charters and inclusive air tours covering the Caribbean, South America, and the Pacific and on November 26 added semipermanent transatlantic authority as well. World marked these unprecedented additions to its franchise by ordering, on December 22—as a Christmas gesture to Pan American, perhaps—three Boeing 747 wide-bodied jets and two more Boeing 707-320Cs to add to its existing fleet of six Douglas DC-6As, together with six newly acquired Boeing 727-100 short–medium-range airliners. Altogether Ed Daly finished the year 1966 in grand style.

He was in high gear now. He had proved to his own complete satisfaction that if he operated efficiently, dispensed with unnecessary ancillary staff, exerted good disipline, and used his own good judgment, World Airways could make money hand over fist. He was very much in command, arguably a dictator, making all the vital decisions, and in fact taking very little advice. This was possibly because he did not need to, for he had an unerring instinct for making the right money-making decisions.

Ed Daly was not the calmest of men, either in his habits or his attitudes. He often displayed the fiery temper and occasional belligerence expected of the Irish. He drank a lot. There were frequent occasions when he threatened to fire subordinates who argued too strongly against his convictions, but the melodrama was rarely translated into the threatened action. He would dominate discussions, and his language was pithy and penetrating. But he was usually right, and his stockholders respected his intuitive judgment. Equally, his employees seldom had any reason for genuine complaint of sustained unfair treatment or lack of upward mobility. World Airways was a successful airline, Ed Daly was its creator, and the staff, especially the select band of highly competent senior executives, worked their tails off as they watched their leader do the same.

As a measure of consolidation of strength, in February 1967

World took a forty-year lease with the Port of Oakland for a new $11 million Air Center and International Headquarters at Oakland International Airport. Shortly thereafter, displaying supreme confidence, both in himself and in his airline, Ed Daly challenged the airline Establishment when, on April 26, 1967, he applied to the C.A.B. for a license to operate a transcontinental scheduled air service for $75.00. With his efficient team, and with the world's newest and most economical long-haul aircraft on order, World Airways could have done the job. The public would have lined up the length of several blocks to buy bargain-priced tickets. But this was before the idea of deregulation of the airlines was even being discussed, much less being put into effect. World Airways was classified as a Supplemental Carrier, and that was that. There was no admission then to the privileged ranks of the scheduled operators who, with the tacit approval of the C.A.B., conducted a de facto—almost a de jure—operation, at substantially higher fares, with aircraft barely half full.

Inevitably, the application failed to break through the impenetrable barriers of bureaucracy which at that time denied entry of a new airline to the scheduled industry. Unabashed, Daly leased three of his aircraft to United Air Lines in October 1967 and also postponed the Boeing 747 order to avoid being burdened with excess capacity. But he was still on the crest of a wave of success in the charter market. Measured by revenue passenger-miles, World was the nineteenth largest airline in the world, larger than such prestigious national flag carriers as Swissair, Iberia (Spain), or QANTAS (Australia) or the medium-sized U.S. domestic trunk scheduled airlines.

In 1968 Daly tried a little diversification. He formed the Worldamerica Investors Corporation and bought a bank, the First Western Bank and Trust Company of California, with assets of $900 million. This was accomplished without issuing stock, for the acquisition was made from bank loans and from World's own funds. In 1974 Daly sold the bank to Lloyd's Bank, of London, for $115 million in cash.

During the same year, 1968, after starting, on July 1, Rest and Rehabilitation (R & R) flights from Vietnam to Australia and Japan, World Airways became the only airline to win the U.S. National Safety Council's highest award in each of four consecutive years. This was on August 20, and the award of a new LOGAIR contract on September 11 may not have been a coincidence. Among other recorded achievements, World delivered to U.S. servicemen in Vietnam the forces newspaper *Stars and Stripes*. This was printed in Japan, and the uncensored news reached a million readers.

During the winter of 1968–69, Ed Daly was involved in negotiations that, if completed, would have concluded in the sale of World Airways to the Insurance Company of North America, of Philadelphia. Daly would have been richer by many millions of dollars, but he pulled out of the deal at the last moment. Even though he would have continued as chairman and chief executive officer of World, he simply could not bear the prospect of relinquishing absolute control.

The next four years were uneventful, by Daly standards. On April 18, 1969, World Airways was granted permanent authority for charters and inclusive tours across the Atlantic, and with most other parts of the world's surface already secured in this respect, Ed Daly's airline literally lived up to its name. World met the same fate as had befallen many of its fellow airlines during the summer of 1970, when the air crew went on strike, staying out from May 14 to July 4, but such temporary inconveniences were brushed aside as Daly's airline grew steadily in both the commercial charter and military markets. On December 15, in a unique operation in cooperation with the United Service Organizations (U.S.O.), World started a Homecoming contract. World Airways offered U.S. servicemen in Vietnam and other points in the western Pacific a $350 round trip Boeing 747 flight from Saigon to Oakland. Twenty-three thousand troops took advantage of this travel bargain, which lasted until December 1971. Daly himself was in evidence at this time, personally delivering items of Christmas cheer to Saigon, including the traditional hams, trees, and turkeys.

In March 1971, World purchased three DC-8-63CF convertible aircraft from McDonnell Douglas, adding three more of these versatile and profitable 252-seaters in 1973. But Ed Daly, relaxing a little from day-to-day strains of running the airline, derived further pleasure from an executive aircraft that he bought in September 1971. This was no hot-rod jet, but an orthodox Convair 440 piston-engined airliner, big enough to be fitted out as a flying World Airways headquarters, with sophisticated equipment so that he could keep in touch with the entire World system, wherever he might be.

*With a leprechaun on its nose and a shamrock on its tail, Ed Daly's
personal aircraft, a Convair 440 named the* Jolly Green Giant, *roamed the
world with its owner for fourteen years, throughout the 1970s and until his
death in 1984.*

The *Jolly Green Giant*, as the Convair 440 was named, was painted
in thirteen shades of green, with a leprechaun by the front door and
a shamrock on the tail, just in case any observer might be unaware
of the owner's origins. It had originally been given to Arthur Godfrey by United Air Lines President W. R. Patterson. It passed to the
state of California, whose governor, Ronald Reagan, decided he did
not need it. The *Jolly Green Giant* roamed the world for fourteen
years and was eventually sold on March 30, 1985.

The early 1970s saw steady progress for World Airways. It
was now deeply involved with the kind of business that had become its bread and butter, the long-haul contract airlift operation
in support of U.S. military forces in distant lands, in this instance
Vietnam. The entire fleet of Boeing 707s was occupied almost exclusively with transpacific flights from 1973 to 1975, largely on R & R
service. In March 1972, the Boeing 747 order, postponed earlier because of market uncertanties—or, to be blunt, the failure of World
Airways to enter the transcontinental scheduled market—was re-

instated, and in December of that year three more McDonnell Douglas DC-8-63Fs were ordered.

In May 1973 World's first 747 made its inaugural charter flight from Oakland to London, and in the same month the new maintenance base was dedicated at the World headquarters in Oakland, which quickly became the center of maintenance and overhaul for most of the Supplemental airlines—and for a few scheduled ones as well. As the third highest of twelve participating bidders World also received a $15.4 million contract from the Military Airlift Command.

While the vast majority of World's activity was strictly under contract, it would have been uncharacteristic of Daly not to do some things in his own way. As the tactical situation grew more desperate in Southeast Asia, so Daly's personal involvement and identification with the human problems intensified. No longer partying in the Caribbean in the *Jolly Green Giant*, he was on hand in Saigon, anxious to help and, if necessary, to take on the North Vietnamese himself.

Between February 15 and 26, 1975, World Airways was one of the commercial contractors called in to airlift supplies into Phnom Penh, the now isolated capital of beleaguered Cambodia. With only three complete crews, working a concentrated shift system, two DC-8-63CFs averaged six round trips a day, carrying 3,493 tons of cargo from Tan San Nhut air base in Vietnam to Phnom Penh. Landings at the Pochentong airfield in Phnom Penh were often extremely hazardous, with enemy rocket fire interspersed with congestion from Cambodian Air Force T-38s, which had priority. There were some casualities among the ground crew. Some maneuvers were made that were not advised in the DC-8 flight manual, such as descents at 4,500 feet a minute, instead of the normal 1,000 feet.

Most of the cargo on these flights was ammunition—described euphemistically and cynically as "hard rice"—and was clearly carried in a lost cause. Ed Daly disagreed with the decision on the nature of the load and was relieved when he was able, from February 27 to March 14, to substitute a "soft rice" airlift, carrying desperately needed staple food for the nearly starving inhabitants of Phnom Penh. During the latter operation, World Airways transported about 10,000 tons of rice, enough for about 60 million meals. A total of 292 trips was made during the twenty-six days of operation; they ended only when, on April 16, 1975, the Khmer Rouge occupied Pochentong airfield.

On March 10, 1975, just before the end of the Cambodian rice airlift, the North Vietnamese launched their offensive against South Vietnam, after only two years of precarious peace. With no U.S. forces to provide support, the South Vietnamese defense forces melted away, either through fear or through a complete lack of confidence in the government of President Thieu. By March 29, the North Vietnamese army was at the gates of Da Nang, second city of South Vietnam. The only people left there were civilians and bands of unorganized soldiers.

Ed Daly had brought two Boeing 727s to Saigon, to make twenty flights under government charter to Da Nang to evacuate refugees. With the situation deteriorating by the hour, the U.S. Embassy canceled the contract after only three flights had been made. In one last desperate humanitarian gesture, Daly decided to carry on independently. Against official advice, he wanted to make one last effort, perhaps in the hope of reassuring the Vietnamese people, who may have felt that the U.S. government had abandoned them, that there were some Americans who cared deeply for their hopeless plight.

Two World Airways Boeing 727-100s took off early on March 29, and the first one, with Daly on board, along with his personal bodyguard, stewardesses, and several newsmen who had hitched a ride, touched down on the main runway at Danang. The intention was to stop, load up quickly, and take off again within ten minutes or so, so that the second 727 could repeat the performance. Daly and his crew thought at first that the airfield was deserted. Then, to quote Jan Wollett, one of the flight attendants, "thousands—and I mean literally thousands—started racing towards us. They were running, they were on motorcycles, they were in vans, they were in jeeps and cars and personal carriers, they were on bicycles—they were coming in anything they could find to get into the aircraft."

This panic-stricken mob reached the rear ventral stair before the 727 had stopped taxying and fought desperately to clamber up the stairs, fighting each other and even shooting their fellow refugees as they clawed their way toward the airsteps or the handrail, the strong trampling the weak underfoot. Ed Daly was on the airstair, and his clothes were almost ripped off him as he tried to control the seething mass of humanity. He used the butt end of his pistol with some effect and drew on the Golden Gloves talents of his youth to ward off desperate clutches that could have pulled him and the World cabin crew off the airplane.

The Boeing 727 never stopped taxying. Miraculously, they were able to haul on board a crew member who had bravely got off to assist with the airfield control, and Ken Healy, the pilot, managed to take off from a taxiway parallel to the runway, hitting a jeep and a pole as he left the ground. The aircraft had also been damaged by bullets and a grenade. It was carrying rather more than its specified load of 133 passengers. Estimates of the number on board varied from 330 to 338, of whom about 60 had scrambled into the cargo compartment, and eight were actually in the wheel wells of the main landing gear.

This landing gear well was the last refuge for desperate people at the end of their tether and at the edge of sanity. Several fell off, including one when the 727 was at an altitude of 600 feet. One was killed when he was crushed by the retractable gear, thereby preventing full retraction and saving the lives of the others in the wheel well. Healy was relieved to discover, as he touched down on Saigon's 14,000-foot runway, that the gear held.

Daly's feelings after this astonishing episode were mixed. He certainly took a few shots of his favorite beverage. His hair, already losing its color, must have gone several shades whiter. He had been able to derive scant satisfaction from his mission of mercy. True, he had brought out a few hundred Vietnamese soldiers and men who might well not have survived otherwise. But his main purpose in going to Danang had been to evacuate women and children, and the harsh reality of the dramatic flight was that the head count showed only eleven of these. Ed Daly's quixotic gesture ended in disillusionment and left on the cavalier Irishman an indelible impression of the frailty of human nature.

His own condition was not good. On the day the shooting stopped—as newspapers described that momentous day—the *Honolulu Advertiser* reported that Daly left Saigon with "a case of double pneumonia, a broken hand in a cast, an infected left eye, and a couple of shattered teeth." He had, like his indefatigable crews, led by Ken Healy and Bill Keating, been going without sleep for seventy-two hours at a stretch. But the old reprobate was not finished yet. Defying orders to the contrary, he returned to the United States with his battered World Airways contingent, accompanied by 218 Vietnamese refugees, including 57 orphan children, for all of whom he took personal responsibility and whom the staff of World Airways took to their hearts.

Their arrival in California did not endear them, however, to the hearts of the U.S. Department of Immigration and Naturalization, which on May 7 attempted to fine World Airways $218,000 for bringing in the 218 refugees. But this excess of zeal in applying the law was soon countermanded in the face of public opinion, which reflected the mood of emergency that overwhelmed people like Daly, who were men of action rather than of words.

It had been the same in Saigon. When Ken Healy was about to take off with his load of fifty-seven orphans, the tower at Tan San Nhut Airport instructed "Do not take off, you have no clearance." Healy claimed afterwards that "he simply didn't get the message in time." Such breaking of the rules was strictly in the tradition of the soldier who disobeys orders and finishes up with both a reprimand and the Purple Heart. And Daly's much-publicized actions, tinged with melodrama, undoubtedly sent a similar shock wave through the corridors of power in Washington, leading to special directives from President Ford.

While some officials fumed at Daly's cavalier attitude toward regulations, the public and the press welcomed his actions as a breath of fresh air and common sense overriding the kinds of bureaucratic attitude they themselves had encountered in other contexts. Congratulatory letters to the press outnumbered critical letters by an enormous margin, and Daly received accolades, gifts, and plaques by the dozen.

The *Oakland Tribune* neatly described both the man and his deeds as a "pistol-packing airline owner, wearing a green beret, dreaming the impossible dream and slicing through red tape with DC-8s and 727s" and seeming "more like a swashbuckling 'Man of La Mancha' than a millionaire businessman." Compared with the activity that inspired such a description, the relative calm following the end of the Vietnam War must have been an anticlimax. Denied the stimulus and challenge of emergencies such as those he met in Cambodia and Da Nang, Daly and World returned to the more mundane work of carrying charter passengers in a rapidly growing tourist market. Then, on October 24, 1978, the Airline Deregulation Act was passed, and the opportunity came at last to enter the privileged ranks of the scheduled operators. Daly promptly added another Boeing 747 to his fleet, but selected the McDonnell Douglas DC-10-30 as the joint flagship type and ordered six, with an option to buy three more.

But this apparently progressive move turned out to be a hollow victory. His luck changed, and things began to go wrong. For a start, World was paying high interest rates for the DC-10s, which raised the basic costs of the scheduled operation when it began, on April 11, 1979. World had been granted, at long last, the routes it had aspired to back in 1967: California (Oakland and Los Angeles) to the East Coast (Newark and Baltimore-Washington), but hardly had the new service got under way when all the DC-10s were grounded during a peak summer period, following the spectacular crash at Chicago's O'Hare Airport on May 25. Then, no sooner had regular flights resumed when the flight crews, the flight attendants, and the mechanics went on strike and stayed out from August to December. Thus 1979, which could have seen Ed Daly leading a former Supplemental airline into a leading position among the elite domestic trunklines, witnessed instead a near disaster.

Worst of all, under deregulation, all the airlines which had formerly claimed that fares could not be lowered to the level for which World had originally campaigned now entered into a fares war, with heavily discounted tariffs everywhere. The supreme irony was that World, a pioneer of low fares, now found itself undersold, as United, American, and T.W.A. made sure that the upstart newcomer did not encroach on their territory.

World's finances went from bad to worse, the result of the combined effect of cutthroat deregulated competition and high interest rates. Services opened on February 27, 1980, on the California–Hawaii market, but this was already heavily oversubscribed. World lost more than $28 million during the year. On May 29, 1981, World began transatlantic service from Baltimore to London and Frankfurt, and although its service and its schedule of fares were immaculate, once again it was in a viciously competitive market—as Sir Freddie Laker would testify. All the North Atlantic scheduled airlines cut their fares ruthlessly to levels below cost to combat at all costs, including the taxpayers', the innovators such as World. Daly's airline lost $20 million in 1981. And so it went, with a record $58 million loss in 1982 and World grimly hanging on by rescheduling its debts, all thoughts of ambitious expansion having been put aside.

During the anxious years, Ed Daly still managed to find some outlets for his attempts to mix humanitarian acts with his business. He echoed an early 1970s operation in the Republic of Mali with another African venture in April 1982, sending a Boeing 747 to Somaliland to airlift supplies, food, and medicine, and to evacuate refugees. Again he was sadly disillusioned, as he witnessed the confiscation of much of the food and its sale on the black market.

Ed Daly died on January 21, 1984, at the age of sixty-one. He had always been a deeply religious man, though by no means a temperate one. Indeed, an English newspaper described his death by stating that "the distillers finally won the war of attrition," and there was some basis for the hyperbole. At his funeral the tributes were numerous, recalling the heroic return from Saigon in 1975. World Airways lives on today, drawing strength from the inspiration of its former leader.

Nobody who ever met Edward Joseph Daly, even for ten seconds, will ever forget him, though the individual recollections may be mixed and not always complimentary. Perhaps the epitaph that he would have liked best was that which accompanied an award, after the Da Nang affair, dedicated by the crew of the *Jolly Green Giant:* "A man of rare qualities, a fist of iron, balls of brass, and a heart of gold."

Frank Lorenzo
Man of Destiny

When Francisco A. Lorenzo, then chairman of the board of Jet Capital Corporation, took over the ailing Texas International Airlines in August 1972, he became, at the age of thirty-two, the youngest president and chief executive officer of any airline of substance in the history of air transport in the United States. His systematic progress toward that position had been a remarkable success story since his start in aviation as a financial analyst with T.W.A. in 1963. His subsequent progress toward greater goals has been marked with no less success and has been just as systematic. But during the decade that elapsed after the Texas takeover, Lorenzo became the most controversial single personality in the airline world, not simply because he created headline news with increasing frequency, but also because he challenged the entire structure of cost-and-revenue relations that had long existed in a closely protected corporate environment and in doing so generated a cause célèbre of historic proportions.

He was able to do so, emerging triumphantly from a prolonged and bitter battle with the unions, as a direct result of disciplined financial and analytical training coupled with a visceral stamina that enabled him to match the courage of his convictions with boldness of action. Underpinning these qualities has been a level of perseverance and determination to match those of Sir Reginald Ansett, a man of similar outlook in Australia, who rated these qualities above all others as keys to success.

Like Sir Reginald, Frank Lorenzo has been accused of being ruthless, to which he would assert that, like an embattled commander of a siege defense, he did what had to be done. As a leader of a body of people, he has always recognized that casualties along the way were inevitable in a competitive environment. A general has to accept losses on the battlefield, on his own side as well as on the enemy's. And so it has been, in the harsh and unforgiving arena of airline deregulation in the United States.

In response to constant challenges and obstacles, Frank Lorenzo just keeps going. Physically fit and light of stature, he maintains his health by regular jogging and occasional participation in long-distance running. But his behavior in the corridors of financial power and manipulation can be likened more to that of a tough and rugged football player like John Riggins, who simply puts his head down and wears out the opposition. At the risk of overplaying the sporting analogy, Lorenzo frequently switches to the quarterback's position and initiates many a spectacular play, running for a dramatic touchdown, albeit punctuating the plays with a few interceptions to prove that he is not quite omnipotent.

Such a man would be expected to be an extrovert, seeking publicity and using the media to publicize his ambitions and generally living a flamboyant life in parallel with the excitement of a spectacular career. As an adopted Texan, he ought to wear a large hat, ride horses, shoot guns, and attend rodeos. The complete opposite is the case. Frank Lorenzo is a quiet-living man to whom privacy is almost a religion. He grants interviews to the press or anyone else only under duress, not because he fears the cameras but because he believes that it is his duty to stand up and be counted from time to time. He is happily married, with three children, and he keeps his family life to himself.

There are no moderate opinions about Frank Lorenzo. He is either regarded with awe, as by the loyal employees who stuck by him during the darkest days and shared much of the risk-taking with him; or he is hated with a deadly passion, as by opponents who misjudged his shrewdness and his underlying determination to win. Most of his employees never get close enough to him to know whether they like him or love him personally, but they certainly respect him. They may not place him on a pedestal, and Lorenzo would not wish them to do so. He is concerned that, at times, individuals have been hurt, caught in the mesh of boardroom battles for supremacy and control of corporate destinies. But he is un-

Frank Lorenzo is possibly the best-known airline leader in the United States today. Since acquiring a regional airline, Texas International, in 1972, he has shaken the industry to its foundations by taking over Continental and Eastern, both important trunk airlines. His confrontation with the powerful pilots' union was a turning point in labor relations in the industry.

concerned by the image of the devil incarnate that has been projected on him by his antagonists, particularly the more vociferous of the union spokesmen. He is very much his own man, impervious to flattery and insensitive to abuse.

Frank Lorenzo was born in Rego Park, Queens, New York, on May 19, 1940. His parents were Spanish immigrants who ran a beauty parlor in Manhattan. Slimly built, dark, and handsome, he worked his way through Columbia University, where he obtained his bachelor's degree in economics in 1961. In traditional American style, he drove a Coca-Cola truck and worked part-time as a salesman for Macy's New York department store during vacations before going on to Harvard to take his master's degree in finance in 1963. Soon after graduation, he joined Trans World Airlines in New York as a financial analyst, and stayed with that company for two years before spending six months in the army.

An important event in his young life was meeting Robert J. Carney, who worked for the investment firm of S. G. Warburg and Company. By this time he had joined Eastern Airlines as manager of financial analysis, and he and Carney founded Lorenzo, Carney & Company in 1966, each investing $1,000 initially. With this modest start, the two partners were able to set up a holding company, Jet Capital Corporation, which in 1967 raised about $1.2 million in additional funds through a public stock offering. Four years later

Jet Capital purchased 460,000 shares of Texas International Airlines for roughly that amount.

In 1971, Texas International was struggling. One of the original Local Service airlines created in the late 1940s by the Civil Aeronautics Board (C.A.B.) under pressure from Congress to bring air service to small communities in the United States, it had been heavily subsidized during its entire existence, for most of which it bore the name of Trans Texas Airways (T.T.A.). It concentrated on service throughout Texas and into neighboring states and operated veteran Douglas DC-3s which, with Texan bravado, it called Super Starliners. A critical public claimed that the company initials stood for Tinker Toy Airways and other less complimentary titles. T.T.A. had never come to terms with the realities of airline operation as a business exercise and, like others in the Local Service category, relied on government support for financial viability.

In 1968 Minnesota Enterprises had purchased controlling interest in T.T.A. and during the next few years introduced Douglas DC-9 twin jets to replace the DC-3s and their turbopropeller Convairliner companions. The name was changed to Texas International (TXI), and new routes were opened to Denver, Los Angeles, and Salt Lake City. But by 1970, when a nonstop San Antonio–Dallas route completed the Texas Triangle, TXI had no fewer than seventy stations on its network, was attracting healthy traffic from only a few of these, and was losing money heavily. On its best routes it had too much competition from trunk carriers; on its poor routes, the improved road system had diluted the traffic, and new commuter airlines were offering superior service with more convenient schedules.

Texas International, in fact, was in deep trouble. The Chase Manhattan Bank, one of its primary lenders, asked Lorenzo and Carney to act as financial consultants and investigate the situation. Starting this assignment in January 1971, they faced a formidable task. The airline had lost $6 million in 1970, slightly more than in the previous year. In June 1971 Jet Capital made an offer to refinance the airline.

Although Hughes Airwest made a counteroffer to acquire Texas International, doubtless seeing an opportunity to fashion a coast-to-coast network thereby, the way was already clear for a Lorenzo-Carney takeover. The other alternative, bankruptcy, was too awful to contemplate, and on January 19, 1972, Jet Capital confidently applied to the C.A.B. for approval to take control. The board approved the acquisition on August 10, 1972, under a refinancing plan that satisfied the Wall Street bankers. This added $1.5 million equity capital, restructured the senior debt, and exchanged subordinate debt obligations for equity securities. Jet Capital assumed 59 percent of the voting control and Frank Lorenzo took over as president.

An interesting aspect of the transaction was that, in the words of W. Lloyd Lane, who served as president during the closing years of the Minnesota Enterprises period, "Our lenders and creditors are allowing us to reshape our financial house totally, and on a voluntary basis." Could this have been a trial run for much larger and more ambitious things to come?

Lorenzo set about putting Texas International's tottering house in order. During the early 1970s, TXI abandoned several unproductive, money-losing routes and streamlined much of the network. Service to small cities served by Beech 99 commuter aircraft was suspended. In March 1973 two more DC-9s augmented the fleet, the first mainline aircraft additions since 1969. Seating layouts were increased and a notable route was added, Houston–Mexico City nonstop. Then, early in 1977, TXI announced its Peanuts Fares program and gained instant notoriety.

And well it might. For this was the first of the deep-discount fares that were later to become popular with many U.S. airlines, large and small. It was a watershed in air passenger tariffs. Essentially, the fares on selected routes were reduced so that formerly empty seats were filled, and even though the yield per seat was much lower, the revenue per flight was much higher than before, when passengers were paying full fares but filling only 30 percent of the seats.

By this time, Texas International had turned the red ink into black. In spite of a five-month strike during the early part of 1975, the company made a goodly profit in 1976, $3.2 million on record revenues of $120 million. More important than the revenues, the costs had been trimmed, the strike having shown that Lorenzo was a determined bargainer, holding firm for greater productivity from the staff. The fleet of aircraft had been rationalized so that it was almost of one type, the DC-9, while efficiency had also been vastly improved by better scheduling and the elimination of many multisegment routes.

During the latter 1970s, TXI had completely reversed its down-at-the-heels image of barely half a decade before. In 1978 the airline world was astonished to learn that Lorenzo had moved to take over National Airlines, a domestic trunk line three times the size of TXI, having purchased 9.2 percent of the stock of National. This alarmed the C.A.B., which could not fathom the basic issues of this mouse-that-roared exercise, and the chairman of National sought the backing of other investors to beat off the attack. But the employees of National, disenchanted with its management, headlined a staff newsletter with an appeal to Lorenzo: "Take Us, We're Yours!"

The *Wall Street Journal* commented that this was "the first case in regulated airline history in which a certificated airline sought approval of a non-negotiated acquisition of control of another certificated airline." The irony was that there was nothing illegal or even unethical about Lorenzo's move. Quite simply, nobody had ever done or even attempted such a thing before, possibly because nobody had thought about it or done the necessary financial homework.

The outcome was that Pan American, which had long coveted the domestic route system of National to link its international gateways, purchased National in September 1978 for $350 million. By this time, Lorenzo and TXI had more than 20 percent of the stock and made a clear profit of $46 million on the deal. As for Pan Am, the need to link its gateways was a dead issue, and the deal was both ill timed and ill judged.

TXI kept up its momentum, earning profits of $13.2 million in 1978 and $41.4 million in 1979. In August 1980, the airline purchased twenty used but immaculate DC-9s from Swissair and Austrian Airlines, two European operators who maintain their aircraft impeccably. Simultaneously, Lorenzo requested permission from the C.A.B. to enter the New York–Washington air shuttle market, the high-density route pioneered by Eastern Airlines in a rare case of regulated originality but now vulnerable to a deregulated challenge.

Recognizing that this kind of air service demanded special treatment, Carney and Lorenzo had created a holding company, Texas Air Corporation, in June 1980. Texas Air thereupon formed New York Air in October, as a sister company to Texas International under the aegis of the parent corporation. New York Air began high-frequency service between LaGuardia Airport, New York, and Washington's National Airport on December 19, 1980.

No sooner had Frank Lorenzo established this bridgehead in the northeast traffic corridor than rumors started to fly that a much bigger airline development was in the works. Out West, in Los Angeles, there was trouble at Continental Airlines, a company which, in former days under the leadership of Robert Six, had been commendably innovative, as far as was legally possible under the rigid control of the C.A.B. Unfortunately, the policies that had been successful for more than forty years under Six's cavalier style of management were suddenly laid bare as the cold winds of airline deregulation changed all the rules—specifically, the balance between revenues and expenditures.

After 1978 Continental found itself under concerted attack by several new airlines that had until then been unable to break through the impenetrable crust of C.A.B. resistance to the idea of competition from lusty young entrants. The Airline Deregulation Act, signed by President Carter in October 1978, opened the flood-gates, and Continental was the most vulnerable of all the domestic trunk airlines, because it suddenly received the full force of direct low-fare competition from formerly intrastate carriers such as Southwest Airlines, P.S.A., and Muse Air.

At least when the airlines bid for hundreds of dormant routes released by the C.A.B., Continental did not lose its head, as some companies did. It set about a sensible rearrangement of its route system. Domestically it closed gaps, rerouted services, and introduced more nonstop segments. In 1979 it began transpacific service to Australia and the southwest Pacific and to Mexico. But in 1980 it dropped the important Chicago–Los Angeles trunk route that had once been its main artery. New hub patterns began to emerge, centered on Houston and Denver.

Nevertheless, the financial situation continued to deteriorate. While Continental joined others in offering dramatic promotional fares, it did so at its peril, because a substantial proportion of its costs were inflexibly high. Robert Six appointed Al Feldman, formerly of Frontier Airlines, president, and attempts were made to trim Continental's costs, but to no avail. Under severe pressure, Feldman committed suicide on August 8, 1981.

One indirect source of pressure was Frank Lorenzo, whose Texas Air Corporation had, during 1981, acquired more than half the stock of Continental Airlines. On November 25, Continental's board of directors, having scrutinized the financial results, which showed a loss of $60 million, even after taking into account $40 million in special credits, decided to "cease resistance" to the Texas takeover bid. A Prosperity Plan, launched in January 1982 and aimed at trimming routes and staff, was a case of shutting the gate after the horse had bolted. Robert Six retired from active service on April 1, 1982, and on June 1 duplicate timetables carrying the slogan "Together We're Even Better" were issued by Continental and Texas International. On July 13 the stockholders voted strong approval of the idea, and in October the financial merger was completed. The new chairman, Frank Lorenzo, pragmatically retained the name Continental Airlines for the merged company, and Texas International officially ceased to exist. But there were Texas ghosts abroad in the corridors of power and in the maintenance hangars.

The management set about the daunting task of putting two airlines together, integrating routes and schedules, and making modest additions, notably in service to Venezuela, as a result of Braniff's demise. The overriding problem, however, was that of costs, particularly labor costs. Negotiations with the various unions were initiated, but there were strong undercurrents of discontent. Continental's employees, at least a vocal and aggressive minority of them, resisted what they felt to be an invasion of sacred preserves of time-honored—and therefore impervious and unchangeable—wage agreements.

On August 13, 1983, the International Association of Machinists went on strike, rejecting an offer to raise wages in exchange for a proportional increase in productivity. In a deteriorating financial situation, Continental offered, on September 14, to give the employees 35 percent of the company's stock, on condition of their accepting an across-the-board agreement to reduce wages and increase productivity. The key to acceptance rested with the pilots and flight attendants, who accounted for 40 percent of the staff but for a substantially higher percentage of the labor costs. At a time when a Continental DC-10 captain was earning $138,000 a year for about twelve hours of duty a week, Continental was losing money at the rate of more than $1 million a day. Obviously Band-Aid treatment had to give way to surgery, if the two sides could not reach agreement.

When Continental met with the Airline Pilots' Association (ALPA) on September 23, 1983, the incredible view of the pilots was that there was "no urgency." Frank Lorenzo took the opposite view. The next day he closed the airline, filing under Chapter 11 of the federal bankruptcy code to reorganize the company and furloughing almost all Continental employees.

This momentous event, unprecedented in the history of commercial airline operations in the United States—or in the world, for that matter—occurred on a Saturday, providing much headline material for the Sunday radio and television news commentators. In a carefully worded statement, Lorenzo said, "Continental patiently and valiantly tried to use the negotiating process to bring costs down to today's marketplace. Continental owes it to its shareholders, employees, and, as importantly, its customers to make Continental cost-competitive and provide for its future—a profitable one." Lorenzo appeared to define the public in the same way that the late C.A.B. had defined "the public convenience and necessity" as including shareholders, employees, and airline passengers.

On Tuesday, September 24, three days after the closure, Continental resumed operations. Overseas routes to the Pacific and to Latin America continued as before, but domestic routes and services were drastically reduced to only 27 percent of former capacity, serving twenty-five cities instead of seventy-eight. The staff was reduced from 12,000 members to 4,000, and in a desperate effort to restore public interest and confidence in the beleaguered airline, introductory fares of $49.00 on any one-way, nonstop segment were offered during the last few days of September and $75 during most of October. Senior captains were paid $43,000, far below Air Line Pilots' Association (ALPA) standards. Nevertheless, about a third of the flying crews accepted the stringent salary economies, observing perhaps that Lorenzo had reduced his own salary of $257,000 to that of a senior captain, but also realizing that half a loaf was better than no bread.

Things came to a head on October 1, when both the pilots and the flight attendants struck, believing that this would shut down the airline. They were wrong. Opinion among union members was far from unanimous, and those loyal to the airline, aided by an unprecedented influx of newly hired employees, were able to maintain services. Surprisingly, and to the chagrin of the unions, only a few Continental flights had to be canceled, and within a week services were back to normal, and the long process of restoring the airline to its former position in the industry had begun.

This had to be done against a bitter, sometimes vicious battle with the unions. ALPA, however, found itself in the position of having to justify its stance to a public which found it hard to believe that any pilot, however well qualified, was worth a salary as high as those that were being paid. Neither did the public take kindly to the prospect of being held hostage by the unions, and few prospective passengers were swayed by the vague arguments presented by the pickets stationed in front of airport entrances. ALPA threatened to fine nonstriking union members $10,000 and paid the striking pilots up to $3,800 a month to man the picket lines.

For its part, Continental began to fashion its new policy. On October 4, 1983, the new employee stock-ownership plan was announced. Three days later, the new pilot-employment policy was introduced, Lorenzo noting that its terms were better than those of the rejuvenated Braniff, which ALPA had accepted. On October 13, a new range of coach fares was set at less than half those of almost all the competing airlines, which had to invent various special discounted fares, tightly bound with restrictions, to compete.

Painstakingly, and with careful analysis of market potentials and operating costs, Continental began to rebuild. The meager 27 percent of its former domestic capacity had risen to 50 percent by the beginning of November and to 64 percent by February 1, 1984. Of its fleet of 106 jet airliners, 64 were in use. And the tide turned emphatically in Frank Lorenzo's favor by a ruling of the Federal Bankruptcy Court on January 17.

Judge R. F. Wheless, Jr., denied a motion by the unions to dismiss the Chapter 11 petition, saying that "the primary purpose in filing these proceedings was to keep the airline operating so as to best utilize its going-concern value. The management of the company owed this obligation to its shareholders and to its creditors" and "the unions have not satisfactorily demonstrated that there was any reasonable alternative under which the airline would keep operating, and this court finds that there was none." Contrary to union claims, Wheless noted that "Continental was unable to pay its debts as they matured" and that "one of the purposes of the bankruptcy code is to give a business an opportunity to catch its financial breath."

By this ruling, Frank Lorenzo was entitled to feel vindicated of the charge that he was a blatant union basher. Matching this sentiment with deeds, he attempted to resume negotiations, offering work-sharing programs, part-time employment, liberal leave, and other innovative ideas to break the impasse. But the pilots' union demanded that Continental displace all pilots hired since the strike began, refurlough the Continental pilots who had returned, and demote all pilots promoted since the strike. This was clearly unacceptable, simply as a matter of ethics.

Lorenzo was in fact able to ignore the strident campaign still being conducted by the pilots' union. There was still tacit support of the union from the flight attendants, though their enthusiasm was waning. Continental expanded steadily, consolidating and augmenting domestic services, opening routes to Canada, and improving the transpacific route to Japan by starting direct Honolulu–Guam and Guam–Tokyo segments in the spring of 1984. Philip J. Bakes, formerly a general counsel of the C.A.B. and before that a counsel to the U.S. Senate Antitrust Subcommittee and an assistant special prosecutor in the Watergate Case, was appointed president and chief operating officer of Continental on April 18. After a long period of tight utilization of its existing fleet, the first of the new low-operating-cost McDonnell Douglas MD-80s were delivered in June.

At the end of the year, the same Judge Wheless confirmed emphatically that the law was on Lorenzo's side. In turning down an appeal by the International Association of Machinists, he reiterated "Continental could not compete in the existing marketplace if it had to continue to pay compensation so substantially in excess of its effective competition. . . . Without reduction of its labor costs, Continental would not be flying today and its current employees would be out of a job, at least out of this job."

The first half of 1985 witnessed a series of events wholly in Continental's favor, confirming that Lorenzo's supreme gamble—or calculated risk—had come off. On January 14 he presented to the U.S. bankruptcy court the elements of the plan, not merely to reorganize the airline as stipulated, but to repay all creditors 100 cents on the dollar. This in itself was something of a precedent. Specifically, claims totaling $757 million would be paid within thirteen years, and all secured debts would be paid off within ten years.

In this more optimistic financial climate, the relations with labor improved. The machinists having accepted the wisdom of the courts, the flight attendants ended their strike on April 17, and some of them were privileged to work the inaugural Continental transatlantic service from Houston to London on April 28.

Lorenzo's main cause for satisfaction on the labor front, however, was from an indirect and possibly unexpected source. The pilots' union, ALPA, had indulged in the unsavory practice of encouraging its members to spy on Continental's operations and to report gleefully a long list of alleged misdemeanors to the Federal Aviation Administration (F.A.A.) in an effort to convey the impression that Continental was an unsafe airline. In this reflection of K.G.B. practices, ALPA must have been delighted at an anti-Continental documentary television program by C.B.S. that turned the practice of generalizing from the particular into a fine art.

The ALPA campaign was a complete failure. After a comprehensive investigation of all the allegations and in a reversal of the common habit of damning with faint praise, the F.A.A. exonerated Continental with faint criticism. In a special press release dated June 11, 1985, it characterized Continental's deficiencies only as "the kind that have been found occasionally during inspections of other carriers." The report emphasized the thoroughness of the investigation, left the reader in no doubt that Continental was probably the safest airline flying in the United States, and by implication criticized those responsible for wasting so much of the administration's time.

And so the good fortune continued. On August 26, Continental Airlines received a petition from more than 90 percent of its working pilots requesting an end to their affiliation with ALPA. Clearly, the apparently all-powerful union, feared by nonunion pilots and airline managements alike, was facing its first real challenge since its inception. Further nails were knocked into the ALPA coffin on September 11, when U.S. bankruptcy judge T. Glover Roberts disallowed huge union claims against the airline, and on September 16, when the local leaders of ALPA at Houston instructed striking pilots to cross the picket lines and return to work. On October 31, 1985, the ALPA strike was over, slightly more than two years after it had begun.

But there was no end to the bitterness. Continental had asked for no quarter, had received none, and was in no mood now to give any. In a public statement it expressed the hope that "the end of the strike will mean termination of the strike benefits ALPA has been paying to imprisoned felons who were apprehended while committing ALPA-funded terrorist acts against working pilots" and suggested that ALPA should tell its members to cease their use of the Fifth Amendment in investigations into other criminal acts.

Thus, during a wild period of intense confrontation between an airline and one of the most entrenched and powerful unions in the world, Frank Lorenzo had come out on top and in so doing had assured the continuance of a low-fare policy for Continental that would not be threatened—as fare policies had so often been threatened in the past—by irresponsible unions representing special interests. It has been argued that up to a third of the benefits of efficiency bestowed by jet aircraft were never passed on to the public because they were absorbed by extortionately high salary increases granted to the pilots by acquiescent airlines. Continental itself calculated that before September 24, 1983, between forty and fifty passengers had to be carried on every aircraft flight, just to pay the crews. That date, therefore, may go down in airline history as one just as important as those that marked the passage of the Kelly Act, the establishment of the C.A.B., and the introduction of jet airliners.

While 1985 was a year of outstanding success for Frank Lorenzo on this all-important issue of labor costs and its weight in the delicate balance of revenues against expenditures in a free market, other events during the same period confirmed that his decisionmaking and inspired judgment could sometimes fall short of perfection, a comforting thought for those who were beginning to believe that he could, if challenged, walk on water. Between June and August 1985 he made a bid to acquire Trans World Airlines (T.W.A.) through the holding company, Texas Air Corporation. If consummated, the resultant merger with Continental, together with New York Air on the East Coast and the newly formed Continental West on the West Coast, would have put Lorenzo in the big leagues, on the same footing as the giants of the industry, United, American, Eastern, and Delta.

But that pleasure had to be deferred, because Carl Icahn, a New York financier, outbid Texas Air and played a trump card by making a deal with the T.W.A. unions, who of course were vigorously opposed to Lorenzo after their humiliating defeat in the Continental affair.

Undeterred, Lorenzo tried again to expand the Texas-Continental empire by putting in a confident offer for Frontier Airlines, the former Local Service and regional airline that shared the Denver hub with Continental and United. Once again he was outbid, this time by Donald Burr, a graduate of the Lorenzo organization in Texas who had founded a new airline, PEOPLExpress, which was threatening to take over where Lorenzo left off.

In a gracious if perhaps cynical gesture, quite unusual in the cutthroat business environment, Texas Air commented, when conceding victory to Burr, "It is gratifying to see airline deregulation working to return to shareholders such rewards," a reference to the handsome financial terms that had saved Frontier from almost certain extinction—doubtless with the comforting thought that Texas Air numbered itself among the shareholders who made a profit on the deal. Perhaps Lorenzo had a premonition that he would have the last word and would be in control of Frontier less than a year later.

The year 1986 began quietly enough, with a new route, a direct connection between Vancouver, Canada, and Hawaii, opened on November 17, 1985, getting under way in time for the new world's fair in the British Columbian city in the summer. Litigation toward release from Chapter 11 proceeded along an even course, with hopes of a clean sheet also by the summer. Then, at 3 A.M. on Monday, February 24, Frank Lorenzo finally pulled it off. In a takeover bid timed with precision and executed with Lorenzo's usual cool determination, Texas Air successfully bid for the heart, soul, and assets of Eastern Airlines. At his third attempt, Frank Lorenzo, in a corporate amalgamation that created an airline conglomerate ranking below only United and American in size, achieved the status of becoming the single most influential person in the U.S. airline industry, possibly in the world.

There were some interesting aspects to the case. Frank Borman, former astronaut and ostensibly a charismatic leader, had been able to keep Eastern's financial head above water only by a succession of palliatives. He had extracted wage and salary concessions with the promise that prosperity was just around the corner, but it wasn't, and the staff had had enough. During the month of February, Borman had actually come to terms with the pilots, who possibly reflected that even a pay cut would still leave them well provided for, because Eastern scales were high. But Borman could not reach agreement with the International Association of Machinists and Aerospace Workers (I.A.M.), headed by Charles Bryan, who had been heavily critical of Borman's management. That Borman and Bryan did not see eye to eye was common knowledge, and with bankruptcy staring Eastern in the face, Frank Lorenzo appeared at the door.

During the bitter Eastern internal discussions that had lasted, almost without a coffee break, from Friday, February 21, the writing was on the wall for Frank Borman when Bryan declared, "I'd just as soon take my chances with Lorenzo." This was quite a tribute to a man who, only a few short years before, had been branded as a union hater, union baiter, and worse. Bryan recognized him as a tough opponent, but an honest one, who stood by his agreements once they had been wrestled over.

A dedicated protagonist of the free market, Lorenzo has been sneeringly referred to as a New York carpetbagger—and that is one of the milder epithets. His peers in the airline boardrooms are always alert to his every move and watch with apprehension any sign or suggestion that he is eyeing one of their strongholds. The airline industry has said farewell to such former leaders as Pan Am's Trippe, Eastern's Rickenbacker, and American's C. R. Smith. These were men of dominating corporate stature and charisma who ran their empires almost single-handedly. They handed over the reins of power to administrative machines, presided over by men whose names mean little to the public at large and not a great deal more to the employees themselves, who feel often that they are mere cogs in those machines.

In many instances the top men are regarded as faceless figureheads, but this can certainly not be said of Frank Lorenzo, who now controls the fortunes of the third largest airline group in the Western world. In a business environment that is in striking contrast to that of the days of yore, one man's personality is felt from the boardroom to the basement, from the mail room to the maintenance shop. If there is a man of destiny in the airline world today, that man is Frank Lorenzo.

Postscript: Since this essay was written Lorenzo has steered Continental completely free of bankruptcy, consummated the Eastern Airlines deal, and actually acquired PEOPLExpress, and Frontier Airlines along with it. The Texas Air empire is now the largest in the Western world.

Donald C. Burr

The People's Airline

During the sixty years or so during which the U. S. airline industry has grown from a few shoestring mail carriers to the gigantic industry it is today, there have been quite a few occasions when an individual airline has expanded at a surprising rate. As it has done so, a leader has sometimes emerged from a small band of pioneers to attain fame and fortune and to become widely known, not only among his peers in the industry, but also by the general public.

One airline that was an instant lusty infant of airline deregulation was People Express, founded by Donald Burr. The fact that this airline burst like a comet on the airline scene, only to disappear in a cloud of Lorenzo's dust, does not erase the memory of its achievement. For in a traveling environment in which the lowest possible fare levels were considered to be in force, Burr forced them even lower, and his revolutionary zeal will long be remembered.

In the old days, during the formative period before World War II, such men were personified by characters such as C. R. Smith, the decisionmaker of American Airlines; Eddie Rickenbacker, the flamboyant publicist of Eastern Airlines; and Howard Hughes, who led T.W.A. to greatness. In the postwar airline world, names such as those of Robert Six, the great opportunist of Continental, and Frank Lorenzo, the Texas miracle-worker who usurped him, spring to mind. But no individual has entered the competitive arena of air transport in the United States and succeeded so quickly and so strikingly as Donald Calvin Burr, whose single-minded faith in basic principles, combined with an unorthodox approach to management, enabled him to project his com-

153

Donald Burr's has been a memorable success story of airline deregulation. Less than two years after the 1978 Deregulation Act, he created PEOPLExpress, which, within five hectic years, rose to join the ranks of the country's leading airlines. His unique management and staffing policy, in which every member on the payroll was considered an equal, eventually proved to be unworkable.

pany, People Express, from a parochial handful of short-haul routes to a nationwide and international network of considerable stature within a mere five-year span.

Burr's basic principles consisted essentially of a conviction that, first in a post-deregulation era in which new fare schedules had been forcefully put into effect by the new entrants such as Muse Air and Southwest Airways and internationally promoted by Sir Freddie Laker and those who sought to emulate his Skytrain, there was scope for even lower fares and that the theory of price elasticity would prove him right. Second, so as to be able to match the low fares with low costs, he put into effect a style of management the like of which had never been witnessed before in the airline industry—possibly not in any other industry either.

Such success would suggest the background of a brilliant academic start in life, and indeed Burr's credentials were more than adequate, if not outstanding. His upbringing was straightforward and orthodox, following the almost predestined course of a middle-income family who believed in educating their children and launching them into worthwhile and remunerative careers.

Donald Burr was born in South Windsor, Connecticut, on May 8, 1941, the third child of an electrical engineer, his mother the local assistant postmaster. He did all the right things—sang in the church choir, was prominent in the youth group, married a pretty girl, Brigit Rupner, at the age of twenty, and took a lively interest in airplanes. He went to Stanford University and Harvard Business School and earned a private pilot's license.

While at Stanford he met an investment banker, W. Peter Slusser, and the chief of the New York Stock Exchange, Keith Funston; this meeting undoubtedly helped to set the course of his future career. He joined a small securities firm on Wall Street, the National Aviation Corporation, and in 1972, at the age of thirty, he became its president.

The next year he met Frank Lorenzo of Texas International. Once a struggling Local Service airline, dependent on subsidy, Texas was reviving under Lorenzo's firm and shrewd stewardship. Always looking for sharp executives to spearhead his company toward greater goals, Lorenzo hired Burr, who became chief operating officer in 1978. In June 1979 he became president, but he resigned six months later to pursue independent ambitions of his own. His timing was immaculate. The Airline Deregulation Act had been signed into law in October 1978, and the way was clear for a man of ideas to put them into effect.

Before 1978 the way would not have been clear. The Civil Aeronautics Board (C.A.B.), representing the government, and the Air Transport Association, representing the established group of certificated airlines, would have turned Burr's applications into a legislative obstacle course, while the Air Line Pilots' Association would have bristled at the suggestion that the crews should be hired at a minimum salary or should perform any duties other than those actually associated with flying the aircraft.

Voluminous reports would have been drafted and tabled at the endless hearings to prove that, on any route in the United States, the traffic was matched by the necessary capacity and that the mere suggestion of lower fares was preposterous. The applicant would have been required to prove enormous financial resources, previous operating experience, and a corporate background. Reputable supplemental airlines had tried for years to break down the bureaucratic barriers, all to no avail and at heartbreaking expense. But Donald Burr was different.

For several years, even before deregulation, the idea of a hub-and-spoke route system had been freely and enthusiastically promoted in the airline industry, and several companies were converting their mainly grid networks into new patterns. United, for example, concentrated more and more on making O'Hare Airport, at Chicago, into the aerial crossroads of the United States. Other rivals sought to emulate this effort—T.W.A. at Kansas City and St. Louis, American at Dallas–Fort Worth, Delta at Atlanta, Northwest at Minneapolis, and so on. Burr's problem was to find a hub that was not already spoken for. His former employer, Lorenzo, had cornered the market at Houston, Western had turned its attention to Salt Lake City, and Eastern reigned supreme in the East, especially in the densely traveled Boston–New York–Washington corridor. And Lorenzo was looking at the corridor shuttle market too.

Donald Burr made a selection that owed nothing to luck and certainly nothing to the failure of the other airlines to grasp the opportunity. It was there all the time, staring them in the face, but none was prepared to depart from the rigid orthodoxy that had dictated airline decisions ever since the original route awards of 1938. The entire business community and the long-suffering traveling public always complained bitterly about the inadequacy of New York's LaGuardia Airport to cope with the heavy traffic, especially during the rush hours, at the same time protesting that John F. Kennedy Airport was too far away. Yet just across the Hudson River—no barrier to enterprising transport authorities for at least a century—was Newark Airport, which New Yorkers had had to use before 1940, when LaGuardia was opened, and which had now undergone a complete renovation, expansion, and general facelift. Because it was in New Jersey and regarded faintly as being on the wrong side of the tracks it was strangely shunned, almost ostracized, by the airlines, large and small. Yet it was geographically closer to Lower Manhattan than New York's other airports. By LaGuardia and Kennedy standards, it was uncongested, and there were fewer delays. Parking was comparatively easy, and public transport into downtown New York was cheaper and quicker. Newark seemed to be holding a full deck.

While others procrastinated, Burr acted. He formed People Express Airlines in Houston on April 7, 1980, together with two former employees of Texas International. It was the first completely independent airline to be formed after the passing of the Air-

line Deregulation Act. In August he sold the idea of a Newark hub
to the San Francisco venture capital firm of Hambrecht & Quist.
He had to overcome a certain prejudice, extolling the virtues of the
New Jersey Transit express buses that charged $4.00 for a trip to
New York, departing every fifteen minutes, twenty-four hours a
day. His problem was, as he succinctly expressed it, "Most financial analysts don't take the bus."

William Hambrecht had surprised Burr by the alacrity with
which he had absorbed the arguments in favor of Newark and
deeply discounted fares. Armed with the promise of financial support, Burr now had to put his ideas into action. He approached
John J. Dickerson, Jr., general manager of the New Jersey airports
under the jurisdiction of the Port Authority of New York and New
Jersey, seeking a home for People Express. Dickerson had not been
enamored of aspiring airline operators, most of whom had displayed an unfortunate tendency to fold up almost as soon as they
had taken up residence. Burr, however, ended up with the North
Terminal of Newark Airport. This had been vacant since 1973,
when newer and better terminals had been built. Burr described it
as a ghost town, commenting that "what didn't fall on your head
bit you in the ankle."

Coincidentally, Frank Lorenzo was forming New York Air at
the very time that Burr was exploring the empty corridors of Newark. New York Air, with its Big Apple insignia, would operate out
of LaGuardia. Had Burr been aware of Lorenzo's plans, it would
have made no difference. People Express was on its way.

On October 24, 1980, Burr obtained the C.A.B. certificate to
operate an interstate airline. Since he had applied for it only in
July, the speed with which the board granted it must have set a
new record, especially for a summer vacation period. Within a
month, Hambrecht & Quist came through with the financing to the
extent of $24 million by the issue of 3 million shares. Burr
promptly invested the money in seventeen Boeing 737-100s bought
from the German airline, Lufthansa. They cost him a little more
than $4 million each, while a brand new aircraft would have cost
$10 million. He recruited staff members in large numbers and from
all disciplines at the very time that thousands of airline employees
had been laid off as the first casualties of the Airline Deregulation
Act. They were willing to accept nonunion wages, but more than

that, they were prepared to accept working practices which, in former days, would never have been contemplated, much less promoted as a condition of employment.

Burr's philosophy of industrial relations was based on a corporatewide system in which there were no hierarchy and no different levels of seniority. Everyone was a manager. Pilots were flight managers; ground staff were customer service managers; engineers were maintenance managers. People Express had, in fact, 3,500 managers. Observers of the People Express way of doing things could have been forgiven for assuming that the entire staff were members of a cooperative club. They moved about from one job to another, broadening their knowledge of airline operations. Pilots were to be found helping passengers with their baggage or assisting at the check-in counters. Such goings-on were not, of course, reported to the Air Line Pilots' Association.

In exchange for these utterly democratic forms of behavior, there was ample compensation. All People Express employees held stock in the company; in fact, it was a condition of employment. And they shared in the profits. By learning a variety of jobs, they gained wide experience, and those who cared to absorb the many disciplines and departmental responsibilities soon found themselves qualifying for more senior positions, having escaped from the confines of specialization that so often restrict initiative and curiosity and condemn otherwise capable minds to stereotyped careers.

With such a revolutionary team, Burr moved People Express into Newark early in 1981, took delivery of the first three Boeing 737s, and began service on April 30. The company traded under the name PEOPLExpress and displayed the double-profile "people" profiles on the tails of the aircraft. The first routes were carefully chosen, to three medium-sized cities which, in Burr's opinion, were receiving inadequate service from the incumbent carriers. Thus, Columbus, Buffalo, and Norfolk were linked with Newark—that is, New York—at a fare level regarded almost with incredulity by airlines such as Eastern and American. PEOPLExpress's fare to all three places was cheaper than the normal fare to cities much closer to New York, such as Boston or Washington, whether by air, by train, or by bus.

During the summer of 1981, as more aircraft were delivered, PEOPLExpress expanded to other cities, under the same criteria of selection: Jacksonville, Baltimore, Syracuse, and Indianapolis, plus Boston, which, however, was hardly medium-sized or lacking adequate air service. Possibly Donald Burr was testing the temperature of deeper waters and contemplating a challenge to the Eastern Shuttle. At least, under deregulation, he did not have to grind his way through the frustrating procedures of route applications, examiner's reports, hearings, and testimony that had in the past characterized the C.A.B. obstacle course for an entrepreneur willing to risk his resources in a bold enterprise.

Then, on August 3, 1981, just as the new airline was beginning to be accepted and New York customers were beginning to discover that Newark was not halfway to Philadelphia, the air traffic controllers went on strike. Their union had, however, misjudged the situation badly. As government employees, they were ultimately responsible to the president of the United States. Ronald Reagan held strong views on such conduct and took strong measures. He fired them all. This caused a crisis, which threatened for a while to curtail the scope of the airline industry. The Federal Aviation Administration (F.A.A.) reduced the permissible flight frequencies at many congested air hubs, and the New York trio of airports, LaGuardia, Kennedy, and Newark, was severely affected. As a newcomer, PEOPLExpress had no grounds for preferential treatment, and the strike and its effects could not have come at a worse time.

Burr and his planning staff took an extraordinary gamble, requiring imagination, courage, and—as some would later claim—clairvoyance. On October 25, 1981, the 737s took off from Newark at dawn, before any F.A.A. restrictions at that airport took effect, flew to Buffalo, Columbus, and Baltimore, all uncongested and therefore unrestricted, and thence to Sarasota, Florida. On November 21, the same basic pattern was started with West Palm Beach as the destination.

Essentially, this unusual routing kept to the PEOPLExpress principles: the destinations were not the prime resorts of Miami and Tampa, but they were resorts just the same and less congested. Above all, the one-way fare was $59.00, which was almost irresistible to the good citizens of the air-service-starved Northern cities. Such a cheap way of seeking Florida sunshine must have been expecially attractive to those trying to keep warm in Buffalo in the winter of 1981–82. The outcome was that PEOPLExpress built its loads up to 85 percent, recouped the losses sustained during the worst weeks of the controllers' strike, and recovered its equanimity, confidence, and poise.

During 1982 there was some route development—to Pittsburgh in March; to Melbourne, Florida, in April; and, in November, into the New England cities of Burlington, Vermont, and Hartford, Connecticut. The addition of Melbourne gave PEOPLExpress four Florida destinations, but such a move had been overshadowed by the dramatic entry into Washington on August 3. On that date, Donald Burr threw down the gauntlet to the well-established Eastern Air Shuttle, as familiar to New Yorkers as the Staten Island Ferry, and to Frank Lorenzo's newly established New York Air, which had started service on December 19, 1980. Burr's trump card was the low fare, available at selected hours of the day, of $19.00 one way. The fact that a passenger had to pay $3.00 for each bag checked and 50 cents for a cup of coffee on board was hardly a deterrent.

In August 1982, Donald Burr had received a strong vote of confidence from the best of sources. A second public stock offering was launched by Hambrecht & Quist, this time in company with the distinguished investment firm of Morgan Stanley. More Boeing 737s were added to the fleet, including five of the -200 series, from the Canadian airline CPAir. The first was delivered on November 9, just in time not only for the opening of service on November 15 to Burlington and Hartford, but, far more important, to Dulles International Airport at Washington, D.C.

Once again, Donald Burr was ahead of the game. When Dulles opened, in 1962, it quickly came to be regarded as a white elephant, too far from the center of Washington to compete with the conveniently situated National Airport and suitable only for the sparse intercontinental or transcontinental traffic by four-engined equipment that was not allowed to use the downtown airport. But by the late 1970s, in common with all great seaports, railroad termini, or airports serving major population centers throughout history, Dulles began to spawn its own hinterland. Residential, commercial, even manufacturing development in the vicinity of the airport accelerated and, spurred by the construction of a high-speed access road, Washington began to grow outward toward the once remote airfield.

Concurrently, Washington National Airport, which had been

bursting at the seams for a decade or so, displayed acute signs of saturation, and motorists, limousines, and buses alike began to show a distinct preference for the uncluttered access to Dulles over the congested approaches to National Airport, with its horrifying parking problems. In short, instead of suffering the indignity of contempt as a white elephant, Dulles suddenly acquired the prestige of a potential major air hub. PEOPLExpress, with a battery of gates at both Washington airports, became an important force in the New York–Washington air corridor.

If completing a solid link between New York and the national capital in 1982 was a significant departure from the original policy of seeking poorly served destinations, 1983 was to witness an even more dramatic move. PEOPLExpress entered the world's largest single air market, the North Atlantic, confidently brushing aside any apprehension of the volume and intensity of the competition. Burr's conviction that low fares would always bring rewards held true in this market just as surely as in any other. The success of the Laker Skytrain had proved that. Laker's unfortunate collapse on February 5, 1982, had been caused partly by Sir Freddie's overconfidence, partly by bad luck, especially with currency exchange rates, but most of all because many other airlines had penetrated his market with low fare policies of their own. With Laker removed, the competitors had raised their prices again, to recoup losses sustained in the bitter anti-Laker battle, and the way was clear for another low-fare operator.

The C.A.B. approved Burr's application for a route to London in March 1983 with a speed that probably drew cynical comment from Laker, who had had to fight for years for the privilege. Burr sent Harold Pareti to London to negotiate the British operating and traffic rights from the Civil Aviation Authority (C.A.A.). There followed an amazing demonstration of the effectiveness—if there was any ever doubt—of a low-fare policy. On May 20, Pareti, who had not yet received official approval from the C.A.A., called a press conference at the American Club in London. Before an army of press, radio, and television reporters, he announced that PEOPLExpress would start to take bookings on May 23 and begin flights to Newark on May 26, at a one-way fare of $149—a little more than £100 in English currency. The response was overwhelming. Within twenty-four hours, every flight was solidly booked for the next two months. The aircraft were Boeing 747s, formerly owned by Braniff, another defunct airline, and now fitted with 390 economy-class and 40 premium-class seats.

The interval from the gleam in Burr's eye to the inauguration of service could not have spanned more than about six months, an astonishing contrast to the inertia-laden years that characterized the pace of airline route development in the pre-deregulation era.

With the prized London route now tucked under its belt and with hordes of standby passengers willing to sleep all night at Newark for a chance to visit Europe at a price they could afford, PEOPLExpress now surged forward with even greater momentum. During the summer of 1983, the first Boeing 727-200s, also from the Braniff stable, began to arrive, and after deployment at first to supplement the 737s, they carried the people profile into Houston, bastion of Frank Lorenzo's Continental Airlines, on October 1. The fare was $69.00, the lowest New York–Texas fare ever offered the air-traveling public, not counting Continental's loss-leader introductory package immediately after its temporary closure.

For eight months there was a lull and then the storm broke. During the summer and fall of 1984, PEOPLExpress opened service to eight more major cities in the United States, with a combined metropolitan population exceeding 40 million. Two routes were transcontinental: to Los Angeles, on June 15, and to Oakland (serving San Francisco) on September 28, both served with Boeing 747s and both at a challenging fare of $119.00. The Midwest and the Great Lakes were scooped into Burr's fold: the Twin Cities on June 1, Chicago on August 22, Detroit on September 5, and Cleveland on October 18. Service to Miami began on September 5, to break into Eastern's entrenched Florida market, at $79.00, while Denver, on November 15, at the same fare, opened up the Rocky Mountains to a new stratum of mountaineers and winter sports enthusiasts who could enjoy the thrills of the Rockies at a cost that would have taken them only to Vermont before. PEOPLExpress wound up the year with a Christmas treat: Orlando and Disney World on December 19, at the now standard $79.00 Florida fare, and by April 1985 the airline was serving no fewer than nine destinations in the Sunshine State.

The headlong pace continued during the whole of 1985, on a broad front. No fewer than nineteen cities were added to the network during 1985. By the end of the year the fleet of fifty Boeing 727-200s and twenty-two Boeing 737s were supplemented by six

Boeing 747s. Major cities added were Cincinnati, Atlanta, St. Louis, New Orleans, Dallas, and San Diego, and these were served mainly, if not exclusively, by the 727s, which were also to be seen carrying the PEOPLExpress insignia to Montreal. During the summer months, the 737s were deployed to a new group of cities in the Appalachians and the Piedmont: Birmingham, Charlotte, Columbia, Raleigh-Durham, and Nashville, and there was expansion to other New England and Great Lakes points.

The Boeing 747s were used on the London route, together with the two transcontinental routes to Los Angeles and Oakland (later switched to San Francisco) and to Denver. Then, on September 8, 1985, a second transatlantic route was opened, to Brussels, this time at the astonishing fare of $99.00. By the end of the year, Donald Burr was challenging almost every airline in the country on its home ground, having added American's Dallas–Fort Worth hub, Delta's Atlanta hub, and T.W.A.'s St. Louis hub as direct opponents in the competitive arena, at every point throwing down the gauntlet of low fares as his principal weapon.

Whether or not Burr had set himself a target for the number of cities to be served by PEOPLExpress in a given time will perhaps never be revealed. But the cold statistics reveal that within four and a half years of the opening date of April 30, 1981, a neat, round fifty cities in the United States had received the benefit of the Burr brand of low-fare service. At only two, Indianapolis and Atlantic City, was service subsequently withdrawn. Whether by coincidence or not, 1986 witnessed a change of policy in route expansion. Instead of opening new routes, PEOPLExpress added batches of routes, simply by taking over other airlines.

Several medium-sized airlines, with histories going back to prewar days or to the immediate postwar period, were committed to high salary levels, largely because of the normal effect of long-service increments, and they were also burdened with other costly procedures as a legacy from pre-deregulation operating conditions. Also, the plethora of commuter airlines that had sprouted prolifically during the 1970s were also feeling the chill winds of reality as air passengers contrasted the low fares of the new deregulated airlines with the commuter levels that were often cynically set at what the market would bear, often in monopoly markets.

One of the effects of airline deregulation, therefore, was to produce a kind of Darwinian survival-of-the-fittest environment. The

1978 act hit some of the airlines as a giant meteorite or a severe ice age may have struck life on earth, and many of the species, especially those reared in the dinosaur mold, became extinct. Some survived by transmutation, or by the natural process of evolution, if they were smart enough. Others, unfit or unable to cope with the change, became prey to the predators.

The idea that an airline founded only in 1980 could take over one that traced its history back to 1946 would have been regarded with sheer disbelief by the C.A.B. of old. And very few industry observers or commentators would have given the idea a second thought either. When Frank Lorenzo's Texas International, a mere Local Service or regional airline, took over Continental, an old established trunk line, just at the time that PEOPLExpress was getting under way this was something of a revolution. When Lorenzo acquired Continental, in July 1982, Burr had not yet opened service to Washington. Yet little more than three years later, on November 22, 1985, PEOPLExpress acquired Frontier Airlines, actually winning a takeover battle with Lorenzo, who would dearly have liked to add the Denver-based former regional airline to the Continental–New York Air group. As it turned out, however, Lorenzo was to have the last laugh.

In one inspired act, Donald Burr had expanded his catchment area to encompass almost the entire Rocky Mountain and Western states. Frontier had developed from three small Local Service airlines in the late 1940s to become a large regional airline. Formerly operating a series of meandering routes across all the Western states on a wide-meshed grid, the airline had adapted to the hub concept and had transformed its operations into a concentrated array of spokes radiating from Denver. Even though competing against the giant United Air Lines and the aggressive Continental Airlines, Frontier held its own, partly because of its strong identification as the traditional airline of the Rocky Mountain area. PEOPLExpress suddenly found itself with two hubs instead of one and with connections to several more cities in the West, including Seattle and Vancouver, as well as to other points in Canada, and to the southern tier of states from California to Texas.

Burr's appetite for expansion continued unabated into 1986. On January 31, he acquired Provincetown-Boston Airlines (P.B.A.), the oldest of the commuter airlines, which had existed in a special

C.A.B. category since 1949, long before the word *commuter* was applied to an airline. John van Arsdale, its founder, had hit upon the idea of transferring his aircraft from the New England area around Cape Cod to Florida during the winter season. Airline traffic during the winter was healthy in Florida at a time when aircraft were frozen up or flying empty in the North, so this annual migration was wholly beneficial.

P.B.A., in fact, derived more of its traffic and revenue from the Florida operation than from the New England network. But it had fallen on hard times in 1985, when the F.A.A. grounded it for shortcomings in pilot training and maintenance. This did not deter Donald Burr, who seized an opportunity to consolidate his grip on the Florida market. By acquiring P.B.A., PEOPLExpress increased its Florida station count to fourteen.

Almost simultaneously, on February 5, Burr announced an interline agreement with Britt Airways, a commuter airline of more recent origin than P.B.A. that served every small community within a 200-mile radius of its two minihubs at Chicago and St. Louis. By February 26, Britt had become a fully owned member of the PEOPLExpress team.

As Donald Burr and PEOPLExpress continued its apparently inexorable expansion, mowing down all in its path, there were a few doubters, most of them in the orthodox segment of the airline industry, who dared to suggest that the Burr style of management would eventually have to give way to a more of a traditional hierarchy, with a genealogical edifice that recognized strata of responsibility and control. To operate a tight little spoke network in the eastern states was one thing; to manage an organization that flew more passengers than some of the largest airlines was quite another. As PEOPLExpress had grown, so would its management have to go through a process of evolution, if not revolution.

During the first quarter of 1986, the critics were, to some extent, vindicated by the announcement of declining financial fortunes. There was a certain satisfaction among the less favored fraternity, who were beginning to believe that Burr could do no wrong, to observe signs that this confident front-runner might be showing signs of strain.

The critics were right. On September 15, 1986, in a terse announcement, it was declared that Texas Air Corporation, presided over by the remarkable Frank Lorenzo, had agreed to buy PEO-PLExpress, together with all the assets of its subsidiaries, including Frontier Airlines. The bubble had burst.

Burr's management style, which had created a permanent game of musical chairs, had proved unworkable. The problem was that no one remained long enough in one position to acquire a thorough grounding in a specialized task. Consequently, departmental inefficiencies abounded. Confronting a crisis Burr was almost entirely on his own, like a general deprived of an officer corps, served only by a host of well-meaning but sadly ill-equipped troups.

There are already indications that another upstart airline may be following in the footsteps of PEOPLExpress, though perhaps not necessarily on quite the same scale. The U.S. industry as a whole cannot absorb many such phenomena. Donald Burr, be it remembered, was a protegé of Frank Lorenzo, at Texas International, and now the process has repeated itself. Harold Pareti had risen in the PEOPLExpress ranks to become president of the airline he had joined along with other former colleagues at Texas International when Burr founded it. He was not president for long. Appointed in July 1984, he resigned in January 1985. By fall of the same year, closely following the example set by Burr, but in a different personal style, he had raised substantial capital, had acquired a small fleet of Boeing 737s, had chosen his hub airport—Dulles International at Washington—and had begun service to a few selected points on October 10, 1985. The new star on the horizon is Presidential Airways. To watch the present-day rebels and reformers such as Lorenzo, Burr, and Pareti go about their work, devising ever sharper ways to cut costs, trim waste, and increase efficiency, all the time offering better service to the public, is to witness the direct relation between the protagonists of deregulation and the long-term beneficial effects of unfettered private enterprise.

PEOPLExpress will be remembered as yet another airline that broadened the benefits of air travel. Thanks to "Peoples" many simple folk have taken transatlantic trips who would never have done so otherwise. In the annals of airline history its contribution to the rediscovery of Newark Airport and its pace-setting efforts to establish Dulles International Airport as a domestic hub in its own right, serving the national capital, will also be recognized.

▶▶▶▶▶▶▶▶▶▶▶▶▶▶▶▶▶▶

Canada

▶▶▶▶▶▶▶▶▶▶▶▶▶ ▶▶▶▶▶
◀

▶▶▶▶▶▶▶▶▶ ▶▶▶▶▶▶▶▶▶▶▶▶▶

Grant McConachie

A Man of His Time

Grant McConachie was not one of the distinguished group of almost legendary pioneer bush pilots who first brought the benefits of airline service to Canada. But this is not to discredit or to disparage him. The key word in the statement is *pioneer*, for there were Canadian flyers who had many years of experience behind them before McConachie began his eventful career. But when he started his airline in the mid 1930s, the air transport industry of Canada was in a sorry state. Those companies that managed to eke out a precarious existence were mainly bush operators, or at best regional airlines with limited horizons, uncoordinated and unconnected, except by surface transport. Their objectives were to provide local air service, and none seemed to have the vision or incentive to expand beyond its own parochial boundaries. Although a latecomer into the field, McConachie was the exception. He had vision, drive, ambition, and determination, all of which combined to distinguish him from the crowd—apart from his unique charm, which was no small asset in itself.

When McConachie inaugurated his first scheduled service, as late as 1937, Canada was, incredibly, still two years away from starting its first transcontinental airline. By this time, four were spanning the United States, and Pan American was about to start service across the North Atlantic. While the rest of the world was operating twenty-one-seat airliners such as the Douglas DC-3,

Pictured here with a ski-equipped Fokker Universal, Grant McConachie built his United Air Transport to become a key component of Canadian Pacific Airways, which for many years was the only airline in the Dominion carrying the flag of free enterprise in the face of rigid state control.

which was in service on every continent except the Antarctic, Canada was still soldiering on with time-expired aircraft of an earlier generation. The country was still myopic, its vision clouded. In contrast, when Grant McConachie reached out to the Yukon Territory, his eyes saw opportunities beyond the Klondike. His mental binoculars were focused on faraway China.

To be fair, of all the countries in the world Canada was in the best position to do without air services. Its total population was at that time about 10 million, roughly the same as that of New York or London, and about 90 percent of them lived within 100 miles of the U.S. border. All the big cities of the East, such as Montreal and Toronto, were linked with Winnipeg, on the prairies, and Vancouver, on the Pacific by two of the finest railroad systems in the world. The justification for a transcontinental air service was slender, especially since the trains provided good amenities by offering not only comfortable travel but, in the West, incomparable scenic attractions as well. The Canadian Pacific Railway (C.P.R.), in fact, had built up a corporate empire around its railroad system, with hotels, shipping lines, and a host of affiliated industries. The C.P.R. was a national institution, not particularly interested in airlines, although, in the early 1930s, it had acquired control of Canadian Airways, the biggest of the fragmented concerns, which hardly seemed to justify its name.

Not until 1937 did the Canadian government decide to enter the airline business, and even then it did so half-heartedly. When Trans-Canada Airlines (T.C.A.) was founded, with the stock vested in the government-owned Canadian National Railways, its first fleet consisted of Lockheed L-10 Electras, later supplemented by Lockheed 14s, aircraft that were already being relegated to secondary status by all the leading airlines of the United States and even by European carriers. While T.C.A. performed a solid function in the wartime transatlantic airlift, using converted Lancaster bombers, it was hardly a front-runner. Such conservatism seemed to be inbred, and the reluctance to take risks gave Grant McConachie the opportunities he needed to put into effect the vision he had cherished for Canada when his Ford Tri-Motor first flew into Whitehorse and the Orient was in his sights.

Canada just could not make up its mind where it was going—or, indeed, whether it had any place to go—in the world of commercial aviation. Grant McConachie knew exactly where he wanted to go. In fulfilling his own ambition he also gave his country a sense of purpose and pride, and more than any other single Canadian he put Canada firmly on the world airline map and flew its flag proudly in the big cities of five continents.

Grant McConachie's story was not altogether unusual during his formative years. It was a typical Huckleberry Finn type of early development, with a twentieth-century aviation slant, and one which did not indicate particularly that he was destined to become a great leader of men. Indeed, his youth and adolescence were marked by waywardness and a reluctance to acquire knowledge in the orthodox sense. But there was evidence that he possessed in abundance two of the qualities that are said to be important ingredients of the formula for success: the willingness to take risks and the enjoyment of good luck. Indeed, his capacity for risking his neck in a manner that defied the laws of life expectancy and financial survival were matched only by his ability to take in stride the benefits of successive strokes of good fortune, the odds against which would have driven many a bookmaker to despair.

Grant McConachie was born in Hamilton, Ontario, in April 1909, but nine months later his parents moved to Edmonton, in far-away Alberta. His father held a fairly responsible position in railroading, so young Grant grew up in an environment of machines and metal and the grease and the smells that go with them. During his early school days he spent as much time in sports and in earning spare cash by working at part-time jobs as he did attending classes. After a confrontation with his father after he had run away from home and from school, he finally buckled down, passed his Grade Ten examination, and, after some more hard work on the railroad, registered in the Faculty of Engineering at the University of Alberta, at the age of eighteen.

During this same year, 1927, he was taken up on his first short flight in an airplane, and, like many other youngsters during the year that Lindbergh dramatized the allure of flying, Grant McConachie was bitten by the bug. In 1928 he tried to join the Royal Canadian Air Force, but he became ill with scarlet fever and missed his chance to enroll. He also failed his university examination. After another spell of hard physical work, which his muscular frame absorbed readily, he learned to fly at the Edmonton Aero Club. Even his martinet flying instructor was forced to admit that McConachie was a born airman. He was taking people for rides at five dollars each before he had qualified with the statutory thirty hours of flying time required before carrying passengers for hire or reward.

His consequent temporary grounding provided him with an opportunity to test out his natural charm and disarming smile, for he was back in the air again within a few days, performing hair-raising stunts at the annual air show. Shortly afterward he took a passenger across to the United States, simultaneously breaking three sets of regulations—customs, immigration, and rules of the air—in both countries. But again, his smile and his ability to talk his way out of trouble saved his license. He was still only twenty-one, and the next year, as if to supplement his coming of age, the arrival of Wiley Post and Harold Gatty, using Edmonton as a staging point on their famous round-the-world flight, set the seal on Grant McConachie's career objectives. For he shrewdly observed—and remembered—that the *Winnie Mae* had arrived from Alaska, to the northwest, rather than along the central Pacific route.

The early 1930s were depressing for Canadian airline promoters. The promising Prairie Air Mail, pioneered by Western Canada Airways and taken over in 1930 as a division of Canadian Airways, had been discontinued by the spring of 1932. But this did not deter Grant McConachie in his ambition to become an airline pilot. In fact, he did rather better than that. He persuaded his Uncle Harry to put up $2,500 to buy a Fokker Universal, and they formed an unsteady partnership as Independent Airways. This Uncle Harry was, to put no finer point on it, a man who lived by his wits, or, to put it more bluntly, a con artist. Yet Grant persuaded him to part with $2,500, which was a measure of his remarkable ability to sell his ideas through the sheer force of his personality and disarming enthusiasm.

Independent Airways was anything but glamorous. During the early months of 1932, in three months of intensive flying, Grant McConachie logged 600 hours of flying, hauling fish from an Alberta lake to the railhead at Edmonton. During that time, in addition to building up his bush-flying experience, he also became adept at repairing minor breakages on the Fokker with improvised methods and materials. This included repairing a ski axle by whittling a branch of a tree to fit inside the two broken axle parts and binding them together with birch splints encased in wet caribou thongs. All this concentrated effort enabled McConachie to earn the $2,500 necessary to repay his Uncle Harry. But he was chagrined to learn that his long-suffering Fokker needed an $1,800 overhaul. No records exist of the cost of caribou hide replacement, or of any hazard pay claimed by mechanics charged with overhauling an aircraft that had been hauling fish for a solid three months.

To recoup his money, Grant went barnstorming during the

summer of 1932 and recruited a White Russian refugee, Prince Galizine, and his wealthy Maltese wife as partners in Independent Airways. McConachie was probably less interested in the intriguing international aspects of the management team than in the fact that the Galizines owned another Fokker and a de Havilland Puss Moth. But McConachie flew no fish that winter. Immediately after clinching a $100,000 contract to fly fish from another lake, he crashed in one of the Fokkers, breaking his legs in seventeen places and fracturing both hips, plus assorted fingers, ribs, and kneecaps.

McConachie's amazing resilience to this horrifying experience was matched by his own ideas on the way to cure a certain stiffness in the leg, once the doctors had been persuaded not to cut it off for fear of gangrene and had jury-rigged him back together again. No matter how much he tried, he just could not manage to bend his leg. And so he threw a party and after a few stiff shots of gin hit on the solution. He would lie on the table with his leg sticking out over the end, and one of his mechanics would jump on it. In his own words: "Well, it just lifted me right off that table like a cart wheel and hurled me up in the air and on to the floor—which was quite a leverage because I weighed two hundred and twenty pounds at the time. And there I was on the floor, writhing around in pain. And now completely sober, too!" Unbelievably, after a few days, when the swelling had abated, the knee had loosened up, and after another accidental fall, it was back to normal.

In February 1933, McConachie received a mysterious telephone call from a man named Barney Phillips, who, in a manner beloved of fiction writers, knew of a secret source of gold in the mountains of northern British Columbia. He even had the classic map left by Dirty Tom just before he died with the secret of Black Mike McLaren's strike. Phillips hired McConachie to fly him to the site, to the north of Takla Lake. He took Phillips and three prospectors to Two Brothers Lake and left them there with meager supplies, intending to return. But he arrived back to find the creditors chasing Independent Airways, which promptly went out of business. He hired a Junkers monoplane, with its pilot, but this aircraft also made a forced landing and was unfit to proceed all the way to Two Brothers Lake. He finally succeeded in finding a relief aircraft and flew provisions to the Phillips party, arriving only just in time to save them from starvation.

Impressed by McConachie's style, Barney Phillips proposed that they should go into partnership. He would provide the finance, McConachie would provide the flying experience. And so, in August 1933, United Air Transport was born, with Grant McConachie, twenty-four years old, as its president.

The first task was to obtain some aircraft. Luckily a local air-prospecting company, Northern Exploration, had also gone bankrupt, and the newly founded United was able to pick up two Fokker Universals at ten cents on the dollar. One of these, almost a derelict, was at Prince George in a deplorable state. The engine had been completely stripped of any part that could be unbolted or otherwise removed. Incredible as it may seem, an appeal to the local citizenry restored the assorted parts to their owner, whose mechanic was able to reassemble the Wright engine.

Acquiring another Fokker, to make a grand fleet of three, United Air Transport airfreighted all the machinery and parts needed by the mining company at Two Brothers Lake during the winter of 1933–34. But then Barney Phillips died suddenly, so McConachie formed a new partnership with the younger Barney, the eighteen-year-old son. McConachie having now been exposed to the perils of undercapitalization, transitory markets, and crash-prone aircraft—not to mention a crash-prone pilot who learned only by hard personal experience of the hazards of ice formation on wings and propellers—the partners registered the aircraft in their mothers' names, so that the company itself owned almost no assets.

The first years of United Air Transport were not exactly epoch-making, but they were eventful in the manner that seemed almost inevitable with Grant McConachie at the helm. In 1934, for example, he bought a Ford Tri-Motor from Harry Oakes, a self-made millionaire living in cantankerous luxury on an estate near Niagara Falls on the proceeds of an Ontario gold mine, where he had literally struck it rich. McConachie wore the crotchety Oakes down with his charm. More important, he sliced the price down from $55,000 to $2,500. He flew the Ford back to Edmonton after making two forced landings, one of them in a churchyard, where the sturdy machine plowed its way through the gravestones. The problem was ice on the wings—another lesson for McConachie, but he had brought home the biggest aircraft registered in Canada. This in itself was a reflection on the state of Canadian commercial aviation, for this was the year that, across the border, both the Douglas DC-2 and the Sikorsky S-42 flying boat made their maiden flights.

Although the three-engined Ford multiplied the cold-starting problems by three and mechanics sometimes despaired of repeatedly pouring hot oil into the engines at temperatures down to 68 degrees (Fahrenheit) below freezing, the Old Tin Goose earned its keep. During the three month winter season of 1934–35, it hauled a million pounds of fish.

On May 16, 1935, McConachie took the Ford on a spree, almost as a holiday after its soul-destroying repetitive fish hauls. He obtained a charter contract to fly a rich passenger from Calgary to Vancouver for $1,000. Of course, he selected the Ford, the pride of the fleet. All went well until, over the Rockies, he once again came close to disaster because ice built up on the wings as he flew through clouds. He managed to turn about and changed course to land at Grand Forks, British Columbia. He received a hero's welcome when he finally arrived at Vancouver, for this had been, incredibly, the first flight over the route. But it had been a near thing, and McConachie's luck had once again saved both his skin and his reputation.

Two months after the Vancouver episode, Grant married Margaret McLean, of Scottish ancestry, whose father had farmed in the Peace River country of northern British Columbia. Their honeymoon was spent at Takla Lake, a haven of serenity, also in the northern part of the province; it might have been more enjoyable had the barge bringing all the furniture and provisions for the newly erected cabin not been sunk en route.

After the end of the 1936 fish haul, Grant McConachie found an opportunity to cash in on his original bargain purchase of the Ford. He flew it north to Whitehorse, in the Yukon Territory, and sold it to George Simmons, of Northern Airways, for $8,000—a clear profit of $5,500—plus an excellent Fairchild FC2W2 worth about $10,000. The Fairchild, as the Ford had done earlier, quickly notched its place in United Air Transport's checkered history. It was used to demonstrate the airline's qualifications to fly the air mail between Fort Nelson and Fort St John, in the Peace River district, which was connected to the rest of Canada by air.

Even that demonstration flight was marked with typical McConachie unorthodoxy. Not wishing to fly empty, he filled the rear of the aircraft with fresh fruit, eggs, and other supplies for the isolated community at Fort Nelson but was alarmed to find that the weight had depressed the pontoons, so that the force of the water during taxying had prised open their inspection caps. Again, the McConachie charm—"You have the unique distinction of being the first, and I hope to God the last, passenger we've submerged" he told the postal inspector—turned away wrath, and at last United Air Transport had a mail contract to provide some stability to its uncertain and sporadic sources of income.

The next step was the historical beginning of the first full passenger and mail service by air between Alberta and the Yukon. United Air Transport's Ford Tri-Motor floatplane inaugurated service on July 5, 1937, from Edmonton to Whitehorse, via Fort St. John, Fort Nelson, and Watson Lake (Lower Post). McConachie at first met opposition from the incumbent Whitepass company, which owned the stage line to Dawson, capital of the Yukon; the railroad to Skagway, on the Alaskan coast; and the river boats to Dawson. Whitepass, in fact, owned Whitehorse, and the way to Dawson was blocked—or so Herb Wheeler, the tough and uncompromising boss of Whitepass thought. He even bought aircraft himself to stop McConachie by fair means—and there were strong rumors that he resorted to some foul means as well. But McConachie won him over, as he did everyone else, and Whitepass and United came to a mutually advantageous working agreement.

Even at this time, Grant McConachie had his eyes firmly focused on the Orient. He had never forgotten Wiley Post and the revelation of the great circle route to Japan. But there was work to be done, not to mention the effort to disseminate a vision that was far beyond the grasp of most Canadians—Canadian politicians in particular.

Much of the work was just steady development, such as the construction of airports to replace the rough strips that could be used for only a brief period of the year in northwestern latitudes. Fort Nelson claimed the honor of building the first airstrip for wheeled aircraft in the entire area. Gradually the need for skis in the winter and floats in the summer diminished. Meanwhile, the fortunes of United were none too good, and McConachie drew once again on his secret weapon: his devastating ability to charm his way out of any difficulty. He persuaded the Imperial Oil Company of Canada to provide $100,000 of revolving credit on fuel supplies—and even claimed a rebate from the government on receipted notes. Not content with this coup, he extracted from the Canadian Car & Foundry company three handsome Barkley-Grow floatplanes for a token one dollar each, the rest to be paid from future operating revenues. Astonishingly, Can Car never pressed for payments and was eventually reimbursed only when McConachie sold the aircraft to make way for larger ones.

To his astute wheeling and dealing, McConachie added more samples of his remarkable luck. Because of the shortage of funds, he had taken a gamble and insured only two of the United fleet of ten aircraft, selected at random. On November 3, 1938, three aircraft were lost, for various reasons, in one day. Two were the ones insured and the third was salvageable. In December of the same year, he ordered three ungainly Fleet biplane freighter aircraft. He took the precaution this time of insuring them, by a telephone call placed to United headquarters. He watched one of the Fleets go up in flames at Chicago just as he was about to take off on a demonstration run. Fortunately the insurance formalities had been completed an hour earlier and McConachie himself was lucky to walk away from the burning wreckage. Then in June 1939 the second Fleet crashed at Lower Post (Watson Lake), and McConachie canceled the order for the third.

In spite of these calamities, he still had his "dear old lovely-ugly, profit-making Ford, McConachie's money-in-the-bank freighter," as Ronald Keith neatly described this veteran machine. But he hadn't reckoned with being attacked by the Air Force. In the spring of 1939, the Ford was on the ramp at Vancouver Airport, minding its own business, when a pilot trainee in a Hawker Hurricane rammed it amidships, destroying it as surely as if it had been charged by a Tiger tank. Informed by the local commanding officer that he couldn't sue the Crown, McConachie nevertheless took action. The court awarded the airline $52,000 for loss of contracts, plus costs. It also collected $5,200 in insurance.

By this time, United Air Transport had merged with another airline in a neat action that consolidated two regional route systems. On August 4, 1938, United merged with Ginger Coote Airways, formed by a gentleman of that name, doubtless one of the same disposition as McConachie himself. Ginger Coote operated from Vancouver to Fort St. John via Prince George. The first segment of this modest network linked the western part of United's bush services to Vancouver; the second linked the western with the eastern main line from Whitehorse to Edmonton. The amalgamated system, Yukon Southern Air Transport, was in the shape of an inverted Y and connected British Columbia and Alberta—that is, western Canada—with the Yukon, with connections to Alaska.

To this description, if it had been made by Grant McConachie in the year of the amalgamation, would undoubtedly have been appended "and beyond," because he had not forgotten the unique strategic importance of the area he served as it related to the great circle route to the Orient. Neither, incidentally, had Pan American, which had secured a flank by developing Pacific Alaska Airlines. And in fact, in February 1940 McConachie struck up a working relationship with that U.S. Chosen Instrument for developing air routes overseas. In April of the same year, he negotiated with Amtorg, the Soviet overseas trading agency, for the right to fly down the coast of eastern Siberia, and he even announced his intention to start a service to Vladivostok.

But it was not to be. There were signs that, had the war ended quickly, such a development might have been logical. In fact, the Canadian-U.S. Joint Defence Board cooperated in the modernization of the vital air route between Edmonton and Whitehorse, a critical link on the land-based air route between the lower forty-eight states and Alaska. McConachie himself flew the Pan American route between New York and Bermuda to gain over-ocean flying experience. But he was whistling in the wind. The war quickly escalated, so it became obvious that all intercontinental plans would have to be postponed indefinitely.

In the case of Yukon Southern, there were other reasons that those plans, and any others for that matter, would have to be put off. The airline's credit had finally run dry; traffic was depressed, so no money was coming in; and in fact the war was of little help, except that McConachie was able to obtain aircraft, such as Lockheed Lodestars, and spare parts on the grounds that his communications activity was vital to the war effort.

He was not alone. All over Canada, small airlines had managed to survive in localized situations, usually as short air extensions of branch railway lines. Mackenzie Air Service operated a long lifeline north of Edmonton to the Great Slave Lake mining region and onward to the tiny communities in the Northwest Territories. But none of the others could boast more than a hundred miles or so of route mileage. One company, Canadian Airways, was simply a collection of small routes tacked on as appendages to the transcontinental trunk rail line of the great Canadian Pacific Railway. The C.P.R. had subscribed to a large block of stock in Canadian Airways as long ago as 1930 but had shown little interest in getting into the aviation business.

But now, in 1941, possibly spurred into action by the creation of Trans-Canada Airlines, a government-owned affiliate of C.P.R.'s archrival, the Canadian National Railways, the giant Canadian conglomerate began to think more seriously about air transport. It began to mop up all the small airlines, starting with Mackenzie in 1939, and by mid 1942 it had amalgamated no fewer than ten companies into one. Yukon Southern was purchased on January 13, 1941; its employees became members of the 81,000-strong Canadian Pacific community on May 16, 1941, and the whole assortment became Canadian Pacific Airlines (C.P.A.) on July 1, 1942. It was capitalized at $4,000,000, and L. B. Unwin was the first president.

In its mopping-up process, the C.P.R. had taken many famous bush flyers under its wing. Taking on ten airlines with ten presidents and their teams of executives was difficult enough. But to take on hardy pioneers such as Punch Dickens and Wop May, not to mention men of means such as Leigh Brintnell, was to court trouble because of the personal rivalries. Whether or not Grant McConachie's neutrality during the infighting was a factor is a matter of conjecture. Undoubtedly his engaging charm had not deserted him as he moved into the middle echelons of a giant corporation, and his clear-cut ideas of traversing the Pacific, whether to China by the northern great circle route or to Australia by island-hopping via Hawaii and Fiji, must have singled him out as man of vision.

At any rate, when Canadian Pacific was founded, Punch Dickens was appointed vice-president and general manager of the airline in Montreal, while McConachie was general manager of the all-important western lines. The latter was located in Edmonton, but McConachie reported to W. M. Neal, senior vice-president of the C.P.R. One version of the Dickens-McConachie relationship could have been that Dickens watched the dollars and cents while McConachie spent them. On the other hand, it could also have been an example of the contrast between two types of accountant: the one who always asks "How much will it cost?" and the other who asks, more penetratingly, "How much will it earn?"

During World War II, in a steady development that did as much to change the pace of airline development as did the more familiar transition from bush planes to modern airliners, airports were built all over northwest and central Canada, partly to support the construction of the Alaska Highway supply line, and partly—in response to McConachie's campaign based on hard-won experience—to make the change from floatplanes and skis to year-round wheeled operations. C.P.A. was an integral part of the Canadian war effort. It organized the Atlantic Ferry Service and ran it until the Royal Air Force took over, and it operated seven flying schools and five overhaul plants for the British Commonwealth Air Training Plan.

Behind the scenes, McConachie was campaigning for his cause. In typical flamboyant style he scored a personal triumph by winning over W. M. Neal to the view that the great Canadian Pacific dynasty should not be concerning itself with bush operations but should have far more dignified goals, in keeping with its slogan calling itself "the world's greatest transportation system." He did this on an occasion when he had been called to Montreal to be reprimanded severely for leaking the news to the press that C.P.A. was losing money heavily. McConachie neatly switched the emphasis, pointing out that operating dozens of different types of inefficient bush aircraft was a certain way to lose money and that the airline was doomed unless it changed its policy and concentrated on mainline routes. Instead of receiving a reprimand, he identified himself as a candidate for higher office.

When the war ended, events followed swiftly. The Liberal government, under C. C. Howe, had ordained, in March 1944, that the railways should divest themselves of their air interests, conveniently ignoring both the issue of the state-owned transport organizations that owned airlines, and the ethical implications. In 1946 Neal was elected president of C.P.A. succeeding Unwin, and he appointed McConachie his assistant. These two put into effect McConachie's scheme to prune away the dead wood of the system, retaining only the healthy roots and stems. On February 1, 1947, W. M. Neal succeeded D. C. Coleman as president of the C.P.R., and six days later Grant McConachie became president of C.P.A. He was thirty-seven years old.

He was now in a position to turn his transpacific dreams into realities. He began his campaign during 1948, at the political level, to overcome the Canadian government's Chosen Instrument policy, which came close to giving T.C.A. a monopoly. McConachie tried his usual convincing presentation, complete with a globe and a piece of string to demonstrate the principles of the great circle route. Once again, however, he was blessed with luck, for he may not have got the ministerial nod had it not been for the reaction from T.C.A. The Chosen Instrument did not wish to fly the Pacific, believing the venture to be too much of a financial risk.

Prime Minister Howe laid down two conditions, which McConachie cheerfully accepted. He was obliged to purchase a fleet of Canadian-built North Stars—Douglas DC-4s, manufactured under license, with Rolls-Royce engines—and, so as to provide a reciprocal service with the Australians, who were flying to Vancouver, he was asked to open a route to the southwest Pacific as well.

So far, so good. Now Grant McConachie began to face forces that were resistant to his powers of persuasion. He had to negotiate, on behalf of Canadian Pacific and as representative of his government, the right to operate to both China and Australia. China was almost out of the question. A civil war was raging there, and the prospects of an amicable agreement with a regime leaning heavily toward Moscow—which controlled the airspace between Alaska and China—faded. In Australia he came up against a ruling party so strongly committed to the policy of state control that it had created its own national airline and would agree to a deal only with Canada's equivalent operator, T.C.A.

Circumstances combined to provide McConachie with an opportunity to put on a star performance. Almost as a consolatory gesture, the Canadian delegation was invited to a luncheon by the Australian prime minister, Ben Chiffley, who had risen to political eminence because of his work on the railways and because he was a strong union man. He regarded the Canadian Pacific Railway as a bunch of bloated capitalists. In response to Chiffley's cordial speech, in which he wondered how McConachie had become president at the age of thirty-seven—possibly he thought that it was a case of sheer nepotism—McConachie brandished his union card and described the way he had started work by clearing the railway ash pits. He had literally risen from the ashes to become a top executive. Chiffley was charmed, impressed, and prepared to

change the Australian position. Once again the McConachie charisma had come through; but who else would still have been carrying his union card on such an occasion?

The November mission to Australia was quickly succeeded by
one to the Orient just before Christmas. Accompanied by Wop May,
he was successful in obtaining the rights in Japan, still under Allied control, directly from General Douglas MacArthur. At their
meeting McConachie hardly got a word in edgewise. MacArthur
did all the talking. But C.P.A. received its permit without any problem.

The situation was slightly different when they arrived in
Shanghai to deal with the Nationalist government, still hanging on
by the skin of its teeth. This time, the necessary approval was forthcoming mainly, it appeared, because Wop May happened to know
a trusted retainer from the days of the 1911 revolution under Sun
Yat-sen. May made his pitch to General Morris "Two-Gun" Cohen,
of Jewish descent and now a senior general in the Chinese army
and a veteran of the Nationalist party. For once McConachie did
not have to put on an act.

At first the Pacific routes were a struggle. As T.C.A. had predicted, the normal air traffic potential was simply insufficient to
fill the aircraft. But C.P.A.'s and McConachie's luck continued. In
the north, the airline received a contract in support of the U.S. military airlift to and from Korea. All the top brass found the C.P.A.
standards so far superior that it became the preferred airline. On
the southern route, McConachie had realized, with characteristic
intuition, that there were opportunities to create a new air travel
market: tourism. C.P.A. did a roaring business carrying sun-
starved Canadians to the beaches of Hawaii.

Grant McConachie was never a man for economic analysis or
market research. He sincerely believed that, backed by intuition
and instinct, big decisions would invariably be followed by success, sooner or later. The problem, as he saw it, was not to obtain
the ingredients, but simply to decide to make the cake. Arguably,
his convictions in this respect were upheld not because of the shortcomings of market research, but because the opposition played his
game, providing overconservatism to augment his overconfidence
and optimism. T.C.A. played into his hands.

Having handed the Pacific to C.P.A. on a plate, it then gave
him South America. T.C.A. had developed vacation services to the

Caribbean with commendable verve and in January 1954 had opened a service to Mexico City, via Tampa, Florida. C.P.A., meanwhile, had started a Vancouver–Mexico City–Lima route in October 1953. T.C.A. decided to pull out of its route, allowing C.P.A. to take over, in exchange for giving up local services in Quebec. The Lima service was extended to Buenos Aires in 1956.

Across the Atlantic, the Canadian government actually did agree to C.P.A.'s persuasive arguments to operate a polar route. But this had to be to Amsterdam, because T.C.A. protected its London and Paris gateways into Europe. Nevertheless, direct service from the West Coast of North America proved to be more popular than T.C.A. had expected. McConachie enjoyed the pleasure of inaugurating a one-stop Vancouver–Amsterdam service on June 4, 1955, and two years later, on May 30, 1957, added a route across the central Atlantic, to Lisbon, opening up the joys of the Mediterranean to Canadian tourists.

McConachie and C.P.A. had thus managed to construct a worldwide network—one of the longest in route mileage of all the international airlines—largely by default. Its next objective was to obtain a transcontinental route from Vancouver to the large cities of eastern Canada. For the first time, his intuition-backed rhetoric was of no avail. He was confronted with a systematic market and economic analysis prepared by a well-known British—and therefore impartial—airline economist, Stephen Wheatcroft. C.P.A. had sought five round trips and had glowing plans. It received only one, which it duly started on May 4, 1959, with the Bristol Britannia turboprop airliner, which, for a brief period, enjoyed its reputation as the Whispering Giant until the jets took over. Later C.P.A. was able to consolidate its position into one of free and open competition, but McConachie never lived to enjoy a commercial environment in which he would have thrived.

In one respect, McConachie's instincts failed him. He was never a good judge of aircraft from an economic standpoint and overruled his advisers, one of whom commented in 1962, when C.P.A. announced a loss of $7.6 million for the year, that the airline had been run on "a mixture of glamour and gasoline for twenty years." He had, for example, wholeheartedly advocated the first Comet I, an airliner which, even had it been delivered, could not have flown the critical Vancouver–Hawaii segment with a commercial payload. When the first one crashed at Karachi on a delivery flight, he talked his directors into ordering the Comet II, but his hopes were dashed by the two historic Comet crashes in the Mediterranean within months of the decision.

In the tidying-up process the Mackenzie River services were handed over to a regional airline in 1959, but McConachie would not let go of the original United–Ginger Coote–Yukon Southern heritage in Alberta and British Columbia. In answer to T.C.A.'s direct service from the Prairie Provinces to London, begun in 1958 from Winnipeg, he started one from Calgary early in 1961. In late August of that year, the Canadian government actually approved a direct polar service from Vancouver, Calgary, and Edmonton to London, and Canadian Pacific announced the news publicly on September 30. But at the last moment, the British government refused permission for a second Canadian airline to operate in London.

Douglas DC-8 jets entered service in 1960. Of course, McConachie's were "Super-DC-8s." Asked how they differed from T.C.A.'s, which seemed to the lay public and technicians alike to be the same type, he explained, disarmingly, that his were simply DC-8s with C.P.A. markings.

In the spring of 1964, the silver lining appeared from behind the black cloud of Canadian bureaucratic intransigence. The minister of transport announced that C.P.A.'s route system was recognized as comprising permanent spheres of influence. The weight of restriction was lifted, and further overseas destination points were added during the latter 1960s. In April 1970 the transcontinental frequency was increased to seven round trips a day. The years of toil were over and an era of expansion began.

Grant McConachie, whose instincts had created a great airline system, did not live to see the official recognition of his efforts. On June 29, 1965, he died suddenly of a heart attack in Long Beach, California, at the age of fifty-six. Only a few months earlier he had joined the enthusiasts for the supersonic airliner and had placed deposits on three of the Mach 3 U.S. SSTs. Such a decision was typical of the man, but the accounts department of C.P.A. must have been relieved when that ambitious project, doomed from the start to economic failure, was canceled.

Had he lived he could not have coped with the meticulous bookkeeping and corporate disciplines necessary for a large international and trunk airliner to survive in an age when financial viability rested on careful attention to every detail, and the complexities of the administration were such that instinctive decisions could not be tolerated. The sheer magnitude of the operation now left little scope for the element of luck. Decisions had to be made by boardroom professionals rather than by gifted individuals.

The irony, of course, is that without McConachie's inspiration, toughness, and ability to squeeze blood out of so many stones during the dark days of the postwar years, when the Canadian government wanted no part of Canadian Pacific Airlines, there would have been no administrative organization, no magnitude of operation, and no boardroom. Grant McConachie created all three, and during the years of his individualistic stewardship, he *was* Canadian Pacific Airlines. He was the Man of the Hour on many occasions, and for two critical decades, he was the Man of His Time.

Maxwell Ward

Bush Service to
Royal Doulton

Few visitors to the handsome suite of offices in the modern, stylish Wardair headquarters at Toronto International Airport would think of Maxwell W. Ward, now clearly a successful business man, as once a somewhat irresponsible bush pilot, flying a flimsy three-seater on operations of questionable legality and at high risk. Yet that was how Max Ward began his long climb up the ladder of success, and his story is one of the dreams come true of the airline industry.

He has never forgotten his early years and still reminisces with obvious pride of the struggles of the early days, not only in learning to survive physically in the unforgiving climate and inhospitable terrain of Canada's Far North, but also in learning the hard lessons of financial survival in a fiercely competitive world. Neither has he lost an enduring respect for the hardy pioneer bush pilots. The great names of immortals such as Punch Dickens, and Doc Oakes, and Wop May are enshrined on the noses of the great flagships of Wardair's fleet of wide-bodied jets.

None of this is surprising, if Max Ward's background and early tuition in aviation affairs are borne in mind. He was born in Edmonton in 1921, and throughout his childhood the names of Dickens, May, and others were familiar to the young boy who was mad about airplanes. So were the identities of the fledgling airlines of western Canada, Mackenzie Air Service in particular, for it was based at Edmonton, and its aircraft appeared to set off on an adventure to the north each time they took off. Western Canada Airways

187

Maxwell Ward carried the enthusiasm of an independent spirit into the jet age, as a latter-day reflection of the bush-pilot opportunism of the old-time Canadian pioneers. Wardair is Canada's third largest airline today.

and United Air Transport, run by Punch Dickens and Grant McConachie respectively, operated out of Edmonton, to provide an indelible impression of the importance of air transport on the mind of a young enthusiast.

Inevitably, when Canada entered World War II, in 1939, young Max was quick to join the Canadian Air Force but was disappointed to be posted, not to a flight training school, but to an observer school, where he suffered the indignity of being assigned to guard duty. But he finally achieved his ambition to fly, in Tiger Moths, and graduated to Cessna T50s, at Claresholme, Alberta, ready to take on the might of Nazi Germany.

Unfortunately, this was not to be. When his class, sixty-four strong, were graduated, two, one of them Max Ward, were selected to become flight instructors. He was posted to Moncton, New Brunswick, and trained other pilots to go overseas. At Moncton he flew Harvards and Ansons, and he ended the war at St. Catherines,

Ontario, in Yales and Norsemen. He had thus spent four years as an instructor and as a consequence was a highly skilled pilot. But he sometimes reflects that, had he been cannier, he could have protested bitterly against the prospect of not being sent to the battlefront, and armed service psychology being what is was, he would probably have got what he wanted, a more adventurous service career and a flirtation with danger.

When the war ended he found these experiences soon enough. At first he joined with one Jack Moare in providing general flying services at Edmonton, using a war-surplus Cessna T50 Crane, but this partnership was short-lived. In the Canadian Northwest, bush pilots were in great demand after the war, nowhere more than at Yellowknife, on the northern shore of the Great Slave Lake in the Northwest Territories and the gateway to Canada's Arctic North. Max Ward decided to set up shop at Yellowknife.

There, in 1946, he formed his own company, Polaris Charter Company, with a fleet of one de Havilland Canada D.H. 83C Fox Moth, fitted—as all aircraft had to be in those conditions—with interchangeable wheels, skis, and floats. When Ward went to Toronto to buy the aircraft from the manufacturer, he had only $1,500, but a friend lent him the additional $1,000 necessary to put down as the first payment on the $10,500 Fox Moth. So great was his affection for this, his first airplane, that some thirty-five years later he fashioned a restoration out of parts of three different aircraft plus a newly built fuselage.

Max Ward learned to maintain the Fox Moth himself, taking practical lessons from Ernie Mills, a hardened veteran who made it clear that he intended to demonstrate procedures once only, after which Ward was on his own. With the admonition "If anything goes wrong, I'll bat you!" always uppermost in his mind, Ward learned how to take an engine apart blindfolded and accepted the discipline of doing the maintenance checks thoroughly, with no short cuts. In the Frozen North, such methods were absolutely essential, for a forced landing could place a pilot in a precarious situation, in temperatures substantially below zero, hundreds of miles from the nearest habitation. To be able to cope with emergencies, not least in mechanical matters, was a vital ingredient of survival.

While Max Ward was conscientious in practical matters such as this, he was not really good at the administrative side of things, and in fact, throughout his subsequent career, he was always a bit impatient when it came to dealing with representatives of government. In the case of Polaris, the problem was fundamental: he had failed to obtain an operating license, and by order of the Air Transport Board he was obliged to go into partnership with another operator.

As a footnote to this episode, it was a reflection of the state of aviation in Canada in those days that the Air Transport Board consisted in effect of two men, Romeo Vachon and Dan McLean, both of whom were former bush pilots. The sympathy between them and Max Ward, following in their footsteps, was such that he received no more than a slap on the wrist, a regulatory procedure which may account for the fact that one of Wardair's Boeing 747s is named the *Romeo Vachon*.

In 1947, therefore, Max Ward joined up with George Pigeon, who owned a Stinson Station Wagon, and the business was aptly called Yellowknife Airways. The Fox Moth was lost in a crash, but Ward borrowed $5,000 to put toward a $35,000 Bellanca Skyrocket, built under license in Edmonton. With this sturdy aircraft the little airline, armed with Pigeon's license, flew bush services to hunters, trappers, prospectors, and miners in remote outposts of the Canadian northlands. They transported supplies, people, medical teams, and doctors, often in potentially hazardous circumstances.

Ward is pragmatic in his assessment of the qualities of a good bush pilot. He dismisses the idea that a bush pilot should be daring, taking chances, and seeking to challenge the hand of fate. The daring ones, he claims—with experience and evidence to support his opinion—didn't last very long. The mortality rate was high, although it was not the flying itself that accounted for the fatalities. Weather, poor maintenance, bad judgment—these were the elements of potential disaster. In the North the weather was always the paramount enemy of the bush pilot, and Max Ward insists that there is a golden rule to be observed when confronted with deteriorating conditions: just land at the best place possible, make a cup of tea, radio your position, and wait for the low ceiling or storm to clear.

In the Northwest Territories, the bush pilots usually learned the hard way, by some experience or other that made them converts for life to the principles of caution and avoidance of any course of action that involved a foreseeable risk. Ward himself once broke his own golden rule and paid the penalty. Late in November

This picture of ground staff loading oil barrels onto a Wardair de Havilland DHC-2 Beaver at Yellowknife, in the Northwest Territories of Canada, vividly illustrates the demanding operating conditions in the far north. Note the complete protection for the engine and for the mechanics whose task it was to start it.

1948, he had to deliver a man to the Hudson's Bay post at Bathurst Inlet, just north of the Arctic Circle. He also took along a second passenger who wished to visit his father, a trapper, about halfway along the route, at Muskox Lake. Delayed for a while at the Lake, because the trapper was out with his lines, they took off rather late in the shortened day and with instruments rendered unreliable because of the stop. Nearing Bathurst Inlet, they ran into ice-particle fog, and in deteriorating visibility—they had run out of daylight completely, as well as fuel reserves and sense of direction—they ricocheted off the top of an uncharted hill and luckily came to earth with only a broken landing gear. Having picked up some furs from the trapper, they were able to keep warm in a makeshift tent under the Bellanca wing and with an improvised aerial made radio contact with Yellowknife. The D. H. Beaver sent to rescue them at first got lost, but six days later help arrived, and the Bellanca was repaired and flown out. Every bush pilot in the Canadian North can tell such stories, but the ones left to tell the tale are the ones who carried their emergency kits and supplies and checked them regularly and who kept their aircraft in tiptop condition and their radios faultless.

Max Ward became disenchanted with the life at Yellowknife, for by this time he was married and had two children. But even though the family moved up to join him, he decided to leave what was not exactly a flourishing business, fascinating though it might be compared with more sedentary occupations. He wound up Yellowknife Airways in 1949 and to clear his debts went into the construction business at Lethbridge, Alberta, keeping his flying hand in working part-time for Associated Airways.

But he was itching to get back into aviation, and in 1952 he founded a new company, Wardair, with a new single-engined DHC-3 Otter, which cost him $25,000. This particular Otter was the fifth one off the production line and was the first to be used in airline operations. Ward made sure that he obtained an Air Transport Board operating license; it became effective on June 6, 1953, which may be taken as the official starting date of Wardair.

Gradually the company expanded. After three years it still boasted only thirteen employees, but the fleet had grown to five DHC-3 Otters and one DHC-2 Beaver. Then in 1957 Ward purchased a Bristol Type 170 Freighter, an ungainly-looking aircraft, which, however, could carry large bulky loads of up to six tons or forty-four passengers. Fitted with special oversized tires, it was ideal for operating in the primitive conditions of the Canadian North, coping with semiprepared landing strips on the tundra or, during the winter, on frozen lakes. This aircraft, able to lift consignments that were too big or awkward to fit into the typical bush aircraft of the Otter or Beaver type, was so successful that Wardair built the fleet up to five. It also operated a Supermarine Stranraer for a short while in 1959, and this actual aircraft is preserved in the Royal Air Force Museum in England.

The year 1961 was a watershed in Max Ward's and Wardair's lives. By one decision, inspired by a shrewd amalgam of intuition and good judgment, the airline changed course completely during a period of less than twelve months. To the surprise—and a little expressed incredulity—on the part of some of his contemporaries, Max Ward acquired a Douglas DC-6A convertible pressurized airliner, which could carry ninety-one passengers or about fourteen tons of freight. Leased from Canadian Pacific Airlines, this relatively modern, demanding aircraft did not seem to be suited to the operating conditions in the North, and indeed it could not be used at all north of Yellowknife during the summer, when the ice and snow melted and landing strips became marshland.

Prospects for other work for the DC-6 type of aircraft did not appear promising at that time. The Canadian air transport industry had been a late starter, its national airline, Trans-Canada Airlines (T.C.A.), having been founded only in 1937, as a state-owned national carrier, and Canadian Pacific Airlines (C.P.A.) having become the second flag carrier in 1942, through the amalgamation of about a dozen small companies, or the remnants thereof. The government had jealously guarded its own airline, and C.P.A. had only been able to move out of its early regional airline status by picking up overseas routes that Canada wished to serve reciprocally with other countries, but that T.C.A. either did not wish to operate, because it thought them uneconomical, or could not operate, because it had insufficient or unsuitable aircraft. C.P.A. had operated its original services as branch connections with the main trunk transcontinental railroad operated by its sister company, and only in 1959 had it gained access to the coveted transcontinental air route—and then only with restricted frequency.

Access to Canadian scheduled routes, therefore, was almost out of the question, for when C.P.A. obtained its Vancouver–Winnipeg–Toronto–Montreal route, it disposed of most of its remaining feeder services. Those that were workable had been picked up by provincial companies; those that were hopelessly uneconomical, mainly because of improved surface communications and transport, were closed down.

Wardair's DC-6 was not exactly the last word in competitive aircraft at that time either, although it was by no means obsolete. All the big airlines of the world were using second-generation piston-engined airliners—DC-7s and Super-Constellations. Canada, in fact, was in the van of progress; C.P.A. actually inaugurated its transcontinental service in 1959 with the new four-engined British turbo-prop, the Bristol Britannia, and T.C.A. responded the following year with the Vickers Vanguard, also a four-engined British turboprop.

The outlook appeared to be nothing but blue sky for the incumbent national airlines, with no prospect of competition from small fry such as Wardair in the foreseeable future. Indeed, C.P.A. itself had only gained a foothold in the established order by a combination of good fortune and public support of a traditional and famous name. But from the obscurity of the legal machinery that governed Canadian commercial aviation came the proverbial cloud no bigger than a man's hand. In the very same year that Max Ward bought his DC-6, the Canadian Air Transport Board extended the Class 9-4 international charter authority to include the affinity rules—that is, a charter airline could carry a complete load of passengers belonging to a club or organization that did not exist primarily for the purpose of travel. Thus, if the Edmonton Bridge and Whist Society wished to charter an aircraft, then split the cost among its members, it could legally do so, and the price per seat worked out to about half the cheapest fare then offered by any of the scheduled airlines.

Late in 1961 Max Ward obtained a Class 9-4 license and moved his headquarters from Yellowknife to Edmonton. He changed the name of the company to Wardair Canada and set up two divisions, the International and the Northern operations. In 1962 Wardair Canada then proceeded to operate nine affinity charter flights between Canada and Europe. Refueling at Sondre Stromfjord, in Greenland, the trips took nineteen hours each way. But at the price they were paying, the club members did not object to the arduous journey, and in fact, from the very beginning, Wardair's policy was to offer all its patrons amenities and comfort comparable to those in normal scheduled economy service.

During its first season, the DC-6 carried 712 passengers across the Atlantic at an average load factor of 87 percent—some twenty-five points higher than that of its scheduled contemporaries. In the second year, 1963, a DC-6B passenger aircraft was obtained from the Dutch airline, K.L.M., and almost 3,500 happy Canadian club members flew the Atlantic. By 1965 the figure had risen to almost 6,000, and in 1966, by which time the fleet had been augmented by a smart 119-seat Boeing 727-100 three-engined jet, this was doubled.

Some indication of the change in fortunes for Max Ward and

Wardair can be gleaned from the fact that the Boeing 727 cost $5.5 million. Only ten years earlier the total fleet of small aircraft could not have been worth half that. Such was the headlong pace, in fact, that in April 1968, a 183-seat long-range Boeing 707-320c joined the fleet, and a sister ship was added in March 1969. With such capacity and with apparently unlimited demand, Wardair prospered. Revenues grew from well under $1 million in 1962 to almost $16.5 million in 1970.

The charter market garden, however, was not entirely full of roses. Wardair actually lost money in 1970 and was obliged to raise its fares the following year, nevertheless maintaining them at a level far lower than those of its scheduled competitors. Even so efficient an airline as Wardair must have found difficulty in breaking even during the trough season, but even after the increase, the fare of $178 for the round trip between Toronto and London during October and November must have been one of the world's best bargains. In the summer it was only $237, against the scheduled $602 economy class and $366 excursion.

The last fare had been introduced by the scheduled airlines on the highly competitive North Atlantic route in an effort to stave off the threat of the growing number of charter airlines, both in Europe and America, which were making inroads into the hitherto hallowed air of the flag airlines of North America and Europe. Not that such healthy and vigorous competitors as Max Ward feared competition. In fact they thrived on it. But the charter airlines, those outside the Establishment, faced a form of competition that was more insidious. Wardair suddenly found itself in what Max Ward politely described as difficulties with the Canadian government, which alleged that Wardair was not covering its passengers with adequate insurance. Ward had no objection to complying with any law or regulation, but he did object strongly to what he described as the government's "irresponsible and unnecessary" methods of ensuring a solution. The plain fact was that the government's T.C.A. (now Air Canada) wanted the Atlantic to itself, and little Wardair was making too many waves, splashing about in the pond in an alarming way.

The regulatory environment improved in 1973, when the government of Canada, along with those of the United Kingdom and other European countries, recognized that the affinity rules were subject to so much abuse that it introduced a new form of charter tariff, the Advanced Booking Charter (A.B.C.). These were open to travel agents as well as to the clubs whose bridge players, tiddlywinks enthusiasts, or bird-watchers had been taking advantage en masse of the former regulations.

True to form, Max Ward responded almost immediately by purchasing larger aircraft to meet the forecast demand for greatly increased traffic. The first 456-seat Boeing 747 was delivered on May 2, 1973, and was followed by a second giant jet in December 1974. By 1975 the annual passenger total exceeded 500,000, with a consistent pattern of mainly A.B.C.s in the summer and inclusive tours—complete air travel and hotel packages—during the winter months.

On January 1, 1976, Wardair went through a complete corporate reorganization. Wardair Canada became the parent holding company for several subsidiaries. The main one was Wardair Canada (1975), and others were Wardair (U.K.), set up to take advantage of the growing demand for Canada-bound traffic from Great Britain, and International Vacations Ltd., a travel agency that could now legitimately sell tickets under the A.B.C. rules. Also, Wardair Jamaica was registered in Jamaica to operate a hotel, to complete the cycle of the inclusive tour-package process.

But like all other charter operators at that time, on both sides of the Atlantic, Max Ward felt that his kind of airline was being unnecessarily, perhaps vindictively, handicapped by an alliance of government agencies and scheduled airlines which, while overtly competing in the commercial arena, were covertly trying to do everything they could to make life difficult for the nonscheduled operators. In Wardair's annual report for 1975, these handicaps were itemized. They included the requirement of sixty-day advance booking for A.B.C. charters, with passenger lists to be submitted, together with other operating and technical data, to both Canadian and foreign governments; the restriction of a charter flight to only one point of origin, with no intermediate traffic stops; the refusal to allow A.B.C. loads to be mixed with inclusive tour passengers on the same aircraft; the requirement that inflexible return flight dates be fixed for A.B.C. traffic; and the prohibition of mixing Canadian passengers with foreigners on the same aircraft.

Max Ward went on to state, "The volume of paper which must be processed to assure the governments, both Canadian and foreign, that we are complying with these many restrictions would shock you, the shareholder, and the costs of processing the paper are of course considerable."

Responding to the tide of public opinion and prodded by Max Ward whenever he had the opportunity, the government did relax its position somewhat toward the end of 1977 by proposing A.B.C. travel within Canada. But this was a palliative, and Canada continued to lag behind the legislation being enacted by the Civil Aeronautics Board in the United States, by the Civil Aviation Authority in the United Kingdom, and by other European governments. In fact, Wardair was not able to begin domestic A.B.C. service until 1980.

Wardair was now consolidating its technical and operating position. By now it was an airline of considerable stature, operating charter flights from six Canadian cities, not only to the United Kingdom and Europe, but also to the United States, including Hawaii, to the Caribbean, and to Mexico and Latin America. The Dominion Capital, Ottawa, was added to the network in 1977. During the same year, a new hangar and maintenance headquarters opened at Edmonton, able to accept Boeing 747s in 120,000 square feet of hangar space, with adjoining shop and offices. A sizable investment in additional aircraft was committed, and during 1978 and 1979 two more new Boeing 747s were added, together with two long-range McDonnell Douglas DC-10-30 wide-bodied trijets.

Late in 1978, the Canadian government made further regulatory improvements, eliminating the last two of the handicaps listed by Max Ward in his 1975 annual report. But these did not attack the nucleus of the problem, as Ward pungently commented: "too late to be of any value during 1978 and even then fell far short of expectations. As a result, Canada's regulatory environment is far more restrictive than that found in the U.S. or in most parts of Europe." He went on to observe, "a substantial number of travellers departing from, or travelling to Canada select routes via the United States. This loss is directly felt by the charter airlines serving Canada." Toronto-bound tourists or visitors could fly to Detroit or Chicago and make a quick connection by train, or their relatives could easily meet them across the border.

Late in 1979, two actions, one by the company itself, the other by an air transport authority under siege, set the seal on Wardair's future. On October 19, Max Ward finally closed down his beloved Northern Division, still based at Yellowknife. Through the years, the Otters and Beavers had given way to Twin Otters. A Grumman Gulfstream had been added in 1977, offering a standard of luxury to rich Edmonton oilmen that was in striking contrast to the austerity of the early days. De Havilland's latest product, a Dash Seven four-engined short takeoff and loading (STOL) turboprop had joined the division in 1978. But business activity had declined, a projected pipeline project had been abandoned, mining activity was sluggish, surface transport had been vastly improved, and an application to operate scheduled regional routes had been rejected. And so Wardair decided to become entirely a charter airline and sold its fleet of bush aircraft.

The timing was excellent. The very next month, the Canadian government capitulated, possibly realizing what Max Ward had been telling them for ten years: that expanding the air travel market to all strata of fare-paying passengers and devising sensible means of improving the efficiency of the operation to meet the travel demand, without artifically contrived restrictions, could only benefit the whole country. Thus in November 1979—more than a year after the U.S. Air Deregulation Act had been signed into law by President Carter—the Air Transport Committee of the Canadian Transport Commission made significant changes in the Air Carrier Regulations, in effect removing all the remaining handicaps listed in Max Ward's visionary analysis of 1975. Had the commission taken note of Max's advice then, it could have been ahead of the game. But in February 1980 it relaxed even further by authorizing the domestic charter services that had never really got under way in 1977, when the idea was first proposed.

Altogether, the winter of 1979–80 was a busy one for Wardair, whose staff must have been encouraged by the final victory of common sense against the dead hand of bureaucracy. The company made a number of refugee flights from Malaysia, under contract to the Canadian government, and also entered the Moslem Hajj market, flying pilgrims from Cairo to Jeddah for the annual pilgrimage to Mecca. But the significant date in the Wardair calendar of this period was May 8, 1980, when full domestic A.B.C. charter service was introduced on the densely patronized Toronto–Vancouver route, quickly followed by similar services from Toronto to Edmonton and Calgary and from Montreal to Calgary and Vancouver.

During the early 1980s, sniping continued between Ward and the Canadian aviation authorities, which sometimes found allies in other regulatory agencies. In February 1982, for example, the Ontario Securities Commission ordered Wardair to revise its tax-payable method of accounting to a tax-allocation basis—that is, to make provision for deferred taxes. In the long term, this made no difference in the amount of tax paid; it was merely typical of the bureaucratic irritants with which independents such as Wardair had to contend.

In 1982 Wardair sustained its second successive heavy financial loss—exceeding $10 million—even though traffic and revenues had increased. The basic problem was that a world economic recession had adversely affected long-distance air travel, and the charter airlines suffered the most. Like many other charter airlines, in both the United States and Europe, Wardair was more vulnerable than its scheduled rivals to the effect of declining demand, mostly at the lower levels of the fare strata. Scheduled airlines were cushioned against the worst effects because a large proportion of their clientele, the first-class and business travelers, was less sensitive to any decline in discretionary income, and only a small proportion of their total market was severely affected.

Furthermore, during the long years of struggle to provide cheap fares to an ever larger sector of the traveling public and to prove the basic logic of innovative marketing methods to meet the specialized demand, Wardair and its fellow charter airlines had had to watch their scheduled rivals cynically erode their birthright. Scheduled airlines offered low fares, on the same or nearly the same terms as the charter carriers, but were permitted to tailor the capacity so as to exploit the situation as it suited them, often simply to fill otherwise empty seats. The charter airlines, in contrast, were not allowed to provide services that could be said to border on the definition of *scheduled*.

On February 22, 1984, Wardair submitted recommendations to the Air Transport Committee, in a well-argued protest against the rigid two-airline policy practiced in Canada. It expressed grave apprehension at the effect of U.S. deregulation policy, whose repercussions were being felt throughout the world. After many years of inertia and complacency, the world airline industry was being forced to be more competitive through greater efficiency. The implication of the reasoned arguments was that, throughout the formative years leading up to the new deregulated world, Wardair had led the way in preparing the air industry of Canada for the stiffer challenges and therefore deserved a degree of recognition, and indeed reward, for its efforts.

In a complete about-face from its policy of less than a decade before, the Minister of Transport announced significant changes in air policy on May 10, 1984. Restrictions were relaxed, almost to the point of removal in some instances, for both scheduled and charter airlines. Wardair suddenly found itself being treated on an almost equal basis with those airlines from which it had in the past been separated in an invisible caste system.

Under the terms of a revision of the bilateral air agreement between Canada and the United States, a new scheduled international route from Canada to San Juan, Puerto Rico, was added. And because of Wardair's impeccable record of service in the Caribbean market, not to mention its efficient marketing organization for catering to the tourist industry, it was designated by the Ministry of Transport as Canada's scheduled airline to serve the route.

Almost exactly a year later, on May 9, 1985, in a decision that must have reduced Canadian aviation conservatives to a state of near apoplexy, Wardair was officially designated Canada's second scheduled air carrier to serve the United Kingdom. The broad authority permitted service from ten Canadian cities to London, Manchester, and Glasgow. Impartial analysts, however, would applaud the move as the only one that was ethically possible. By its many charter programs since 1982—when it carried barely 700 passengers across the Atlantic—Wardair's transatlantic total was now many hundreds of thousands annually, with the United Kingdom as the primary market. In twenty-three years—slightly longer than the customary period—Max Ward's airline had come of age.

During these two hectic decades, Max Ward had never allowed reductions in costs to be made by reducing standards of service or passenger amenities. Even in the early years, when it was fashionable to sneer at charter airlines because of charges—usually spurious—of poor onboard standards, Wardair served its charter passengers meals on Royal Doulton china. As a new Canadian scheduled airline enters the market, the incumbents will have to look to their laurels, as new standards of comfort will be evident, and the customer will have a wider choice.

Wardair will also be meeting the challenge confidently with the knowledge that in 1984 it made a record profit of $50 million, as if to celebrate its newfound status. The established Canadian airlines, Air Canada and C.P.Air, will have nothing to fear from the new levels of efficiency forced upon them, and as well-organized corporations they will continue to thrive. But as they speculate on what course they might have taken, left to their own devices, they may reflect that it was Maxwell W. Ward who threw down the gauntlet of low fares before the Canadian aviation authorities and eventually dragged them, kicking and screaming, into the world of mass air travel.

▶▶▶▶▶▶▶▶▶▶▶▶▶▶▶▶

The
United
Kingdom

▶▶▶▶▶▶▶▶▶▶▶▶ ▶▶▶▶▶
◀

▶▶▶▶▶▶▶▶▶▶ ◀ ▶▶▶▶▶▶▶▶▶▶

Edward Hillman

The Cockney Sparrow

Edward Henry Hillman was born in 1890 at Laindon, Essex, and began his career as a farmer's boy, earning no more than the standard wage for that occupation during the early part of the century, a few shillings, or less than a pound a week, hardly enough to provide bare subsistence. Before the Great War he had already joined the cavalry, "chiefly to secure three good meals a day," a natural progression from a world of horses. He was in the retreat from Mons, and he reached the rank of sergeant major. Apparently he was shrewd enough to realize that four-legged transport was destined to give way to four-wheeled locomotion. By the end of hostilities, he was a chauffeur in the diplomatic service, and he must have been a good driver, for he was put in charge of a Rolls-Royce. In later life— though not so many years later, considering the circumstances—he would be driving his own Rolls.

Intrigued with the emerging patterns of public transport, he pursued a vigorously independent course, which was to become a crusade within a few years. Following in the footsteps of other famous airmen, Hillman set up a small bicycle business, then worked as a taxi driver, and later began a car-hire service in London. He realized that the taxi owners, not the drivers, made all the money. In 1928 he had scraped together enough money, first to buy a London taxi, and then, in 1928, his first motor coach. With this slender asset he proceeded to launch a motor coach service, Hillman's Saloon Coaches, in Essex. He opened his first route on December 7, 1928, from Stratford, in East London, to Chelmsford, via Romford and Brentwood. This was the period in Britain when there was an unre-

Former cavalryman, taxi driver, and bus operator Edward Hillman stands proudly in front of his de Havilland Puss Moth at Maylands airfield, northeast of London, in 1932. Within two years he was challenging Britain's flag airline, Imperial Airways, on the prestigious London–Paris route with another small aircraft which brought great success to its builders, and which he played no small part in its promotion and design.

stricted road traffic boom, and bus services and long-distance coach services proliferated everywhere. In 1931, by the time Hillman entered the aviation business, the boom was at its height. Hillman's buses and coaches ranged throughout Essex, especially to seaside towns such as Clacton, and he claimed to own about 300 coaches, although the actual number was probably smaller.

During this period he must have demonstrated a degree of thrift bordering on parsimony. His fares to the public were low, and he achieved them by keeping his costs down, not least in wages. He did not regard driving a bus as a particularly demanding profession, therefore not demanding a generous salary. In this he was in line with most other bus and coach operators, and the latent strength of the Transport and General Workers Union was still only a gleam in Ernest Bevin's eye. Hillman's attitude was later to be carried over into his airline, for he saw very little difference between a bus driver and a pilot. In his view, pilots were just bus drivers who were privileged to fly airplanes. He even wanted to qualify as a commercial pilot himself, because "these bloody pilots of mine . . . won't fly because the weather is bad. I want to be able to get in and fly it myself." Eric Starling, later to become Gandar Dower's renowned chief pilot, observing Hillman's generous paunch, pointed out that there were strict medical tests.

Edward Hillman was inspired to start his airline at least partially because in 1931 the government applied strict curbs on the unrestricted development of passenger coach and bus transport and directed the industry to organize itself into regional groups. Hillman, along with a fellow freebooter, W. L. Thurgood, who operated the People's bus service on the northern fringes of London, was forced out, and his bus services were absorbed by London Transport. He received £145,000 in compensation for what was in effect a compulsory purchase. Within three years of starting his bus and coach company, he had founded Hillman's Airways, in November 1931. On Christmas Day of the same year, he launched his first air service, a charter flight in a de Havilland Puss Moth, from Maylands, a small airfield near Romford, Essex, which he rented from a local farmer. With Edward Hillman, idea and deed were often simultaneous.

On April 1, 1932, Hillman began a regular scheduled service from Maylands to Clacton-on-Sea, using a "fleet" of two de Havilland Fox Moths in addition to his Puss Moth. Today the journey takes about an hour and a half up the A12, and even in those days, a Hillman coach would probably have negotiated the trip in little more than two hours, even having to drive through Brentwood, Chelmsford, and Colchester. Bypasses around cities had not yet been thought of, much less superhighways. His airline flights would have been regarded by passengers more in the nature of a novelty, almost an adventure, rather than as a serious means of traveling from one place to another. For Hillman, however, the trips to the seaside resort may have been just his way of groping his way toward something more ambitious. Romford to Clacton was just the training ground.

On March 11, 1932, he had already surprised the dignified people at de Havilland by buying the two Fox Moths. He had visited the

Stag Lane airfield, the headquarters of de Havilland before its move to Hatfield, and found himself in some fairly distinguished company as the Fox Moth was demonstrated. His unkempt appearance seemed out of keeping with his mission, but there was nothing wrong with his credit rating. He paid on the spot, and de Havilland was to see him again the following year.

On September 24, 1932, he was honored at a ceremony at Romford. Bill Courtnay, well-known aviator and splendid publicity man, introduced Edward Hillman to the aviation community and others who wished to join the fun. Hillman was greeted by the lord mayor of London and many other distinguished officials, who had been escorted to Maylands Aerodrome by a small squadron of air force fighters. There were a civic reception in Romford Market Square and a smart luncheon at the White Hart Hotel. There were speeches and toasts. Hillman's was the briefest, in which he apologized unaffectedly for his lack of education and ended quickly by wishing everyone "Good 'Ealth."

Hillman claimed he had been to the great University of Life, which was presumably the same one that drew its students from the School of Hard Knocks. Certainly, Hillman was poorly educated, and he had probably left school—as farmers' boys invariably did—at a very young age, without having shown a great inclination toward academic achievement. When shown a contract by the de Havilland salesmen, Hillman was said to have blinked at it and asked one of the salesmen to read it to him. But this did not necessarily suggest that he was illiterate to the degree that he signed his name with an X.

For Hillman, like many another low-bred minor celebrity, was no fool; he possessed a native intelligence that overrode his limitations in academic learning. He was thrifty, disciplined, hardworking, and did not tolerate inefficiency. He was particularly tough with his pilots, who were poorly paid, but they did not seem to mind, for they undoubtedly enjoyed their work. He shrewdly selected pilots from former air force noncommissioned flying crew or those who loved flying so much that they would almost fly for nothing. There were no flight-deck prima donnas working for Hillman. They knew that their boss worked as hard as they did and on a cold night was known to meet a flight back from Paris with a mug of hot tea in his hand for the pilot

The Fox Moths had performed during 1932 to Hillman's complete satisfaction, and the growing air-mindedness sweeping through Britain in the early 1930s encouraged him to expand his air business. He realized that he needed a large aircraft and went back to de Havilland. His specification was quite simple. The new airplane was to be twice as big as the Fox Moth, but still flyable by only one pilot. This turned out to be a neat biplane designed by Arthur Hagg and powered by two Gipsy Queen engines. It was called the Dragon and sold for £2,899, an astonishingly low figure, considerably lower than the price of the nearest rival, the Airspeed Ferry. It could carry six people quite comfortably, or eight, if they carried no luggage. The price included eleven instruments, tool kit, log book, instruction book, and a few sundry items. The six seats were extra, £105 the lot. Hillman was later heard to complain that "De Havillands charged me fifty quid [pounds] to fit it out with a bleeding shithouse, fifty bleeding quid for a shithouse."

The impression has been widely held that Hillman "designed" the D.H. 84 Dragon, but this was not absolutely true. The Iraqi Air Force had also approached de Havilland at the same time to discuss the possibility of a light general-purpose trainer. Nevertheless, Hillman can take credit for having placed the initial order, and for having inaugurated the first service of a most successful line of aircraft, one for which de Havilland justly became respected in almost every corner of the world. The Dragon would doubtless have been a natural twin-engined development of the famous single-engined Moth line of aircraft. Hillman simply acted as a catalyst. His instinctive competitive flair and the low airline-operating costs that he demonstrated were of inestimable benefit to de Havilland. As long as Edward Hillman was flying its aircraft in his inimitable fashion, the manufacturer hardly needed to advertise.

The D.H. 84 Dragon made its maiden flight on November 24, 1932, and Hillman took delivery of the first one off the line on December 20. The famous pilot Amy Johnson broke a bottle of champagne on G-ACAN to christen it *Maylands*. Hillman's chief pilot, Harold Woods, flew joyrides all day, six passengers at a time.

Hillman's Airways started a twice-daily service from Maylands on April 1, 1933. The fleet of Dragons thereupon ushered in a new age of air transport for Great Britain. Hillman charged £3.10.0 (£3.50 in today's money) for the single journey; £5.10.0 (£5.50) round trip; or £4.15.0 (£4.75) for a special weekend excursion. These fares compared favorably with those charged by Imperial Airways on the Croydon–le Bourget link. True, Imperial was operating the huge thirty-eight-seat Handley Page H.P. 42 biplanes, but these were so slow that there was time to serve five-course meals during the London–Paris trip. They were supposed to epitomize luxury air travel, but Imperial's fare, one way, was the same as Hillman's for the round trip, so Hillman had a distinct edge, even though his pilots looked like bus drivers and there were no meals. "I don't want no subsidy nor no high-falutin pilots and toffee-nosed flying hostesses." It was a clear case of paying your money and taking your choice. To put the situation in perspective, Hillman was offering a trip to Paris and back for just a little more than the average working man's weekly wage.

On April 1, 1933, Hillman also reopened his seasonal service to Clacton and added one to Margate a week later. The next year, having held his own against Imperial, Hillman challenged another organization of substance, Railway Air Services (R.A.S.). This group supplemented the trunk rail lines that linked London with Scotland and Northern Ireland and was owned by the Big Four railway companies of Britain. It was originally intended as an air service to speed up journeys from the southwest to the Midlands and the North, where the rail service was notoriously circuitous and slow, but in 1934 routes were opened to radiate from London.

R.A.S. opened its London–Birmingham–Manchester–Belfast–Glasgow trunk route on August 20, 1934, and it was perhaps an unintentional compliment to Hillman that the de Havilland D.H. 84 Dragon was at first the standard equipment. The railways had the advantage of a post-office mail contract, and although Hillman had begun his service to the north a month earlier than R.A.S., on July 16, 1934, he had to suspend it on July 30. Undaunted, he augmented the Paris service by an extra daily flight, making it thrice daily. By this time he had added the improved D.H. 89 Dragon Rapide and again was first into service with the new type. De Havilland could not have wished for a better salesman.

Hillman continued to promote his self-imposed image as a rough diamond but nevertheless liked to be seen as a successful man. Once, when at de Havilland, one of the salesmen there, a young man of independent and inherited wealth, tried to impress Hillman by showing him his new Rolls-Royce, which had a special body of which only three existed. Hillman's only comment was "Blimey, just like mine!" He owned one of the other two.

Hillman's route had been London–Liverpool–Isle of Man–Belfast, because he felt that the Irish Sea crossing offered the best advantage for air travel over surface modes. The R.A.S. route aimed to serve both Northern Ireland and Scotland. But before the end of the year, Hillman too had obtained a mail contract, and on December 1, 1934, he reinstated his domestic trunk service, this time omitting the Isle of Man and adding Glasgow. Both Hillman and R.A.S. thus served Northern Ireland and Scotland, using the same equipment, the former serving Liverpool and the latter serving Birmingham and Manchester en route to Belfast and Glasgow. He also leased one of his Dragons to E. L. Gandar Dower in September 1934 to start a service from Aberdeen to the far North of Scotland and to the Orkney Islands. The farmer's boy had achieved air parity with the railroad monopoly.

He did not live to indulge in the cut-and-thrust competition for air routes that was to develop during the latter 1930s before the outbreak of World War II. He died on the last day of 1934, a victim of a coronary attack. He had always suffered from high blood pressure, and in his later years he was red-faced and rotund, carrying too much weight, considering his ailment. But he suffered from what in recent years has become a common affliction—an inner compulsion to keep working long hours, every day of the week, in a continuous effort to attain ever greater objectives.

Had he lived, there is no knowing what Edward Hillman might have achieved. His spirit lived on for a while in the airline that he had so energetically launched, for the momentum was still there. On December 19, 1934, shortly before he died, Hillman's Airways became a public company. The 400,000 five-shilling shares—25 new pence, or 35 cents in today's money, but worth considerably more in those days—were taken up within an hour. But sadly, the shareholders received no dividends. In fact, Hillman's executors had to sell his own large block of shares on behalf of the family. These were purchased by the large banking house of Erlangers, which was subsequently to be closely involved with airline financing in Britain.

During the summer of 1935, the Romford–Paris service frequency was increased to four times daily and the Glasgow service to twice a day. The base of operations was transferred from Maylands to Stapleford, near Loughton, just a few miles north of Romford. Both Maylands and Stapleford, which became known as the Essex Airport, may sound as though they are miles away from London in the rural fastnesses of East Anglia. In fact, the sites of these now defunct airfields are both about the same distance from the center of London as Heathrow and considerably closer than either Gatwick or Stansted.

During the same summer, Hillman's started new routes from Stapleford to le Zoute, Brussels, and Antwerp, thus providing a comprehensive service to Belgium. This started on June 21, and Ramsgate was included in the route on July 15. Meanwhile, a branch service had been opened from Liverpool to Manchester and Hull on June 6.

Hillman's Airways' last timetable appeared on October 6, 1935, just before the British Airways takeover. The one-way fare from London to Paris was £4. The schedule shows the departure time from King's Cross Coach Station at 8:30 A.M. to connect with the aircraft departure from Essex Airport at 9:30. The de Havilland biplanes reached le Bourget at 11:15, and the arrival time at the terminal in rue Edouard VII was 11:45. The total journey between the city centers thus took 3 hours 15 minutes, half an hour less than Imperial's. To beat that even today would require a fortuitous combination of light traffic on the M4 motorway and the Péripherique, plus benevolent air traffic controllers at Heathrow and Roissy.

Within a year of his death, Hillman's Airways had disappeared. In the aforementioned struggle one of the contenders for a goodly share of the British internal air routes was a financial group called Whitehall Securities, which had an arrangement with the Railways group aimed at dividing the domestic spoils between them, while Imperial fulfilled its overseas obligations. Whitehall Securities established British Airways on October 1, 1935, by merging Spartan Airlines and United Airways, and on December 11 of the same year it pulled Hillman's into its net.

Edward Hillman's great achievement was that within the remarkably short period of three years he had developed a successful airline and had instinctively grasped the essentials of airline economics. He was the true entrepreneur, who was simply in business to make a good living for himself, at the same time to provide the proverbial better nail. His particular Emersonian objective was better service to the public, and for him the public was not the film star, cabinet minister, or business executive customarily pictured climbing the steps to board the Imperial Airways Handley Pages.

Edward Hillman's clientele were the average wage earners, and his entire approach was to try to bring the joy and convenience of air travel to that stratum of the public. Perhaps even his base at Romford symbolized this objective, for it was a small grass field, with just a few modest wooden sheds for the passengers' convenience. Also, Romford was in Essex, the side of the metropolis whose hinterland was the East End and docklands of London, at the opposite end of the social spectrum from the southern and western stockbroker belts adjacent to Croydon and Heston, the bases of Imperial and British Airways respectively.

There were many independent free spirits in Britain during the 1930s and to them can be given the greater share of the credit for developing a system of internal air routes. Some were bus operators, Sword, Thurgood, MacBrayne, and others, but none compared with Hillman for having the vision to realize that the Imperial Airways approach would never bring air transport to ordinary people. And while the other independents competed only with surface transport, rail, road, and ship, Edward Hillman took on the British flag airline.

In many ways, he was the prototype of Sir Freddie Laker, who was to attain much greater fame and notoriety half a century later. Hillman's £3.10.0 Romford–Paris service in 1933 was comparable to Laker's £59 Gatwick–New York Skytrain in 1981, in that they both challenged the Establishment. Both charged low fares, both fixed their own terms of employment without reference to unions, both were forced to operate from London's secondary airfields, and each was responsible for starting the first services by a British airliner that may fairly be judged to have achieved worldwide success. In 1933 Hillman launched the D.H. 84 Dragon, which could pay its way without subsidy and could be maintained by any competent mechanic. Thirty-two years later, Freddie Laker launched the BAC One-Eleven for British United Airways with much the same criteria, albeit at a different level of technology.

Edward Hillman did not live to enjoy the success he deserved. But during his short life—he was only forty-four when he died—he had helped to bring aviation heads out of the clouds and down to earth. His methods were rough, even primitive, but after his all-too-brief injection of inspired initiative, British air transport was never quite the same again.

▶▶▶▶▶▶▶▶▶▶▶▶ ◀ ▶▶▶▶▶▶▶▶▶▶

Capt. Edmund E. Fresson

The Honorary Orcadian

Edmund Fresson was born in England on September 20, 1891, and although he first took an interest in aviation as early as 1908, he was not able to pursue it as a career for several years. On leaving school, he joined a firm of tea merchants and was sent to Shanghai in 1911, at the relatively early age of twenty. When the Great War erupted in 1914, he volunteered for the Royal Flying Corps but became ill and did not succeed in his ambition to become an airman until three years later.

He was finally accepted, in Canada in 1917, and was posted for flight training at Camp Borden in November of that year, learning to fly in a Curtiss JN 4 Jenny. Returning to England, he did coastal patrols from Norfolk and was a flight instructor at Duxford. He left the service in June 1919 but remained in the reserve.

Ted Fresson then returned to China, and he resumed his association with airplanes when a Major Willie McBain, also a former member of the R.F.C., arrived in Shanghai with a 160-horsepower Armstrong Whitworth biplane—either an F.K. 3 or an F.K. 8. Fresson assisted in assembling it and later flew it for hire and reward.

At the end of 1923 a Chinese faction, representing one of the regional semiautonomous administrations—if such autocratic rule could be so described—approached Fresson for advice about the

Edmund Fresson is seen here in front of his de Havilland D.H. 84 Dragon, with which his Highland Airways opened service between Inverness and Aberdeen in 1934. He was responsible for developing air services throughout the Orkney and Shetland Islands, using diminutive grass fields as airports.

establishment of an aircraft factory at Taiyuan, in Shanxi province. The result was that Fresson received a contract to build a prototype, which, if successful, would be followed by a production run of fifty. Ted Fresson left the tea business, ordered materials and equipment from Aircraft Disposal Company, and, with the help of a German engineer, designed a general-purpose biplane, which made its first flight in 1925.

The mid 1920s, however, were the period of conflict in China between numerous so-called warlords. There was much intrigue, the German Junkers company interceded in Shanxi, and that was the end of Fresson's enterprise. Surprisingly, bearing in mind the sometimes chaotic circumstances of the time, he did receive compensation.

Ted Fresson left China, returned to England, and in 1928 joined Berkshire Aviation Tours, operated by F. J. V. Holmes. Then, in January 1929, together with other air-minded associates, he founded North British Aviation Company, at Hooton Park, Cheshire, close to Liverpool. North British acquired two Avro 504Ks and began operations on March 29, 1929.

In 1931, Captain Fresson flew one of the Avros on a joyriding tour to the north of Scotland. During this trip—on August 22, to be precise—he flew across the Pentland Firth from Thurso to Kirkwall and instantly realized that there was a natural demand for an air service across the stretch of water that divides the Orkney Islands from the Scottish mainland. In contrast to other mainland-to-island prospects farther south in Great Britain, the Pentland was often cursed with violent storms, dirty weather generally, and rough seas in particular. The boat trip was often most unpleasant, if not an ordeal, so airsickness on a twenty-minute flight did not seem too bad a risk by comparison with the almost certain seasickness that afflicted even experienced seafarers in those parts.

During 1932 Fresson devoted himself to the task of surveying possible trans-Pentland routes, flying a de Havilland Gipsy Moth. He selected airfield sites and sought financial support. The latter was eventually forthcoming, after much frustrating campaigning, from Macrae and Dick, motor vehicle dealers of Inverness, and from the North of Scotland and Orkney and Shetland Steam Navigation Company. Even in those days, Scottish transport interests seem to have adopted a sensible "if you can't beat them, join them" attitude. So, with help from land and sea, Highland Airways was registered on April 3, 1933, in Edinburgh, with capital of £2,675. Fresson was the managing director, doubling as chief pilot.

Wisely realizing that, in this sparsely populated region of the British Isles, traffic density would not be at the same level as on the London–Paris route, Fresson obtained a small Monospar ST 4 aircraft, able to carry only three passengers. This diminutive miniairliner, however, christened *Inverness*, had two engines, which could be comforting when it was halfway across the Pentland Firth with half a gale blowing up. Wasting no time, Fresson started scheduled service on May 8, 1933, from Inverness, the unofficial capital of the Scottish Highlands, to Kirkwall, via Wick, county towns, respectively, of Orkney and Caithness. Three days later, an additional route was started from Kirkwall to Thurso, on Scotland's far northern coast, opposite Orkney, and the only other town in Caithness. During the first three months, not a flight was missed, in spite of many days of fog.

Fresson's airfields matched his aircraft, and any of them would be regarded today as inadequate even as ramp space for a Boeing 747. The one at Inverness was a grass area—as were all airfields, large or small, in 1933—but had the important advantage of being only five minutes' walk from the center of town. Those at Kirkwall, Wick, and Thurso, while a little farther into the countryside, were nevertheless only a few minutes' ride away by car, bus, or bicycle from their respective town halls or post offices.

To judge the kind of innovative strides that Fresson was making, some account should be taken of the contemporary transport environment. To travel from London all the way to Inverness by train in the early 1930s was almost as rare an occurrence as to fly from London to the Falkland Islands today. To continue on, by the final segment of the London, Midland, and Scottish Railway, by the daily train, which stopped at every station, was akin to taking a branch line train in the Australian outback. Fresson's 1 hour 20 minute Monospar trip from Inverness to Kirkwall, saving as it did no less than nine hours over the surface alternative, was therefore a dramatic demonstration of the value of scheduled airline service in the far north of Scotland.

Incidentally, in spite of the small size of the Monospar it was able to carry a specially designed pannier beneath the fuselage, for which Fresson paid £70. One of its main purposes was to deliver copies of *The Scotsman* newspaper from Inverness to the remote fastnesses of the United Kingdom, for the Highland Airways service permitted delivery of the precious written word a full day earlier than had previously been possible. In the early days of domestic air service, newspapers, in fact, were one of the categories of air freight most commonly carried, and airlines were even formed for the sole purpose of providing quick delivery. As late as 1933—or, for that matter, even today—no educated Scot would be without his *Scotsman* as the source of the only true word, and if for no other reason, Highland Airways and Captain Fresson were regarded in the Orkneys with as much respect as the entire British Broadcasting Corporation.

The Thurso service had to be closed down during the winter of 1933–34 for lack of traffic, even though the single fare was only

£1—which, however, was almost a week's wage for most working people in the Orkneys. The short trans-Pentland trip had to be fitted in during the aircraft's ground time at Kirkwall between northbound and southbound Inverness-originating flights, and this was difficult during the short winter day in the northern latitudes because Kirkwall is almost as far north as Anchorage, Alaska.

The year 1934 witnessed the flowering of Highland Airways from a cautious, quasi-experimental one-man operation into a full-fledged airline, with a staff of three: pilot, engineer, and groundsman. With the beginning of the new season, a new de Havilland D.H. 84 Dragon, G-ACIT *Aberdeen*, opened a new route from Inverness to the city of that name on May 7. The Dragon offered passengers the luxury of not having to carry their suitcases on their laps, as they did in the Monospar. Planning the new service was not without difficulty. Simultaneously with Fresson's efforts in the far north, a fellow visionary and free spirit, Eric Gandar Dower, had staked his claim at Aberdeen and had built the airfield there, metaphorically with his bare hands. Understandably, he retained the exclusive rights at that field, near the village of Dyce, for his own airline, Aberdeen Airways. Fresson had to use a field at Seaton, near the Bridge of Don, which, fortuitously, was actually closer to the center of Aberdeen than Dyce.

Rivalry between Fresson and Gandar Dower was keen from then on, although the two were never actually recorded as having fought a duel. Nevertheless, they wrestled grimly for pride of place as Scotland's leading local airline promoter. Fresson exacted mild revenge on Gandar Dower by refusing him permission to land at Highland Airways fields, and Aberdeen Airways had to seek separate landing grounds, just as Fresson had had to shop around in Aberdeen. The official Air Ministry information circular, for example, stated quite firmly that Wick airfield was private, controlled by Highland Airways, and that "a full schedule in respect of this landing ground will not be published, since the licensee reserves the site for his exclusive use and no facilities are available for unauthorized aircraft." The Scots are not known for mincing words, and this was plain language, directed at Fresson's rival in Aberdeen.

On May 29, 1934, after about eighteen months' procrastination by the Post Office, which seemed not to have believed Fresson's impressive service record, Highland Airways began a nonsurcharged air mail service between Inverness and Kirkwall, the first such service in the entire British Isles. It was flown by Fresson himself, and when it arrived at Kirkwall, a thousand people were there to greet the de Havilland Dragon. The occasion was the Orkney Islands equivalent in miniature of the scene at le Bourget, Paris, when Lindbergh arrived with *The Spirit of St. Louis* in 1927. On the return flight from Kirkwall to Inverness, Fresson carried 1,200 letters. Subsequently Fresson was justifiably proud of his record of punctuality and regularity. He would maintain the schedule even if he was the only occupant of the aircraft, and crofter and fisherman alike would set their watches by his passing.

No less important for the Orkney Islands was a new service started on August 6 of the same year, using the trusty Monospar. It took off from Kirkwall and made subsequent flights, by various itineraries, depending upon traffic, demand, weather, or the state of the airfields, to Longhope, on the island of Hoy, and to small fields on the islands of Stronsay, Sanday, Rousay, Westray, and North Ronaldsay. Such were the appalling weather conditions at times that flights to these tiny communities were possible only during the summer months—and this restriction applied to the steamship services as well.

North Ronaldsay, the most northerly of the Orkney Islands, wanted Fresson to operate there and invited him to take the boat from Kirkwall and look for a possible landing site. He found two fields that would be adequate if joined together. As he explained to the islanders, "This would take time because the hedge has to be removed, a ditch filled in, levelled, and so on." "Rubbish," said the head man of the island. He ordered every fit man to be at the field first thing the following morning. By lunchtime the job was done.

Highland Airways disappeared after World War II, by absorption into British European Airways. Few services to these outer Orkneys were subsequently maintained, and to some points none at all, until Loganair, a latter-day Highland Airways, resumed operations in the 1960s. This alone is some indication of the pioneering enthusiasm of Captain Edmund Fresson and other Scottish airline promoters of his ilk during the formative years of the British domestic scheduled airline network.

In 1935, when Highland Airways resumed service on a through route from Aberdeen to Kirkwall, via Wick, Fresson had to find another airfield at Aberdeen. This was not only because of further intransigence by Eric Gandar Dower, but also for the curious reason that the site was required by the local authorities for the Highland Show. No doubt there would have been some danger from low-flying cabers. In any event, Fresson had to move to a field at Kintore, no less than ten miles northwest of Aberdeen, which in those days was considered a long way to go to catch an airplane. Dyce Airport was along the same road, halfway to Kintore, a circumstance that must have given a great deal of satisfaction to Eric Gandar Dower and a great deal of irritation to Edmund Fresson.

On June 1, 1935, the Highland Airways mail service was advertised as being extended to the Shetland Islands, but this was somewhat deceptive, because the segment between Kirkwall and Lerwick, county town of Shetland, was served by ship. Highland did not operate the Kirkwall–Thurso route in 1935, and the trans-Pentland service was performed by Aberdeen Airways, with the island terminus at Stromness, the other Orkney town. Continuing the tit-for-tat rivalry, Gandar Dower had to build his own Thurso airfield at Clardon, almost next door to Fresson's former field at West Murkle.

Admirable though Fresson's pioneering efforts were, however, he could not continue independently, simply because Highland Airways was losing money. Although the environment was in theory ideal for air transport, the actual potential revenue was simply not sufficient. The Orkney Islanders did not maintain their letter-writing tempo after the inaugural service out of Kirkwall, and the industries of the area were largely self-sufficient, generating little business traffic. Tourism was nonexistent, and there was a limit to the number of subscribers to *The Scotsman*. Neither did Fresson have Eric Gandar Dower's resources. When the latter lost money on his airways operation, he was able to sell another piece of property in London to reinforce the finances of Aberdeen Airways. Rather than close down, Fresson was obliged to merge with another, better endowed, airline group.

On April 4, 1935, United Airways had been formed in London, backed mainly by a financing corporation, Whitehall Securities, which had decided to enter the airline business, first forming United, whose services were primarily between London and Blackpool. It then began to buy other domestic companies, and on September 30, a master plan took shape as Hillman's Airways and

Spartan Air Lines merged with United to form, at first, Allied British Airways, which then, on October 29, changed its name to British Airways.

Truth to tell, many of the early British airline pioneers—a surprising number of them former omnibus operators who had been thrown out of business by a rationalization of the national bus and coach industry into large groups—were easily picked off by the Whitehall Securities group. Independent men such as Edward Hillman, W. L. Thurgood (Jersey Airways), John Sword (Midland and Scottish Air Ferries), and even Ted Fresson, of Highland Airways, were vulnerable. Typically, they had exhausted their slender capital, were perilously close to losing money, and the only alternative, short of bankruptcy, was to close down. Eric Gandar Dower was almost alone in being able to resist the pressures of a takeover bid, because of independent sources of wealth.

Thus, Captain Fresson merged with United Airways as early as June 1935, although this was not widely publicized at the time, because he continued to operate under the Highland Airways name. In October, when the amalgamated companies became British Airways, Fresson and the residual operations of the other Scottish independent, Midland and Scottish Airways, adopted that title for the winter, but in 1936 they reverted to operating under their own company names.

One of the advantages of being part of a well-financed group was that the resources to obtain better aircraft were available, and Fresson was thus able to add a de Havilland D. H. 89A Dragon Rapide to his fleet in 1935 and a second one in 1936. After reopening the Aberdeen–Wick–Kirkwall route on May 4, 1936, Fresson extended it on June 3 to Sumburgh, the new airport at the southernmost tip of the main island of the Shetlands.

Typical of the rivalry between Fresson and Gandar Dower at the time was the latter's reaction when learning of the planned extension of Highland Airways to the Shetlands. One day before Fresson, Gandar Dower's chief pilot, Eric Starling, not only began service, but in November the following year inaugurated the mail service, under a contract with the Post Office, as well.

As Starling remarked, "Fresson, of course, was hopping mad"—which was probably putting it mildly, for Fresson had been planning the route carefully for many months. And to compound the agony, the British Air Ministry had refused to install radio at either Sumburgh or Kirkwall, a decision which, in retrospect, was extraordinary, considering the immense social service the fledgling airlines were providing for some of Britain's remotest communities. The local authorities also refused to bear the cost of employing control officers, which was again surprising, considering the enthusiasm with which they had welcomed Fresson in the first place.

The supreme irony was that Fresson's Highland Airways supplied the control officers at a total cost of £350 a year and also paid for the upkeep of the airfields. But the installation of radio technically made them available for public use, and Highland—somewhat unfairly in the circumstances—had to give up its monopoly rights, in spite of having been refused permission to use Dyce Airport at Aberdeen. Kirkwall's radio was in operation by May 1936 and Sumburgh's by the following month. But Inverness did not reach that stage of high technology until the following year. And Eric Gandar Dower, who owned Dyce, saw no reason to install radio and thus permit all and sundry, including Edmund Fresson, to use his airfield.

Right from the beginning Captain Fresson had realized that the Western Isles, those many islands off the western coast of Scotland, were as much in need of air service as the Orkneys and Shetlands. On March 8, 1934, he took the D.H. Dragon G-ACIT from Inverness to Stornoway, the chief town of Lewis, but was never able to obtain permission to build an airstrip. This was partly because the only suitable ground in the vicinity was on a golf course, which in Scotland is considered to be hallowed ground. But Fresson made charter flights, partly for the convenience of the local council members of Stornoway, who needed to attend meetings of the Ross and Cromarty County Council at Dingwall, near Inverness.

On August 12, 1937, Highland Airways and Northern and Scottish Airways merged to form Scottish Airways. Northern and Scottish had been formed by yet another omnibus operator, George Nicholson, late in 1934, and had taken over the routes in the west of Scotland when John Sword was forced to abdicate under pressure from the railways. They had alleged a conflict of interest because of his former association with the Scottish Motor Traction Company, which was linked with the railways. At this time, 50 percent of the ownership was taken up by the London, Midland, and Scottish (L.M.S.) Railway and its bus-operating Scottish associate, David McBrayne.

Thus a rare battle was waged for the Scottish airline skies, although happily the D.H. Rapides were not equipped with machine guns. Indeed the opposite was the case. The pilots themselves, who kept up an amazing record of regularity with the flimsy canvas-and-wood biplanes of that era, developed a camaraderie that sustained both their senses of humor and their well-being—as well as, on occasion, their record of regularity.

Eric Starling tells a charming story of how, when he was with Gandar Dower at Aberdeen, a much-needed spare part would usually come up on the overnight train from the de Havilland factory at Hatfield, north of London, which happened to be on the same railway network, the London and North Eastern Railway (L.N.E.R.). Landing gears gave them special trouble, and sometimes a friend in Highland Airways would oblige by sending the necessary spare component on the evening local train from Inverness, thus saving a precious twelve hours or so. On one occasion, Eric Gandar Dower, who knew there was a landing gear repair job to be done and that the morning departure would therefore be delayed, was surprised to observe the Dragon leaving on time, at 9 A.M. Any suspicion of fraternizing with the enemy would normally have produced a strong reaction, but this time G.D. discreetly remarked "Perhaps it's best if I ask no questions."

Flying in the north of Scotland was undoubtedly different in those days, especially with the legendary and ever-present Scottish mist. Overnight hangarage was almost essential for—again to quote Starling—"a soggy wet Dragon would be one passenger short and ten miles an hour slower than specification." As for the Monospar G-ACEW, this little airplane made some remarkable flights, not least one by Fresson—who else?—on May 13, 1937. On that day he carried one passenger from Orkney to Fair Isle, an isolated rocky islet twenty-seven miles east-northeast of North Ronaldsay, the outermost island of the Orkneys. The occasion was also to deliver newspapers marking the accession of Edward VIII, and Fresson himself described the scene as a "three quarter circle of cliffs 300 feet high and the length was 275 yards. If I boshed the landing there was a nice little drop over the edge." Very few landings were made there, except by some foolhardy seagulls, for many years. The navy started to build a landing strip there only just before the end of the war, and later the aforementioned Loganair put the is-

land and its famous sweaters in closer touch with the rest of the
world.

John Stroud, the doyen of British aviation writers, claimed
that the Monospar was a good airplane in bad weather when gales
could reach seventy miles an hour or so and that it showed no tendency to blow over on the ground in very high winds. Not noted for
making exaggerated statements, Stroud observed that "at times it
must have had precious little ground speed when battling with
headwinds." This could quite possibly mean that, like certain D.H.
Rapides which witnesses at Gibraltar have sworn were actually losing headway when observed against a fixed point on the Rock, the
Monospar was quite capable of flying backward, given the right
winds. Hyperbole apart, there was an occasion when Adam Smith
defied the gales to bring much-needed supplies to North Ronaldsay. On his next trip, the total population, all 160 of them, were at
the little airfield to greet him and present him with a silver cigarette case.

Considering that it was built mainly of wood and canvas, the
de Havilland D.H. 84 Dragon also showed amazing resilience. The
one that joined Fresson's fleet in 1933 and that started the service
to Aberdeen, flew throughout World War II and was finally retired
by British European Airways after the conflict. It was sold in 1984
at an auction of the contents of the Southend Air Museum and finally found its way into the Science Museum in London. All the
British prewar domestic airlines had a great affection for the
Dragon, and partnerships of shrewd pilot and well-built airplane
bestowed upon such companies as Highland Airways and Aberdeen Airways a perfect safety record.

There were, of course, some near misses. Adam Smith, a veteran Highland Airways pilot, recalled that once when trying to fly
from Glasgow to Inverness—this would have been after the amalgamation—he was forced to a height of 17,000 feet in an unpressurized Dragon. When he finally found a hole in the clouds through
which to descend, he noticed that the land was on the wrong side.
He had been blown from one coast of Scotland to the other and was
near Ullapool, in the far northwest, instead of in the vicinity of the
Moray Firth in the northeast.

One of Fresson's pilots crashed two Dragons, sending up the
insurance rates of Highland Airways and earning the pilot the nick-

name of St. George the Second because he slew two Dragons. The pilot joined Imperial Airways.

When, on the rare occasions that even Fresson's hardy pilots felt that discretion was the better part of valor, there was a mutual understanding that if the weather was too bad for Highland Airways, it was too bad for Aberdeen Airways too. Eric Starling recalls that "if we [he and Adam Smith] decided not to go, we'd go into Aberdeen together and get plastered." This was apparently as much a case of mutual insurance against the fear of being upstaged as it was for mutual enjoyment.

But these inebriated diversions were exceptions to the rule. Highland Airways maintained an amazing record of regularity, which continued after it had become Scottish Airways. Such was the reputation established by Captain Fresson, however, that even though the name "Scottish" was painted on the airplanes, the official name was seldom used, either by the staff or by the public. Fresson remained with Scottish Airways and subsequently with the Associated Airways Joint Committee group during the War. He also remained with the temporarily rejuvenated Scottish Airways until February 1, 1947, when all the domestic airlines of the United Kingdom except Channel Islands Airways and the recalcitrant Gandar Dower, who followed shortly thereafter, were taken over by British European Airways.

Captain E. E. Fresson could easily have accepted a sinecure under the new nationalized system. In a strange mixture of capitalist laissez faire and socialist bureaucracy, Highland Airways, which Fresson had managed to sustain as a viable operation with very little help from a parent corporation, suddenly became top heavy with staff and departments, often duplicating those at the head office in London. The managing director of B.E.A., Gerard d'Erlanger, could not understand Fresson, and the feeling was mutual. But while Fresson's bookkeeping losses were modest, d'Erlanger's were unbelievable.

During the entire period, from the founding of Highland Airways in April 1933 and for the next fourteen years under its various names and administrations, Captain Fresson's individual personality had been the common denominator. Memories of the operations, adventurous and unusual though they were, have gradually receded. Stories of derring-do in the far north were seldom disseminated even as far as Edinburgh and Glasgow, much less south of the Scottish border, where climate and conditions are more benevolent.

Scottish Airways and Allied Airways continued operations right through the war. They did close temporarily at the outbreak and were pulled in to help in the evacuation from France in 1940. Since radar stations, naval bases, and service airfields were appearing all over the islands, however, Winston Churchill directed that the airlines should continue, because, with their specialized flying techniques, they were best suited to keep regular communications open.

The name of Fresson, who died on September 25, 1963, is still a watchword throughout the Orkney and Shetland islands, which first received, through his initiative, the inestimable advantage of dependable air service. And at the Kirkwall airport today, there is a special little monument to one of aviation's lesser known folk heroes, who, in his own way, was something of a public benefactor.

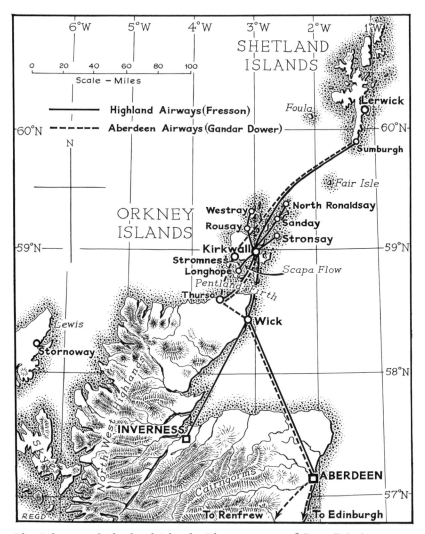

The Orkney and Shetland Islands. *These outposts of Great Britain were several days removed from Edinburgh or London until Edmund Fresson and Eric Gandar Dower connected them to the mainland by a system of air routes. Many of the smaller islands possessed airstrips no longer than a football field.*

Eric L. Gandar Dower

Actor Turned Airman

Eric L. Gandar Dower was one of those rare men who are naturally gifted, able to excel in almost any field of activity that takes their fancy. He enjoyed the benefit of inherited wealth, his grandfather having established a family fortune in real property after immigrating to England from Eastern Europe. Eric's father continued the good work, with the result that his son, born in 1895, went to Brighton College, one of Britain's best public—private, in American terminology—schools.

He was fascinated by airplanes at an early age. The Rheims air meet in France caught his attention in 1908. The following year, at the age of fourteen, he motorcycled from Brighton to Dover to see Blériot's aircraft after its epic flight across the Channel. And while at Brighton College, he once played truant to visit the first British Flying School, which had been established at Amesbury, on Salisbury Plain. He made his first flight in 1913 as a passenger, from Shoreham, near Brighton, and landed in the grounds of the Roedean School for Girls.

Aviation was only one of the versatile Gandar Dower's interests. He was a good sportsman, excelling in cricket and football, and would doubtless have played for Sussex, possibly for England, had he put his mind to it. He also possessed a natural literary talent, expressed in some early poetry and a consuming interest in amateur dramatics. This led to his attending the Royal Academy of

Dramatic Art—the prestigious RADA—in October 1914, but by this time the Great War had broken out, and in March 1915, he joined the Royal Naval Air Service as a flight sublieutenant.

But the theater was his first love, and as soon as the war had ended, he went back to it and established himself as a competent actor of great promise. Using the stage name of Eric Leslie, he quickly graduated to a well-known Shakespearean touring company promoted by Mr. (later Sir Philip) Ben Greet. His performances drew good reviews everywhere he went, and by 1921 he was touring with his own company. E. L. Gandar Dower from the start was one of those who are naturally inclined to manage things for themselves rather than be managed.

During that year he had also written his first play, *The Silent Husband*, but his promising stage career then came to an abrupt end in a curious manner. It was typical of Gandar Dower that, while on a brief holiday at Ryde, in the Isle of Wight, playing in a tennis tournament—which he doubtless won—he dived off the pier into a rough sea to rescue a small boy from drowning. This meritorious performance was recognized when Sir Cyril Cobb, chairman of the London County Council, presented him with the Royal Humane Society's award at a performance of *As You Like It* at the Euston Empire.

This was reported in the press, and the story unfortunately reached the eyes and ears of his father, who was in control of the family fortunes. Eric had been the least businesslike of the family, and for his own good, his inheritance was put in trust until 1923, when he would reach the age of twenty-eight. His father is reported to have declared, in almost classic dramatic fashion—which Eric would well understand—"Stop all this acting nonsense or I will cut you off without a penny." Actually, the sum was £100, or about $500 a year at the rate of exchange at the time, hardly enough to keep Eric Gandar Dower in the manner to which he was accustomed.

Back to school he went, to Jesus College, Cambridge, where he earned a master's degree. While this is no easy task at Cambridge, the chances are that Gandar Dower took it almost in his spare time. During his last year at Cambridge, 1926, the General Strike broke out throughout Great Britain, and industry and transport almost came to a standstill. Eric was one of the adventurous band of cavaliers who had the means to provide transport with their own

Eric Gandar Dower, seen here receiving a commendation from Princess Alexandra, founded Aberdeen Airways in 1934, built the airport at Aberdeen, and fought the railway interests, financial predators, and the post–World War II state airline, in a continuous series of conflicts to retain his independence.

cars and who volunteered to drive buses and to help run London's underground railway.

By one of those whims of fate that control our destinies, it was while driving a London bus down Piccadilly that Gandar Dower chanced to stop at the Royal Aero Club to pick up some mail and there met Robert Cowell Smith, who was a fellow aviation enthusiast. Cowell Smith was a Scot, from Banchory, near Aberdeen, and Gandar Dower was intrigued with his suggestion that there was a need for a flying school at Aberdeen.

With absolutely no reservation or qualification, Eric Gandar Dower can take the full credit for bringing aviation to northeastern Scotland, particularly to its metropolis, Aberdeen. In March 1931, he flew to the Granite City in a Blackburn Bluebird, which immediately became an object of curiosity when stored in some garage space at Aberdeen Motors. He could have charged admission to look at it, so rare was the sight of an airplane in the distant northeast of Great Britain in those days. He bought 200 acres of land at Dyce, a village four miles northwest of the center of Aberdeen, and began to build an airport.

In Gandar Dower's own words: "Work greeted and swallowed us. I was a social disappointment. Invitations to fish and shoot were declined. Society shrugged shoulders and condemned the recluse. Weekends and holidays were burnt up—never less than twelve hours a day. Farms were bought and thousands of tons of rock removed. Burns [streams] were diverted and 650 yards of one encased in a concrete culvert." After three years of dedicated hard labor, Eric L. Gandar Dower triumphantly opened Dyce Airport, to serve Aberdeen and its hinterland, on July 28, 1934.

At that time, the village of Dyce had no electricity. Gandar Dower at first provided his own, with a diesel generator, then had to pay to have the power extended from the neighboring community of Stoneywood. For this privilege he had to guarantee a minimum consumption, and the fact that the good citizens of Dyce received electricity for the first time was not taken into account.

By this time he had also decided to form an airline, establishing Aberdeen Airways on January 2, 1934, with capital of £29,000. It was registered in Edinburgh, with the declared intention to operate scheduled services within Scotland and across the North Sea.

Gandar Dower had built his own airport. Now, to launch an airline he needed aircraft and capable personnel. As to the former, he owned a Short Scion, and with this small machine he took four guests on the inaugural flight to Renfrew, the airport serving Glasgow, on September 10, 1934. The guest list on this historic journey perhaps provides a commentary on the air travel market in Britain in the mid 1930s. Eric Gandar Dower's guests were Viscount Arbuthnott, Admiral Farquhar, a Major Struthers, and J. G. Burnett, a member of parliament. Aberdeen Airways seemed to be going first class.

Gandar Dower had, by this time, hired a pilot, Eric Starling (always known as Eric Allen, to avoid confusion with his employer) whose story is remarkable in its own right.

Eric Starling had just recently learned to fly. Like many a young man of his day with the spirit of adventure in his veins, he took flying lessons at Gatwick, which was then a small grass field on the borders of Sussex and Surrey, south of London. One of the qualifying tests was to make a night flight, without radio, to prove the pilot's ability to navigate solely by the stars or by reference to recognizable lights of towns and any other barely visible landmarks below. On May 16, 1933, Starling set off from Gatwick to Lympne, that great private flying rendezvous close to Folkstone, on the coast of Kent.

To cut a long story short, Starling got lost, and after flying around for a while, searching for a familiar set of lights, he glimpsed a fairly large town, which he did not recognize. Running

short of fuel, however, he was forced to seek a landing, and he decided to bring his aircraft down on one of the well-lit but now deserted streets. He had to avoid the main roads, for these carried a
network of streetcar overhead wires, and indeed, he had to be careful to bring his aircraft down smartly, and to stay down, in one of
the side streets before it intersected with the overhead wires of a
main crosstreet.

Starling landed in a street in Calais, France, in the middle of
the night, with only a slight mishap as his wing caught a lamp standard. He thereby became an instant celebrity of dubious distinction. He was treated most courteously by the French authorities,
not even arrested for dangerous driving, but he had to pay for the
repair of the lamp standard. His biggest problem was to ship the
aircraft back to England, with no papers to prove that it had ever
left the country.

The sequel to this remarkable episode was that Eric Gandar
Dower heard of it, went down to Gatwick, and hired the other Eric
on the spot. The latter's main qualification to be chief pilot of Aberdeen Airways was, "You're as mad as I am."

Gandar Dower's constant companion at this time was a Miss
Brunning, known as C.B. to her friends, who was always at his side,
keeping the books, and continually providing advice, which as often as not was ignored. Eventually they were married, although
this was more in the nature of a financial precaution, British death
duties being what they are, rather than in recognition of the sanc-
tity of marriage.

Aberdeen Airways began a daily service from Aberdeen to
Renfrew, using the Scion and sometimes a de Havilland D.H. 84
Dragon leased from Edward Hillman. Hillman had named it *Maylands*, the name of his airfield at Romford, Essex. Now it was re-
christened *Starling* in tribute to Aberdeen's other Eric. The pilots
normally followed the railway lines for navigation and were handicapped by the complete absence of radio aids in that region. While
the eastern side of Scotland is not the most mountainous in that
land, there is no lack of mountains and hills, interspersed with
large estuaries from the North Sea, all combining to provide
weather and visibility of a most uncertain nature.

Edward Hillman and Eric Gandar Dower, at opposite ends of
the social scale, had much in common. Both were fiercely independent, running their own shows and overcoming apparently impossi-

ble odds—as much from bureaucracy and opposing vested interests as from technical shortcomings—to achieve their objectives. In Hillman's case, ground transport was no problem, for he already had a fleet of 300 motor coaches. Gandar Dower had to buy a bus to persuade thrifty and cautious Aberdonians to go out to Dyce to ride in an airplane. In the early days traffic was so sparse that he found that a small car would suffice. He even collected passengers from their own homes.

Miss Dunning reported that in the first week of operations receipts from selling tickets had been £8.15.0 (£8.75 in today's currency) and that expenditure had been £450, hardly a promising beginning. The lack of enthusiasm for air travel was understandable. There was little comfort on the Dragons, which were built of wood and canvas and were very draughty. There was no heat, and rugs were a necessity. Flights were often bumpy and airsickness was not unknown. The excellent rail service between Aberdeen and Edinburgh, warm, comfortable, and invulnerable to the uncertain weather, suffered no dilution of traffic.

Gandar Dower quickly realized that the marginal improvement in journey time in good weather would not compensate for the irregularity and discomfort of air travel compared with the rail service on an overland route. He was forced to cut the service to Renfrew down to twice weekly in the winter of 1934–35 but, undaunted, sought other, more logical outlets for his airline.

Accordingly, on May 27, 1935, Aberdeen Airways began daily service from Aberdeen to the Orkney Islands, via the far north of the Scottish mainland, in the county of Caithness, at Wick and Thurso. Although there was an airfield at Wick, Gandar Dower had to build one at Thurso, and because Kirkwall, in the Orkneys, was the preserve of Captain E. E. Fresson's Highland Airways, he had to rent a field at Stromness, the only other town in Orkney.

This service gave the public something it really needed. The journey by air from Aberdeen to Orkney was only a little more than an hour by D.H. Dragon, whereas the meandering rail journey and trans-Pentland Firth boat ride combined to make a trek of more than eleven hours, with the possibility of seasickness thrown in. The air ferry from Thurso to Stromness took only 15 minutes, while the trip took 2½ hours by boat.

Operating a fledgling airline in the north of Scotland in those days required versatility. Pilots sold tickets and made out their own loadsheets. They deliberately overweighed passengers if there was some concern about field length and conditions, and under-weighed them if there was a good strong wind. Starling reports "we frequently flew with the trimmer fully forward and still had to push on the stick to keep level. When we started carrying mail in the Rapides, we would take all the seats down out of the port side, put the passengers in, and then stack mailbags on the left side nearly up to the roof. I used to take the fire axe up front so that I could get out if anything went wrong."

Gandar Dower always paid great tribute to his pilots, who—in striking contrast to Edward Hillman's disparaging viewpoint—he realized were the backbone of his operation. He was always pre-pared to sing the praises of his pilots, who "knew every blade of grass between Aberdeen and the Moray Firth and on to Wick."

During 1935 also, starting on June 11, Aberdeen Airways be-gan a daily service to Edinburgh, connecting with North Eastern Airways, which had started a service between the English and Scot-tish capitals. North Eastern was obliged to terminate its opera-tions in July and did not reopen until the end of the following year; the suspension of service was the result of an unsavory episode in the annals of British transport.

The railways had, for a whole century, monopolized intercity travel throughout the British Isles. Not until after the Great War was there a real threat from the roads. Motorized traffic was still a novelty in the early part of the twentieth century, and only in the early 1920s were buses and coaches developed to be efficient enough to challenge the trains. By 1930, however, long-distance coaches were enabling poor people to travel from the industrial Midlands or from London to seaside towns at an incredibly low price. For about a pound, a Londoner could travel to Devon and back, and such was the popularity of this road traffic, together with competitive local bus services all over the country, that the railways felt the first breath of competition.

No sooner had the road threat been contained, largely by re-strictive legislation that rationalized into regional groups the prolif-eration of madly competing coach companies, than the threat of in-dependent airlines raised its ugly head. The railways did not worry too much about such people as Edward Hillman, who was con-cerned with battling Imperial Airways. But they regarded the com-bination of North Eastern and Aberdeen Airways as a diabolical plot to destroy their birthright, because the air routes of those two companies precisely paralleled the main trunk route of the London and North Eastern Railway (L.N.E.R.). The route of the *Flying Scotsman*, as the 10 A.M. train from King's Cross Station had been popularly known since time immemorial, was sacrosanct, and to fly over it was the railway equivalent of sacrilege.

Of course, the percentage of air traffic diverted from the railways by the airlines was hardly measurable, but having had their fingers burned once by the motor coaches, the rail executives moved with alacrity to nip the threatened aerial attack in the bud. The word went out to all travel agents that if they sold airline tickets, the privilege of selling rail tickets would be withdrawn. While the agents sold only a small proportion of the rail tickets, they sold a high proportion of the air tickets, and such an action was potentially crippling to the likes of Eric Gandar Dower.

To compound his problems, the Aberdeen Corporation tried to take over, by compulsory purchase, Dyce Airport, the one that Eric Gandar Dower had almost literally built with his bare hands. It cost Eric £5,000—and the sale of another property in London, no doubt—to resist this flanking attack. All these irritations were fought against a financial situation that was far from healthy and would have deterred all but such a person as Eric Gandar Dower, who had both the obstinate determination and the means to back it up. As Aberdeen Airways steadily lost money, Gandar Dower steadily sold more property in London to keep his airline afloat.

In spite of the opposition, it continued to expand. On June 2, 1936, the Orkney route was extended to Shetland, with Eric Starling making the inaugural flight in a new de Havilland D.H. 89 Dragon Rapide. Even with stops, the 1-hour-35-minute Aberdeen-Shetland flight compared favorably with the 18-hour sea journey. North Eastern, meanwhile, had reopened its East Coast trunk service from London, on November 2, 1936, with stops in northern England but terminating at Perth, the gateway to the Highlands, in preference to Edinburgh.

Gandar Dower changed the name of his airline from Aberdeen Airways to Allied Airways (Gandar Dower), in March 1937. This was in preparation for a route expansion, which introduced an intriguing new element to his operation. On July 12 of that year, Eric Starling took off in a new D.H. 86B Express airliner from Newcastle to Stavanger, Norway, to inaugurate direct service across the

North Sea to Scandinavia. The 2½-hour flight from Newcastle was timed to connect with the new streamlined L.N.E.R. express train, the *Coronation*, and at Stavanger, the Allied D.H. 86 connected with the D.N.L. (Norwegian Air Lines) service to Oslo, and thence to Stockholm and Copenhagen. The London–Oslo journey could be accomplished within a day, whereas it took almost two days by ship.

On November 23, 1937, Eric Starling—who else?—carried the first air mail to the Shetland Islands, an interesting commentary on the axiom that charity should begin at home, for by this time, air mail had been carried to the farthest points in the British Empire for several years, and the Empire Air Mail Scheme, under which all letters were carried by air, without surcharge, was to open less than three months later.

Relief came at last to Gandar Dower on October 21, 1938, when the British government established the Air Transport Licensing Authority to regulate the airlines, thus reassuring the railways that free-for-all competition would not arise and providing security for the airlines by allocating them spheres of influence in which to operate. Allied received confirmation in all of its routes radiating from Aberdeen to Thurso, Kirkwall (Orkney), Stromness (Orkney), and Shetland. In December of the same year, a government White Paper gave details of subsidies to be paid to the airlines for providing essential domestic services, and Allied Airways (Gandar Dower) was one of the chosen few.

Possibly the most satisfactory development of the government policy regarding internal air routes was that it specifically criticized the action of the railways in banning agency ticket sales and put a stop to this despicable practice. Eric Gandar Dower's trials seemed to be at an end.

This happy state of affairs—an operating environment which would permit an efficient airline to grow and prosper—was short-lived. Less than a year later, on September 3, 1939, World War II began in Europe, and all internal airlines shut down immediately. After protests, Allied Airways was allowed to resume operations at the end of September, but by this time all the pilots except one had joined the Royal Air Force and the ground staff was depleted.

When the Associated Airways Joint Committee (A.A.J.C.) was formed, on May 5, 1940, to coordinate internal air services during the period of emergency, Allied was not included in the airline group, which was centered on the Railway Air Services organization. Gandar Dower had a separate agreement with the secretary of state for air and operated under contract directly with the government. The services of Allied were of great importance, serving as they did the Orkney Island group, which surrounded the great Royal Navy base of Scapa Flow.

At the end of the war, on December 31, 1945, the contract with the government was terminated. The next few months were to prove heartrending for Eric Gandar Dower. Not one to suffer fools gladly, he was now inundated with fools from every direction. The ethics of the Lands Department of the Air Ministry, responsible for derequisitioning land, were highly questionable over the matter of sovereignty of Dyce Airport. The problem of who should own the other airfields was almost moot, as most had been destroyed. And overshadowing the entire scene, the postwar Labour government introduced a rigid system of nationalized airlines, denying the right of any private person or company to operate a scheduled air service.

To mention the smaller problems first, the war put an end to air service to Thurso and Stromness. In the former case, a junior army officer had conscientiously ordered a team of bulldozers to cut trenches across the field to stop German air forces from landing—possibly a laudable gesture early in the war, in view of Thurso's proximity to Scapa Flow, but of little satisfaction to Gandar Dower, who had built the Thurso airfield. Thurso's hangar and offices had been requisitioned and all Gandar Dower's possessions had been destroyed or lost. At Stromness, the Norwegian army had taken possession and rendered the field useless to aircraft, while the Navy removed the hangar for use as a cinema.

These were minor problems, however, compared with the situation at Dyce. The airport had been requisitioned for wartime use, but when the war was over, to Gandar Dower's astonishment the Air Ministry blandly informed him that it was going to keep it. Furthermore, adding insult to injury, it now proceeded to charge him for the use of his own hangar and for permission to land at his own airport. He must have regretted the honorable way in which he had kept his books during the war, making only a token claim for services rendered under its contract with the government. He could easily have made a number of justifiable bookkeeping entries, not to mention paying himself a salary, and could have made a small fortune out of the war, as some others in his position would have done.

Of course, with the nationalization of the airlines, Allied Airways (Gandar Dower) was a nonoperating company after World War II. Eventually, on April 12, 1947, it was absorbed by the newly formed British European Airways (B.E.A.), under a price settlement that Gandar Dower described as generous. The negotiations with B.E.A. were in marked contrast with those of the Air Ministry, the War Office, and the Admiralty, which dragged on for twenty years. When these claims were eventually settled, in 1966, after a postwar period twice as long as the entire operating history of Aberdeen/ Allied Airways, including the war, the interest paid on the accumulated amount of compensation was a paltry 2 percent, from which income tax was deducted.

To illustrate the parsimony of the authorities, the 200 acres at Dyce were acquired from Gandar Dower at a price of £186 an acre. Local grass pasture sold for £300 an acre.

Eric Gandar Dower whiled away the time after the war by being elected the Conservative member of Parliament for Caithness. His preoccupation with parliamentary duties probably helped him to forget the bitter and harrowing litigation departments, which seemed bent on denying him a fair deal. There were many acrimonious negotiations, and saturated as he was in frustration—he was described by a colleague as a belligerent Robert Morley—these could not have helped his cause. The prolonged confrontation was reported to have reached a minor crisis on one occasion when the Air Ministry requisitioning team was met outside the hangar at Dyce by Eric Gandar Dower brandishing a shotgun.

Not all his life, however, was spent in blood, sweat, and tears. During the 1930s, he frequently flew for pleasure, and he competed four times in the King's Cup Air Race around the British Isles. He never won the race, but he claimed a unique record. Because of the sickly smell of leaking petrol in the closed cockpit of one of his aircraft, he was sick over four different countries, England, Ireland, Scotland, and Wales, all on the same day.

Throughout the rest of his life, Eric Gandar Dower never recovered spiritually from the mental battering he had received from the railways, the local councils, the War Office, the Air Ministry, the Admiralty, and the Labour government. Bitterly reflecting upon the twenty-seven years it took him to make an acceptable settlement of the compulsory purchase of Dyce in 1939, he observed: "Just think . . . how they hacked out of our lives the youth and the ability to use whatever virtues we possessed."

Asked if he would have chosen another career if he could live his life over again, his response was instantaneous: "I would have stuck to the stage. They could not have nationalized me out of that."

Sir Freddie Laker

The One and Only

Frederick Alfred Laker was born on August 22, 1922, in the lovely cathedral city of Canterbury, England. His parents were scrap dealers, and when he was five years old, his father deserted his mother, who was left to make ends meet by running a small general store and to marry again, happily. At the age of sixteen Freddie joined Short Brothers, builders of the famous Empire flying boats, in nearby Rochester, as a tea boy. He had already shown his business acumen at that early age, having made a profit running his school tuck shop; now he made money selling tea at a penny a can, while serving his early apprenticeship in aircraft engineering. When the Shorts' factory was bombed in 1940, he joined General Aircraft as an aircraft fitter.

Eternal optimist though he was, he could never then have dreamed of the spectacular course his subsequent career would take, much less of the far-reaching effect of that career on the world's airline industry. More than that, his mother could never, in her wildest imagination, have believed that her tea-boy son would one day be knighted by the Queen of England. Nor could either of them have thought that Freddie would also be a living example of the old adage "the higher they climb, the harder they fall."

But for the first forty-two years of his hardworking life, the path was ever upward, as he chose a sometimes belligerently independent course through the tortuous labyrinth of airline politics that have been the scourge of the British airline industry since it was born in 1919. During four postwar decades, Freddie Laker at first became known in British airline circles for his forcefulness, la-

Sir Freddie Laker poses cheerily in front of one of his beloved DC-10 Skytrain aircraft, with which he launched the first no-reservations transatlantic airline service in 1977. Forced out of business by an alliance of banks and ruthlessly competing airlines, he established a formula that others have since copied with conspicuous success.

ter drew the attention of a wider British public to become one of the best-known airline personalities in Europe, and finally became a household name throughout the entire world. Throughout the whole period, he was always well liked, even though his frankness and directness were somewhat alarming to those used to a more orthodox and sedate manner of doing business. At the time of his downfall, his popularity had reached hero-worshipping proportions of almost Churchillian magnitude, and he was known to be a great favorite of the prime minister.

Freddie Laker's wartime years were not particularly distinguished. He joined the Air Transport Auxiliary (A.T.A.) as an engineer and ferry pilot and did a fair amount of flying in almost every type of aircraft used by the Royal Air Force, in fulfillment of the A.T.A.'s function as logistics support in delivery flights from North America to Europe. He married Joan, his first wife, in 1942, and his daughter Elaine was born two years later. When the war ended, he spent part of his time buying and selling anything that caught his fancy, part of the time with London Aero Motor Services. His instinct led him to advise his boss, Bobby Sanderson, to sell his share of the business.

In 1947, Laker had amalgamated—some would have suggested the word *legitimated*—his various sidelines to form Aviation Traders (Engineering), at Bovingdon, about thirty miles northwest of London. The next year, at the age of twenty-six, he was angling for the purchase of no fewer than twelve Handley Page Halton airliners from the state airline, British Overseas Airways Corporation (B.O.A.C.). They were going at a bargain price—£42,000 for the lot—but Freddie could come up with only a tenth of the money himself. Then by chance he met Sanderson in a London pub, and his former boss lent him the balance.

This was not such a great deal as it sounded, and Freddie was probably as busy with the birth of his son, Kevin, as with flying his Haltons. For these aircraft were not exactly the most sought after, having been produced only as a stopgap measure to sustain B.O.A.C., the British national airline, in the immediate postwar years while the aircraft industry was struggling to its feet and new, modern aircraft were still in the design stage. The Haltons were not even the favorite interim aircraft of B.O.A.C., which was glad to get rid of them.

Luck favored the brave. During 1948 and 1949, the Russians, of all people, came to Freddie Laker's assistance by provoking the famous Berlin airlift. By shutting the frontier between East and West Germany, and between the western and Soviet zones of Berlin, the Soviet Union stimulated an unprecedented airlift. At the time, all the independent airlines in Britain had been scraping along at best, picking up the few crumbs from the state airlines' table, denied, as they were, the right to operate scheduled services. Now the independents suddenly found themselves in demand, and Aviation Traders was in the thick of the fray.

Although the Haltons did not constitute the largest share of Britain's contribution to the airlift, they had a goodly share of it. The government contracts were not particularly generous, but the work was intensive, and it suited Freddie Laker down to the ground. He made a lot of money and immediately provided evidence of the flamboyant style that was to be his trademark for the rest of his career. He bought his first Rolls-Royce, brand new, and moved Aviation Traders to Southend.

The Haltons were scrapped as soon as the Berlin Airlift was terminated. But Laker was active thereafter on several fronts, converting Royal Air Force (R.A.F.) surplus Halifaxes for the Egyptian

Air Force, reactivating Surrey Flying Services, and purchasing Fairflight from Air Vice-Marshal Donald Bennett.

Laker merged Fairflight and Surrey Flying Services to form Air Charter, which continued to provide air-freight service into Berlin, at first with Avro Yorks, later with reengineered Avro Tudor 1s. One of Freddie Laker's long-forgotten achievements was to obtain an unrestricted certificate of airworthiness for this ugly duckling of the postwar era, putting it into service on February 14, 1954, and operating it successfully all over the world until June 16, 1959.

During the 1950s, under his energetic and imaginative direction, Aviation Traders was involved in several other interesting projects. It converted Bristol Freighters for another Laker enterprise, Air Charter, which he had purchased in 1952 to expand into the air charter business with specialized aircraft. Air Charter began car-ferrying operations from Southend to Calais on April 14, 1955, extending to Ostend on October 17, 1955, and to Rotterdam on October 1, 1956. Laker was not the pioneer of this unique type of airline service. Silver City Airways, operating from Lympne to le Touquet, had been the first to carry automobiles across the English Channel, on July 14, 1948. But Laker shrewdly judged that there was enough automobile traffic for two airlines, especially if they served different markets.

Aviation Traders was not always successful in its projects. Laker bought 252 obsolete Percival Prentice training aircraft, hoping to sell them at a profit after converting them for private use. But this project was a failure, for he sold only 20. In 1957 the prototype of Aviation Traders' own design, the ATL 90 Accountant, with two Rolls-Royce Dart Turboprop engines, was offered as a twenty-eight-seat feeder aircraft to meet the elusive DC-3 Replacement specification, but it failed to obtain the government's financial support, essential for the success of such an ambitious project. Later, after Laker had dropped the idea, the Hawker Siddeley 748, which sold in hundreds throughout the world, was said to have had an uncanny resemblance to the Accountant.

On January 1, 1959, Airwork, a British independent airline of long standing, backed by shipping companies, purchased the Laker businesses. The car-ferrying operations were reorganized as Channel Air Bridge. Freddie Laker joined the Airwork board, and put £800,000 in the bank, some of which he withdrew to invest in his hobby, racehorses. Only two years later, on July 1, 1960, Airwork

The McDonnell Douglas DC-10 was chosen by Sir Freddie Laker to operate his historic Skytrain service, which provided a transocean air route on the same basis as any short-haul no-reservations shuttle service.

joined with the Hunting-Clan group of airlines and other related companies to form British United Airways (B.U.A.). Although the Airwork and Hunting-Clan groups were both backed by powerful British shipping interests, Freddie Laker emerged as the managing director—equivalent to president in the United States. Miles Wyatt represented the shipping people as chairman.

Until this time, all the independent airlines had been severely limited in what they could do and were restricted mainly to charter and contract operations—in carrying troops, for example. In effect, competition was nonexistent until 1952, when the new Conservative government allowed a more liberal interpretation of the law. An impartial seven-man Air Transport Advisory Council (A.T.A.C.) granted seven- and ten-year licenses for the independents to operate scheduled services, provided there was no "material diversion" from the state corporations, B.O.A.C. and B.E.A. Then, when the Conservatives won another election in 1959, the A.T.A.C. was replaced by the Air Transport Licensing Board (A.T.L.B.) and the independents at last had a chance to obtain routes of substance other than a few crumbs.

Typically, Freddie Laker took full advantage of the opportunity that was now offered. In 1960, he ordered four VC-10s and in May 1961 ten BAC One-Elevens, both types from the British Aircraft Corporation (B.A.C.). The much-underrated four-engined VC-10s were to upgrade the long-haul intercontinental routes of B.U.A., especially to South America, B.U.A. having leaped in where B.O.A.C. had feared to tread, because it was losing money there. The One Elevens were for the new European service, a few routes having been granted by the A.T.L.B., much to the dismay of the state corporations, which had hitherto enjoyed a complete monopoly.

Freddie Laker was the first to order the B.A.C. One-Eleven, which was the first of the second-generation twin-engined jets, the French Caravelle having pioneered the twin, as well as the novel idea of mounting the engines on the rear fuselage. British European Airways (B.E.A.) meanwhile had ordered the larger de Havilland Trident but had stupidly changed its mind over the specification. Laker's order came just at the right time for B.A.C., B.E.A. having compromised the Trident's chances of success in overseas markets, both by delaying the project, thus giving Boeing a golden opportunity, and, by making it smaller, making it less efficient against the Boeing product. Sure enough, the One-Eleven, which went into service with B.U.A. on April 9, 1965, became a greater success than the Trident, selling more than twice as many, mostly overseas, including the United States. Because of his prompt order, without procrastination, and with the correct customer specification just at the right time, Freddie Laker can take much of the credit for the success of the only British jet airliner to be exported in measurable quantities.

The middle 1960s were eventful—as usual for Laker—on both the business and personal fronts. British United Airways merged with the Britavia Group, the main operating division of which was Silver City Airways, the other car-ferrying company. The two car-ferrying companies were merged and were supplied with larger specialized aircraft, the ATL 98 Carvair. These were old Douglas DC-4s, converted by the Aviation Traders workshops at Southend, to permit five cars to drive in through the nose, the flight deck having been moved into a bulge on the top of the fuselage. The Carvairs were ugly, like the three-car Bristol Freighters before them, but they worked, and they provided further evidence of Laker's characteristic ever-active flair for innovation.

This was in 1962, the same year in which he fired 500 engineers for working to rule to obtain £1-a-week pay raise. Laker was never a union man.

Soon afterward he had a severe dispute with the B.U.A. chairman, Miles Wyatt, and left to pursue his own career. Independence thereupon took on a sharper meaning, for Laker would no longer be competing against state airlines; he would be competing against the powerful independent airlines, which had now rationalized themselves into two main groups, one of which was B.U.A. His straightforward approach and humble background did not sit well with the well-bred, public school–educated—private school–educated, in U.S. terminology—directors, and he could not expect—and he certainly did not solicit—any help from his former independent colleagues.

On February 8, 1966, Laker Airways was formed with share capital of £211,500, held by Mr. and Mrs. Laker, plus £4,000,000 in loans. Laker's standing with the banks was good enough to raise such an investment, permitting him to buy three new B.A.C. One-Elevens, and two Bristol Britannia long-haul turboprops from B.O.A.C. By this time, he knew the charter market backward and found business easily, even against the healthy competition. All the independent airlines were now flourishing on the crest of a wave of inclusive air tour traffic that permitted a fair percentage of the population of the United Kingdom to spend a couple of weeks each year on the Spanish, Italian, or Yugoslav beaches. The One-Eleven, incidentally, was ideal for this trade. It could make two round trips every twenty-four hours between Britain and the Mediterranean, and its size was equivalent to the capacity of two normal buses, which were an important ancillary element of the inclusive tour package.

Laker Airways started business, under contract to Air France, on July 29, 1966, using two Britannias purchased from B.O.A.C. He then proceeded to expand into the tourist market. He bought Arrowsmith Holidays, based in Manchester, in 1967, and Lord Brothers, of London, in 1968. Although in Britain it is now taken for granted that the air charter airlines work hand in glove with the tourist agencies, few remember that it was Freddie Laker who squeezed the last penny of efficiency out of the system. His main improvement was to introduce time charters, which were for a whole year, with a fixed number of hours guaranteed at a basic rate and a sliding scale of reduced rates for extra hours flown. This permitted the tour organizers, who quickly arranged similar contracts with hotel keepers on the Costa Blanca (near Valencia) or in Tenerife, to offer almost impossibly low inclusive holiday rates during the winter months. The business was good for everyone: the airlines, which kept their aircraft flying during the trough season at marginal cost levels; the tour operators, whose business expanded enormously; and the public, who found it cheaper to take a winter holiday in the south of Spain than to stay at home. Freddie Laker sold the entire capacity of his three B.A.C. One-Elevens for two years ahead, before February 27, 1967, when he took delivery of the first aircraft.

On the domestic front, Laker's affairs were not quite so smooth. In 1968, he was divorced from Joan, having met his second wife, Rosemary, while visiting South Africa.

During the same year, using two Boeing 707s acquired in February 1969, he joined the ranks of owners of the independent airlines which had been able to do a roaring trade in the so-called affinity charters across the Atlantic Ocean, mainly to and from the United States. Under U.S. civil aviation law, which was even more restrictive and discouraging to new ideas than the British, one way a nonscheduled airline could get into the large-volume passenger business was by contracting with special groups for a series of flights. The special groups had to be set up for reasons totally unconnected with air travel. An amazing number of such groups mushroomed, however, to create an entirely new market. Chess clubs, birders, football clubs, these and many others with even less plausible qualifications supplied hundreds of thousands of transatlantic passengers, and because the contracted airlines had long-term guarantees of full loads and could fly at all times of the day or night, however inconvenient, they were able to charge unbelievably low rates.

The whole thing was a farce. It was a clear case of the application of a regulation that could never be enforced. It was difficult to prove that a member of the Santa Monica Soccer Club did not know the difference between a soccer ball and a rugby ball, or that the president of a chess club had never heard of a queen's gambit. Freddie Laker was one of many who felt that this particular law was an ass and devised an idea intended to put cheap air travel, the great virtue of the affinity charters, on a sound and legitimate footing, without the subterfuge necessary to overcome the defensive mechanism of the price-fixing International Air Transport Association (IATA).

On June 15, 1971, he announced his application to the British Air Transport Licensing Board for the right to operate a service which he called Skytrain. In complete contrast to the procedures of the scheduled airlines, or even the affinity tours, there would be no advance reservations—this was the "train" element of Skytrain. Also, like normal travel in many trains, there would be no special meal service on board except minimal refreshments. Prepackaged meals could be purchased before boarding. For aspiring transatlantic passengers who just wanted to get there and back and were unmoved by the big airlines' advertisements of luxury seating or seven-course meals, Laker's Skytrain Boeing 707s would be just as good as anyone else's. The difference was the fare: £37.50 one way—about $100 at the then rate of exchange—with a reduction in winter. This was about a quarter of the normal economy class fare and about a sixth of the first class. It was even substantially lower than the cheapest excursion rate that the scheduled airlines offered for all kinds of groups of various sizes and for various periods, all very confusing to the man in the street.

The great joy of Skytrain was its simplicity. No phony football clubs, no reductions for groups of seventeen traveling after 10:30 P.M. on Tuesdays, Thursdays, and Saturdays for seventeen to thirty-one days. Just turn up at Victoria Station, London, for the train connection to Gatwick Airport, or at the airport itself, bring your money, buy your ticket, and climb on board.

This whole idea, the essence of which was its down-to-earth simplicity, left the entire airline industry in a state of shock for a considerable time. Of course, everyone objected—the British government, the U.S. government, the British airlines, the U.S. airlines—and IATA did not take too kindly to it either. One of their problems was that they could not figure out exactly what they were objecting to.

For Freddie Laker had spotted the true nature of the London–New York route. The traffic density was high enough for it to be regarded the same way as any other pair of cities that generated more than two million passengers a year. When he applied for Skytrain in 1971, transatlantic air travel as a whole was running at about 14 million passengers annually, of whom about a fifth flew between the biggest traffic hubs on each side of the Atlantic. The Brazilians had introduced the world's first no-frills, no-reservations shuttle service between Rio de Janeiro and São Paulo on July 6, 1959, and the idea has been followed on dense short-haul routes in the United States, Europe, Japan, and Indonesia. Laker realized instinctively that the qualifying criterion for a no-reservation air shuttle was high traffic density and that the 3,440-mile range of London–New York made no difference to the basic economic principles involved.

When the incumbent airlines recovered from their initial bewilderment, they screamed to their respective governments. The British and U.S. authorities were, of course, directly involved and had to thrash the matter out. But other airlines and their protective governments in Europe did not look too kindly on Mr. Laker either, for he was tempting potential travelers from at least half a dozen countries to take a trip to London to save money on the whole journey to America. As the Duke of Edinburgh later quipped "Freddie Laker is at Peace with his Maker, but with IATA he's persona non grata."

During the 1970s, litigation dragged on. The British A.T.L.B. turned down Skytrain in 1971, and Laker promptly appealed. His appeal was upheld but was later reversed by the new civil aviation minister, to allow the new Civil Aviation Authority (C.A.A.), which replaced the A.T.L.B., to consider the matter. The C.A.A. granted a license, but only from Stansted, officially London's third airport, but in practice quite inconvenient for Londoners for it was forty miles away to the northeast. But the British government designated Laker a flag carrier, and this obliged the U.S. government to grant him a permit. Meanwhile, he had purchased two wide-bodied Douglas DC-10s and put them into service on the Mediterranean sunshine routes on November 21, 1972.

But in 1973 the U.S. Civil Aeronautics Board (C.A.B.) denied Laker a permit until he had paid fines for breaches of the affinity charter rules. This was bureaucracy gone mad, for the breach was more by the legislators than by the legislated. Undoubtedly Laker had broken the rules, but only by subjecting all his passengers to a complicated questionnaire, under oath, could he have established their affinity qualifications. Every operator in the business was at least as guilty.

The C.A.B. recommended approval in 1974, but President Nixon, who had to sign off all international route awards, failed to act. Laker filed antitrust actions against the four opposing British and U.S. airlines, but under pressure from B.O.A.C., Peter Shore, the Labour government's trade secretary, issued what were euphemistically called guidelines to the C.A.A. to cancel Laker's Skytrain license. In 1976 the House of Lords, however, reflected British public opinion by urging Shore to withdraw his so-called guidelines, and the High Court and the Appeals Court also ruled against Shore. After eight years of fighting a rearguard action by the Establishment, Freddie Laker had had to prove that a minister of the Crown had, in effect, broken his own laws before the way was finally cleared.

On the domestic front, Laker had married his third wife, Pat, in 1975, his stepdaughter, Betinna, having been born two years earlier. But then tragedy struck the Laker household when his son, Kevin, was killed in an automobile accident, in a new Aston Martin his father had given him for his birthday.

On June 15, 1977, President Carter, an advocate of airline deregulation, signed the necessary papers. On September 26, Skytrain was finally launched, and not from Stansted. One rumor had it that the queue for tickets stretched from Victoria Station all the way to Gatwick. Laker himself flew on the first flight, which was, in fact, only 70 percent full. But it was a wide-bodied Douglas DC-10, equipped with 345 seats, and, at the £59 fare— inflation and the declining value of the pound had made its mark since the 1971 application—there was no shortage of passengers to fill the seats during the months to come.

For the first year, Skytrain was an unqualified success, and Laker made an estimated $2,000,000 clear profit. But where others may have waited a year or so, to ensure that this was no temporary phenomenon, he plunged forward with more ambitious plans. He extended the Skytrain service to Los Angeles on September 26, 1978, and on April 10, 1979, he placed orders for ten Airbus A-300s and five more DC-10s—he had already bought more of the latter, to make a total of eleven.

This was a bad year for the McDonnell Douglas trijet, for on May 25, 1979, in possibly the most spectacular airline tragedy in history—it occurred at Chicago, the busiest airport in the world, in broad daylight—an engine fell off an American Airlines DC-10, which then crashed out of control. The subsequent inquiry as to the cause exonerated the manufacturer, but every DC-10 operator in the world suffered, for the Federal Aviation Agency (F.A.A.) grounded the entire fleet. Freddie Laker, however, was one of the stoutest defenders of the aircraft, and he joined the other British and European airlines that agreed as a group to fly the aircraft, having inspected their own DC-10s and found nothing to support the suggestion of defective construction. Nevertheless, the affair could not have come at a worse time, for Skytrain was only just getting under way and could not afford any setbacks. Laker estimated that he lost $13,000,000, and this was probably no exaggeration.

Such business problems were shrugged off by the effervescent Laker, whose native optimism was now tinged with a certain overconfidence. But such was his friendly personality, with never a suggestion that he was any different from the boy who had sold tea at Short Brothers before the war, that all his extroverted activities and sometimes outrageous statements merely seemed to make him more popular. He was even forgiven by the Labour government, which had given him so much trouble. On June 3, 1978, he became Sir Freddie Laker, although anyone meeting him next day would never have known it. Capping off this personal triumph, his second son, Freddie Allan, was born, but not long after, he was saddened when his mother, whom he loved dearly, died.

Laker Airways needed the Airbuses because Laker was convinced that the Skytrain formula was right and that many short-haul routes within Europe were dense enough to justify the no-reservation air-shuttle principle. He initiated a campaign, both with the licensing authorities and the public, to start a network throughout Europe, and to show that he meant business, he had to be prepared to start the services if the licenses were granted. But he encountered unspoken opposition from every official quarter. Even when the British gave him permission to fly from London (Gatwick) to Zurich in March 1981, the Swiss did not distinguish between Gatwick and Heathrow and would permit only British Airways, the incumbent Heathrow airline, to operate. Laker considered this unethical, possibly illegal under the terms of the Treaty of Rome, which was supposed to remove bureaucratic transborder restrictions in pursuance of the objective of a

United Europe. He was beginning to find, however, that national protectionism was alive and well throughout the Continent.

He also ran into trouble where he thought he might succeed, in a wholly British negotiation and with the comforting knowledge that the new Prime Minister, Margaret Thatcher, regarded Sir Freddie as a crusader for private enterprise who could do no wrong. The issue was expanded sevice to Hong Kong, to which corner of the diminishing British Commonwealth the long-held British Airways monopoly of service to and from London was collapsing. The route was a peculiar case in international air law. Although airlines had to fly over or stop at foreign points, it was strictly a domestic route, at least for traffic between the two points, and all decisions were made in London. There was a Hong Kong Air Transport Licensing Authority (A.T.L.A.), but until then it had never done more than rubber-stamp decisions made in London. Now, a dormant A.T.L.A. awoke from its slumbers, possibly reminded of its powers by vested interests in Hong Kong.

The British C.A.A. had already, in 1980, rejected his application to start a Skytrain service to Hong Kong, and it had also rejected another Laker bid for rights to offer service to Australia. The British independent airline British Caledonian Airways and the Hong Kong-based, British-owned, Cathay Pacific Airways received the nod for the Hong Kong route, even though the secretary of state for trade granted Laker's appeal for London–Hong Kong. Now, in June 1981, he tried again, this time at the Hong Kong end, not only for a route to London, but also for one across the Pacific to Vancouver. This was part of a grand—some would suggest grandiose—plan to start a round-the-world Skytrain. Operating via Hong Kong and the United States or Canada, the entire route would need licensing authority from only two countries, the United Kingdom and the United States. In this case, even though the old-school Hong Kong legislators were not enamored of Laker's flamboyant style, the A.T.L.A. did grant him the route. For both routes, Laker needed two route certificates, but he received only one for each, and that was not enough.

These plans and ambitions were being conducted against a background of falling business. By the end of summer 1981, rumors were spreading that not all was well with Sir Freddie. The whole airline world was undergoing a recession and the average load factor—the percentage of seats filled—was plummeting, nowhere more spectacularly than on the North Atlantic, where more than forty scheduled airlines, not to mention the nonskeds, were competing ruthlessly for the diminishing business.

On top of this, many of the established airlines, supported or encouraged by the governments of the countries they represented, suddenly found ways and means to offer fares at about the same level as Laker's. The U.S. Department of Justice and the National Air Carrier Association thought the new fares were "predatory" but T.W.A. and Pan American took the view that they had "to guard the store." Earlier they had resisted vehemently the mere idea of offering any fare lower than their own special excursion rates, often producing learned and scholarly reports to prove the point. In Laker's words "One has to wonder about the integrity, honor, and truthfulness of those who stood up day after day for six years and swore on a stack of bibles that such a service couldn't be operated." To quote another, later, commentary "the big airlines, blaming Laker's low fares for much of their problems, had deliberately set out to bring him to heel (although they will deny stoutly to their dying day that they ever wanted him to crash completely)."

Large loans had been taken out to finance Laker's new Airbuses and additional DC-10s. One of the problems was that the loans were in dollars, whereas most of Laker's income was in pounds, and the pound was declining in value. The customary measures were taken by the banks to reschedule the payments, and McDonnell Douglas offered help by offering to inject capital—until it realized that it would be financing Airbuses thereby. Even the Bank of England could do nothing to combat the inexorable truth that the 1981–82 winter season was appalling for North Atlantic traffic and that Laker was losing money hand over fist, although the prospects for 1982 were excellent.

But—contrary to implications made at the time—the lenders were not pressing Laker for payment. He had never defaulted on a single progress payment, always paying principal and interest on schedule. The principal payments for September 1981, January 1982, and March 1982 had been postponed with full agreement by the lending institutions. Not a single debt was overdue.

Nevertheless, Laker Airways ceased operations on February 5, 1982, and all Laker's scheduled and tour operations stopped immediately. Hundreds of people were stranded and thousands lost money on prepurchased tickets. Some other airlines helped passengers to get back home, in the hope that eventually something could be salvaged from the official receiver. Possibly for the first time in his life, Freddie Laker was completely demoralized, having been cynically and callously betrayed by a large number of business associates in whom he had placed his trust. Almost to the last minute, he had put on a brave front while trying to sell his tour business in an effort to obtain some ready cash. Completely exhausted, he was not even making his customary rounds with his staff, one of whom remarked on his lack of interest in them, "We have worked on loyally and . . . nobody has bothered to thank us or even to say goodbye."

The next day, in a decidedly odd situation in that Laker was far from bankrupt, the receivers were called in, headed by Bill Mackey, who had been appointed by the Clydesdale Bank. The problem was awesome. Debts alone came to $270 million. The assets consisted of twenty jet aircraft, including eleven good DC-10s—but the market for any aircraft during this time, much less second-hand ones, was depressed. A week later, most of the employees were dismissed, just a few being retained to service the aircraft, which were disposed of with almost indecent haste.

Then followed one of the most extraordinary episodes in airline history. Here was a man who flamboyantly bought a new Rolls-Royce every year, kept a string of racehorses, spent his Christmases on his yacht on the Mediterranean, and was almost a stereotype of the entrepreneur who had gambled and lost. Yet he suddenly emerged as an underdog, evoking widespread sentimental sympathy. He was publicly supported by Prince Michael and—until she executed an about face—Margaret Thatcher and by millions of British people, excluding trade union organizers, who did not care for Laker's style of master-and-servant relationships, informal and friendly though they were. "Save Laker" funds sprang up all over the country. Although the receivers discouraged them, millions of pounds were either subscribed or pledged, and the money continued to flow in for weeks. But of course it was never enough. A billion pounds would not have diverted from their course those who were determined to put Laker down.

In a last-ditch effort, financier Roland Rowland tried out a plan to revive the Laker airline—to be called the People's Airline, although Rowland insisted on retaining the name Laker. This would have been a smaller airline, leasing perhaps five or six DC-10s. But it was hopeless. Laker blamed the banks for "talking him into the Airbuses." But, to be fair, nobody had ever talked Freddie Laker into anything.

Laker was not entirely the victim of circumstances or even of lack of judgment. He had himself to blame, at least in part. He had been so overwhelmed by the initial success of Skytrain that he did not pause to put the Laker Airways house in order by recapitalizing the enterprise or analyzing his financial results in detail. He had ordered A300 aircraft before he had the scheduled routes on which to operate them and even when his chances of receiving those routes were slim at best. But from the way the money was rolling in for the 1982 Mediterranean tour program, full use would have been made of the A300s.

But there was another side. British Airways' debt was running at $350 million at roughly the same time that Laker was going under. And Pan American was in such deep trouble that three years later it had to sell its entire Pacific network for $750 million to remain solvent. The European airlines were wondering how many of their high-priced seats would be empty if Freddie Laker established a foothold on the Continent.

The whole affair thus revealed the questionable ethics of governments that subsidized flag carriers with losses higher than Laker's, taxed the public to make up those subsidies, direct or indirect, then stood idly by when the recipients of the subsidies lowered fares to an uneconomic level, simply to torpedo Skytrain. Laker's efficiency could have sustained the low fares as long as the subsidized airlines did not raid his chosen territory and steal his traffic—traffic that had not existed before he came along.

A month or so after the Laker collapse, Robert Beckman, Sir Freddie Laker's American lawyer in Washington, D.C., began to collect evidence to support his conviction that, during the bitter winter of 1981–82, the IATA competitors had "smelled blood and moved in for the kill" in more ways than one. Both British Airways and Pan American, which had previously remained aloof from the Laker-level fares of the charter airlines, had introduced a $249 London–New York round-trip fare on October 16, 1981. With the advantage of a dense spoke network of hub traffic feeding into Heathrow Airport, British Airways and Pan Am, joined by T.W.A., were able to outsell Laker, who had no feeder traffic at Gatwick.

Then, as the new year began, the suppliers of Laker's flagship aircraft, the McDonnell Douglas DC-10, and its engine manufacturer, General Electric, began to receive what John Brizendine, president of the commercial aircraft division of McDonnell Douglas, called a series of nastigrams. They came from British Caledonian, SABENA, U.T.A., K.L.M., Lufthansa, Swissair, and S.A.S. The messages all contained a common denominator, ranging in tone from a strong hint to an outright threat, to the effect that, if McDonnell Douglas and G.E. helped Laker in any way, future orders might not be forthcoming from old-established customers.

All these charges were carefully documented by Beckman, and by November 1982, he had persuaded the liquidator, Christopher Morris, acting on behalf of Touche, Ross & Company, to file an antitrust suit in the U.S. District Court at Washington to the amount of $350 million, which, if settled in the plaintiff's favor with triple damages, could amount to a staggering $1.1 billion. Most of the originators of the nastigrams were named, together with British Airways, T.W.A., Pan American, and the two manufacturers for good measure.

One intriguing aspect of the threatened litigation was that British Airways was seriously embarrassed in the process of preparing to transform itself from a state-owned corporation to a private one, and obviously nothing could be done in this direction as long as a court case was outstanding.

In January 1983, several of the airlines filed counterclaims in London, challenging the right of the liquidator to sue in a U.S. court. At first the British court granted the injunction, much to the displeasure of Judge Harold H. Greene in Washington. But in May the British High Court overturned the injunction, only to have that decision reversed again by the Court of Appeal. Morris then took the case to the House of Lords, which decided in his favor, and the way appeared open for the arguments to be taken up in Washington.

As the months passed into 1984, speculation ebbed and flowed as to who held the advantage, with Sir Freddie Laker consistently putting on his customary bold front, declaring, in no uncertain terms, that he wanted his airline back. After much procrastination, with legal expenses mounting, and a grand jury also having been called to investigate possible violations of U.S. antitrust laws, President Reagan intervened. He ordered the Department of Justice to call off the investigation, and this had the effect of weighing the scales on the sides of the defendants, who were thus relieved of the threat of criminal proceedings.

Eventually, on June 12, 1985, an out-of-court settlement was made in Washington. The accused would pay the liquidator $48 million, of which British Airways would contribute $32.5 million. This was less than 5 percent of the $1.1 billion triple damages but was ample to provide full refunds for Laker's former employees and ticket holders who were owed large sums. The settlement offer included a provision that Sir Freddie should receive a personal settlement of $8 million, on condition that all subsequent claims on the defendants should be dropped. In time, settlements in cash or in kind, to the value of $300 million, were made.

The offer was open until August 20, and for several weeks Laker held out. But he finally bowed to the inevitable, and the cause célèbre passed into history. There were many side issues, such as Rowland's threat to claim damages against what the People's Airline might have made during the next ten years, and Beckman continued to file suit for damages on behalf of certain former Laker employees who had genuinely suffered as a direct result of the airline's collapse. But to all intents and purposes, the Laker affair was over, to the enormous satisfaction of most of the European IATA establishment.

There may never be another Skytrain. It was wonderful while it lasted, and such was Laker's fame and personality that he hardly needed to advertise. His standard of service was always as good as that of any economy-class airline. He was not the first to offer low fares across the Atlantic; that honor goes to the gypsy charter operators of the early 1960s. But more than any other single person or organization, he legitimated the entire conception of a stratum of airline fares as far below economy class as economy was below first class. Other airlines, notably PEOPLExpress in the United States and Virgin Atlantic in the United Kingdom, have followed in his low-fare footsteps. The public may never again Take a Laker, but he will never be forgotten as a crusader for low fares, a cheerful iconoclast who challenged the Establishment and, more than any other single person, opened up the Atlantic air travel market to the common man.

Postscript: PEOPLExpress has ceased to exist as an independent airline, having been absorbed by Texas Air Corporation.

▶▶▶▶▶▶ ▶▶▶▶▶▶▶▶ ◀ ▶▶▶▶▶▶▶▶

Sir Adam Thomson

Flying Scotsman

Sir Adam Thomson is probably better known in Great Britain, and much of Europe, than any of the occupants of his equivalent seat behind the revolving door of the chairman's office at British Airways, the much larger and politically dominant flag carrier, and he is almost as well known to the general public as the flamboyant and deliberate publicity seeker, Sir Freddie Laker.

Yet he was a late entrant to the field of airline operations, arriving on the scene long after many other independent spirits such as Gordon Olley, Sammy Morton, Taffy Powell, and Freddie Laker. He founded his airline, Caledonian Airways, only in 1961, after several independent airlines in Britain had already folded, and started scheduled service only after he had purchased British United Airways in 1970.

The combined British Caledonian Airways accounts today for only about 15 percent of the total British air transport effort. As the so-called British Second Force airline, it is therefore—by government decreee—a poor second. Nevertheless, it can still claim to rank among the world's top thirty airlines, by most statistical units of measurement.

Thomson's biggest contribution to the British, or indeed the world air transport industry, however, was that he did more than any other single person to provide respectability to the charter, or nonscheduled, segment of the airline fraternity. To a happy band of

259

intuitive individuals, he brought the qualities of respectability, dignity, and discipline, to the extent that, at the creation of the Second Force, a fairly substantial scheduled airline was taken over by his smaller charter company.

Adam Thomson was born in Glasgow on July 7, 1926. His father had been invalided out of World War I and worked on the London, Midland, and Scottish Railway (L.M.S.), first in the shunting yard, later as a timekeeper. Because of his father's infirmity, Adam's mother was the driving force of the family. She was determined, in spite of the severe financial belt-tightening necessary in those days for such an ambition, that her son should receive a good education.

She was successful. Adam attended Rutherglen Academy in 1938, Coatbridge College in 1941, and the Royal Technical College in 1943, all in or near Glasgow. At first he contemplated a career in mechanical or electrical engineering, but from an early age he wanted to become a pilot. When he was seventeen, by which time the tide of World War II had been decisively turned, he joined the Royal Navy as a trainee pilot in the Empire Training Scheme. He obtained his wings in Canada and, after advanced flying conversion in England, signed on "to the end of the present emergency," which enabled him to keep flying until March 1947.

Soon afterward, with the aid of two friends, he made arrangements to acquire a Supermarine Walrus. The idea was to give joyrides from areas of water such as large lakes or from suitable beach locations and to carry mail to fishing fleets. But this project never got off the ground, or indeed the water, as acquisition of the aircraft never came about.

During that summer he became a flying instructor and charter pilot at Cowes, and later at Bembridge, in the Isle of Wight. Early in 1950 he was flying de Havilland Rapides for Newman Airways, based at Croydon and Ryde, and operating charters to the Channel Islands. He was flying on the old "B" license, which permitted him to fly with passengers, but a change in the air regulations obliged him to obtain the new Airline Transport Pilot's License, so he went through the Air Service Training School at Hamble.

Although intuitively still wishing to start an airline, he had to go through a self-imposed apprenticeship. In 1951 he joined British European Airways (B.E.A.) as a first officer on Pionairs (converted C-47s, former R.A.F. DC-3 Dakotas); then in 1953 a spell with West African Airways Corporation, based at Lagos, Nigeria, as a captain

Sir Adam Thomson, seen here simply as Captain Thomson while in West Africa in 1953, built up a small charter company to attain the status of Britain's Second Force airline. He was the first to offer, on a wide scale, cheap transatlantic fares under the Affinity Group Charter rules.

on the de Havilland Dove and the homely Bristol 170 Wayfarer. Returning to England in 1954, he flew mainly Handley Page Hermes four-engined airliners for the Britavia–Silver City Airways group.

This was a period in the history of the British Commonwealth of Nations during which the area of sovereignty could be described as the Empire upon which, in spite of Sir Winston Churchill's protestations to the contrary, the sun was beginning to set. The Britavia part of the group was active mainly on trooping contracts linking the homeland with military units in Asia and Africa, happily almost entirely on noncombatant garrison duties. These contracts were reasonably lucrative, so several British shipping companies, with the blessing of the government, were encouraged to invest in the independent airlines. For his part, Adam Thomson, pilot, doubled on the Hermes and on the Bristol 170 car ferrying services across the English Channel.

By a chance meeting with Jean Rodgie, a former stewardess on the Hermes Singapore run, he was introduced to John de la Haye, then working with Harold Bamberg's Eagle Airways. De la Haye, a native of Jersey, in the Channel Islands, and like Thomson formerly with British European Airways, was interested in starting charter flights from Europe to the United States. Thomson had already proposed various holiday packages to Africa and the Far East, and the two ideas seemed to have something in common. Thomson and de la Haye met at the Skyway Hotel near Heathrow Airport in the late summer of 1960, and the idea of forming an airline was born. Jean Rodgie, whom Thomson remembers with gratitude as the catalyst to the meeting, was eventually to become the chief stewardess of the company that came into being as a result of this historic meeting.

On April 27, 1961, Caledonian Airways was founded in Glasgow. The capital was £54,000, of which a substantial proportion was held by Thomson, de la Haye, and a few friends; about a quarter by a group of Scottish investors, including Marshal Gibson and James McWilliam; and the remaining quarter by a group of Scots-Americans, headed by Murray Vidockler. For a short time during the initial efforts to get under way, Max Wilson, who had formed the Overseas Visitors Club, was also associated with Caledonian as a major shareholder.

This club was an important pioneering innovation. To overcome the restrictive regulations governing the British independent airlines, such a club enabled members to qualify for air charter flights and permitted the independent airlines to organize their programs more efficiently by using the clubs as ticket agencies. It was the harbinger of a future mass movement of people who were later to form the segment of the air-traveling public known as the Visiting Friends and Relatives (V.F.R.) traffic.

Caledonian Airways made its first flight with paying passengers from Barbados to London on November 30, 1961, appropriately on St. Andrew's Day, in honor of Scotland's patron saint. On the day before, the aircraft, a Douglas DC-7C leased from the Belgian national airline, SABENA, had flown from Brussels to Barbados on a simultaneous proving and positioning flight. Caledonian's contract with the Belgians was wholly satisfactory. The fixed monthly lease rate was relatively small. The remainder of the leasing charge, including maintenance, was fixed according to hours flown, not elapsed time. If Caledonian did not fly, little was lost on the aircraft depreciation account.

On December 3, Caledonian positioned the aircraft at Luxembourg, and Adam Thomson himself flew it to Lourenço Marques (now Maputo), via Khartoum, returning via Lagos and Lisbon. The destination, in Portuguese East Africa (now Mozambique), was close to the South African frontier, and the majority of the passengers did not originate in Luxembourg. An equal number were destined not for Portuguese East Africa but for Johannesburg. This was a typical device to which progressive and innovative charter airlines had to resort in the 1960s to overcome the cartel tariff-fixing of the national air carriers, which were staunch members of the International Air Transport Association (IATA).

On December 21, 1961, just in time for the Christmas holiday, Caledonian made its first group charter flight to New York. Captain Bill Williams, with Thomson as copilot, piloted the westward flight. Next day, on what must have been a celebratory journey, with John de la Haye on board, they changed places. Not too often does the chairman of the company fly his own inaugurals. Most of the passengers belonged, perfectly legitimately, to a club, the Knights of Columba.

Transatlantic air charter flights by nonscheduled foreign airlines were then limited to six a year per airline by the U.S. Civil Aeronautics Board, although U.S. airlines were not similarly limited. Thomson does not claim, by any means, to have been the first to have operated these. Harold Bamberg's Eagle Airways, certain U.S. Supplemental airlines such as World and Saturn, and even scheduled operators such as B.O.A.C. and Pan American Airways, had made periodic charter or nonscheduled crossings. The mere idea of nonscheduled activity was actually considered in the airline business to be faintly unrespectable, bordering closely on the illegitimate. Charter operators were regarded by their scheduled rivals as having been born on the wrong side of the airline blanket and deserving to be treated accordingly. John de la Haye recalls that on one occasion, such was the attitude of aviation officials that the head of the Traffic Section of the U.S. Civil Aeronautics Board rejected a transatlantic tariff proposal on the grounds that the application used the abbreviation *Ltd* instead of spelling the word out in full. Another was rejected on the grounds that it was submitted on paper of the wrong size.

Less than six months after opening service, Caledonian Airways reached the nadir of its fortunes. Its sole aircraft, the DC-7C *Star O' Robbie Burns*, crashed at Douala, Cameroon, killing all 111 people on board, including the chief pilot and Adam Thomson's good friend Bill Williams. The elevator springtab mechanism had jammed, locking this vital control. The defect was later the subject of a mandatory modification. This, the only fatal crash in Caledonian's quarter-century history, would normally have been disastrous for a fledgling airline, but Caledonian was made of sterner stuff. At the time of the accident, the suspension of service over such a limited one-aircraft operation was not critical, even though all operations were suspended for about a month until arrangements could be made with SABENA for a replacement DC-7C.

At the beginning, Caledonian's business consisted of a little of this and a little of that. After the accident, in February 1962, only thirteen revenue hours were flown. From March onward there was the odd trooping contract, although larger independents received most of those; there were long-haul charters to Africa, summer vacation packages to the Mediterranean, various ad hoc charters, and the annual Hajj movement of pilgrims to Jeddah. Then, later that year, came an opportunity that was to change the airline's entire stature and put it firmly in the direction of commercial success, at the same time registering Caledonian's place in airline history.

On the initiative of John de la Haye, in a case handled by Leonard Bebchick, Caledonian's energetic lawyer in Washington, the airline had applied, in August 1961, to operate an 1,800-hour charter program, under Section 402 of the U.S. Civil Aeronautics Act. Until then only occasional individual charter flights had been applied for or granted, so this application created a precedent to an agency known to be protective of the scheduled airlines and their grandfather rights. In what became known in aviation circles as the Caledonian Case, the C.A.B. granted a Foreign Air Carrier Permit under Section 402—to the surprise of many close observers of the commercial aviation scene. The hearing was on August 13, 1962, and in June 1963, after grave deliberation and resistance to objections by Pan American and T.W.A., President Kennedy ratified the permit, his approval being necessary because it concerned a foreign air route and was therefore a matter of federal concern and policy.

From this moment on, Caledonian never looked back. The permit allowed almost unlimited affinity-group frequency—although with a clause limiting groups originating in the United States—and the DC-7C fleet was quickly increased to four, with two DC-6Bs added in 1964. The number of transatlantic charter passengers increased from 8,100 in 1962–63 to almost 37,000 in 1965–66. The additional aircraft allowed extra capacity to be allocated to the European inclusive tour programs, general charters, and trooping. Bristol Britannia long-range turboprops were added in the spring of 1965, and the inaugural transatlantic charter was flown with this fine aircraft on May 8 of that year. Transatlantic services were added from Manchester to New York, as well as from London and Glasgow.

In February 1965, Caledonian applied to the British Air Transport Licensing Board (A.T.L.B.) for two permits. One was for a low-fare scheduled service from London and Prestwick to New York, along the lines of that of the innovative Loftleidir, the Icelandic airline. The other was for a transatlantic Inclusive Tour license, similar to the European licenses covering the charter business. Only the latter was granted, and the program was not quite so successful as had been expected, because B.O.A.C. and other airlines, spurred by the new competition, introduced promotional fares at the same time. The U.S. Supplementals, however, were not yet in this business, which continued to be primarily a European speciality.

Such was Caledonian's success, and such was the management's confidence in its ability to maintain the momentum, that it ordered two 189-seat Boeing 707-320C jet airliners in November 1965. The first one took off on a revenue-earning flight from Gatwick Airport on January 16, 1968. The Boeings were used not only over the North Atlantic but also to the Far East. Long-distance charters to Singapore were highly successful. At first operated from Luxembourg, they were soon transferred to London, and the frequency increased to a daily service when more Boeings were delivered during the late 1960s. The service was very popular, both with the Singapore authorities and with Australian travelers seizing the chance to visit the home country for the first time at a reasonable price. For the essence of the journey was the low fare: Caledonian charged £186 for a Boeing 707 round trip to Singapore, whereas the IATA one-way economy fare was £224. For the V.F.R. contingent, who were prepared to trade time to save money, moreover, Ian Ritchie, Thomson's marketing director, and a travel agent, Gilbert Brown, came up with the idea, originally to fill in the winter trough period, of chartering a Soviet ship, which they were able to do at a favorable rate, to provide the link between Singapore and Sydney.

The prospects on the North Atlantic seemed unlimited. New airlines were entering the burgeoning market every few months, either from Europe or Asia, or from the ranks of the U.S. Supplementals. Thomson thought it high time that Great Britain had a second scheduled operator, to counter three U.S. certificated airlines: Pan American, T.W.A., and Seaboard World, the last specializing in cargo. But the A.T.L.B. turned down the transatlantic application from Caledonian, which with statistical evidence, claimed already to be Britain's second largest transatlantic passenger carrier. The airline was flying more passenger-miles than B.E.A. and carrying more passengers than B.O.A.C.

The airline had also gained a substantial reputation, and an enviable one, not only by the best advertising method in the world—word of mouth—but by deliberately emphasizing its Scottish image and ancestry. Its insignia was a lion rampant, the symbol of Scotland; the stewardesses wore a selection of genuine Scottish tartans, while the menus on board had a distinctly Scottish flavor, especially on Burns night, when the haggis was much in evidence.

In short, Caledonian became known as the airline which, provided that the passenger needed a complete inclusive tour, with hotel and other ground amenities included, offered the best bargain. But even this was less important than the other device, the V.F.R. flights of the type promoted by Max Wilson's Overseas Visitors Club. If the passenger had plenty of time to spare—and this applied to retired folk visiting their children across the Atlantic and to teachers during the long summer holiday—then the V.F.R. flight was an ideal solution, especially because of the price. For Caledonian could offer a round trip for less money than a scheduled airline could offer one way, simply because it filled the airplanes instead of only half filling them and because its overhead costs were immeasurably lower. The latter unseen advantage was not because the direct costs—fuel, maintenance, crew, airport charges—were any less, but because Caledonian's marketing costs were minimal. The clubs did almost all the agency and marketing work for nothing.

These clubs, in fact, became a significant factor in the development of the air travel business, to the extent that, indirectly, they changed the entire attitude toward tariff-fixing. Caledonian's efforts during the early 1960s were the little cloud arising out of the sea in the ensuing fares war. It gradually worked itself up to the proportions of a large cloud, then broke like a storm over the entrenched bulwarks of the IATA fare structure, which was designed to force airline passengers to pay whatever was needed to support a predetermined and outdated, not to say top-heavy, airline organizational system.

If laws are intrinsically bad, the public will soon find a way to circumvent or evade them, and so it was with the various types of charter. The group of legitimate clubs, which had taken advantage of the clause in the regulations that demanded that to take advantage of the travel privileges the club must not ostensibly have been formed for the purposes of travel and touring, was augmented by a host of others.

These clubs applied the well-known test of whether a lemon was good or bad. Was there anything illegal about *first* forming, say, a chess club, or a birding society, or even a Glasgow-based supporters club for the Los Angeles Dodgers, thus complying with the regulations, *then* offering travel privileges to its members?

In practice, the answer seemed to be no. Such groups sprang up everywhere, on both sides of the Atlantic. In the United States as well as in Britain, with the active support of Caledonian Airways, they strengthened their stature by becoming associated with the Council of British Societies. This was an old-established prewar society with impeccable credentials, and it greatly increased its membership through the attraction of the V.F.R. flights. The word got around that the only sensible way to fly across the Pond was to join a club. By filling the aircraft and making use of it the full twenty-four hours of the day, Caledonian's aircraft were booked a year ahead, a situation guaranteed to allow airline planners to sleep well at night.

At $189 round trip from Los Angeles to London—cheaper than one way to New York—who cared whether the terminal at Los Angeles was across the tracks and of a standard inferior to the smart architecture of the scheduled terminals?

By this time Adam Thomson was firmly in control. He had fulfilled his ambition to form an airline by the age of thirty-five and had bought his first Boeing 707 when he was forty. Now at forty-two he moved into high gear. True, he had to relinquish absolute financial control. His stake in Caledonian had been diluted when he had to find the money to buy the Boeing. The capital had been increased from shipping interests on the Clyde—Donaldson, Lyle, Hogarth; from Great Universal Stores; and from the Industrial

Commercial Finance Corporation, an investment agency of a consortium of banks. But Thomson retained managerial control, through powers conferred to Airways Interests (Thomson), a voting trust, amicably agreed to by the voters. *Trust* was the key word, for the owners of Caledonian had complete confidence in the chairman of the board.

As the decade of the 1960s drew to its close, Adam Thomson not only steered his airline through an unprecedented period of growth but also into an airline takeover of national—later international—importance, and in so doing he transformed the British airline industry, until then completely dominated by the two state-owned airlines.

On the traffic side, Caledonian carried three times as many North Atlantic passengers and four times as many inclusive-tour holidaymakers in 1969 as in 1968. Imaginative marketing efforts included Swinging London Weekend flights by Gerry Herod's Travellers International for New York theater or night-club devotees, doubtless traveling as members of the Manchester United Supporters Club, Brooklyn Chapter.

True, the Bureau of Enforcement of the U.S. Civil Aeronautics Board filed a complaint against five transatlantic airlines. Although Caledonian was one of the defendants, the main culprits were the new airlines that tried to gain some of the V.F.R. traffic that Caledonian had generated and flagrantly broke the rules. The essence of the complaint was that certain passengers could not produce evidence that they belonged to any registered club. The reaction of the airlines involved was one of amused disdain. The chairman of the C.A.B. was likened to King Canute trying to turn back the tide or to trying to spit into the wind. Leonard Bebchick thought the threat to be ludicrous, and in his statement in the Caledonian 1968–69 annual report, Thomson stated tersely: "We agree fully with his conclusions."

Caledonian Airways had far more important things to consider than the undignified bureaucratic wriggling in Washington. Two large British independent airlines suddenly collapsed in 1968, and the Scottish operator took up much of the slack, including many stranded passengers. Once again, word-of-mouth publicity contributed to Caledonian's image, one satisfied passenger remarking that the crew "never behaved like people who were doing you a favour"—which they really were, as Caledonian donated the aircraft, returning stranded Californians to Los Angeles and Britons to the United Kingdom.

Even more important considerations were just across the horizon. Better than any other independent airline chief, Adam Thomson recognized the opportunity, not only as a natural opportunist—"We will be accused of pleading our own case. We make no bones about it. We are"—but in relation to the stuttering progress of the British civil aviation industry as a whole. In an almost statesmanlike commentary in a message to his employees, he reviewed the full implications of what became known as the Edwards Report.

In 1967 the government had appointed a committee, under the chairmanship of Sir Ronald Edwards, to study the whole future of the British airline industry. Thomson correctly observed, "It may well lay down a pattern that will govern the development of British aviation for the next 20 years or more." He recalled that almost thirty years had passed since the findings of the Cadman Committee had led in 1940 to the formation of B.O.A.C., that Britain had failed to develop a coherent postwar policy, and that "successive governments have done no more than patch up a policy which pays little but lip service to private enterprise. We hope that Edwards will revolutionize this." He was prophetic, for Edwards did bring about a revolution—a moderate revolution, but one that marked a change in British aviation policy which has never been reversed.

The long-awaited Edwards Report was published on April 1, 1969, and one of its far-reaching recommendations was that Great Britain should create a Second Force airline, large enough to add variety, if not direct competition, to the policies that motivated the course of British airline progress. Although several other British airlines, notably Donaldson, British United, Lloyd, and British Midland, had joined in the booming Atlantic market during the latter 1960s, Caledonian was clearly the industry leader among the British independents. All the implications of the Edwards Report seemed to be, in fact, that Caledonian and British United Airways (B.U.A.), which operated a mixed bag of scheduled routes as well as charters, should merge to become the Second Force.

British United had been formed in July 1960, by a merger of Airwork and the Hunting-Clan group, backed by shipping interests. In January 1962, it had purchased the Britavia group, for whom Adam Thomson had formerly flown, and had thus mopped up all but a few of the aspiring postwar independent British airlines. Only Skyways and Eagle were outside the B.U.A. orbit, at least in scheduled operations, and Eagle had already folded.

But not all was well, in spite of the imposing installations at Gatwick Airport, which suggested that B.U.A. was almost the size of its Heathrow rivals, B.O.A.C. and B.E.A. To its credit, largely because of the initiative of one of its directors, Freddie Laker, it had become the launching customer of the British Aircraft Corporation's B.A.C. One-Eleven, the only British jet airliner whose sales even approached break-even numbers. It had also taken over B.O.A.C.'s loss-sustaining South American routes and after four years of arduous work had managed to make them profitable, using British Vickers (now B.A.C.) VC-10s. But its structure was unwieldy and too diversified in the context of the Edwards recommendations.

Of the British United shares in 1969, 98 percent were held by British and Commonwealth Shipping, owned by the Cayser family. Anthony Cayser and Adam Thomson had already been holding discussions, which had reached an advanced stage. Both felt that a Caledonian–B.U.A. merger would fit in precisely with the objectives of the Edwards Second Force. The basic premise was to amalgamate the demonstrated Caledonian flair for innovative marketing with B.U.A.'s established routes and solid technical base at Gatwick, destined to become not only London's second airport, but an important international air hub in its own right.

In a bizarre turn of events, one of the British newspapers disclosed that Nicholas Cayser had been negotiating with the state airline, B.O.A.C. This contravened the presumptions of Edwards, and the storm of protest led to debate of the issue in the House of Commons on March 17, 1970, when the Conservative opposition laid down a motion of censure against the ruling Labour government. Quite remarkably, the president of the Board of Trade, Roy Mason, who was supposed to be briefed on such matters, announced publicly that "he was not aware of the Caledonian negotiations" and that he would give the Caledonian–B.U.A. plan a chance of success.

This was an historic debate, because the unanimity of views of all parties led the Conservatives themselves to withdraw their motion of censure. The way was clear for the merger.

This was put together by the merchant bankers, Kleinwort Benson, and the Industrial Commercial Finance Corporation, the same that had helped Adam Thomson to buy his first Boeing 707.

The official date of the merger—strictly, the purchase of B.U.A., the larger airline, by Caledonian, the smaller of the two—was, with neat timing, St. Andrew's Day, November 30, 1970, exactly nine years after Caledonian Airways had made its first revenue-earning flight with a leased aircraft. The price of B.U.A. was £6,900,000.

With a combined fleet of 31 aircraft—VC-10s, Boeing 707s, and B.A.C. One-Elevens—and operating as British Caledonian Airways, Adam Thomson and his new team set about the formidable task of turning the ideal of a Second Force into a reality. On March 31, 1971, in compliance with the spirit of the Edwards Report, British Caledonian Airways, or B-Cal, as it was becoming known, took over B.O.A.C.'s West African network. Other short-haul routes were added, notably from London (Gatwick) to Paris on November 1, but in fact no serious inroads were made into B.E.A.'s comprehensive European web, least of all to its London (Heathrow)–Paris route.

The most important addition to the Caledonian system was a scheduled service across the North Atlantic to supplement the nonscheduled flights. The British government granted licenses to operate to both New York and Los Angeles on February 18, 1972, and amid a blaze of publicity, the inaugural service to New York left Gatwick on April 1, 1973. The planeload of guests and passengers, including Earl Mountbatten, were piped aboard the Boeing 707 *Flagship Bonnie Scotland,* and the sense of a great occasion was hardly marred by its having to be diverted to Boston because of foul weather in New York.

By an odd twist of fate, the legislation that followed the Edwards Report excluded British Caledonian's authority to operate its charter flights to Singapore, and an amendment, or exemption, from the licensing requirement was required. Thus the Singapore service became known as the Exempt Charter Service. Unfortunately, this also permitted direct competition on the same basis from B.O.A.C. and from Singapore Airlines/M.S.A. and formed the basis of what later became known as Advanced Booking Charters (A.B.C.) and Advanced Purchase Excursion (APEX) fares. For its part, British Caledonian covered its bets by joining with Saber Air, a Singapore charter airline, and opened daily service on its behalf on January 1, 1973.

British United Airways had already fashioned a domestic network in the United Kingdom, culminating in the establishment of intercity jet service from London to Belfast, Edinburgh, and Glasgow, with B.A.C. One-Elevens, on January 4, 1966. To this was added a service to Manchester on November 1, 1973, which, with one to Brussels on June 4, 1974, consolidated an efficient hub system linking the long-distance routes from five continents with a short-haul spoke network at Gatwick.

The Caledonian Airways group had expanded to include associated airlines overseas, such as Gambia Airways and Sierra Leone Airways, a large travel agency—Blue Cars, later Blue Sky,—about a dozen hotels, and other aviation-related activities. This expansion in all the essential components of the transport system required a considerable outlay. But the omens were not good for the expectation of immediate rewards. Just as the expansion program got under way, British Caledonian was assailed on all fronts. During the early 1970s, the oil price increase imposed on the whole world by the Organization of Petroleum Exporting Countries (OPEC) hit the airlines severely. B-Cal's entry on the North Atlantic was opposed emphatically by rivals who were not about to greet the newcomer with enthusiasm and sympathy. There was a devaluation problem in Argentina, source of much of the Latin American revenue, and the hopes of a more widely based European route system as a result of the Edwards recommendations had not materialized. British Caledonian suddenly found itself facing financial disaster and inevitable extinction.

Adam Thomson faced the crisis grimly and took some hard decisions. He acted swiftly, effectively, some would say ruthlessly. But, rather as Frank Lorenzo did in the crisis at Continental a decade later, when the only alternative would have been to close down an important airline, he did what he had to do. Within a period of only a few weeks, he pulled British Caledonian out of the North Atlantic scheduled market (on October 31, 1974), grounded five B.A.C. One-Elevens, and reduced the size of his staff by more than 15 percent, from 5,500 to 4,675. He trimmed management by 30 percent, and several of the senior members, including Guinane, Bates, Crosbie, and de la Haye (who was ill) left for a period. Frank Hope had already departed a little earlier. British Caledonian licked its wounds, struggled on in the markets it had retained, did a record business on the Hajj, and adjusted to a new level of service, adopting a more wary attitude toward its future.

Thomson also had to mark time, for a new British Labour government had called for a Civil Aviation Review, to reevaluate airline policy. The result was not exactly world-shattering for British Caledonian, but at least it knew where it stood and was able to make long-term plans and to order a new generation of aircraft accordingly. Under the circumstances—because a Labour administration would be expected to favor the state-owned airline, British Airways—Thomson felt that the minister of transport, Peter Shore, was quite fair in allocating routes on a spheres-of-influence basis, especially in allowing B-Cal to retain British authority to fly to Houston and Atlanta, which at the time were not part of the United States–United Kingdom bilateral agreement.

British Caledonian was still denied access to New York and Los Angeles and had thus to pay dearly for clipping its own wings in 1974. But gradually the tide turned. Under the new dual-designation U.S. gateway arrangements that arose out of the Bermuda Two bilateral agreement signed on July 23, 1977, there was some compensation in being offered direct access to Houston, Atlanta, and—later—Dallas/Fort Worth. Crumbs though these may have been from the master's table, they were sizable crumbs. All three destinations were in the prospering southeastern quadrant of the United States, and each city was the center of a highly developed regional hub system, acting as a feeder to the long-distance routes.

Additionally, British Caledonian had been allocated the northwestern South American group of routes, taking over services to Caracas, Bogotá, and Lima from British Airways late in 1976, so that a new transatlantic network was in prospect. Thomson had had to swallow a bitter pill, however. His old adversary, Freddie Laker, who had campaigned vigorously in his characteristically flamboyant style, had seized the opportunity to attack on all fronts, seeking support for his cause from politicians and the public alike. Laker actually took the minister to court and won his case to be designated as the third British scheduled operator to the United States, thereby inheriting the cherished routes to New York and Los Angeles, partly on the grounds that, since British Caledonian had voluntarily surrendered them, he should be given his chance to launch the innovative Skytrain service. This development, incidentally, had the residual effect of negating the former spheres-of-influence policy introduced by Labour's Peter Shore.

British Caledonian moved into wide-bodied service in 1977. The airline took delivery of its first long-range McDonnell Douglas

DC-10-30 in February 1977 and introduced it on the West African routes the following month. The second DC-10 having been delivered soon afterward, the North Atlantic charter program opened in May with wide-bodied comfort and Caledonian cabin-service standards. On October 23, service began on the new route from Gatwick to Houston, an order was placed for two more DC-10s, and a group trading profit of almost £10 million was announced.

Adam Thomson had been made a Commander of the British Empire in the 1976 New Year's Honours List. Quite apart from the personal satisfaction that he must have enjoyed on receiving such recognition, he must have been reasonably well pleased at the thought that his airline was holding its own against stiff competition. British Caledonian had gained a new foothold in the United States and had entered the wide-bodied era. But he was bitter about the Laker affair and did not mince words. With a certain clairvoyance in respect to the route to Los Angeles, he stated in his report to the shareholders in April 1969 "This route is better served by B-Cal's proposal to cover all sectors of the market, first class, executive, thrift, and cargo, than by the one-class Skytrain type of service. Time will show this view to be right and when it does that the Civil Aviation Authority should not allow Laker Airways gradually to change its mode of operation to that proposed by B-Cal whose license it revoked." Prophetic words indeed, in the light of subsequent events.

During the closing years of the 1970s, in fact, British Caledonian went through a remarkable transformation, unrecorded by newspaper headlines but nonetheless as significant as the award of any major route. Between 1976 and 1980 the airline changed from a primarily charter, or nonscheduled airline into a predominantly scheduled one. The charter traffic percentage declined from 52 percent to 12 percent during that period. At the same time, the introduction of wide-bodied DC-10s proceeded apace, and by 1980 these aircraft were carrying 55 percent of the total revenue-earning capacity.

The catastrophic American Airlines crash at Chicago on May 25, 1979, severely affected passengers' acceptance of the DC-10 for a while, but—in one of the very few matters upon which Thomson and Freddie Laker were able to agree—British Caledonian maintained complete faith in the integrity of that aircraft. Thomson even contemplated taking legal action against the U.S. Federal Aviation Administration for not allowing the aircraft into the

United States for a period of several weeks, causing severe loss of revenue to all DC-10 operators.

Another development during the summer of 1980 was the announcement that the number of international passengers at Gatwick Airport had risen to rank London's second airport as the fourth busiest in serving the European international market, surpassing Amsterdam and exceeded only by Heathrow, Orly (Paris), and Frankfurt. British Caledonian's steady and continuous growth had contributed greatly to this surprising result.

All things considered, Thomson was poised to enter a new decade with a certain élan. New routes were opened to no fewer than four long-haul destinations—St. Louis, Atlanta, Dallas/Fort Worth, and Hong Kong. Of these, the Atlanta route, opened on June 1, 1980, with six DC-10 round trips a week, was the most important transatlantic addition, while the Hong Kong route reinstated British Caledonian's presence in the Far East, which had waned since the heady days of the Singapore exempt charters. Although Thomson was doubtless pleased that Sir Freddie had been denied access to Hong Kong by the authorities in the Crown Colony, he was up against stiff competition from British Airways, which had occupied the route as a monopoly since time immemorial, and from the other newcomer, Cathay Pacific, from Hong Kong itself, with consequent built-in advantages of market identity and an efficient feeder system from every city in the western Pacific.

The London–Hong Kong route is a curious anomaly in the legalistic world of ICAO's framework of the Freedoms of Air. Both termini are British, and it is therefore an unusual kind of domestic route, free from any obligation to require international landing rights from a British operator, at least until China assumes sovereignty. Because of geographical circumstance, however, it could not, until recently, be operated without recourse to one or more international freedoms, such as overflying or nontraffic landing at a point en route. Nevertheless, London–Hong Kong traffic, spurred by the multiple-airline competition on this unusual domestic route, has grown swiftly. Imaginative scheduling, standards of service, and an energetic fares war produced positive results for all the participants, and the benefits to the British traveling public were such as had not been experienced in many a long day.

During 1981 British Caledonian's financial results were disappointing. Besides Freddie Laker's transatlantic Skytrain, a host of other newcomers had joined the fray, so more than forty airlines were operating scheduled service between Europe and North America. Unfortunately, this was a desperate period for the world airline industry as a whole. Airlines were cutting fares with gay abandon, and the Atlantic sky was almost a free market. Laker at first thrived, but he overreached himself, expanded too ambitiously, and rashly bought European Airbuses for routes that he did not have. In a classic example of "How are the mighty fallen" Sir Freddie was forced to cease operations abruptly on February 5, 1982. After unnecessary delays from the U.S. authorities, British Caledonian at last returned to Los Angeles on May 21, 1982.

The Falkland Islands War put an end to service to Argentina and also to Chile, so the South American east coast service was curtailed to terminate at São Paulo. The northwest South American service was pulled back to Bogotá, with, however, San Juan, Puerto Rico, now added as a stop en route. Such route manipulations weighed, on balance, in British Caledonian's favor, at least in the profit and loss account.

Now another threatening cloud appeared. The British government announced its intention to turn over the state airline, British Airways, to private investors. As a great supporter of private enterprise, Sir Adam Thomson—he had been knighted by Queen Elizabeth on March 29, 1983, in the New Year Honours List—quite naturally regarded this threatened development with alarm. One of the comforting thoughts he had always nursed during times of crisis was that, mighty though British Airways might be, with its enormous fleet, massive route network, and excessive staff, it was inefficient. During the Skytrain period, it had run up unbelievable debts, mainly by cutting fares to match Laker's.

He expressed his views, as usual, in incontrovertible logic: "Moves have already begun with the support, last year, of the state airline's loss of £545 million. We object most strongly, however, to our main competitor being bailed out after making losses on a scale which would put a private company out of business, then being groomed to appear financially attractive to investors, without any consideration whatsoever being given to the effect of this action on British Caledonian Airways." No doubt Sir Freddie Laker, stoutly fighting a rearguard action in the courts, would even have had some sympathy with Sir Adam's case, bearing in mind that British Airways had been one of the worst fare-slashers, stealing

Skytrain traffic while it was losing money hand over fist at the tax-payer's expense. Some of the other airlines that had also believed in a low-fare policy suffered from traffic diversion, and one or two of them even collapsed.

While British Airways excused itself on the grounds that all the airlines were losing money, especially on the North Atlantic routes, Thomson was able to report, "Throughout the worst years in the history of the international airline industry we have continued to be the fastest-growing scheduled service airline in Europe." Thus, with good Scottish thrift echoed by consistently satisfactory financial results, compared with which those of British Airways looked like the national debt, he felt that the new Conservative government, under Margaret Thatcher, should give him a fair shake.

British Caledonian made its case to the government, in discussions with both senior ministers and the Civil Aviation Authority and in a series of publications whose superb presentation, in well-chosen words and well-designed maps and charts, were models of their kind. Among these, the one published on January 31, 1984, *A Competitive Strategy for British Air Transport in Private Ownership*, made the arguments so succinctly that the Gold Book—as it became known, from its striking cover—could have served as a blueprint for British air transport for the next quarter-century.

The case was made passionately but with systematic logic. British Caledonian did not seek equality with British Airways, nor did it challenge the status of the latter as the British Chosen Instrument. It pointed out that, in spite of the recommendations of the Edwards Committee, British Airways still accounted for 83 percent of the scheduled service output and that of the remainder, B-Cal's was only 13 percent and the demise of a number of struggling independent companies clutching for the residual 4 percent was no surprise. The point was made that Britain's Second Force was thus a very poor second, and the corresponding percentage relation was less extreme in all the other leading airline countries.

Demonstrating an approach that went beyond British Caledonian's self-interest, the reports observed that Gatwick's position as a major airport serving London was also an important issue to be addressed. Coincidentally, Gatwick served only 14 percent of London's air traffic, and the Gold Book contained an admirable map showing the catchment areas of both Heathrow and Gatwick, not only for London, but for the whole of southeast England, and reminding readers, some of whom seemed not be aware of its relevance, that the M25 Orbital Road, almost completed, would change the patterns of airport accessibility.

In summary Thomson stated, "Under the circumstances it must be a nonsense for a Government dedicated to supporting private enterprise to create an instrument that will undoubtedly undermine those who have built the existing independent sector." The main thing British Caledonian asked for was a better share of Europe, including all the Iberian peninsula, the Polar route to Tokyo, the Caribbean and South American sphere of influence, and a modest share of the routes to India, Canada, and the Middle East. The entire package was estimated to bring British Caledonian's annual passenger boardings to a level equal to about 34 percent of those of British Airways and the number of weekly flights to be 35 percent.

The case was a good one and should have appealed to the Thatcher government. But British Airways had its supporters too, and the debate developed into a political dispute. Norman Tebbitt, secretary of state for trade, supported British Airways, while Nicholas Ridley, secretary of state for transport, and other members of the Cabinet backed Thomson. Ridley asked the advice of the Civil Aviation Authority, which thereupon instituted the Civil Aviation Review. In substance the C.A.A. supported Thomson's case, recommending in its report CAP 500, dated July 16, 1984, a substantial transfer of routes from British Airways to British Caledonian, subject to the latter's proof that it could generate the funds to support such expansion—for the transfer of only 15 percent of British Airways' traffic would require B-Cal to double its output. Thomson was able to demonstrate that he could raise £150 million in additional equity capital, plus £240 million in loans for additional aircraft.

For the British airline industry, which had stumbled forward in fits and starts since the end of World War II, too often the victim of successive government vacillation, sometimes the battered ball in games of political football, and occasionally its own worst enemy, this was, in the title of one of the handsome British Caledonian documents, the Historic Opportunity. To its eternal shame, the British government threw it away.

It took precious little note of the logic of British Caledonian's case, the principles of competition that it espoused, or the C.A.A.'s recommendation. Sheltering behind assertions that British Airways' status as the designated carrier, under scores of bilateral agreements, determined much of the international policy, it also ignored the C.A.A.'s view that British Airways was a monopoly within the meaning of the Fair Trading Act of 1973 and that the state airline's revenue was "earned from higher fares than the Authority would approve, were the U.K. the sole regulator."

In a travesty of what would have been judged to have been good common sense had the politicians accepted even half of British Caledonian's recommendations, the British government made the kind of decision which, had it been made by a Labour administration, would have brought accusations of socialist bias and drawn a vote of censure in Parliament from self-righteous defenders of competition. But there was, it seemed, a great deal of difference between a state-owned airline and a state-owned airline that was about to be given into private hands.

The net result was that British Caledonian was offered routes to Saudi Arabia in exchange for the transfer back to British Airways of its routes to Latin America. In the circumstances, with the British Airways privatization policy an important factor, Sir Adam Thomson felt that there was cause for satisfaction in that after a determined fight he was able to retain routes to the U.S. gateways and to Hong Kong and was also to reenter the New York market. The withdrawal from Brazil and the Caribbean and the inauguration of direct service to Riyadh, capital of Saudi Arabia, took place on March 31, 1985. A month later, British Caledonian returned to New York. And on January 23, 1986, the Civil Aviation Authority granted authority for B-Cal to initiate a service to Tokyo.

Altogether, however, this was a shabby outcome of a once promising development that could have changed the face, for the better, of the entire British commercial aviation scene. The Second Force's share of the airline market went up modestly from 13 percent to 15 percent, hardly a cause for great rejoicing. But there were no recriminations at Gatwick, where Sir Adam and his B-Cal team face the future with confidence. After all, for an airline that was founded only in 1961, had entered the scheduled market only in 1970, and had actually withdrawn from the lucrative North Atlantic arena in 1974, things could have been a great deal worse.

As for Thomson himself, he has cause for quiet satisfaction. He has certainly fulfilled his youthful ambition to form an airline and can look back on some notable achievements. Perhaps the turning point was January 31, 1962, when Caledonian filed his application for a U.S. Section 402 foreign permit and put the whole business of Visiting Friends and Relatives into top gear. He has come a long way in the twenty-five years since then, from rebel to reformer to aviation statesman. As British Airways goes through its reconstruction under the dictates of privatization, it would do well to keep constantly on the alert. For Sir Adam Thomson, representing the Second Force, is watching every move, and, as if to underscore his determination, British Caledonian became, in November 1986, the first airline in the world to order the MD-11, McDonnell Douglas's technologically advanced successor to the already highly economical DC-10.

▸ ▸ ▸ ▸ ▸ ▸ ▸ ▸ ▸ ▸ ▸ ▸ ▸ ▸ ▸ ▸ ▸ ▸ ▸

Europe

▸ ▸ ▸ ▸ ▸ ▸ ▸ ▸ ▸ ▸ ▸ ▸ ▸ ◂ ▸ ▸ ▸ ▸ ▸

▶▶▶▶▶▶▶▶▶▶▶▶▶▶▶▶ ◀▶▶▶▶▶▶▶

Marcel Bouilloux-Lafont

The Shattered Dream

In this book there are many stories of men whose lives progressed along the rags-to-riches course. There are accounts of rich men who became even richer and of those who went from rags to riches only to revert to a level of income far removed from their earlier afflu-ence. The case of Marcel Bouilloux-Lafont, however, was unique. He was a great airline man who actually went from riches to rags, through no fault of his own. True, he did not die a pauper, but com-pared to the comfortable security of the financial empire over which he once ruled he was poor—and certainly he was spiritually weak—at the end of his life.

Furthermore, Bouilloux-Lafont was no ordinary airline pro-moter, seeking to cut a niche for himself in some corner of the world or in some segment of airline activity that seemed to have been over-looked, ignored, or suppressed. He was extraordinary, possibly the most visionary of all the airline promoters who came to prominence during the formative years of the air transport industry.

In a few short years, from 1927 to 1931, he built the largest and most prestigious airline in the world. Then, at the very mo-ment that he stood poised to assert the world leadership that was within his grasp, he was ruined, put out of business by political-industrial intrigue in France. His good name was destroyed, he lost an immense fortune, and his great airline was reduced to a mere shadow of its former self.

Marcel Bouilloux-Lafont (center) built Aéropostale to become the largest airline in the world by 1930. Poised to pioneer the first North Atlantic air service, he was forced into financial ruin in 1931 by a political-industrial intrigue engineered by jealous rivals. In this picture he is seen with his chief pilot, the famous Jean Mermoz (left), and with Sr Angel S. Adami, a famous Uruguayan air pioneer (right). The picture was taken at the Montevideo airport, constructed by the Bouilloux-Lafont organization.

Marcel Bouilloux-Lafont was born in Angoulême, France, on April 9, 1871. He was educated at the College of Étampes, then at the University of Paris. He began a career as a lawyer but later joined the business that his father had founded in 1855. He became prominent in business, owning property and investing in banks and other commercial activities, not only in France but also in South America, particularly in Brazil, which he first visited in 1907 and where he built docks, railways, apartment houses, and other installations. He was an intense French patriot, and his determination to succeed in South America was motivated in part by memories of the bitterness generated between France and Germany during World War I, the Great War that transformed the way of life and the social conduct of the whole of Europe.

During the mid 1920s, as an adjunct to his commercial activities within South America and because of his need to travel frequently between that continent and Europe, he became interested in commercial aviation. At the time, a French aircraft manufacturer and airline promoter, Pierre-Georges Latécoère, was trying to extend his airline route, which already linked France with what was then French West Africa. His ambition was to cross the South Atlantic from Dakar, Senegal, to a point in Brazil and along the coast of eastern South America as far as Buenos Aires, the Paris of South America and a great capital city in its own right. His airline was the Compagnie Générale d'Enterprises Aéronautiques (C.G.E.A.), also known as the Ligne Latécoère, or simply La Ligne.

One of the popular fallacies of aviation history is that the Germans were almost exclusively responsible for the early development of airlines in Latin America. During the early period, immediately following the Great War, the French were just as active and at least as successful. Only in the mid 1920s, when the remarkable little Junkers-F 13 metal airplane demonstrated its ruggedness and resistance to the severe operating conditions of the South American jungles, mountains, and tropical waterways—not to mention the termites that besieged the wooden airplanes—did German-sponsored companies gain the ascendancy.

Latécoère's airline represented one of the efforts to expand French influence throughout South America. C.G.E.A. was one of the first as well as one of the finest airlines in the world. Based at Toulouse, in the south of France, it was operating scheduled mail services to Algeria and Morocco as early as 1919 and had extended its routes to Dakar by 1925. The ultimate destination was Argentina, a prosperous country at that time whose standard of living during the interwar period was equal to that of many European countries.

Latécoère's route development was encouraged and subsidized by the French government, but the fleet, consisting mainly of aged aircraft of almost vintage design, was barely adequate. His seaplanes, flying boats, and landplanes were all produced in his own factory. But he lacked the necessary foreign authority to achieve his goals, seemed unable to discern the proper approach in South America to obtain such authority, and did not appear to have a cohesive plan for crossing the South Atlantic.

The Brazilians, who controlled a large section of Latécoère's cherished Paris–Buenos Aires route, were not being deliberately obstructionist. Because of the vast size of the country—larger in area than the forty-eight states of the United States—and its coastline stretching along half the east coast of South America, to grant operating rights to a foreign airline would have had far-reaching implications. Years later, when the airline countries of the world thrashed out a formula of flying privileges that became known as the Five Freedoms of the Air, the Brazilian bone of contention in the 1930s was a prime example of cabotage—the freedom to operate with full traffic authority wholly within the boundaries of a foreign country. Cabotage in the air is very seldom exercised today, and the privilege is jealously guarded. Little wonder that in the 1920s Brazil watched the foreign airlines carefully, whether they were from Europe or from the United States.

In December 1926, a frustrated Latécoère sought help from Bouilloux-Lafont, whose business success in Brazil had drawn widespread attention. In an historic meeting, Bouilloux-Lafont is reported to have said, "I have never before invested a sou in aviation; but you are French, I am French, all my resources and energies are at your disposal." On April 11, 1927, Bouilloux-Lafont bought Latécoère's airline and renamed it Aéropostale, a word that is revered today in France with romantic passion, even by Bouilloux-Lafont's enemies and detractors, who try to pretend that he never existed and to transfer the credit for his achievements to others.

The French business tycoon did more than buy an airline. He inherited a tradition. The company had been run by an efficient and indefatigable tyrant, Didier Daurat. C.G.E.A. was Daurat's whole life. His devotion to to La Ligne was intense, and his team of pilots became a collective legend in their own time. Jean Mermoz, one of the great pioneer airmen of all time, is held in the same esteem in French aviation circles as Lindbergh is in the United States—and with some justification. Antoine de St. Exupéry is possibly better known, not only because of his exploits as a pilot, both in peacetime and in war, but mainly because he could write even better than he could fly.

Latécoère's Ligne was supported by a heavy subsidy, paid according to a generous formula by the French government to carry the mails. This was not unusual during these exploratory and developmental years of air transport. All airlines that aspired to win international spoils, not to mention prestige, on behalf of their governments, were paid subsidies. Germany, France, Italy, Great Britain, and the United States all subsidized heavily the airlines that carried the mail. Sometimes the contributions were euphemistically described as mail payments but they were subsidies just the same.

The Latécoère fleet was easily the largest of any airline in the world, at least in numbers, if not in quality. It certainly had good pilots and a good organization, and to these priceless assets and Didier Daurat's discipline, Bouilloux-Lafont was to add initiative, drive, and leadership. He inherited a good airline and made it into a great one. His greatest secret was knowing how to negotiate with Latin American governments, and he combined this knowledge with a determination to succeed.

To operate the important Brazilian section of the Paris–Buenos Aires route, Latécoère had originally obtained the necessary authority, in October 1925, through a subsidiary company. But the authority was not ratified, partly because the Germans were campaigning effectively, establishing the renowned Condor Syndikat as the agency for German airline enterprise in South America. Condor obtained Brazilian operating rights in January 1927, gaining a head start on C.G.E.A., whose special position was not confirmed until March.

Bouilloux-Lafont took complete control of C.G.E.A. in April 1927, Latécoère retired from active participation in the airline, retaining only a small nominal shareholding and transferring his interests to the building of a line of fine flying boats at Biscarosse, near Bordeaux, and selling aircraft to Bouilloux-Lafont. Bouilloux-Lafont, meanwhile, with characteristic energy and drive, set in motion, with his own funds, an extensive development program, with a budget of US$1.5 million which, in 1927-equivalent purchasing power, would represent $25 million today.

During this period, when world airlines were in their infancy, operations were still somewhat hazardous and certainly very costly. Little revenue could be earned from passengers, for the high fares needed to cover operating costs deterred all but the wealthy—and the adventurous wealthy at that—from undertaking long air journeys. The main source of revenue was mail. Having already inherited the French and Brazilian air mail contracts, Bouilloux-Lafont negotiated one in Argentina in June 1927, to carry 25 percent of the mail to Europe. Subsequently he obtained other mail contracts—from Chile and Paraguay in 1928, Venezuela in 1929, and Bolivia and Peru in 1930.

Much of his considerable investment was spent in building the essential infrastructure to support the airline. In South America in the 1920s, most of the governments were either completely impoverished or had other priorities. The airlines were expected to provide their own ground services. Accordingly, Paul Vachet, one of Aéropostale's best pilots who also had a flair for practical organization on the ground, undertook the massive task. Under Vachet's direction, the airline established flying-boat bases, airfields and emergency landing grounds, hangars, lighting and radio installations. Vachet's chain of ground support spread all the way from the island of Fernando de Noronha, off the northeastern tip of Brazil, to Argentina and Paraguay. Such was the thoroughness of this pioneer work accomplished in the late 1920s that traces of it can still be found along the coast of Brazil today, where many airports were developed from the foundations laid down by Vachet. Incidentally, the other French airlines, which received government subsidy on the same basis as Aéropostale, were not burdened with this obligation.

Aéropostale inherited—that is to say, purchased—close to two hundred mail-carrying aircraft. All were built or modified by Latécoère, but their performance for South American operations was woefully inadequate. To cross the Andes between Buenos Aires and Santiago, Bouilloux-Lafont had to order two Potez 25s, which could cruise at an altitude of 6,000 meters. Flying from Africa to Brazil with a payload, however, was still beyond the grasp of heavier-than-air aircraft of the 1920s. The famous airship *Graf Zeppelin* was establishing a good reputation as the lighter-than-air solution to long-distance flying, for passengers as well as for mail. The first regular airplane all–air mail flights across the South Atlantic were not achieved until February 1934, when Deutsche Lufthansa inaugurated its historic service by the ingenious device of stationing ships equipped with catapults in mid ocean to provide the Dornier Wals with mid-ocean depots.

Nevertheless, Aéropostale inaugurated a mail service from Toulouse to Buenos Aires on March 1, 1928, and extended it to Santiago on July 15, 1929. The 3,000-kilometer transocean section across the South Atlantic from Dakar to Fernando de Noronha was performed by fast destroyers on loan from the French Navy. In spite of this surface-borne segment, necessitated by the range limitations of the available aircraft, Aéropostale offered Paris–Buenos Aires mail service in eight days, which compared favorably with the sixteen days taken by the fastest ocean liner. Seeking to miti-

The Latécoère 38 was ordered in 1930 by Marcel Bouilloux-Lafont expressly for his developing transatlantic service and to expand Aéropostale's network northwards from South America to the Caribbean and the United States. The development of this aircraft was neglected, for reasons that have never been fully explained.

gate a technical limitation, in November 1928 Bouilloux-Lafont ordered six new ships, designed especially to provide faster service across the ocean. The first of these entered service in 1930.

Such was the effect of Aéropostale's performance that businessmen in New York discovered that the quickest way to send mail or packages to Argentina was to ship them to France and hand them over to Didier Daurat's intrepid team of pilots based at Toulouse.

Rivalry for South Atlantic air mail honors between France and Germany intensified. Bouilloux-Lafont consolidated his position in Argentina by creating Aeroposta Argentina as a local subsidiary in September 1927. By establishing a locally registered company such as this, and also companies in Uruguay, Brazil, and other countries, he overcame opposition on both the political and the personal fronts. German competition was in evidence when the *Graf Zeppelin* made a survey flight from Friedrichshafen, Germany, to Rio de Janeiro in May 1930 to demonstrate the practicability of a regular passenger-carrying airship service.

Even the great German airship was scooped, however. On an historic flight on May 12, one week before the *Graf Zeppelin* left Friedrichshafen, Jean Mermoz flew a new Latécoère 28 floatplane, the *Comte de la Vaulx*, across the South Atlantic. He flew nonstop from St. Louis, Senegal, to Natal, Brazil, in 19 hours 35 minutes. On this single occasion, mail was delivered from Paris to Buenos Aires in only four days, a triumph of French enterprise and organization. More specifically, it provided dramatic evidence of the great potential of Aéropostale.

Strangely, Mermoz is remembered vividly by the French aviation fraternity today, and his colleague Saint-Exupéry is almost deified, but the man who was the driving force behind both the flight and the airline that promoted it is not only widely forgotten in France today, but his memory is being deliberately suppressed.

Bouilloux-Lafont was rapidly expanding the Aéropostale empire in South America. A local network had been opened in Venezuela early in 1930, Chile was linked with Peru and Bolivia in October of that year, and service from Venezuela to Trinidad was begun in January 1931. In less than four years, Bouilloux-Lafont had created an airline organization that served nine countries in South America. Plans were afoot to open a route from Natal to Caracas via the French, Dutch, and British Guianas. Colombia and neighboring Ecuador, where the Colombo-German airline SCADTA was solidly established, were the only countries on the entire continent that were beyond Aéropostale's grasp.

By the end of 1931, Bouilloux-Lafont had also acquired a substantial interest in the Compagnie Transafricaine, which had been established in 1929 to operate air services across Africa from Algiers to Madagascar via the Belgian Congo. The considerable subsidy paid to Aéropostale was generous, but no more so than that paid to other French airlines. Aéropostale, moreover, had built its own infrastructure, whereas the other airlines relied on facilities provided by the countries served en route—in British India, for example. Such was the strength of Bouilloux-Lafont's carefully constructed system that his aircraft were flying almost as many miles—and receiving almost as much subsidy—as the other four French airlines put together.

Suddenly, on March 31, 1931, in a decision that shattered the aviation world of France and elsewhere, Aéropostale was placed under a state of *liquidation judiciaire*. One U.S. writer later described the event: "Government subsidy was withheld through political intrigue, and the company went into bankruptcy." This succinct statement referred to an orchestrated campaign by French industrialists and politicians to get rid of Marcel Bouilloux-Lafont.

The agreement between Aéropostale and the air minister, Victor Laurent-Eynac, signed on August 2, 1929, was never shown to the Chamber by the minister. Consequently, the Chamber was never given a chance to ratify the agreement—a quite extraordinary political circumstance. The subsidy, paid in arrears, was withheld. To make matters worse, the worldwide repercussions of the Wall Street crash in 1929 and political problems in Brazil adversely affected Bouilloux-Lafont's financial reserves. The monies subscribed by the French public by a bond issue and allocated to the provision of the great infrastructure, new aircraft, and new ships were suddenly deprived of adequate security.

Although legally the French *liquidation judiciaire* falls short of bankruptcy, the effect on the victim is the same and is far more severe than the now familiar Chapter 11 clause of the U.S. bankruptcy laws. Bouilloux-Lafont was a broken man.

The French government apparently wished to acquire an interest, amounting to about a third of the share capital, in the entire French airline industry, at the same time reorganizing it into three systems. This was in accordance with the time honored custom of *blocage*, whereby the government could acquire a shareholding if a commercial activity affected national policy or military strategy. Bouilloux-Lafont seemed to have been caught up in this survival of Napoleonic law, although another interpretation is that certain industrial interests invoked the principles of the law for their own ends.

If Bouilloux-Lafont's independence seemed truculent, there was a reason. The other four French airlines were heavily backed by French aircraft manufacturers. Air Union's board included Breguet, Blériot, and many other well-known aviation names, CIDNA's included Potez, and S.G.T.A. was synonymous with Farman. Latécoère, of course, had formerly been one of this exclusive club that built aircraft for its own airlines, but Marcel Bouilloux-Lafont was not a member. Vigorously independent, he was nevertheless every bit a patriot. He felt strongly that he had built his airline for the glory of France. But the financial resources, leadership, and management skills were his and no one else's. The other airlines, in contrast, had no need for ships, they obtained aircraft from parent manufacturers and paid next to nothing for their infrastructure. By falling in with the government's plan, the other airline promoters, who had their manufacturing plants to fall back on, had everything to gain from a captive market. Bouilloux-Lafont had nothing to gain and everything to lose.

But these considerations, involving a sense of justice as much as a code of ethics, meant little to the forces that were determined to destroy Aéropostale and to get rid of Bouilloux-Lafont. The decision of March 31, 1931, in effect ostracized the entire Bouilloux-Lafont family, turning them almost into outlaws. Marcel himself seldom visited France thereafter, except for essential business matters. Such was the animosity prevailing at the time that poor André Bouilloux-Lafont, Marcel's son, was caught up in a scandal when he indiscreetly made accusations against the head of CIDNA and Gnôme et Rhône, Paul-Louis Weiller. The accusations, based on false evidence supplied by an *agent provocateur,* purported to show that the German airline, Deutsche Luft Hansa, a Spanish group, and Weiller were planning to establish a transoceanic airline to supersede Aéropostale. André had obtained a declaration of authenticity of the documents from a qualified graphologist and had shown them to government officials. At the subsequent trial, other graphologists then declared that the documents were false, and the *agent* suddenly reversed his evidence and declared that the documents were false. André was then charged with having deliberately used the documents to defame the parties mentioned—who included a senior member of the French aviation ministry—and was convicted.

The whole affair was most unsavory and seems to have bordered on a severe miscarriage of justice. It was certainly an additional cross for Marcel Bouilloux-Lafont to bear. It could have been written off as just a routine historical incident, albeit a colorful one involving a clash of personalities. Life is full of injustice, and arguably, because of his determined, even obstinate independence, Marcel Bouilloux-Lafont paid an extortionate price. Perhaps he should have swallowed his pride, accepted the 33 percent government shareholding, and continued to run his airline. But if that too was in the government's plan, why did it condone the systematic campaign of defamation? And what was the reason for the peremptory manner of the March 31 announcement, which left no flexibility for maneuver, discussion, or appeal?

Two years later, on May 17, 1933, four airlines, Air Orient, Air Union, CIDNA, and S.G.T.A., merged to form the Société Centrale pour l'Exploitation de Lignes Aériennes (SCELA). This was the preliminary sparring before the formation of Air France on August 30, 1933, when SCELA purchased Aéropostale's assets.

Bouilloux-Lafont's airline, by now only a shadow of its former self, had been kept flying by a committee, concentrating only on the trunk route to Buenos Aires and Santiago. SCELA, representing the power of the French aircraft industry, now proceeded to acquire it by outright purchase, in 1933. It engulfed Aéropostale's 130 aircraft, its four modern ships, all its ground installations, its base at Toulouse, a good organization, and the finest team of airline pilots in the world. For these assets—half the French airline industry—it paid 77,250,000 francs, which it was permitted to pay off in fifteen annual installments *without interest.* At the end of the payment period, taking into account the declining value of the franc, this was equivalent to the cost of a good dinner for Air France's Board of Directors, which, as a matter of record, was a who's who of the French aircraft manufacturing industry, supplemented by the French banks and representatives of the Republic. By the device of first forming the SCELA association and only then purchasing Aéropostale's assests while in *liquidation judiciaire,* the ousting of Bouilloux-Lafont was a model of Machiavellian ingenuity.

The tragedy is that French authorities who so callously disposed of an irritant to their master plan did not realize that, at the same time, they were surrendering a unique opportunity to gain world airline supremacy, for the Aéropostale promoter's vision reached farther than Latin America, on which he already had a firm grip, or Africa, where his plans were in an advanced stage. Trying to prevent the Germans from obtaining a strategic advantage, Bouilloux-Lafont became involved in international negotiations with Portugal, so as to secure landing rights in the Cape Verde Islands and—later—in the Azores. As a direct result, a series of events occurred in rapid succession that suddenly placed him in a privileged position. To put no finer point on the situation, Marcel Bouilloux-Lafont was poised to dominate about two thirds of the world's international air traffic at that time.

During the years between the two world wars, the leading European countries still held sovereignty over much of the Eastern Hemisphere. Portugal still retained considerable possessions in Africa and offshore islands in the Atlantic. With no airline of its own, it sought assistance. Bouilloux-Lafont was in a perfect position to help. He simply had to add spurs to his existing West African coastal route to serve all the Portuguese territories in Africa, and he quickly moved to take advantage of his priceless strategic assets.

The manner in which this would be accomplished was to be by a joint Franco-Portuguese company, Sociedade Portuguesa de Estudos e Linhas Aereas (SPELA), formed by Portuguese private interests, the French aircraft engine manufacturer Gnôme et Rhône, and Aéropostale. By drawing upon Aéropostale's resources and experience, SPELA would develop a network to the Portuguese colonies in systematic stages.

It was an industrial-political masterstroke. The SPELA agreement was signed on September 16, 1930. Bouilloux-Lafont and Paul-Louis Weiller, head of the Gnôme et Rhône engine company, thereby pulled off a coup that hit the other air countries of the world like a thunderbolt. In exchange for services rendered, the Portuguese government granted to SPELA—that is, to Aéropostale—the exclusive landing rights in all Portuguese territories. The mainland of Africa under Lisbon's sovereignty did not hold great strategic importance, but the offshore islands such as the Cape Verdes and, more dramatically, the Azores, certainly did. For Pan American, Deutsche Luft Hansa, and Imperial Airways, the key staging point on the North Atlantic air route was suddenly off limits.

Here was a fascinating situation. Only two countries, Britain and France, possessed all the necessary assets to plan a North Atlantic air service. They had the technical ability to develop aircraft, and they ruled over territories on both sides of the North and Central Atlantic, thus permitting the establishment of bases and termini without hindrance. Two other countries, Germany and the United States, had the technical potential but lacked territory and could be denied landing rights, as indeed they were during the 1930s. Two more, Portugal and Denmark, had the territory but not the technical resources. SPELA alone had had the best of all worlds, Aéropostale supplying the technical ability and operational talent, and Portugal supplying the vital island aircraft carrier at the Azores, then considered essential for developing a transatlantic route, at a time when aircraft could not cross any ocean nonstop.

As Aéropostale began the year 1931, Bouilloux-Lafont had undoubtedly realized what an unprecedented opportunity had fallen into his lap. Paul Vachet was already establishing an infrastructure in the Caribbean to comply with Bouilloux-Lafont's plans for the route from Trinidad to the French West Indies. France's flying hero, Jean Mermoz, was preparing himself for the conquest of the North Atlantic. Had the French government given Marcel Bouilloux-Lafont half the support that Britain, Germany, and the United States gave to their national airline leaders, he could have been the first to develop a North Atlantic air route.

But his visionary plans came to nothing. The link from Brazil to Venezuela, the extension to Lima, the final completion of the West Indies route—even these logical steps were frustrated when, on France's day of aviation infamy, March 31, 1931, the French government abruptly suspended the agreed-upon subsidy to Aéropostale.

There is yet another fascinating side to the Bouilloux-Lafont story. Victor Laurent-Eynac had become France's first air minister when the Poincaré government created the Air Ministry in 1928. He signed the world's first bilateral agreement in 1929, exchanging selected landing and overflying rights with the British. He also encouraged the development of large flying boats for transoceanic use, and almost all these were constructed by none other than Pierre Latécoère.

Much publicity accrued to the Latécoère 521, a large four-engined craft, which, however, did not fly until 1935. Its development was delayed until, by the time it was almost ready, in 1939, World War II had started. Another Latécoère four-engined flying boat, the Type 300, designed for the South Atlantic, made its maiden flight in 1931 but did not go into intermittent semiregular service until 1934.

Behind the much-publicized development of these aircraft, however, was the curious—almost bizarre—episode of what can be described as the mystery of the Latécoère 38. A twin-engined flying boat, very much like the famous Dornier Wal in general appearance, the Type 38 made its first flight at Biscarosse on August 24, 1931, having apparently been built to an Aéropostale specification, with the express objective of carrying mails across the South Atlan-

tic. All indications were that it was a better aircraft than the
Dornier.

On January 1, 1931, the Latécoère 38-2 received its certificate
of navigation (equivalent to today's certificate of airworthiness).
On February 15, Aéropostale sent a flight engineer, Louis Cavaillès,
to evaluate the aircraft. But on March 31, when Aéropostale was
forced into *liquidation judiciaire,* all work on the Latécoère was
abandoned and Louis Cavaillès spent the next eighteen months fishing, literally, off the pier.

Unbelievably, this fine aircraft, which apparently had the potential to open the world's first transoceanic air service, possibly as
early as late in 1931, was allowed to corrode in the back of its hangar at Biscarosse. Possibly the authorities who had taken charge of
the Aéropostale affairs thought that the Latecoere 300 or the
Couzinet 70 *Arc-en-Ciel* landplane were better solutions. In the
event, neither of these aircraft was a success, and in any event, to
neglect another contender for such a prestigious objective was inexplicable, unless deliberately contrived.

Marie-Paule Vié-Klaze, the French aviation writer who has
compiled the definitive history of the Latécoère flying boats, put it
this way: "Aéropostale's affairs were not in good shape in 1931, but
the aircraft, having been ordered by the Government, had certainly
been paid for, at least in part. There is no explanation as to why the
aircraft should be neglected. After the departure of Cavaillès, it
slowly rusted away at the back of the hangar and finished up on the
scrap-heap."

In discarding so irresponsibly a golden opportunity to place itself in the forefront of airline development throughout the world,
what did the French government and its chosen airline representatives actually do? As narrated here, Aéropostale was ruthlessly disposed of, rather in the manner of killing a goose that was laying
one golden egg after another. Bouilloux-Lafont's enemies did not
want the eggs, they wanted the carcass. Cynically undervaluing his
carefully garnished assets at about a third of their value, they gave
his great airline the coup de grace when it was swallowed up by
SCELA on August 30, 1933, to form Air France.

The Portuguese government promptly canceled the SPELA
contract on October 7, 1933, and the Azores were subsequently
open to all comers, notably Deutsche Lufthansa—the three words
of the name had been reduced to two that year—which used the

mid-Atlantic islands as a base for an impressive series of survey flights to New York from 1936 until the outbreak of World War II in 1939.

Competition between France and Germany was, in fact, eliminated. By the end of 1933, Air France had come to terms with Lufthansa, establishing a pooling agreement under which mail services across the South Atlantic alternated between the national airlines. During the summer of 1931 the *Graf Zeppelin* had made three round trips to Brazil, with full loads of passengers, and the frequency was increased thereafter until airship services ceased in May 1937, following the *Hindenburg* disaster. Overflying rights for German aircraft across all French territories were waived, and the sight of the symbolic swastika must have given old Marcel much anguish. As a sincere patriot, he must also have regarded with suspicion the idea of German flying boats using the Azores as a base and flying regularly to New York.

In 1931 Bouilloux-Lafont had been on the brink of securing air traffic rights, many of them on an exclusive basis, to cover about half the air routes in the world. Considering that air transport itself was barely a decade old, this was a stupendous achievement. During an all-too-brief period of four years, from 1927 to 1931, he had assembled the four essential elements necessary to guarantee success: solid finance—from his own resources as well as from the customary mail subsidy; efficient administration and staff—the world's best; good equipment—the Latécoère 38 would have been the new flagship of the world's biggest airline fleet; and a good route network—the world's longest. To this he added the element, rare in that era, of a superb infrastructure of airfields, radio, and navigational aids.

After the mortal blow of March 31, 1931, Marcel Bouilloux-Lafont tried to retain his dignity and self-respect while attempting to salvage something from the wreckage of a once great institution. He was able to sell off the subsidiaries in Venezuela and Argentina so as to pay off some of his debts. He also sold his house and lands in France to pay off his creditors there. He was never again active in aviation circles, either in France or in Brazil, where he spent the rest of his life, almost alone, with a few of his family and acquaintances. He made occasional visits to France to try to repair some of the damages of his personal financial crash, but for the most part he lived quietly in a small hotel in Rio, having had to sell his large house in the most fashionable part of the city. He died in the Hotel Natal on February 2, 1944, and his death was marked honorably— as was his due—by the Brazilian newspapers.

The obituaries made passing reference to his airline interests and thereby omitted to pay proper tribute to this remarkable leader of men. He had demonstrated a grasp of the essentials of transoceanic travel that antedated such intercontinental plans as Juan Trippe's for Pan American, Albert Plesman's for K.L.M., or George Woods-Humphery's for Imperial Airways. Had he been allowed to continue his dynamic course, he could have completed the airline conquest of the North Atlantic. France, rather than the United States, could have assumed airline dominance during the years leading up to World War II, had that country chosen to follow Bouilloux-Lafont's inspired lead.

There are still a few of the older generation of aviation people in South America who remember Marcel Bouilloux-Lafont with affection, recognizing the debt that the airline industry in that continent owes to him. Some airline pioneers have been justly recognized for their achievements; some have received greater recognition than their achievements justified; but there can be little doubt that, for what he did, and for what he conceived for his country, no single man has been so underappreciated or underrecognized. No one deserves a place in the airline hall of fame more than Marcel Bouilloux-Lafont.

Alfred Eliasson

Airline of the
Sixth Happiness

Many ordinary folk on both sides of the Atlantic commonly believe that Sir Freddie Laker was the first to offer very cheap fares—lower than the scheduled service economy or excursion fares—between the two continents. This misunderstanding has arisen because of Laker's superb promotional flair. He did not deliberately set out to deceive; he simply sold a good product. The question of who was first was unimportant when his main concern was simply to sell tickets and make a profit.

Aircraft and airline people, however, will recall that the first cheap fares between the United Kingdom and the United States were launched by the British charter airlines, led by Caledonian Airways, who found a chink in the regulatory armor of the stout defenders of the fare-fixing policies of the International Air Transport Association (IATA). Like Fred Laker, Adam Thomson, head of Caledonian, was also knighted by the Queen of England to continue to fight the good fight on behalf of the affinity tour group organizers.

Laker's success, quickly followed by disaster, was achieved in the late 1970s, Thomson's during the late 1960s. But the real pioneering of North Atlantic bargain air fares was carried out in the 1950s and from an unexpected location. The little country of Iceland, so much on the fringe of Europe that it is often forgotten to be part of the continent, politically if not geographically, launched the first cut-rate fares across the Atlantic on June 12, 1952. The name of the airline was Loftleidir, "Sky Trails," and the most prominent of the three men who founded it was Alfred Eliasson.

Unlike Laker and Thomson, Eliasson will not receive an accolade, because his country had, several years earlier, renounced the Danish crown and achieved independence for its fewer than 200,000 people. This fierce sense of independence is reflected in the determination of its leaders, whether politicians or businessmen. The British Navy may well remember Iceland's stout defense of its fishing grounds, and the world of IATA airlines treats Loftleidir with no less respect.

Alfred Eliasson would be the first to protest that he did not start Loftleidir on his own. The founding fathers were a triumvirate, consisting of Eliasson, Kristinn Olsen, and Sigurdur Olafsson. Of the three, however, Eliasson was to emerge as the most influential, becoming the managing director of the airline. Olafsson retired from the company after a short tenure of office, while Olsen became director of operations, but Eliasson took on wider responsibilities and was for many years the driving force. He was to influence the airline's policy even thirty years later, when he became one of another triumvirate, the executive committee of a greatly enlarged Icelandic airline, headed by a new generation of leaders.

Alfred Eliasson was born on March 16, 1920, was graduated from the Icelandic business college in Reykjavik, then started a taxi firm with a small fleet of cabs. A few years later he left Iceland to go to Canada, where he learned to fly at Johannesson's Flying School in Winnipeg. He received his commercial certificate in 1942 and completed his training for a captain's rating later that year. He served as an instructor pilot with the Royal Canadian Air Force until December 1943, when he decided to return to his native land with two Icelandic friends, Olsen and Olafsson.

The three young pilots founded Loftleidir, with the support of some local businessmen, on March 10, 1944, with capital of 160,000 Icelandic kronur ($22,000). They started operations with a single Stinson Reliant seaplane, flying around the perimeter of the island, calling at the tiny communities which at that time—as some are even today—were completely cut off from the capital, Reykjavik, or even from one of the few towns on the island, except by sea. Although the heavily indented coastline, with its fjords almost rivaling those of Norway in grandeur, offered safe harbor from the worst Atlantic storms, the weather was nevertheless atro-

Alfred Eliasson, center, cofounder of the Icelandic airline Loftleidir, in front of the Douglas C-47 that had been abandoned on an Icelandic glacier after a crash landing. Eliasson and his team dug it out of the snows, dragged it to level ground, salvaged it, and sold it for a comfortable profit. Such enterprise created the first low-fare operator on the North Atlantic air route.

cious, and there were few navigational aids. But little Loftleidir was providing an essential and much-appreciated service, not only for normal passenger and freight work, but also for emergency flights such as for medical evacuation or a flying doctor service, and to help the local fishing communities by spotting shoals of fish.

The Loftleidir service must have been successful. The company bought a Grumman Goose and a second Stinson Reliant and carried a total of 484 passengers during the first twelve months of an operation that, by the standards of countries blessed with more gentle terrain and a kinder climate, could hardly be called scheduled. But it was a service, and the Icelanders loved it.

This is not to imply, however, that the trio of former Royal Canadian Air Force pilots were the pioneers of airline service in Iceland. Iceland had a notable, if transitory, history in this respect. In September 1919, the year when other European countries with far greater resources and traffic potential were just coming to grips with the new mode of transport, Flugfelag Islands (Icelandic Aircraft Company) began a modest service from a small grass field near Reykjavik. The aircraft was an Avro 504K, purchased from the Danish airline, and it made a few sightseeing trips before being sold back to Denmark the following year.

A second company of the same name was formed in June 1928 to operate seasonal services to all the fjords around Iceland, using Junkers-F 13 floatplanes leased from the German airline, Deutsche Luft Hansa. A Junkers-W 33 was added in 1929, but the services ended in 1931, during a period of economic belt-tightening all around the world. The aircraft were returned to Germany, and in an interesting sequel to the episode, Luft Hansa, aspiring to create an air route to North America using the northerly route, via Iceland and Greenland, subsequently reminded the Danish minister for Iceland—then a Danish territory—that it had written off the lease charges but that Germany was entitled to most-favored-nation treatment because of its earlier operational support—not to mention the debt.

Iceland's first sustained airline was Flugfelag Akureyrar (Akureyri Airline Company), which was formed in the northern town of Akureyri in June 1937 and began scheduled service with a Waco YKS floatplane between Akureyri and Reykjavik on May 4, 1938. The company moved to Reykjavik in 1940, was reorganized as Flugfelag Islands, and proceeded to expand, increasing its capital, extending domestic routes, and buying more aircraft, including two eight-seat de Havilland Rapides in 1943. In October 1944 it added a Consolidated Catalina equipped with twenty-two seats and in 1945 was able to report a total of 7,000 passengers carried. The Catalinas had also made several overseas flights to the United Kingdom and to Copenhagen.

With the end of World War II, Flugfelag purchased more aircraft, Douglas DC-3s, Catalinas, a Grumman Goose, and a Noorduyn Norseman. Also it leased twenty-four-seat Consolidated Liberators (bombers converted for commercial use) from Scottish Aviation, which it used to begin a scheduled service from Reykjavik to Prestwick, Scotland, and on to Copenhagen, on May 27, 1946. When Eliasson and his colleagues entered the Icelandic airline market, therefore, a well-established airline had already been organized and was proceeding to develop services to all the countries of Europe with which Iceland had commercial and ethnic relations.

But the newcomer, Loftleidir, did not seem to be particularly overawed by this competition and strove to demonstrate that it was able to match its rival, particularly in the matter of providing the flying equipment necessary to provide the best service. The Icelandic government, meanwhile, did not favor one company over the other, commendably allowing the two groups of entrepreneurs to seek their own independent salvations.

In the beginning, Loftleidir pursued the familiar European path. Although Iceland had become independent from Denmark in 1944, close ties still remained with that country and, to a lesser extent, with the other Scandinavian countries. Flugfelag must have been put on its mettle when, on June 17, 1947, Loftleidir started a Copenhagen service with a forty-four seat Douglas DC-4, named *Hekla*, after Iceland's famous volcano. At first the crews were Americans, but by August 1948 these had been replaced with Icelanders.

The year 1948 saw quite a lot of action. On June 9, Loftleidir introduced a Douglas DC-3 to back up the DC-4; on July 8, Flugfelag put its own DC-4, named *Gullfaxi*, "Golden Horse," into service on routes to Copenhagen, Oslo, and Prestwick; and then Loftleidir topped this by starting a DC-4 service to New York.

This was a demonstration of faith, if there was one in the world of airlines at the time. On February 3, 1948, Eliasson had applied successfully to the U.S. Civil Aeronautics Board for permission to operate to New York and had been granted the privilege on May 26, reflecting a surprising burst of activity in that normally foot-dragging agency. Few in Washington can have taken Loftleidir seriously, feeling that a little Arctic island would pose no threat of competition to the might of Pan American and T.W.A.

In a sense they were right, and somewhat predictably, Loftleider foundered at first. Because of limited funds, not to mention a reluctance of the transatlantic air-traveling public to go the long way around, Loftleidir was unable to maintain service regularly. Neither was there, at this time, any tourist base in Iceland to attract visitors. Hotel accommodations were limited, and a tourism infrastructure was nonexistent. Most of the world still thought of

Iceland as a country of Eskimos and polar bears, only slightly more hospitable than the Greenland icecap.

The situation did not look promising in 1950. Loftleidir decided to withdraw its ambitious venture to the United States, and Flugfelag appeared to consolidate its position on the European routes and gain the ascendancy. The latter airline had started a route to London in May 1949, and it then joined IATA as a gesture of attaining legitimacy in the airline world as a whole, a move that was perfectly proper, indeed necessary, because of the power of the large European airlines, notably the Scandinavian Airlines System (S.A.S.), the consortium owned jointly by Denmark, Sweden, and Norway, to control fares and routes.

By the end of 1950, the three pilots' airline venture was at such a low ebb that they withdrew from international participation altogether, confining their routes to the Icelandic fjords and the Westman Islands, a tiny group off the south coast. Until Loftleidir arrived on the scene, the islanders could visit the mainland only by sea, often a hazardous undertaking in the winter. Eliasson and his companions made a deal: if you will build an airfield, they said to the islanders, we will provide a service. And so a strip was carved out of the volcanic rock, and the subsequent regular air service helped Loftleidir to establish a good reputation, which must have sustained it during some difficult times.

Loftleidir established another kind of fame in 1951, with a remarkable operation. In September 1950 a Dakota Rescue Aircraft had landed on the Vatnajökull Glacier, the largest in Europe, in an effort to rescue the crew of a Loftleidir DC-4 that had crash-landed there. All efforts to salvage the aircraft had failed, so it was abandoned and the crew returned to base. The Dakota—the military version of the ageless Douglas DC-3—was left to the mercy of an Icelandic winter, and all that could be seen of it the following spring was a mound of snow.

Between April 8 and May 6, 1951, a team of Loftleidir staff, led by Eliasson, dug the DC-3 out of the snow, hauled it sixty miles down the glacier, and flew it back to Reykjavik. As might have been predicted, the inspection report noted a number of defects, mainly wrinkles and dents in the fuselage and wings, and stated that the tail wheel and ski attachments needed to be replaced. But otherwise the aircraft was repairable, and in November it was registered in Iceland, appropriately christened *Jökull*, "Glacier," then sold privately in Spain for a sum reported variously as $44,000 and $75,000. Whatever the amount, the salvage had required only a negligible outlay, and the company made a handsome profit from a bold speculation. In so doing, they also contributed to the folklore of the famous DC-3.

This addition to the meager Loftleidir bank account came about in 1952, a year of great decisions. On January 3 its regular domestic services were suspended, because the Icelandic government decided that the traffic was insufficient to justify the deployment of two airlines. Having suspended its first international service and lost its DC-4, Loftleidir thus had no scheduled routes at all. Loftleidir and Flugfelag had always squabbled about who was getting the best deal from the aviation department, and the official responsible may have decided to make his life easier by allocating individual routes to each airline, thereby ending the controversy.

At least if grandfather rights were a factor, the government was strictly impartial, for it raised no objection when Loftleidir, which had sold all its small aircraft, resumed service to New York with a DC-4 leased from Braathens S.A.F.E., the Norwegian airline owned and operated by the shipping company of that name. It was a courageous, perhaps a desperate, decision for the financially insecure Loftleidir. To attract traffic, fares were set about 16 percent lower than those of the IATA transatlantic airlines, but at first the results were hardly earth-shattering. From the inaugural date, June 12, 1958, until the end of the year, only 1,748 passengers were persuaded to take advantage of the lower fare package.

The Loftleidir management may not have done much calculation of the elasticity of demand, but it was convinced that there was a market for low-fare traffic across the Atlantic. Accordingly, on January 1, 1953, Loftleidir announced a new bargain. Quite simply, the transatlantic round-trip fare from New York to Scandinavia was set $100 lower than the lowest charged by the IATA carriers. True, by the circuitous route via Iceland, the journey took much longer. The DC-4s were also slower than the DC-6Bs, Constellations, and Stratocruisers of the big airlines, and the ride was a little less comfortable, because the DC-4s were unpressurized.

But for people who saved for several years so as to be able to afford the minimum fare to visit a relative across the ocean, or for students who had plenty of time but not plenty of money, Loftleidir's package was attractive. More than 5,000 passengers chose the Icelandic newcomer in 1953, and the word began to be passed around.

The working arrangement with Braathens was conducted on the Loftleidir side by K. J. Kristjansson, O. Olason, and Gunnar Gunnarsson and on the Braathens side by Einar Fröysaa, R. Klemetsen, and J. Raad. It permitted passengers to connect from New York to Reykjavik by Loftleidir, then to fly on to Stavanger and Oslo in another DC-4, leased from Braathens. A Norwegian crew took over the aircraft at Stavanger or Oslo and flew it on to Göteborg, Copenhagen, and the Far East, while the Loftleidir crews left the flight at Hamburg, Germany. Theoretically, the Loftleidir-Braathens partnership chould provide a cheap flight from New York to Hong Kong, although few passengers are likely to have made this journey. In any event, Braathens was obliged to terminate its Far East service in 1955, the full implications of what Braathens and Loftleidir were doing having sent palpitations through the hearts of the members of IATA, especially S.A.S.

But Loftleidir was too busy to worry about such matters. Business was booming. On January 1, 1954, a subsidiary company, Icelandic Airlines, was formed in New York to cope with the explosion of traffic, which doubled in that year, then doubled again by the end of 1956.

During the latter 1950s, there was a noteworthy injection of expertise by the Braathens organization, which had considerable influence in business and political circles in Norway. Loftleidir benefited by gaining managerial experience, operational advice, and technical consultancy from Braathens. Thanks largely to this stimulant, Loftleidir was able to reintroduce through service to several points in Europe—Göteborg in 1954, Glasgow in 1956, Luxembourg in 1955, London in 1957, Amsterdam in 1959, and Helsinki in 1960. These destinations were to be curtailed later, but the benefit of the Loftleidir fare schedule was plainly evident. To cope with the demand and to raise the standards a fleet of five pressurized Douglas DC-6Bs came into service, the first on December 7, 1959, with the result that 40,000 passengers used Loftleidir in 1960.

The success of the Icelandic airline rested not only on its deliberate and by now carefully calculated low-fares policy but also on its shrewd exploitation of international traffic rights as laid down in the codes set by the International Civil Aviation Organization (ICAO). Under the terms of the so-called Five Freedoms, originally recommended after much wrangling at the Chicago Conference of 1944, airlines could normally carry traffic under mutual arrangements between pairs of countries. The Third and Fourth Freedoms allowed airlines to carry traffic to and bring traffic from each other's countries while the First and Second Freedoms dealt with overflying and emergency landing rights. The much-coveted Fifth Freedom allowed airlines to carry traffic between two foreign countries, a privilege jealously guarded, especially by those countries that could use such rights for bargaining purposes.

Although Loftleidir may not have been the first to recognize the opportunity, it was certainly the airline that derived the greatest benefit from an apparent evasion of the provisions of the Five Freedoms, specifically the fifth. Loftleidir could, under the Fourth Freedom, bring passengers from the United States to Iceland, then, after a smart change of aircraft and flight number, transfer those passengers onto a flight from Iceland to a European destination under the Third Freedom. In so doing Loftleidir was not breaking any rule but when, as a matter of convenience and common sense, it simply flew the same aircraft straight through, with only a nominal stop at Reykjavik, this seemed to be breaking the spirit, if not the letter, of the ICAO rule.

At least this is what the airlines who were domiciled in those countries served by Loftleidir thought, and through their respective governments, they protested vigorously against what became known as the Sixth Freedom activities of this renegade upstart. The result was that in 1962, the same year in which Loftleidir moved its operational base to the larger airfield at Keflavik, about fifteen miles west of Reykjavik, the fares east of Iceland had to be fixed according to the levels set by IATA, of which organization, of course, Loftleidir's rival, Flugfelag, was a member.

But this restriction applied only to countries that subscribed to the price-fixing ideals of the long-established flag carriers of Europe and the North American airlines. So Loftleidir concentrated its efforts on little Luxembourg, the western European principality squeezed between Belgium and Germany, which, quite firmly, did not subscribe to the principles of IATA. One reason it could take its independent course with equanimity was that geographically Luxembourg was ideally located to serve a huge population in northwestern Europe, being more or less equidistant from Amsterdam and the cities of the Netherlands, Brussels and almost the whole of

Belgium, northeastern France,and particularly the densely populated industrial area of the Ruhr, in western Germany, together
with commercial German cities such as Düsseldorf and Cologne.

The theories of the elasticity of demand were more than vindicated. In a single year, 1962, Loftleidir's traffic almost quadrupled,
and in 1963 the transatlantic passenger count reached 73,300. The
word was getting around that the amount of money saved by flying
Loftleidir would go a long way toward paying the hotel bill at the
other end. Luxembourg began to find itself firmly on the western
European travel map. The airlines that forced Loftleidir into the
principality may have wished they had not interfered.

There is nothing like a little healthy competition to promote
initiative and to open up closed minds. In 1963 the IATA carriers
lowered their fares so that the difference between Loftleidir's and
theirs was only 16 percent instead of twenty percent. But they were
helpless in influencing the Luxembourg flights, where the saving
could be anything up to 30 percent, depending on the ultimate destination. In a compensatory move, and as a further promotional
gambit, Loftleidir introduced a bargain stopover package in Reykjavik. Arguably, twenty-four hours in a remote capital not noted
for tourist attractions of the popular kind was not much of a bargain. But passengers quickly discovered that the woolen clothing,
particularly the unmistakable Icelandic sweaters, were a bargain
at any price, and the aircraft were noticeably more tightly packed
on the onward legs of the journey across the northern perimeter of
the Atlantic.

By this time, of course, all the major airlines were operating jet
airliners, whose average speeds of 500 miles an hour and smooth tur-
bine-engined ride were incomparably superior to Loftleidir's now
outmoded piston-engined DC-6Bs. The technical differential had
been imposed upon Loftleidir, because one of the conditions under
which it was permitted to defy all the orthodox customs by its outrageous practice of the Atlantic Sixth Freedom was that its equipment
should be of a demonstrably lower standard, as befitted the lower
fares. The U.S. Civil Aeronautics Board, under pressure from Pan
American and others, tended in principle to approve this view, although Loftleidir never went so far as to challenge it. International
litigation could have raised all kinds of issues, including the conditions under which U.S. forces were allowed to maintain a heavy mili-

tary presence in Iceland. Fortunately, the sides never came to blows over Loftleidir's apparent defiance of all the conventions.

By the mid 1960s all the big airlines were bringing in the latest fan-engined models of the Boeing 707s and Douglas DC-8s, and Loftleider, by this time operating independent of Braathens, felt that the time had come to act in its own defense. No longer having to scrimp on financing or having to dig aircraft out of the snow to reinforce the fleet, it put into service a fleet of five Canadair CL-44 turboprop airliners. This was a Canadian-built version of the British Britannia—the Whispering Giant—which had come so near to worldwide success before being eclipsed by the swift introduction of the big jets. The CL-44 was longer than the Britannia and had Rolls-Royce Tyne engines.

Maintaining its momentum in improving its flying standards and its capacity, Eliasson's technical team, advised by the American consultants Dixon Speas Associates, came up with an enterprising, though little-known innovation. The fuselage of the CL-44 was lengthened by fifteen feet, making it possible to increase the seating from 160 to 189. Loftleidir quite brashly called these aircraft, officially designated CL 44Js, the Rolls-Royce 400s. Entering service on May 29, 1964, they were at the time the largest aircraft plying the North Atlantic route.

The response to the Reykjavik stopover idea had been so encouraging that Loftleidir built its own hotel at the Reykjavik airport, which it opened on May 1, 1966. With 108 rooms, it could deal with the increased demand, which grew further when, in October of the same year, the stopover privilege was increased to forty-eight hours and excursions to the hot springs near Reykjavik, to the ancient site of the old Icelandic capital, Thingvellir, and to the Gullfoss, an impressive waterfall, a scaled-down Niagara, were included. Loftleidir also introduced a free twenty-four-hour stopover in Luxembourg for those passengers who wished to visit the principality before proceeding to their ultimate destination.

Recalling the fictional establishment symbolizing a haven of comfort and rest in war-torn China, the Loftleidir Hotel in Reykjavik might well be dubbed the Inn of the Sixth Freedom.

With more and more people flocking to Loftleidir to take advantage of cheap fares, interesting stopovers, and bargain shopping, the traffic grew. In August 1967 Loftleidir carried its one-millionth passenger, who was almost certainly from one of the younger age groups, for by this time, the Icelandic pioneer had become known as the hippie airline because of its popularity with that notoriously impecunious yet adventurous element of society. The term, when applied, was usually intended in a derogatory sense, but it did Loftleidir little harm, for its very use reminded others of the economic levels at which the Icelandic airline's fares were set.

In 1968 the last of the piston-engined DC-6Bs was retired, but these aircraft were put to good work with an associated company, Flughjalp (Flight Aid), formed to assist in flying supplies to Biafra, the Nigerian province that rebelled against the central government of that country, leading to a disastrous civil war and attracting worldwide sympathy for the hardship that was the result of the conflict. Maintaining this praiseworthy charitable enterprise after the Biafran crisis had ended, Flughjalp donated the whole fleet of DC-6Bs to Peru in 1970 for earthquake relief.

In parallel with this admirable activity, Loftleidir engaged in a flurry of simultaneous commercial expansion. In 1969, it acquired the operations of International Air Bahama (I.A.B.), a low-cost Bahamian airline, that flew between that country and Luxembourg. I.A.B. operated a Boeing 707, but this was exchanged for a DC-8. In 1970 two of the stretched DC-8-63s were acquired, without infringing the specific understanding with the American authorities that Loftleidir's own equipment would be one step behind the world's main-line standards. For this was the year that the wide-bodied jets came into service on the North Atlantic, first with Pan American, and with all the big flag carriers, from both North America and Europe, in hot pursuit.

The acquisition of I.A.B. had been a shrewd tactical move. It provided Loftleidir with a fallback position, had the U.S. authorities chosen to be vindictive. In the event, the Civil Aeronautics Board permitted Loftleidir to operate DC-8-63s, but with a traffic quota restriction.

During 1970 also, Loftleidir participated in forming Cargolux Airlines International, an all-cargo airline based in Luxembourg, which was becoming a traffic hub for northwestern Europe. Other investors in Cargolux were a Swedish shipping company and Luxair, the local airline. Loftleidir's main contribution was in the form of some of the CL-44J fleet, under various leasing agreements. The CL-44s were retired from passenger service with Loftleidir on

November 5, 1971, on which date Stockholm replaced Göteborg as the terminal in Sweden.

Going from strength to strength, with the ability to deploy its assets internationally, Loftleidir transferred its main overhaul base from New York to Luxembourg in January 1972 and began service to a second gateway to the United States, Chicago, on May 2, 1973. This was of special importance for the Sixth Freedom airline, for this Great Lakes city could draw upon a catchment area containing a large percentage of the Scandinavian immigrants to the United States. Far more important, however, as one of the largest cities in the United States it was a natural choice on the basis of demographic analysis. Even more important was the access to Luxembourg as a European hub, for Chicago's direct air service to Europe was confined to far fewer destinations than New York's.

Operational developments such as new airliners and new routes neatly disposed of, Loftleidir now became engrossed in a far-reaching corporate reorganization within Iceland, quite simply the merger with Flugfelag. For some years the existence of two companies, each with a claim to represent its country as the official carrier, had been something of an anachronism. Most European countries other than the very largest had only one airline each, and that was customarily state-owned or state-controlled. For all international air routes, in fact, except nonscheduled or charter services, the three Scandinavian countries had operated in a rare example of a successful international airline consortium, on the theory, well-founded, that in the competitive world of European scheduled airlines, divided they would have fallen, but united they could conquer. It did not escape the attention of some observers, incidentally, that while S.A.S. was protesting Loftleidir's alleged breach of Five Freedom ethics, passengers were flying from America to Copenhagen by S.A.S., and then proceeding to other cities by the same airline—a case of the pot calling the kettle black.

On June 28, 1973, in simultaneous meetings of the boards of Loftleidir and Flugfelag it was agreed that the two companies would be merged into one, to be called Flugleidir. But both airlines, for the time being, retained their separate identities, with Flugleidir as the holding company. The official day of founding was July 20, and on August 1 the company began its work. During the fall of 1973 the two airlines coordinated their international services and merged their overseas offices and installations. On

March 1, 1974, an executive committee was appointed, and, significantly, two of the three members were from Loftleidir. Alfred Eliasson was one, Sigurdur Helgason, formerly Loftleidir's vice-president in New York, was the second, and Orn O. Johnson, managing director of Flugfelag, was the third.

When, on February 6, 1976, a special independent committee announced the distribution of the shareholding of the merged airline, the majority, 53.5298 percent, went to Loftleidir, leaving 46.4702 percent for Flugfelag. The accuracy of the calculation needed to achieve all these decimal places is a tribute to the impartiality, not to mention the devotion, of the committee, which must have assessed the value of every paper clip. That Loftleidir emerged from the investigation with such strength was a true accolade to Alfred Eliasson. Without diminishing the contributions of his cofounders, it was his drive and imagination which, in little more than two decades, had held a derelict airline together, pulled it up by its bootstraps, and made Loftleidir's into a fairy-tale success story. In so doing, he had also made his country, as well as his airline, a force to be reckoned with in the commercial airline world.

The merger was finally consummated in October 1979, and to avoid confusion among the thousands of foreign and non-Icelandic-speaking customers, the airline became known as Icelandair. Almost immediately, far from profiting from the new image it had hoped to create, the renamed airline suffered from what one of its spokesmen described as the triple whammy of economic recession, airline deregulation, and soaring jet-fuel costs. Flugleidir, in fact, incurred heavy losses in two successive years before beginning a solid recovery in 1982.

One disappointment was that the high hopes it had placed on operating the wide-bodied McDonnell Douglas DC-10-30 were doomed. Not only did the introduction of this aircraft on January 4, 1979, coincide with the shortage of public spending power because of the recession, but in May 1979 the DC-10s were grounded, following the spectacular American Airlines crash at O'Hare Airport, Chicago. This catastrophic event was bad enough, occurring as it did at a time when Icelandair's third U.S. gateway, Baltimore, had opened only a short time earlier in the fall of 1978. The Baltimore airport also served the fast-growing metropolitan area of

Washington, D.C., and the adjoining suburbs in Maryland and northern Virginia and was a well-researched location. But the station had to be closed temporarily in 1979, and in the spring of 1980 the single DC-10 was leased to another airline, leaving a tidy fleet of four DC-8-63CFs, which, however, were just about the best money-makers and the most versatile aircraft in the business, short of the wide bodies.

Time magazine wrote off Icelandair, noting that it had peaked in 1977 in carrying 240,000 passengers, and identified the biggest threat as Sir Freddie Laker's Skytrain service and the fare-slashing policies of the IATA airlines, which, in taking desperate and unprecedented measures to fight Laker, had injured Icelandair at least as much. Sigurdur Helgason, who had taken over the airline as its chief executive officer, Eliasson having withdrawn because of ill health, remarked that "North American competition is operating under the law of the jungle." Like good jungle fighters, Icelandair went into hiding. It reduced its transatlantic flights from twenty-three to two a week and laid off about 500 of its 1,700 employees.

But not for long. Ignoring *Time's* requiem to the effect that "Like the flower children it once served, Icelandair is left mostly with memories," the airline staged a remarkable recovery. Service from Baltimore-Washington was resumed on November 7, 1982, and two more U.S. gateways, at Detroit and Orlando, were added in 1984. Detroit, from May 11, opened up new markets in a hitherto poorly served Great Lakes region, while Orlando, from October 26, aimed to provide direct service for Europeans wishing to visit Walt Disney World and Epcot Center as well as the Florida beach resorts. Today, Icelandair is back in the black again.

Alfred Eliasson left a legacy not simply of independence and courage. He instilled into his airline a great talent for ingenuity and the ability to make a virtue out of blind necessity at the same time that he established a sound structural base which could withstand crises such as the one of the late 1970s. Although today Icelandair's Douglas DC-8-70s still maintain the token technical differential from the wide-bodied jets, Icelandair competes on a straightforward basis with the forty or so other transatlantic airlines. But in so doing, it has never compromised its own ideals of offering economic fares to the air-traveling public. The IATA edifice of tariff restrictions came tumbling down to beat off Freddie Laker.

Other newcomers such as PEOPLExpress and Virgin Air took his place. But all the combined forces of the Establishment on both sides of the Atlantic were unable to beat off Icelandair.

Thanks to the traditions, procedures, and principles so carefully nurtured by Alfred Eliasson and his dedicated team during the formative years of Loftleidir, the Icelandic flag airline can confidently take on all comers. Eliasson's successor, a young Sigurdur Helgason, who follows in his own father's footsteps, threatening almost to create a dynasty, probably still has a few aces up his sleeve.

▶▶▶▶▶▶▶▶▶▶▶▶▶▶▶▶▶▶

Latin America

▶▶▶▶▶▶▶▶▶▶▶▶▶◀▶▶▶▶▶

Lowell Yerex

The Living Legend

After Pan American Airways had established a position of complete dominance in Latin America during the 1930s, it became an airline institution of such strength as to appear invulnerable and impregnable. One man, however, dared to penetrate Pan Am's defenses to the extent that he caused great consternation at the highest levels of the U.S. Chosen Instrument. His activities, furthermore, occupied the attentions of diplomats and officials on both sides of the Atlantic for several years, and the fact that his material resources seldom consisted of more than a couple of dozen old airplanes, all of which had seen better days, was all the more remarkable.

Lowell Yerex was born in New Zealand on July 24, 1895, the son of a Canadian doctor who had emigrated to the South Pacific, where his seven children became known as "the American kids." The family moved back to the United States, and he and his brother Lincoln were educated at Valparaiso University in Indiana. He taught school at a rural community for a short while, but at the age of twenty-one he joined the Canadian contingent of the Royal Flying Corps and began his flying career the hard way—on the Western Front toward the end of the Great War of 1914–18. In May 1918 he was shot down behind the German lines. He escaped from a prison train, was recaptured, and was released again with the Armistice of November 1918. At an early age he had already demonstrated a capacity for taking risks.

He returned to Canada with a wartime demobilization bonus of £500, then went back to the United States, where, like many returning heroes, he had difficulty in finding a permanent job. He

Lowell Yerex was a New Zealand–born barnstormer who founded TACA in Honduras in 1931 with a single Stinson monoplane. Within a decade he was challenging Pan American for pride of place among the airlines of Central America. His fleet at one time included no fewer than twenty-six versatile Ford Tri-Motors. He is seen here with his personal Bellanca CH-400.

and other members of his family went to California, where he worked in a San Francisco shipyard for a while. He then moved to Texas to become one of the happy band of mad aviators who established the barnstorming brotherhood, stunting at improvised air shows and giving joyrides. He was a member of the Gates Flying Circus, along with Clyde Pangborn, who was later to become a famous American record-breaking pilot, but barnstorming was a hand-to-mouth, not to say life-or-death, occupation, and it died out altogether in the mid 1920s.

He then improved his education in Santa Fe, New Mexico, selling Packard cars for a while and learning to speak Spanish, an ability that was soon to prove useful. During this period he was on the Santa Fe welcoming committee for Lindbergh when the new American hero made his tour of the United States after his famous flight of May 1927. Yerex's International Motor Trucks Company serviced the *Spirit of St. Louis*.

With the onset of the Great Depression, Yerex moved across the border into Mexico, and in 1930 he gained his first experience with an airline whose history would make good fiction were it not true. Corporación de Aeronáutica de Transportes (C.A.T.) had been founded early in 1929 by Theodore Hull, a Los Angeles banker and private pilot who combined his two occupations to start a trunk airline route from El Paso to Mexico City. Operating Ryan Broughams and Lockheed Vegas, his intrepid pilots included the famous Wiley Post, who was able to obtain a Mexican pilot's license, even though he had only one eye, and at least three men who would later run their own airlines: Paul Braniff, Gordon Barry (of the Mexican airline LAMSA), and Yerex.

The way in which Yerex came to start his own company was a combination of opportunism and a stroke of luck. In October 1931, a man named Henshaw hired Yerex to fly a Stinson Junior to Honduras. There Henshaw joined with a Dr. T. C. Pounds, an oculist from Brooklyn, who had started the first air service in Central America in 1923 by carrying air mail from the isolated capital, Tegucigalpa, which was linked with the remainder of the country and the coast neither by rail nor by road. Pounds, described by one writer as "a ruffled W. C. Fields in flying togs," was one of several aviation entrepreneurs touting for business in Honduras during the 1920s. He must therefore have possessed several admirable habits, but paying his pilots was not one of them. Yerex, under contract to Pounds, eventually tired of this arrangement and commandeered the Stinson until he did get paid, in kind, with part ownership of the aircraft. By the end of 1931, he was the sole owner, having proved that the value of his unpaid salary was equivalent to the other half of the Stinson.

Yerex, having already demonstrated that he could organize the transport of mail and cargo better than could his employers, promptly formed his own airline, Transportes Aéreos Centro-Americanos (TACA), with the five-seat Stinson, christened *Espíritu de Honduras*—the Lindbergh touch—as his main asset. Dr Pounds's mail contract expired on February 20, 1932, and he lost it to Yerex, whose new contract took effect on March 16 with a regular service from Tegucigalpa to San Pedro Sula. Almost immediately, Yerex inadvertently became involved in an incident that was the turning point of his career.

During the summer of 1932, Honduras was going through one of the minor revolutions which, in Central America, served as a relief from the monotony of life much in the same way as the World Series does in the United States. Yerex was hired by President Carías Andino as a one-man Honduran air force, whose main duties were reconnaissance over the guerilla encampments in the hills. Occasionally, he was expected to drop bombs, of a most primitive manufacture—large milk cans filled with sundry hardware, with a stick of dynamite in the middle. The bombs were simply dropped through a hole in the floor of the aircraft.

An interesting side note to the episode is that C. N. Shelton, another gringo adventurer whose approach to life was a strange mixture of irresponsibility and self-discipline, refused, as a U.S. citizen, to participate.

One day in June, Yerex and his crew, one Guy Moloney, an Irish adventurer, approached a rebel column at Sierra de Hule, near Tegucigalpa. During a strafing run, Yerex's aerial superiority was marred when an insurgent hit him in the eye with a lucky rifle shot. He managed to fly back to the capital with one eye gone, the other filled with blood from a two-inch bullet wound, and a leaking gasoline tank, ruptured by the versatile bullet. The doctor found that the bullet had also fractured Yerex's skull. After a trip to New Orleans for treatment, he returned to join the ranks of one-eyed pilots and found himself a national hero in the eyes of the president. He shrewdly declined a cash reward in favor of a permanent mail contract for TACA. This was confirmed on February 1, 1933, and he also received certain privileges, such as the right to import aircraft and materials free of customs duty. Because of his standing with the president, he was presumably excused from other forms of additional expense, customary in Central America during those times. At all events, from this moment on, Yerex never looked back; he proceeded to consolidate his position as the most aggressive and innovative airline operator in the region, and he expanded his TACA empire throughout the whole of Central America.

An amusing sequel to this incident was that the three rebel generals whom Yerex had strafed when he lost his eye later took a TACA domestic flight in Nicaragua, from Ocotal to Managua. They recognized the aircraft as being the same as they had shot at and asked the pilot to convey their apologies to Yerex for wounding him, but said that they would return to Honduras some day and shoot him and Moloney anyway.

What sort of man was this Yerex? Slightly handicapped by a stammer, not to mention the loss of an eye, seldom operating anything except flimsy single-engined aircraft or at best second- or third-hand trimotors, with no capital backing except from his own earnings, with no special political influence, except fortuitously, as in Honduras—in short, with none of the elements normally considered essential for successful airline promotion—what kind of man was it who built an airline system that became a household word through Central America and was eventually regarded as a threat to Pan American Airways, the Chosen Instrument of the United States?

During his eventful career, he never smoked or gambled, he drank only as a social necessity, and he enjoyed such middle-class leisure pursuits as reading and playing golf. In this respect, he was quite different from Shelton, with whose life Yerex's was continually intertwined, with one exception. They both liked the company of women, in relationships that were far from platonic. Nevertheless, Yerex was married twice, with reasonable success on both occasions, first to Lillian, back in Texas in the 1920s, and later to Antonietta, daughter of the Honduran minister of education. He had flown impetuously to Belize, British Honduras, to tie the nuptial knot, British style, in 1936. By each wife he had two children. His main virtue seems to have been thrift, which he combined with a certain ruthless determination and an uncanny sense of the way to turn the superior features of air transport to the maximum advantage in Central America.

Yerex had demonstrated a certain business acumen during his early days in Honduras. When he received the mail contract, he was also permitted to sell stamps and to be paid the normal agency discount for such transactions. He also introduced a form of Expreso Diferido—Deferred Freight—whereby a shipper would deposit packages at the local TACA depot, normally a small shack at the airstrip, and they would go out on the next plane available. While this process might take a few days, during the 1930s it was invariably quicker, and infinitely more reliable, than the surface carrier, usually a mule train.

Early on, he had adopted as his company insignia the scarlet, yellow, and blue macaw, one of the colorful native birds of Honduras. In time, the species became known as the TACA bird.

As time went on, Yerex expanded his Honduran operation, concentrating on freight but always available for passengers if they were not too fussy about the accommodation or their fellow travelers. Often they were local farmers or city officials who were given free passes for services rendered. He monopolized airline affairs in Honduras by buying Empresa Dean, the only other company of sub-

322

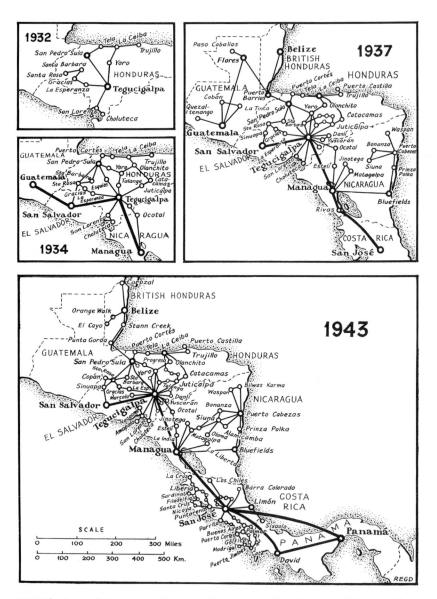

TACA's Central American Empire. *Starting in Honduras in 1931, the New Zealand–born barnstormer-entrepreneur Lowell Yerex seized an opportunity in 1931, while basking in the Honduran president's favor, to create an airline system throughout Central America and to take the local people directly from the oxcart and the mule train into the air.*

stance—and hiring, in the process, none other than C. N. Shelton, who was to carry on the Yerex tradition in the postwar years.

His first foreign venture, in 1935, was to purchase a small Guatamalan airline, Companía Nacional de Aviación, renaming it Companía Nacional TACA de Guatemala. Methodically, he then moved into Nicaragua by acquiring Líneas Aéreas de Nicaragua Empresa Palacios (LANEP) on October 16, 1935, and into El Salvador on August 25, 1939, where the local TACA was in effect the base of the main-line operation that connected the capital cities of the Central American republics. With this last step, TACA, S.A., was also established in Panama City as a nonoperating holding company of the now widespread TACA group, with an authorized capital of $4,000,000. The original Honduran company became TACA de Honduras, and with the acquisition of Empresa Nacional de Transportes Aéreos (ENTA) on January 16, 1940, from Bill Schoenfeldt in Costa Rica, TACA de Costa Rica completed the collection.

During this heady period of expansion, Lowell Yerex operated a bewildering variety of aircraft, almost every one of which flew under two registrations. No fewer than thirty-one different types have been identified as having been in the TACA fleet before Yerex sold all his interest in 1943. There were at least a hundred individual aircraft—the most reliable estimate puts the figure at 108, although the maximum number known to have been available at one time was 46. A pungent commentary on the fleet is the fact that not a single one of these was a Douglas DC-3, possibly considered to be too large and technically complex for TACA's operational style, whatever its fame for versatility may have been elsewhere.

The motley fleet included Stinsons like the one with which Yerex started in 1931 and various single-engined types such as Stearmans, Bellancas, Travelairs, Pilgrims, Wacos, and others of the ilk. Later there were twin-engined types such as the Beech 18, the Curtiss Condor, and various Lockheeds, Models 10, 12, 14, and 18. But Yerex's favorite type, one with which his famous airline has always been identified, was the Ford Tri-Motor, of which he owned 26 at one time or another.

The designers of the Ford Tri-Motor would have been proud to observe the methods by which TACA was able to squeeze the utmost output from the long-suffering airframe. The "Tin Goose" endured what could be described as a form of operational torture.

The maximum load of the Ford 5-AT Tri-Motor was specified as 2,500 pounds. TACA increased this to 5,300 pounds by removing every nonessential item, including the copilot. One Ford was converted to a bulk-liquid carrier for diesel oil by installing a 600-gallon tank that filled the fuselage. Always considerate of the crew, TACA provided a ladder so that the pilot could climb into the cockpit, the normal entrance to which was blocked by the fuel tank. This tank could be filled or emptied in eight minutes, and TACA could haul 2,400 gallons a day between the base storage tanks and an inaccessible mine in Nicaragua.

TACA's feats of logistics with the Fords were truly astonishing. One advantage of the now outmoded form of aircraft construction was that holes could be cut almost at random in the sides or on the roof of the fuselage to provide large doors. The entire equipment for La Luz mine at Siuna, Nicaragua, weighing perhaps 600 tons or more, was airlifted in by TACA's Fords. The items included large Bucyrus mechanical shovels weighing twenty-five tons apiece, which had to be disassembled, cut up with torches, and rewelded at the destination.

Such bizarre operations, which would have given the average Federal Aviation Agency inspector the problem of finding a big enough form to fill in the list of misdemeanors, would have been noteworthy at any normal airport or airfield. But few of Yerex's fields were normal. In fact, the term *field* would be a polite way to describe most of the landing places used as a matter of routine by TACA. Typically, Yerex would make an arrangement with a local community, according to which the local populace would hack a strip out of the local jungle or scrubland. Certain privileges would then be granted to the citizens, who, in turn, continued to provide volunteers to chase cattle off the strips when an aircraft was expected to arrive.

In the mountains, there was seldom a stretch of level ground long enough to allow any overrun, so a TACA aircraft would quite often have to touch down at the threshold of a sheer drop into a ravine and then have to stop before hitting the side of a mountain. Some of the coastal airfields did not have the advantage of good drainage, and pilots had to learn the locations of the soft patches during the rainy season. Mr. Jeppeson, the father of aeronautical charting techniques, would have had to invent special symbols for his airfield charts, had such a luxury been available to Yerex's

Some idea of the operating conditions in Latin America during the formative years of the airlines can be drawn from this picture of an airstrip in Honduras during the 1930s. The bridge was reported not to have been a problem, so long as it was not selected as the point of touchdown.

hardy team of pilots, who flew as often as not because they knew every inch of the terrain below them. They could nurse their aircraft to a safe landing on an average farmyard or building site, and they possessed enough basic instincts, born of hard-won experience, to be able to dispense with weather forecasters.

Curiously, at the height of his Central American operation, Yerex employed only twenty-eight pilots, who kept forty-six aircraft flying. But his workshops at Tegucigalpa and San José were models of inventive engineering skills, and the TACA organization boasted twenty-nine radio stations. In a region where there was no integrated railroad system and the Pan American Highway was as yet only a dream, Yerex provided a transport service that was an essential part of the way of life from the Mexican border to the Isthmus of Panama. As Philip Schleit perceptively observed, the supreme irony of Yerex's achievement was that he may have retarded the development of many of the small republics by removing the need for the governments to provide transport infrastructures. Who needed trains, cars, or buses, as long as there was a TACA?

Yerex's and TACA's style changed irrevocably when TACA Airways, the holding company for the various regional TACAs, was formed in Panama in 1939. Almost immediately, by proclaiming its international aspirations, it triggered the defense mechanism of its potential rival and competitor, Pan American. Salt was rubbed in Pan American's wounds when, on October 1, 1940, American Export Lines, a U.S. shipping company of considerable stature, announced that it had purchased control of TACA for an estimated $2,000,000.

American Export was living dangerously. It made no secret of its ambition to muscle into Pan American's sacred airline territory. The shipping company had founded American Export Airlines in April 1937, had applied to the Civil Aeronautics Board for a transatlantic air route on May 9, 1939, and after much litigation, was granted a certificate on July 15, 1940. When, less than three months later, American Export bought into TACA and applied for a route from New Orleans to Panama and to Guatemala City, it was more than Pan Am's Juan Trippe could stand. For American Export was deftly maneuvering to bypass him with the shortest and most convenient air route from the United States to central and western South America.

Ten days after the TACA purchase, on October 11, a new airline, Aerovías de Guatemala, was founded in Guatemala City. It was managed by Alfred Denby, a U.S. citizen resident in Guatemala and owner of the largest meat business there, but it was financed by Pan American. On November 7, the new airline started operating with Douglas DC-2s, far superior to any of TACA's hand-me-downs. On January 1, 1941, General Ubico, dictator of Guatemala, withdrew TACA's operating franchise.

To put no finer point on it, Yerex lost his shirt in Guatemala, the most important country in Central America, whose capital, Guatemala City, was easily the biggest city between Mexico City and Bogotá. Its strategic importance as a traffic hub rested not only on geography but also on a good airfield with a mile-long runway. Tegucigalpa, on the other hand, however affectionately it may have been esteemed as "Teegoose" by the TACA clientèle, was 3,200 feet above sea level, the same distance as the length of its longest runway, which was also precariously situated in the mountainous terrain.

Yerex was paid five cents on the dollar for his assets in Guatemala, where he had built both an airline network and the necessary infrastructure. Pan American moved in, and Yerex took his airplanes out. On December 4, 1941, the Civil Aeronautics Board disapproved the American Export bid to purchase TACA, and Pan American won its battle for Central American skies, although it was not to be similarly successful on the North Atlantic.

Throughout the entire period of competition with Pan American, Yerex regarded Juan Trippe simply as a worthy business adversary, writing, in retrospect, "I really do not blame Trippe or P.A.A. It is exactly what I would like to do myself." This comment was made out of respect for Pan Am's undeniable success in building an airline empire. Even Yerex, however, who did not stick to the Queensbury rules, would not have stooped to the unscrupulous methods used by the Pan American czar to get his own way. Yet Pan American was less of an enemy to Yerex than the British government, whose appallingly inefficient bureaucracy was matched only by its heartless dismissal of a genuine patriot.

Lowell Yerex was strongly supported by John H. Leche (pronounced Leech), the British envoy extraordinary in Guatemala, who not only recognized Yerex's extraordinary talents and achievements but realized an opportunity that he described in a letter to Lord Halifax as "something very big indeed and . . . [of] such proportions as to be of immense value, strategically, politically, and economically, to Great Britain and the West Indian colonies."

But various reports on TACA circulated endlessly in the corridors of power in Whitehall, London. The Foreign Office, the Air Ministry, the Colonial Office, the Dominions Office, the Board of Trade, the Admiralty, and the Ministry of Information—all these kept passing the proverbial buck with gay abandon or procrastinated on decisions almost as if instructed to do so by Juan Trippe himself.

Faced with ruthless and unscrupulous attacks in Central America, not only attacks on his airline through governmental infiltration by Pan American's agents but also a campaign of character assassination directed at Yerex himself and his staff, Yerex wrote to Clive Pearson, head of the British Overseas Airways Corporation (B.O.A.C.). In an exemplary statement of TACA's position that was accurate and dignified, he offered to sell TACA to the British state airline for $1,000,000. Pearson was impressed with the arguments, the cordiality, and the obvious patriotism displayed in the letter. But bureaucracy prevailed. The British government seemed to be afraid that somehow Anglo-American relations would be adversely affected by a B.O.A.C.-TACA deal and also seemed to be afraid to meet Pan American competition head-on—although there was no evidence that Pan American could compete fairly, since it had never been in the position of having to do so. One British official raised a serious issue: "It is difficult for us to support Mr. Yerex without being quite sure that he is in fact an honorable gentleman." Another was more honest: "There has always been something very fishy about the Air Ministry handling of Yerex and B.O.A.C. handling too. They have always both been averse from helping."

Finally, in a letter to Leche, Yerex expressed genuine regret that he was forced to seek a solution to TACA's future by opening negotiations with parties in the United States. Though he could have been forgiven if he had reacted with indignation, he said, "I will always feel that I have not come up to your expectations and I am very sorry indeed. I hope you will be able to see the situation as it has confronted me." Leche told Lord Halifax that he "was profoundly disappointed that Mr Yerex should have been driven into the arms of the United States," but other commentators were more outspoken. One referred to "a disgraceful exhibition of 'missing the bus,'" while another memorandum from the British Embassy in Washington concluded, "The melancholy truth is that His Majesty's Government were impotent to form a policy until too late."

During this unhappy period Lowell Yerex must have seen the writing on the wall, for, on November 27, 1940, he founded British West Indian Airways (B.W.I.A.) in Trinidad, thereby transferring his attentions from a U.S.-dominated region to what was then a colony of the British Empire and situated as strategically on the east coast route to South America as Panama was on the west.

Once again, he met unbelievable opposition from Great Britain. Although he had everything he needed to establish a British presence in the Caribbean region—good aircraft (Lockheed L.10

Electras), independent finance (his own), and protection from U.S. interference (by a clause in his agreement with American Export)—the British Colonial Office turned procrastination into an exact science. For two and a half years it stalled by demanding interminable amendments to the official agreement between government and airline. There were strong suspicions that Pan American had something to do with the affair. For whatever reason it was a shameful performance.

Watching the sands trickling out, Lowell Yerex was instrumental in the formation of a company in New York to protect his dwindling influence, alternately under attack from the Americans and the British. On January 27, 1943, the Inter-American Airways Agency was incorporated in New York, with T.W.A. holding 70 percent of the shares and Yerex the balance of 30 percent. Negotiations to set up this enterprise, which controlled TACA and B.W.I.A., as well as a new venture, Aerovias Brasil, had started with conversations at a direct meeting with Howard Hughes, owner of T.W.A. These had survived a delicate moment when, at a lavish party given by Hughes, Yerex had unknowingly chatted up Hughes's current girl friend.

By this time, Yerex had also acquired a 42 percent shareholding in a new airline founded in Brazil, with another TACA director holding a nominal 18 percent. Empresa de Transportes Aerovias Brasil, usually known as Aerovias, was incorporated on August 26, 1942, with two Brazilian brothers, Oscar and Roberto Taves, holding the other 40 percent. Even at this late stage, Aerovias added another new dimension to the TACA empire, which was doubtless an important element during the attempt to dispose of it.

Gradually, under unremitting pressure from U.S. members of the TACA board, who continually referred to Yerex and his friends as "British agents," as if Great Britain were an Axis power, Lowell Yerex released his controlling interest in TACA. On May 11, 1943, he sold stock to the value of $2,225,000 to a group of U.S. interests—that is, the Inter-American Agency, thus passing TACA to T.W.A. Shortly afterward, in January 1944, TACA's capital was increased to $5,000,000, at which time Yerex's share was 53 percent. Eventually, during the "night of the long knives," December 13, 1945, he sold the remainder of his stock for $3,000,000.

Nobody knows what may have been in Howard Hughes's mind, or in that of his president, Jack Frye, when he acquired con-

330

trol of TACA, British West India Airways, and Aerovias Brasil. An optimistic cartographer could have made—and did, on timetables published at the time—the new TACA look like another Pan Am empire in Latin America. Elsewhere in 1945 and 1946, as if to show it meant business in its worldwide plans, T.W.A. purchased stock in Philippine Airlines, Hawaiian Airlines, T.A.E. (Greece), L.I.A. (Italy), and Iranian Airways. It also provided substantial technical assistance to Ethiopian Airways, Saudi Arabian Airlines, and T.M.A. (Lebanon). The framework appeared to be taking shape for another worldwide organization that could strengthen T.W.A. in its globe-encircling ambitions, along with its change of name to Trans World Airlines. And TACA may have been part of the scheme.

All these efforts came to nought, however, as did further moves to expand the TACA network in Latin America, in Mexico, Colombia, Venezuela, Argentine, and Paraguay. Only the TACAs in Colombia and Venezuela ever went into operation, and these were disasters. It was a lovely dream while it lasted, but it was never more than a dream. Pan American was too smart and too much experienced in ways of doing business and of controlling affairs in Latin America. Between 1943 and 1945, with the participation of local governments, it set up asssociated companies in Venezuela, the Dominican Republic, Panama, Honduras, Nicaragua, and Costa Rica, and that was that. It already controlled the west coast through PANAGRA and the east coast through Panair do Brasil. It was a precision-built web, and TACA was caught in it.

But Lowell Yerex wasn't caught. He had neatly sidestepped the play when the going got really rough, although unfortunately his marriage to Antonietta broke up—though not for the first time. He retired with his riches to Argentina, settling in Buenos Aires. He promptly became involved in the construction business, building railroads for the Perón government. He made a lot more money, although it was probably never worth very much in that country, where government bills are seldom paid promptly and inflation takes care of the profits.

His wife, Antonietta, rejoined him once more in 1947 but returned to Honduras five years later to work for TAN, the "barefoot airline," successor to TACA that was the brainchild of C. N. Shelton, who had learned much of his trade from Yerex. Twenty years younger than her husband, she tried again in 1958 and stayed for another seven years; she then made a final break, returning once again to TAN.

Lowell Yerex spent much of his declining years visiting or, during the winter months, living in the Hurlingham Country Club, an exclusive, very British club in a metropolis where, until recent years, British influence was very much in the forefront. When he died, of cancer, in December 1968 at the age of seventy-two, he had been living with a twenty-year-old Japanese girl. Because of the provisions of Argentine law, he could leave her only 10 percent of his fortune—perhaps the equivalent of $1,000,000 or thereabouts by this time. Antonietta and his four children were entitled to the remainder, although little of the money is likely to have left Argentina.

Lowell Yerex's ultimate fate as a force in Latin American commercial aviation was a gross miscarriage of justice and a terrible indictment of deceit by his opponents, above all the British government, which betrayed him time after time. Yet he remained intensely patriotic, in spite of repeated slurs on his character. David Yerex, Lowell's nephew, who has uncovered a wealth of damning evidence against bureaucrats and businessmen, both in the United Kingdom and the United States, has pointed out that in 1942 Pan American offered to buy 60 percent of TACA in exchange for a highly paid position in Pan Am—a typical Trippe strategy. Yerex refused because such a move would have given Trippe a total monopoly throughout the Americas, North and South, and would have ended any chance the British may have had to obtain a foothold for a British airline. "But all the thanks he got from the British was continual frustration and opposition."

Possibly the most amazing aspect of Lowell Yerex's colorful and eventful life was that only fifteen years of it were spent building TACA from one single-engined airplane into an organization that Pan American Airways, the Civil Aeronautics Board, the State Department, and almost every arm of the British government felt should be suppressed by extraordinary measures, of questionable ethical standards at best. Yet almost single-handed he made a fortune in spite of the systematic campaign to denigrate, disparage, and ultimately destroy him.

When, in disillusionment, he abandoned TACA because he could do no more, it quickly deteriorated. But Lowell Yerex's shadow still hangs over Central America. He was a legend in his own time.

C. N. Shelton

The Barefoot Airline

Cornell Newton Shelton, as he was rather ponderously christened, was one of the more remarkable entrepreneurs to cross the world airline scene. His sphere of operation was the route from Florida to the west coast of South America, mainly during the 1950s and the 1960s, and the manner in which he chose to perform the operation was innovative, even revolutionary for its time. No respecter of persons or institutions, he challenged dominant commercial interests such as the U.S. Chosen Instrument, Pan American Airways, and powerful government agencies such as the U.S. Civil Aeronautics Board (C.A.B.). Many such free spirits have made the challenges. The difference with Shelton was that he usually won.

C. N. Shelton, or simply Shelton, or C.N., as he was invariably known to his friends and associates, was born in Provo, Utah, of Mormon stock, in 1908. He left home at the age of seventeen without informing his parents, started work in Los Angeles, uncharacteristically creating corsages and selling flowers, and learned to fly in 1927. Returning after an exploratory sortie to Mexico, he met Robert C. Forsblade, who was to be a staunch lieutenant throughout Shelton's stormy career. One of Forsblade's first friendly acts was to borrow $100 from his father when they were stranded in Texas, having gone barnstorming with two Waco 10s they did not own, having damaged the airplanes, and finding themselves stranded without means of support.

In 1931 Shelton took off alone to the Yucatán Peninsula, was grounded by problems with his engine, formed a temporary partnership with a local Mexican auto mechanic, made some more

333

The remarkable C. N. Shelton is second from the left in this vintage picture of the staff of Empresa Dean, a Honduran transport operator of the early 1930s. Having served a tough apprenticeship as a pilot with such pioneer companies, Shelton founded his "barefoot airlines" after World War II, following in the footsteps of Lowell Yerex.

money, and moved on. He then ferried an aircraft from Los Angeles to Honduras—making a round trip of South America via Santiago, Chile, and Buenos Aires en route—and tried to start an airline in Honduras, once again in partnership with Bob Forsblade. But Lowell Yerex had beaten him to that particular happy hunting ground, and the pair moved on to Costa Rica. There they formed an airline with Bill Schoenfeldt, who owned a six-seater, single-engined Fokker. Founded on March 2, 1932, Empresa National de Transportes Aéreos (ENTA) was the first airline in Costa Rica and one of the earliest indigenous airlines in Central America.

These were swashbuckling days for Shelton and Forsblade. On one occasion, on an overloaded takeoff from San José, the engine stuttered and lost power and the Fokker hit a tree, shearing ten feet off the plywood wing and leaving only a perilous two feet of aileron. Shelton managed to bring the aircraft back for a safe landing, then went to find the piece of broken wing, stowed it in the plane, ferried it to an adjoining field where there were repair facilities, and was back flying as usual the next day.

They worked hard and played hard. Shelton was a magnificent drunkard, habitually smashing windows and habitually offering a token $20 to pay for the damage. He was supposed to run ENTA for Schoenfeldt, but he spent all the profits and went to Honduras. He found a job with one of the pioneering airlines in that country, Empresa Dean, and found the environment so congenial that he persuaded Forsblade to join him.

In 1934 the legendary Lowell Yerex bought Empresa Dean as a stage in his grand plan to form a Central American airline consortium, so Shelton and his partner worked for Transportes Aéreos Centro-Americanos (TACA) for a while. Shelton also made his acquaintance with *aguardiente*, described by Philip Schleit as "a rum-like concoction that would make Honduras a major world power if it could be put to military use." To his credit, Shelton never flew passengers while drunk, but his periods of intemperance were too long for Yerex, who fired Shelton in 1938. The police of La Ceiba pulled the latter out of a bar and shipped him to New Orleans, with Shelton firing his pistol in defiant farewell as the boat pulled away.

During this hectic period, Shelton had managed to get married, to Florence Hempstead. The marriage lasted six years, they had two children, and it was Shelton's only legal union. They remained friends for life. Shelton had also begun to show a talent for innovation, when Empresa Dean was still competing with Yerex's TACA, by charging passengers by the pound weight. Yerex found himself carrying all the plump ones. He persuaded Yerex—a man used to doing his own persuading—to adopt instrument flying, an early indication of Shelton's character. Whatever his antisocial habits with the bottle, he was always as sound as a rock on technical matters and a strict observer of regulations affecting safety and operational efficiency.

Upon arriving back in the United States, Shelton quickly found a job with Mid-Continent Airlines, one of the original domestic airlines that qualified as a trunk carrier when the grandfather routes were granted by the C.A.B. in 1938. Mid-Continent operated in the corn country west of the Mississippi but insisted that its newest copilot should leave his pistol at home.

In 1940 Shelton joined Transcontinental and Western Air (T.W.A.)—later to be renamed Trans World Airlines—and soon became involved with that airline's U.S. army contracts in wartime logistics across the South Atlantic. Forsblade was still with him, and such was their level of professionalism that out of the 168 pilots in the South Atlantic Contract Division Shelton and Forsblade ranked first and second, respectively, in the number of hours flown during the 3½-year assignment.

It was while Shelton was serving in this contract work that his acute perceptions saved the day in a dramatic event that was to be the turning point of his career. He had been assigned to the Chinese war theater, in support of the beleaguered Chinese army under Generalissimo Chiang Kai-shek. Flying a Boeing 307 Stratoliner, the world's first pressurized airliner, ordered only by T.W.A. and Pan American before World War II stopped production, he was sent to Chengtu to pick up an important passenger, who turned out to be none other than Mme Chiang Kai-shek. As he started his descent to an airfield that had been designated as a technical and refueling stop, Shelton sensed that something was not quite right with the English accents emanating from the control tower. His hunch was confirmed when small-arms fire broke out, and he went on to land safely at another airfield. The Japanese had taken the airstrip the day before.

Shelton's alert response to the situation had undoubtedly impressed Mme Chiang. She presented him with a personally inscribed silver cigarette case and insisted that he should be her pilot when she accompanied her husband to the summit conference in Teheran with Roosevelt, Churchill, and Stalin. Later he flew her back to Chungking, the new Chinese seat of government, where he was a frequent guest at the Chiang residence and was awarded high honors. During one of his many amicable conversations with Mme Chiang, he mentioned that he wanted to start a little airline in South America but that he had no capital. Mme Chiang thought that financing "could be arranged."

When the war ended, T.W.A. had, among its many other plans, the idea of creating a subsidiary airline in China, much in the same way that Pan American had created subsidiaries in various parts of the world as a means of capturing all the available feeder traffic in the areas it served. Under the visionary leadership of Howard Hughes and Jack Frye, T.W.A. rapidly transformed itself into an intercontinental airline during the years immediately following World War II, and the Chinese affiliate would have fitted in with T.W.A.'s plans to match Pan American's activities in its round-the-world service. Cornell Newton Shelton was to have been president of the Chinese operation, but he had other ambitions better suited to his independent, volatile nature.

One day in 1946, Shelton received a check from the Bank of China for $250,000. He promptly formed C. N. Shelton & Company and resigned from T.W.A. Although in 1948 he flew to Taiwan in his own PBY to find out about the money, Mme Chiang told him simply to carry on, and not until 1953 did he learn that his silent partner was Mr. Kung Lin-kai, who suddenly arrived in Miami and introduced himself. Shelton then decided to devote his entire efforts to running an airline in Latin America.

Not that he had been idle: C. N. Shelton & Company had been wheeling and dealing unsuccessfully in surplus aircraft and had formed Flight Engineering and Equipment Corporation (FEEC) to market, unsuccessfully, a system of instantly installable or removable seats. He had also become thoroughly engrossed in one of his ventures in Central America, where the way of life seemed to suit him best.

In 1946 C. N. Shelton & Company formed Transportes Aéreos Nacionales (TAN), having acquired three war-surplus C-47s (military DC-3s), some route authority from the Costa Rican government, and support from a wealthy family in that country. Unfortunately TAN quickly lost all three of its aircraft; one was lost in an inexplicable crash, fortunately without any passengers on board; one was commandeered by the government to combat a revolution; and one was taken over by the revolutionaries. All his ground equipment, even the office typewriter, disappeared, and so, disenchanted, Shelton moved on to Honduras, where he formed another TAN, with a stated value of $159,000, although under complex Honduran law, there was no rigid check as to how much of this was actually paid in.

Shelton's chief partner in Honduras, apart from the faithful Forsblade, was Miguel Brooks, born in the Middle East, but with an adopted name approved by the president of Honduras, whom he counted as a poker-game acquaintance, which surely did the fortunes of TAN no harm at all. Officially, Brooks held 279 of the 300 shares, Julio Lozano, formerly of Empresa Dean, held 20, and Shelton held only 1. But it was Shelton's company all right.

At first, TAN did charter work to Miami, using a converted

Shelton's Barefoot Airline Route. *By an ingenious evasion of the internationally ordained Five Freedoms rules accepted by the member airlines of the world airline organization, IATA, C. N. Shelton managed to fashion an airline route from the United States to southern South America which paralleled Pan American's at half the price.*

Douglas B-18 bomber and two Curtiss C-46s, with which Shelton had become quite familiar during his Chinese flying days. He also ran a remarkable operation from Catacamas, a small community in Honduras, carrying beef in unrefrigerated C-46s to Havana. The cattle were slaughtered in Catacamas, customarily during the night, only after the aircraft arrived, to permit an early morning takeoff. The C-46s arrived in Havana, "awash with blood," to use Forsblade's words, and no doubt stinking to high heaven. It was a minor miracle that it was ever made usable by passengers again.

On June 12, 1950, the U.S. C.A.B. awarded TAN a full permit to carry passengers to Miami. And on August 1, 1950, Shelton proudly fulfilled his ambition of running an airline for those whom he called the barefoot people. He had always cherished the ambition of bringing the advantages of air transport to the underprivileged peoples of Latin America. For all the much-publicized accomplishments of Pan American Airways, PANAGRA, and the various flag carriers of the larger Latin American countries, very few local people could afford to take advantage of these continent-encircling networks. The fares were affordable only by rich businessmen, politicians, or film stars and on most routes were set under agreements through the International Air Transport Association (IATA), which, in spite of continual protestations, was in effect a vast price-fixing organization.

Shelton saw clearly that few Latin Americans traveled on the airlines in Latin America, and for a Pan American airliner to arrive in Tegucigalpa, Managua, or Panama loaded entirely with U.S. citizens was by no means unusual. At first people were reluctant to fly in Shelton's old C-46s, which they regarded with some justification as converted cattle trucks. But althought the first passenger flight took off empty, he gradually won the public over, and while few of his clientèle were actually barefoot, he opened up air travel to a new stratum of air passengers by the simple device of charging lower fares.

Flying a C-46—never the most forgiving aircraft to fly, especially when one of its two engines quits—was especially tricky in Honduras. At Tegucigalpa the airfield was on a plateau, accessible only by flying up a valley and then descending just at the threshold of the runway. Shelton said it was "like a bird flying up to land on top of a flagpole." At San Pedro Sula the field was an uneven one almost indistinguishable from the adjoining farmland—but with the advantage that it was almost downtown.

During the early 1950s TAN extended its services to Managua, Guatemala City, and Belize, and Shelton began to realize the possibilities of bringing his barefoot airline service to even more people in Central and South America. In 1953 he took the plunge and concentrated entirely on this objective, severing his interest in FEEC by exchanging his share in that company to Kung Lin-kai for 10 percent of TAN. Thereupon he set about the task of devising an airline system that could take full advantage of what has become known as Sixth Freedom rights.

Under protocols defined by the International Civil Aviation Organization (ICAO) all airlines are normally able to exercise the first four of the Five Freedoms of the Air. These four permit overflying or nontraffic stops in a foreign country and flying to and from other countries on a reciprocal basis by designated airlines. The cherished Fifth Freedom permits an airline to fly between two foreign countries; a U.S. airline, for example, may carry passengers between London and Frankfurt. Such a privilege is only granted grudgingly and after prolonged bargaining. But if an airline can take advantage of a fortuitous geographical situation, in which its home base lies athwart a much-traveled air route, it can manipulate the Third and Fourth Freedoms—the right to set up or pick up traffic reciprocally—and combine two routes into one.

So long as Shelton held the right to carry traffic from Miami to Tegucigalpa, he could negotiate further Honduran route authority southward and book passengers through from the United States to all points south, with the minor inconvenience of asking them to stop at Tegucigalpa and to go through the formality of changing aircraft, or perhaps to buy two tickets. In practice, changing aircraft often meant sticking a different identifying label on the aircraft, and the ticketing was no different from writing out a multisector ticket in the normal way. This so-called Sixth Freedom is perfectly legal, as it need break no laws, national or international, but it has caused much heart-searching by members of the international airline community who believed they could write their own laws.

At first Shelton extended TAN's own routes as far south as Lima, Peru, via Guayaquil, Ecuador, as an extension of the route to Managua. This was accomplished through the assistance of Marco Tulio Gonzales, an Ecuadorian lawyer, who was able to arrange the necessary operating permits north and south from Guayaquil. The TAN fare was about 30 percent lower than the Pan American–PANAGRA fare. Curiously, the latter involved an interchange at Panama, whereas TAN's aircraft habitually flew straight through from Lima to Miami, with three stops. TAN's old C-46s competed against the four-engined Douglases of the incumbent operators, and the public paid its money and took its choice: bigger aircraft or lower fares. The businessmen, all expenses paid, took PANAGRA; the barefoot people took TAN.

To combat Pan American's agitation on the Sixth Freedom issue, Shelton and Gonzalez established, in February 1957, Compañía Ecuatoriana de Aviación (C.E.A.), to follow quickly on the heels of Aerolíneas Peruanas (APSA) formed in Lima on September 16, 1956. As could be said of many businesses in Latin America, the manner in which the airlines were financed would not bear too much looking into. But there they were, established as going concerns and combining as neat an airline consortium as ever rang the changes on the various ICAO-blessed Freedom rights. They provided through service from Miami to Central America and all the way down the west coast of South America as far as Santiago, Chile, service to which southerly point was started by APSA on June 17, 1957. By 1961 the group was flying Douglas DC-6s.

Typical of Shelton's innovative practices was his introduction in 1962, with C.E.A., of the world's first "fly now, pay later" plan. Not only did prospective passengers receive a slight discount by being credited with interest accruing on early payments, they were automatically entered in a lottery for further discounts. Shelton also instituted a practice which, unlike the advanced-payments plan, was not repeated elsewhere, so far as is known. To avoid suspicion by alert officials in Miami who might question why a C.E.A. plane was being flown by an APSA crew on a TAN route a robing room was established at "Teegoose"—Tegucigalpa—for the convenience of aircrew who wished to change their airline identities.

Such a subterfuge became unnecessary when APSA obtained its legitimate U.S. operating permit on June 23, 1960, and began DC-6 service to Miami on July 13. Less than three years later, on December 1, 1963, it introduced the first low-fare jet service in Latin America when it put into service the Convair 990, by a narrow margin the fastest jet airliner in the world.

These were heady times for Shelton. His dream of a barefoot

airline business had become a reality. The key to success appeared to be the APSA operation, which, by the injection of powerful Peruvian business interests, was soon to extend its Convair 990 service to every major city in South America, taking advantage of Lima's strategic hub position. By the mid 1960s, the consortium was outselling Braniff and challenging Pan Am. Accordingly, in 1963 Shelton sold his interest in the Ecuadorian C.E.A., a move that, if not a mistake, was at least a misjudgment.

He was elbowed out of control of the airline he had been responsible for creating by Peruvian businessmen who took advantage of the trust which he had always placed on a handshake. They acquired absolute control and proceeded to run the airline in a profligate manner. Reported to be owing $22 million, it finally collapsed, years after Shelton's death, depriving Peru of its national airline, a situation not rectified for several years. Had he lived and been placed in control, Shelton could have made Peru the base of one of the best and most successful airlines in Latin America.

For this cavalier, free-living freebooter was basically a crusader for progress, who fought for the freedom of the air in a disciplined manner. He rightly regarded the legal barriers that were used to handicap his progress as artificial devices being used to restrict legitimate rights. When in 1958 his ten-year TAN operating permit came before the C.A.B. for renewal, his adversaries, Pan American and PANAGRA, thought they had a great opportunity to protest against alleged infringements: the issue of fares (on which they were on weak ground), the Sixth Freedom issue, and the question of Shelton's control of foreign airlines. But on July 20, 1960, the board finally admitted that "TAN is technically correct in its position that there is no legal requirement in its permit or any Board order which it has violated." The TAN-APSA interchange service ceased on September 1, but in any event, APSA had been awarded through service to Miami on the very day of the TAN decision, in which the C.A.B. rapped Shelton lightly on the knuckles for his lack of cooperation at the hearing—by being unavailable when subpoenaed.

There is a strong suspicion that there were many in the C.A.B. who privately admired Shelton. Some may have remembered that Pan American used to ride roughshod over regulations when it suited Juan Trippe's purpose and that Pan Am had indulged in practices similar to those it was now condemning. The C.A.B. investigators, much like those of the Federal Aviation Agency, must have learned with growing respect that, although his aircraft were older and outwardly often down-at-the-heel, they were correctly maintained and professionally flown. Shelton's airlines may not have provided first-class comfort, but they never killed a single passenger.

His financial record, too, was admirable. By using the fleet efficiently, maintaining offices in unpretentious office buildings, and avoiding unnecessary frills, Shelton's low-fare airlines always made a profit as long as he was in control, which was more than could be said for some of his high-priced competitors. One of the glorious ironies of the entire Shelton story was that little TAN, in Honduras, survived, while PANAGRA, its prestigious rival, disappeared down the airline tubes on January 31, 1967, to be acquired by Braniff International, after internecine warfare between PANAGRA's two equal partners, Pan American and the W. R. Grace Corporation. Braniff itself eventually folded, with debts estimated at $733 million.

C. N. Shelton died in Lima on March 15, 1965, at the age of only fifty-seven, and thus did not live to observe these events. His death was undoubtedly caused in part by overindulgence in "mortinis," but his pragmatic attitude toward association with various women is unlikely to have had much to do with it. A contributory cause may have been his acute disillusionment at the way in which some of his Peruvian barefoot people were betrayed by their own countrymen, who callously used APSA to further their own interests. Even the airborne cortege that brought Shelton's body back to Miami turned into a disrespectful party, much to Bob Forsblade's distress. These were the same people for whom Shelton had signed hundreds of chits in Lima hotels for free-loading friends, countless friends of friends, and countless others who never met him and looked down upon him because he was from a humble background and therefore not accepted in the class-ridden society of Latin America.

Shelton owned one suit, which he used only rarely, for going to banks or weddings. He was also part-owner of a topcoat, which he used when visiting Miami in the winter. After he died, the other part-owner probably took lawful possession. It should have been donated to the Smithsonian Institution as a lasting memorial to the man who strived to bring the privilege of air travel to the underprivileged and whose vision, determination, and basic integrity helped to form a lasting link between two continents.

▶▶▶▶▶▶▶▶▶▶▶▶▶▶▶▶▶▶▶▶ ◀▶▶▶

Omar Fontana
O Cavalheiro Gigante

Literally translated, *O Cavalheiro Gigante* means "a giant gentle-man," but this does not exactly sum up the personality of this re-markable airline leader. He is certainly a big man physically, with shoulders like an ox, hands like a lumberjack's, and altogether strongly built, so to describe him as a giant of a man would be fair enough. A precise translation of *cavalheiro* is more difficult, for the word must convey a sense of courtesy and charm, mixed with some old-fashioned gallantry. Perhaps to describe Omar Fontana as an amiable gentleman with a touch of class would be an apt summa-tion of his personality.

Like so many of the independent airline pioneers and promot-ers who have injected new life into a sometimes static industry, Fontana seems to have possessed an instinctive sense of destiny, which he has turned into practical terms by combining it with the courage of his convictions, enabling him to make vital decisions with good timing and shrewd judgment. As in England, where the common people know Sir Freddie Laker better than any other sin-gle airline personality, so it is in Brazil, where Omar Fontana is known to Brazilians far better than anyone else, past or present, in that great airline industry, which has made such a signficant con-tribution to the economic life of the country.

He was born on January 7, 1927, in Joaçaba, Santa Catarina, in southern Brazil. His grandparents had emigrated from Italy and his father, Atillio, had set up a retail business in Santa Maria, Rio Grande do Sul, and later in Joaçaba. Omar was the third of four children, and his mother died when he was only four years old. Later his father married again, and there were two more children by the second marriage. As one of six offspring Omar was by no means given preferential treatment.

Like so many immigrants who had built up their lives by the sweat of their brows, Atillio was determined that his sons should be well educated, and Omar was sent to a boarding school in São Paulo when he was only nine. In one respect, this was Atillio's big mistake, for, one day a bright red airplane flew over the enclosed courtyard of the school. From that time onward, whatever may have been the career the proud parent imagined, Omar's mind was fixed firmly on a life with airplanes, one way or another. In his spare time he began to frequent the Campo de Marte, the local air force base, determined to become a pilot one day. His other ambition was to become a concert pianist.

In 1942, when he was only fifteen, Omar took his first flight, in a yellow Brazilian-built Piper Cub. Reflecting his artistic temperament, he remembers the colors as well as the types of aircraft in his experience, and this aesthetic aspect of his character can be perceived in the striking color scheme of Transbrasil's aircraft today. In May 1945, during his last year at school, he was a candidate for the special reserve squadron of the Brazilian Air Force, ready to start serious training. But the course was canceled because the war ended, and the planned expansion of the air arm was curtailed.

He then went to a private flying school in São Paulo, whence he made his first solo flight. Still in the final months of his ten years at boarding school, he was able to fly only on Sunday. Nevertheless, his first solo flight must have impressed the school well enough, for he was immediately appointed a flying instructor. He was eighteen years old.

By this time—on June 4, 1944, to be exact—Atillio Fontana had founded his own company, moving from the retail business into the production side, by establishing the S.A. Indústria e Comércio Concórdia. S.A. is an abbreviation for Sociedade Anónima, the Portuguese or Brazilian equivalent of a corporation or limited stock company. Concórdia was the name of the small town in Santa Catarina, which, although the citizens of that community did not know it at the time, was to become a household word throughout Brazil. Atillio Fontana abbreviated the name of his company to Sadia, using the first and last letters of the full title.

Atillio's business was prospering, and he could afford to be generous, even indulgent, with his children, although the extent to which this indulgence was taken advantage of by one of his sons, Omar, would not have been to his liking at the time. During the protracted period of financial support endured by parents and students the world over, Atillio sent periodic contributions toward Omar's out-of-pocket expenses, such as for books or other items necessary to what his father thought was a serious course in mechanical engineering. The money was spent elsewhere. Omar had a simple equation: one encyclopedia was equal to five flying lessons.

This continued even after Omar had left school. Still convinced that his son was going to be an engineer, to work in the family business of flour milling and meat packing as it adopted modern methods of mechanization, Atillio sent Omar to a polytechnic institute for two years. But Omar continued to fly at every opportunity, until both sides finally recognized reality and Fontana, Senior, ordered Fontana, Junior, to return home to Concórdia. Here he was offered his first paid job. For about eight months, he worked for the mayor of Concórdia as a secretary-assistant, a position that did not provide much opportunity for flying.

Still determined that one of his sons, at least, should attain some level of academic prowess, Atillio unwisely promised Omar that he could have a car of his choice—even a Rolls Royce!—if he would attend law school. No doubt he had by now despaired and thought that his money was secure, but Omar did, in fact, go on to obtain a law degree and is still a member of the bar. He did not, however, receive the Rolls, but he had no complaint.

He first went to the law school at the University of Santa Catarina at Florianópolis, but after a year or so he transferred to São Paulo, where life became hectic. As well as continuing his legal studies, he was married in 1952, to another law student at his university. They were to have four children, all daughters, and Denilda was to play a significant part in Omar's subsequent business life. Early in 1953, Omar Fontana began to work part-time for Panair do Brasil, then one of the leading airlines of Latin America, going first through the ground school, then graduating as a copilot.

During this busy period, Omar studied at the university in the mornings, worked at the São Paulo office of Sadia in the afternoons, and flew as a copilot for Panair during the evenings and weekends. Consistent with a way of life that was to prevail throughout his career, living with Omar was never dull.

During the summer of 1953, Omar began to translate his love of airplanes and aviation into practical ideas. While still at university, he suggested to his father that the meat-packing business at Concórdia should lease a Panair do Brasil Douglas DC-3, that epitome of aircraft versatility, whose worth is proved by the fact that, fifty years after its first flight, there are still about 1,000 examples still flying. Omar had observed that Panair customarily laid over a DC-3 in São Paulo from Saturday evening until Monday morning, because of the lack of demand for it during weekends. He proposed that Sadia should lease the aircraft and fly fresh meat from Concórdia to the markets of the São Paulo metropolis, now vying with Buenos Aires to be the largest, and certainly the richest, city in South America.

The direct distance by surface transport was not much more than 400 miles, but at that time the roads were not of the best, and the railroad meandered by such a circuitous route that the train engineers were alleged to have surveyed the route themselves because in Brazil they were paid by the kilometer. Either way, meat from the Sadia meat-packing plant took 3½ days to reach São Paulo, whereas a DC-3 could do it in 2½ hours.

The Sunday flights, for which the alliterative slogan *Pelo Ar par seu Lar*—"By Air to your Home"—was adopted, were an immediate success and undoubtedly gave Sadia a promotional stimulant. They also stimulated Omar. During the southbound flights, which were empty, he was able to practice all the emergency drills and other necessary flight training to be able to qualify as a pilot. He moved over from the right-hand seat to the left-hand seat.

Returning to Concórdia, now armed with a law degree, he proposed almost immediately, in February 1954, that Sadia buy its own aircraft, so that it could expand this market of obviously great potential. His father, cautious and skeptical, at first opposed the idea. Controlling at least half the shares, he even threatened to block the vote if Omar took his plan to the shareholders. But with ingenuous charm Omar persuaded his father, who claimed to have democratic principles, to allow the vote to be taken on a one-man one-vote basis. The vote was unanimously in favor and Sadia bought a DC-3 from Panair to do Brasil for $150,000.

If ever Douglas needed proof that the DC-3 was a workhorse, it should have gone to Joaçaba during 1954. The Sadia aircraft made three round trips a day between 3 A.M. and 8:30 P.M. piling up

A truly independent spirit in a land of primarily government- or state-controlled aviation, Omar Fontana created Transbrasil as one of the most innovative of all airlines in South America. This picture of him sampling a DC-10 shows him to be an accomplished pilot, possibly the only president of a major airline in the world who personally checks out his own fleet.

fifteen hours a day, a commendable utilization rate for any air transport airplane, long-haul or short-haul, then or today. In 1954 such an intensity of operation was unheard-of. Always with an eye for detail, Omar saw to it that the refueling was done in São Paulo, where the fuel was cheaper and was mechanically pumped. At Joaçaba it was pumped by hand, straight from the barrel, and refueling a DC-3 could take as much as an hour, thus wasting precious flying time. Every northbound DC-3 carried three tons of fresh meat to an insatiable market.

Concerned about a possible mishap or maintenance requirement interrupting the busy and productive regular schedule of the DC-3, the Sadia board decided, while Omar was away, to order a second DC-3 to serve as a reserve aircraft. On his return, Omar was furious. He demonstrated that, should the faithful DC-3 be grounded for any reason, it was cheaper to hire another aircraft—any aircraft, even a Constellation—than to incur the cost of purchasing a complete substitute. The board canceled the order.

While air freight was clearly more efficient in every respect than any form of surface transport between Joaçaba and São Paulo, Omar Fontana discovered that there were certain handicaps, especially under Brazilian law. He had, for example, to pay twice the price for fuel that the airlines paid. Even worse, because the DC-3 was privately owned, spare parts could not be imported without payment of an exhorbitant customs duty, the equivalent to paying black market prices. A third drawback was that a private company could not provide its own radio or radar installations, and these were badly needed at Joaçaba, for elementary safety if for no other reason.

Unable to do anything about the first two of these problems, Omar felt that a solution to the radio difficulty was possible. Two airlines served Joaçaba at that time, Cruzeiro do Sul and VARIG. He approached Cruzeiro, to discover that it intended to abandon service at Joaçaba and would therefore terminate its radio service. He then tried VARIG and was given a blunt refusal by the local manager. Not one to take no for an answer, he went to the VARIG director in São Paulo and was encouraged to go to VARIG headquarters in Porto Alegre to make his request of the president of VARIG, the great Rubem Berta, himself.

Catching the VARIG Super C-46 to Rio Grande do Sul, the state capital, he presented his case, stressing that little Sadia had no intention of competing with VARIG, wishing only to carry fresh meat to its captive markets. Berta, uncompromising, refused to help. In making this negative gesture, Berta may have had some kind of premonition that this young man before him represented a possible threat in the as-yet-undefined future. At any rate, he said no, very firmly.

In desperation, Omar thereupon said he would start his own airline, without at that time having planned to do so. Berta responded: "Do not insist on doing this; it is only a dream. You, as a small operator, cannot possibly succeed against the strength of the established airlines in Brazil." He might also have added that during this period the many small airlines that had emerged in Brazil during the immediate postwar period were now dying off like flies in the winter and that to create a new airline in an apparently declining market was tantamount to commercial suicide. In any event, Omar replied: "Maybe I will not succeed, but it will not be for want of trying."

Today, Omar Fontana enjoys a quiet chuckle at this memory. The airline that he created, which has been a thorn in VARIG's side ever since, was not only conceived in Porto Alegre, in the very womb, as it were, of Brazil's dominant airline force, but was also inspired by the protectionist attitude of VARIG's leader, who in almost every respect was one of the great men of air transport history. By a piquant paradox, VARIG and Rubem Berta were responsible for the birth of what was to become their most inspired competitor, Transbrasil.

On January 5, 1955, Omar Fontana founded Sadia S.A.— Transportes Aereos. He could not begin scheduled operations as an airline immediately, because there were formalities to be observed with the Brazilian aviation authorities. But he was well prepared. He had the financial backing to ensure stability and investment, he had the nucleus of a fleet and the flying experience to go with it, and he certainly had the drive and initiative to fashion these assets into a working organization. In due course he received from the Ministry of Aeronautics a certificate of operation on August 3, 1955, and a certificate of technical competence on January 20, 1956.

Sadia began scheduled service on March 16, 1956, with the veteran DC-3 (PT-ASJ) on a route from São Paulo to Joaçaba and on to Videira and Florianópolis. A staff of seventeen operated a fleet of two DC-3s and a C-46. At the start Mrs. Fontana made the curtains for the aircraft windows, prepared the box lunches, selected the flight attendants, and chose their uniforms, which last function she still performs. Omar transferred the base of operations to São Paulo as a logical step in locating his airline at the source of perhaps half the business traffic in Brazil.

During the early months, little change was made in the tiny system, except to add a second route from Joaçaba northward to the coffee-growing region of Paraná and northern São Paulo. Concórdia was included when Sadia built its own airport, and then, in November 1957, the network reached to the new federal capital, Brasília, at that time under construction and a magnet to every airline in the land. But apart from these routes, opportunities for expansion were limited, for by this time, every community that could generate even a few passengers a week was to be found on the map of one or another of the well-established airlines. Omar had to content himself with a few local routes in his home state, Santa Catarina.

For a few years in the late 1950s, Sadia operated as an associate of what was then the largest Brazilian domestic airline, REAL, headed by another forceful person, Linneu Gomes, who had also built a vast network from a single route from São Paulo to Rio de Janeiro in 1946. Gomes had approached Fontana with the same kind of pressure as had been exerted by Rubem Berta, to the effect that Sadia could not possibly survive against such powerful competition as REAL, ranked tenth in the world in the number of passenger journeys made, could give it.

Gomes was persuasive and persistent, and Fontana eventually agreed to a cooperative arrangement, but not to complete absorption by REAL, which had been the fate of several other small airlines. Linneu Gomes personally received 50 percent of the stock of Sadia and thus became joint owner with Omar Fontana. But he made this concession only on the condition that Fontana join REAL in a senior position. Accordingly, Fontana became the joint vice-president of traffic and sales and thus gained valuable experience in the administration of a company many times as large as his own. But he had retained his independence of action by not allowing REAL to engulf Sadia, and as part of the mutual understanding with Gomes he expanded his fleet to five DC-3s and two C-46s and spread the route network to Rio de Janeiro and Porto Alegre.

By a strange twist of circumstances, Gomes was later to become an employee of Omar Fontana. REAL, with a fleet of about 120 aircraft, including no fewer than 86 DC-3s, outgrew its strength. For several years it had drawn strength from the lack of a road system in Brazil, but when an automobile manufacturing industry was established in São Paulo in 1957 and Brazilians began to develop their first romance with the Volkswagen, road building and improvement proceeded at an astonishing pace. As soon as a road was completed to one of the regional airline stations, that was the end of air service, and because most of these were REAL's Gomes suffered the most.

VARIG bought REAL in 1961, but not before REAL had had its hour of glory. For it purchased Aerovias Brasil in 1954, with an international route to Miami, had added further U.S. routes to Chicago and Los Angeles in the late 1950s, and had crowned this with a Super Constellation route to Tokyo, opened on July 9, 1960. Omar Fontana had a great deal to do with planning and developing this route, the longest that any Brazilian airline had, but more than two decades were to pass before he was able to fly in international airspace again with his own airline.

In August 1961, when VARIG took over REAL, Omar Fontana bought back Gomes's 50 percent of Sadia and sought fresh capital. At the end of 1962, he acquired Transportes Aéreos Salvador (T.A.S.), based in the city of Salvador, with a network that consisted largely of regional routes within the state of Bahia. The merged group was divided into two operating units: Sadia/T.A.S., serving fifty-four cities in Brazil and run by Fontana, and Sadia, a cold-storage freight operation run by Gomes. The most important outcome of the merger was that Fontana gained access to major cities in the northeast of Brazil, including Salvador, Recife, and Fortaleza. On the map, at least, Sadia was beginning to look like a national airline.

In reality, Sadia was still a regional airline, for its routes were still regional, and the aircraft used to serve them were not of the first-line types used by the leading Brazilian airlines, such as Panair do Brasil, VARIG, VASP, and Cruzeiro do Sul. Nevertheless, Sadia received a valuable stimulant when, at the beginning of 1963, the Brazilian government created the Rede Integração Nacional (RIN) in an effort to provide a sound foundation for a national system of feeder air routes. The demise of many airlines in the late 1950s, the retirement of many old aircraft, and the growing operating costs that ensured financial disaster: all these factors combined to force the government to establish a system of subsidy if Brazil was to retain its airlines. Omar Fontana was one of the beneficiaries.

In February 1964, he startled the Brazilian airline fraternity with a bold campaign to buy a modern aircraft that had been designed especially to be a replacement for the ubiquitous DC-3. Built in England by Handley Page, the Dart Herald was a forty-six–seat, twin-engined turboprop airliner, able to operate from grass strips as well as from paved runways. Fontana quickly found that he would have to call upon every resource of determination and perseverance that he had if he was to overcome the conservative inertia of the government, not to mention the bitter opposition of the established airlines.

Possibly even more important than its field performance was the economical nature of the Herald; Fontana was able to demonstrate that it could operate within the piston-engined fare category and thus qualify for inclusion within the RIN subsidized tariff schedule. But at first he was not allowed to import new aircraft, so he had to lease aircraft, one from a Philippine airline recently bankrupt and another from the manufacturer. At about this time, he also recapitalized Sadia, allowing participation by the employees on a worker-ownership plan.

Negotiations with the various arms of government in Rio de Janeiro—the administration had not yet moved out to Brasília—over the purchase of five Dart Heralds were prolonged. Fontana became so fascinated with the labyrinthine process, involving both government agencies and banks, that he compiled a record of the travel and time involved. He calculated that he traveled to Rio on 234 occasions and spent a total of 1,040 hours at meetings or waiting in anterooms. At the end of this long bureaucratic road, after arranging for additional exports of Brazilian iron ore as a gesture of reciprocal trade, he was finally able to order his five Heralds on January 6, 1965. They cost £1,500,000 sterling ($4,200,000), including spares. To mark the elevation to modern equipment and the retirement of the DC-3s and C-46s, the route network was trimmed from fifty-four cities to twenty-eight. By the time final approval was given to the Herald purchase in February 1966, Sadia had also been admitted to the elite fraternity of the Ponte Aérea, the air bridge between São Paulo and Rio de Janeiro—and incidentally the first air shuttle service in the world. Admission to the club was influenced, so it is rumored, by Fontana's declared intention to introduce the Herald on the route, at reduced fares.

The Brazilian aviation-minded public had hardly digested this development when, in May 1967, Omar Fontana requested government approval to purchase the British Aircraft Corporation's BAC One-Eleven. This was a ninety-four–seat twin-jet and was the first of the second generation short-haul jets, the first generation having been the French Caravelle, used extensively within Brazil. But whereas Omar Fontana had been the first into Brazilian airline airspace with a twin-engined turboprop, in this instance he was scooped by a rival airline, VASP, the São Paulo airline backed by the city, state, and banks of that great city. VASP had moved smartly and, while Omar was carefully selecting the -500 Series of the One-Eleven, it had ordered the earlier -400 series, and had put some leased aircraft into service in January 1968. Sadia's -500s, resplendent in a new multicolored paint scheme—each aircraft was painted in different colors—began work on September 17, 1970.

Although Sadia was still a small airline, Omar Fontana gave it much prominence by his flamboyant approach to marketing. His flair for publicity, evident with his innovative aircraft color schemes, was also confirmed by his launching the Royal Swan service on the One-Elevens, the first attempt to set new standards of luxury on the domestic routes of Brazil. Such extroverted measures were necessary at this time, for none of the Brazilian airlines was thriving, Sadia was losing money, and there were reports of a merger with VASP.

In June 1972 Omar Fontana changed the name of Sadia to the more evocative Transbrasil S.A.—Linhas Aéreas, or simply Transbrasil. At the same time, the decision was made to transfer the headquarters from São Paulo to Brasília. This was said to be a little applied psychology, part of Fontana's effort to identify himself with the federal capital, but the reasons actually were more practical. São Paulo's Congonhas Airport was too small to allow for expansion and Rio de Janeiro's future was uncertain, while Brasília was geographically central, quite apart from its continuously growing importance, not only as the capital but as a city and traffic-generating metropolis in its own right.

Omar Fontana was always in the news headlines, mainly because he was always creating news. On April 16, 1973, Transbrasil was the first airline in the world to put into service the Brasilian-built Embraer EMB-110B Bandeirante, a miniairliner with between twelve and sixteen seats, which aimed to claim a share of the world's commuter airline market. By astute marketing Embraer has been successful in doing just that, and Omar Fontana can thus claim with pride that he helped to launch this little Brazilian airliner and, in so doing, helped to heighten the image of the Brazilian manufacturing industry in the eyes of the world.

Transbrasil was not among the early purchasers of the popular trijet, the Boeing 727, but Fontana was one of the first advocates of the wide-bodied jet for operation on the densely traveled Brazilian intercity routes. In January 1974 he announced that, subject to government approval, he would order two of the European Airbuses, which could carry 230 passengers each, and represented a sensible solution to the problem of traffic congestion. But this order was not taken up, for the government firmly took the stand that this action would destabilize the Brazilian domestic market.

In fact, the whole Brazilian domestic airline industry was in a state of destabilization. Cruzeiro do Sul, one of the oldest airlines in Brazil, was in deep financial straits, and the government made it known that it favored the merger. There was much sparring between aspiring contestants, and Omar Fontana was the first to make an offer, but he could not persuade the National Development Bank to make the required guarantee of 42 percent of the purchase price. The government had actually approved this offer. Later, a proposal that VARIG absorb Transbrasil, as a condition of VASP absorbing Cruzeiro do Sul, failed because Fontana was confident that his own financial problems were temporary, and he refused to sell to VARIG. No doubt Omar also remembered the long opposition of VARIG to his attempts to become established and was none too happy about an unholy alliance now.

He did not allow these complex maneuvers to interfere with the progress of Transbrasil. He joined the ranks of Boeing 727 airlines by putting the QC (Quick Change) convertible freighter version of that airliner into service in 1974 and began night air mail service in the same year, in cooperation with the Brazilian Mail and Telegraph Company. He also established, in 1975, the Transbrasil Foundation, through which the company's 3,000 employees became major shareholders of their own airline, owning up to 39 percent of the total capital, participating also in a corporate social security system.

By Fontana standards, the next few years were uneventful, while Transbrasil consolidated its position as one of the four Brazilian national airlines—although Fontana does not accept the idea that Cruzeiro do Sul is a separate airline from VARIG, which owns it but which maintains the two fleets and accounting systems separately. In company with all the other lines, Transbrasil became involved with the new regional airline system, in which Brazil sensibly set up a group of feeder companies, some of which were closely associated with the trunk carriers. Transbrasil joined the state of Bahia in founding Nordeste, a logical region in which to diversify its activities, bearing in mind its own ancestral connections with Bahia when it took over T.A.S.

In March 1977 Transbrasil's new hanger was dedicated at Brasília. At the time, with 138,000 square feet of space, it was the largest in South America, although it was later eclipsed by VARIG's new establishment at Galeão Airport, Rio de Janeiro. The fleet was standardized by selling off the three remaining Dart Heralds in 1976 and the six BAC One-Elevens in 1978, so by 1979 Omar Fontana could point to a neat Boeing 727 fleet, fourteen strong and resplendent in yet another striking color scheme, all-white fuselage with rainbow stripes on the tail.

The Transbrasil aircraft reflected Omar Fontana's own character and personality. Although they were of the earlier, smaller series of Boeing's best-selling short-haul jet, they were right for the Transbrasil network. While the larger version of the 727 was theoretically more economical to operate, its profitability depended on steady and substantial passenger loads, and with the rival airlines solidly established on most of the densely traveled Brazilian domestic routes, low load factors (percentage of seats occupied) could have been a high risk. The color scheme, of course, was pure Fontana. When he introduced it many airline observers were a little startled. Some shook their heads at the revolutionary design. But today other airlines the world over have turned to similar paint schemes as part of a trend to present air travel in a lighter vein than in the staid old days of navy blue and somber hues.

During the early 1980s the Brazilian government stimulated its commercial airline industry with some bold and constructive policies, and no airline accepted the opportunities offered with more enthusiasm than did Omar Fontana. On October 1, 1980, Transbrasil introduced night services under the Tarifa Economica Noturna (T.E.N.) scheme. This offered the public lower fares and permitted a more intensive—and therefore more economical—use of the aircraft fleet.

On August 15, 1981, this promotional fare idea was augmented by the Tarifas Diferenciadas—Promocionais e Familiares (T.P. and T.F.). The former was for travel during periods of low demand, in an effort to fill otherwise empty seats, while the latter offered substantial discounts to members of the same family traveling together. Shortly afterward, in a move that was of little benefit to Transbrasil, however, because its direct overseas connections were quite limited, Brazil introduced a special twenty-one–day $330 unlimited mileage ticket for overseas visitors. Transbrasil had no overseas routes, and Omar Fontana, having lain fairly low for a few years, decided to do something about it.

Not that this was an ideal time to be speculative. On the contrary, there were good reasons for caution and even procrastination. During 1980 and 1981 Brazil went through a severe economic crisis, which was reflected in bitter and ruthless competition for declining markets in many industries. But the airline industry in Brazil preserved a degree of stability, largely because the government had adopted policies of traffic promotion long advocated by Omar Fontana.

In striking contrast to the agonizing delays experienced in years gone by, response to Fontana's new investment plans was prompt and sympathetic. In 1981 the Coordinating Commission of the Civil Air Transport (COTAC) approved his master plan to modernize the Transbrasil fleet, which was, moreover, by no means antiquated. The investment plan involved the lease-purchase of up to seventeen of the latest generation of Boeing jet airliners to replace the existing B-727s. The proposed total expenditure was $556 million, which was indicative of the strength and stature of Omar Fontana and his airline, far different from the early days, when, as a DC-3 operator, he was not taken seriously by the authorities.

The key to the plan was the inclusion of three Boeing 767-200 wide-bodied twinjets. Equipped with the latest General Electric turbofan engines, in a 210-seat cabin layout, the 767 initiated the first nonscheduled charter flight from Brazil to the United States on July 2, 1983. The previous year, in preparation for this unprecedented development in Brazilian overseas commercial airline operations, Transbrasil Airlines had been founded in Miami, Florida, as a wholly-owned subsidiary. It was presided over by Marise, one of Omar Fontana's daughters. The destination in Florida was Orlando, where Walt Disney World, the famous entertainment attraction, had turned that city from an average provincial center into an international tourist center.

Three days later the Boeing 767 was introduced on Transbrasil's busy Brazilian domestic trunk routes, where it immediately demonstrated Fontana's wisdom in choosing this particular type. Although his rival airlines were operating Airbuses, with 230 seats, the statistics reported by the Directorate of Civil Aviation showed that the 767 was a real moneymaker, with a lower break-even load factor, turning handsome profits for Transbrasil.

In another action, history proverbially repeated itself. In August 1982 Fontana had sought to restore Brazil's position in the international air freight market and had leased a Boeing 707 freighter, capable of carrying forty-two metric tons, from VARIG. Undoubtedly having plans of its own, VARIG canceled the lease agreement in September 1984, giving Fontana an embarrassing sixty days' notice. Acting with characteristic urgency, he obtained four Boeing 707s from a source in the United States and had them converted into a Quick-Change (QC) version, the only such aircraft in the world. Transbrasil now uses these not only on the international cargo flights, but also for the night mail services and on the Ponte Aerea between Brasilia and Rio de Janeiro. But for VARIG's obduracy, Transbrasil's actions would have been less determined and ambitious.

The mid 1980s saw Omar Fontana at full gallop once again. During the summer of 1985, charter services to Orlando peaked at five a week, with originating points as diverse as Manaus, Fortaleza, Belém, even Florianópolis, state capital of Transbrasil's ancestral home, Concórdia. On July 5 the Orlando service was extended to Freeport, the resort city of the Bahamas.

Encouraged by the success of the nonscheduled international enterprise, which had demonstrated Fontana's judgment by proving a complete success within two years, O Cavalheiro Gigante now took a giant step. He applied to the Directorate of Civil Aeronautics (D.C.A.) to be designated the second flag carrier to the United States on the routes he had already established for charter flights, together with routes to Washington, D.C., Atlanta, and Toronto via Freeport and Barbados. All these would be flown by the Boeing 767, which had demonstrated to Fontana's satisfaction that it was as versatile a performer on such long distance routes as it was on the domestic trunk lines in Brazil.

Should the Brazilian D.C.A. be enlightened enough to grant such a request, most of the well-informed traveling public would react favorably, considering such a move to be long overdue. Having taken over REAL in 1961 and Panair do Brasil in 1965, VARIG had monopolized Brazilian overseas air routes. A faithful member of the price-fixing cartel, IATA, VARIG was a law unto itself. Visitors to Brazil had never been able to take advantage of promotional fares, as they could everywhere else in the world, simply because VARIG and its foreign associates, such as Pan American, Lufthansa, and Iberia, perfectly comfortable with their secure business traffic, were not particularly interested in promoting new markets.

Furthermore, international route development was sluggish, not at all consistent with the place in the world of air transport that Brazil should have consolidated. Since VARIG had gained its dominance, the only overseas route development had been to reinstate the route to Tokyo, which Omar Fontana had planned during his short stay with REAL, to add a couple of new points to the existing European network, and to add two low-density routes across the South Atlantic to Africa.

By his visionary challenge to the authorities, Omar Fontana may be doing more than expanding his own domain. He may be reminding a whole country of its missed opportunities and launching Brazil on a new path, to take its place in the upper echelons of the great airline nations, at the same time providing an injection of inspiration, enterprise, and vigor that seem to have been sadly absent from the Brazilian international airline scene for a quarter of a century.

Few airline presidents are as accomplished in the pilot's seat as Omar Fontana. Several of the airline innovators in the past became airline presidents from their early experience as pilots, and several—Howard Hughes, Slim Carmichael, and Orvis Nelson, for example—were possibly more at home on the flight deck than behind an office desk. Not only does Omar Fontana check out potential Transbrasil aircraft personally, passengers on a Boeing 767 flight are likely to hear "This is your Captain—and Chairman of the Board—speaking" in a novel version of the familiar announcement.

The sensitivity needed to fly an airplane is echoed, in Fontana's case, by his musical talents, and he has managed to combine the two by compositions which are related to aviation. His *Fantasia del Aire* and his *Amazonia Suite* have been recorded by Brazilian orchestras, and he is working on a eulogy of the Boeing 767, which may be the first time that an airliner has been so rhapsodized.

For all this to emerge from a man whose physical appearance suggests that he should be the piano mover rather than the piano player is extraordinary. But those who have had the good fortune to meet this remarkable person should not be too much surprised. After all, Concórdia was not exactly the most likely place to found one of Brazil's great airlines.

▶▶▶▶▶▶▶▶▶▶▶▶▶▶▶▶▶▶▶

Asia

▶▶▶▶▶▶▶▶▶▶▶▶◀▶▶▶▶▶

▶▶▶▶▶▶▶▶▶▶▶▶▶▶▶▶▶▶▶▶▶ ◀▶▶

His Highness the Prince Varanand

Prince to Pauper

The subtitle of this profile is perhaps somewhat exaggerated, quite blatantly, to make a point. In the annals of air transport and of the men who created this great worldwide industry, there have been many who trod the fairy-tale path from rags to riches. Some moved from rags to riches and back to rags again, while some, already rich, became richer. And while there were some who lost their proverbial shirts, none could look back upon a romance with the airline business with such disillusionment as a man who lost $50 million.

To lose such a large sum implies wealth in the first place, the kind of wealth normally attributed to kings, oil tycoons, and Eastern potentates. From the last of these broad categories came a most unusual man, one of great charm and natural dignity, possessed of an attractive boyish enthusiasm that sustained him during some pretty dark days, but whose faith in human nature was coupled with an insufficiency of sound judgment, so he was betrayed time and time again and simultaneously stripped of his inherited fortune.

His Highness the Prince Varanand was born in Bangkok, Siam—he insists on this name rather than the now official Thailand—on Saturday, August 19, 1922. His father was His Celestial Highness Prince Chutatuj Taradilok, Gromakhun Petchabune Interachai, the fourth son of Queen Sowapa and King Chulalongkorn, Rama V, of the Chakri Dynasty of Siam. For those unfamiliar with Siamese royal and aristocratic strata, the honor of *Celestial* is

363

The Prince Varanand of Siam served in the Royal Air Force and was a pilot for Thai International Airways before branching out on his own to found a national airline for his country, unfettered by foreign control. But Air Siam foundered in spite of the Prince's valiant efforts. He is pictured here in nostalgic mood outside one of his favorite English pubs, The Bull, at Gerrards Cross.

ranked immediately below that of the king himself; Prince Varanand himself is two levels below that. The term *Gromakhun* is the equivalent of a baronetcy.

As was customary at the time, the young prince was, for the first nine years of his life, permitted to be cared for by his mother, living strictly within the palace grounds. Thereafter, he was separated from both his mother and his nurse—the Siamese nanny— and handed over to a male coach-cum-royal page for training and upbringing in royal protocol.

Because of intermarriage, stemming from the belief that royalty must marry royalty, Veranand's father was physically weak, and he died in 1923, at the age of only thirty-one. At the appropriate age, the prince's uncle, his father's youngest brother, took over the responsibility for his upbringing. Three other brothers also died early in life, and this uncle, by a twist of fate, became King Rama VII, instead of Varanand's father. Varanand himself did not become king because his mother was not of the royal blood. The insistence on the dual royal ancestry prevailed until 1935.

In January 1934 Prince Varanand left Siam to be educated in Europe. He accompanied his uncle, King Rama VII, who, as it turned out, was never to return to Siam. A revolution had taken place in June 1932, and officially, in name only, the absolute monarchy had been replaced with a constitutional one. In practice, all that had happened was that the power had been transferred from the king to an army colonel, who promoted himself to the rank of field marshal and changed the name of the country to Thailand.

Coincidentally, corruption, practiced by almost the entire population, became a national characteristic and a way of life in the new Thailand. This was one of the reasons King Rama VII abdicated, in March 1935.

After a short tour of Italy and France, Prince Varanand was sent to the United States, and in April 1934 he entered Sidwell Friends School in Washington, D.C. In July 1935 he was recalled to England, where he was to remain for almost twenty-five years, including five years spent overseas with the Royal Air Force. He attended a preparatory school, Heath Mount, in Hertfordshire; a public school, Marlborough College; and Magdalene College, Cambridge.

Prince Varanand's first serious interest in aviation developed in 1936, when he watched his uncle, no longer king, take his first solo flight at Heston Airport. Determined to follow in his uncle's footsteps, he began to frequent air displays and to study aviation. At Cambridge, one of his lady friends, having found difficulty in coping with his name, dubbed him Prince Nicky—a friendly nickname that has stayed with him ever since.

In February 1942 he joined the Royal Air Force. In itself this would not arouse special comment, except that he was accepted for service on the exact day that Thai nationals in Great Britain were declared to be enemy aliens. Under Japanese pressure, the new Thailand had declared war on Britain and the United States in January. Although it was proud of its status as the only truly independent country in Asia, resistance to the Japanese onslaught in southeast Asia would have been hopeless, and the country really had no choice in the matter. At any rate, the British government recognized the problem and awarded former King Rama VII and his family the status of Privileged Persons.

Prince Nicky had joined the R.A.F. before he had graduated from Cambridge, and he decided to stay on as a regular officer after the end of World War II. The British authorities helped him to obtain British nationality so that he could be given a permanent commission. Sadly, he had become persona non grata back in Thailand, largely because of his career in the R.A.F. The Thai government had in 1945 become intensely pro-American, to the exclusion of all else. Varanand should have transferred to the U.S. Army Air Force.

On February 29, 1960, after ten years of continuous flying duties, Prince Nicky left the Royal Air Force with a record of one crash, no promotions, and one marriage, which, however, was to end four years later, by which time he had become the father of two lovely children. His premature retirement was unintentionally timed so that he left the service with a gratuity and retirement pay "that would keep me in postage stamps for the rest of my life." In an attempt to flee from nostalgic associations, he emigrated to Switzerland, but there he felt even more the boredom of being unemployed.

He also suffered a strong attack of conscience, leading as he was a comfortable life on proceeds that originated in the country of his birth without doing anything to earn them. During the early 1960s, therefore, he visited Thailand several times, and it was during the course of these visits that he became aware of a developing airline situation in Thailand and subsequently got himself involved in a politico-industrial intrigue of major proportions.

Siam, or Thailand, has a long history of airline development. It can with justification claim to have been one of the pioneers of air transport in Asia, having begun regular mail services as early as 1922, when the Royal Aeronautical Service provided aerial extensions to several of the internal railway lines. Because of its strategic geographical position, Bangkok became a vital staging point on various long-distance air routes during the 1930s, with the Dutch, French, and British airlines including the Thai capital on their services to distant empire destinations. After World War II, attempts were made, partly with American participation, to start indigenous airlines, but these were not successful, even though Thai Airways was the result of an amalgamation in 1951.

This airline survived precariously through a series of alliances with foreign airlines, including Pan American and Northwest, but a sounder solution was found at last when, on December 14, 1959, an agreement was signed with the Scandinavian Airline System (S.A.S.). Besides acquiring a 30 percent shareholding, S.A.S. supplied modern piston-engined equipment—which it no longer needed because of the acquisition of new jets—and embarked on a program of developing Bangkok as an overseas hub for itself.

S.A.S. had been unable to negotiate important traffic rights in the Orient, particularly to Hong Kong, where the British authorities were uncooperative. But with the help of Thai Airways, the difficulties were overcome through the joint operation of Thai Airways International (THAI). International service to Hong Kong, Taipei, and Tokyo, using Thai traffic rights, was opened on May 1, 1960, and within a week THAI was serving the Far East from Calcutta to Singapore.

The device fooled nobody, least of all certain patriotic people in Thailand who were apprehensive of possible exploitation by the Scandinavians. There was a certain logic to their concern. Although Thailand had never been colonized by the Europeans in the political sense, as had almost the whole continent of Asia, the influence of Scandinavia in Thai trading and economics was apparent. The success of Danish teak furniture owes its origins to the supply of the best wood, at the best price, from sources in Thailand. The intrusion of S.A.S., therefore, was interpreted as another ploy by the northern Europeans to consolidate their economic grip on the country.

While any precise cause-and-effect process would be impossible to establish, this feeling was quite real. Within the airline, several Thai pilots, who felt that their presence in THAI was only a token gesture, persuaded Prince Nicky to join them, believing that his ancestry and flying experience could combine to make him a good spokesman and campaigner for their as yet unidentified cause.

The circumstances of his joining THAI were strange. Because the Scandinavians did not believe that a Siamese prince would make the grade and because the Thais feared that he might not and that they would thus lose face, Varanand had to carry out his commercial pilot training in Stockholm in secret and at his own expense. If he made the grade and was accepted by S.A.S. on behalf of THAI, his pay would be retroactive. Fortunately for all concerned, he satisfied the instructors, became a THAI pilot, and got his money back—probably for the last time in his airline career.

At about this time, he met Captain William McIntosh, a British S.A.S. captain and instructor who had managed to remain British, although the airline would have preferred him to have become

Swedish, Norwegian, or Danish. Prince Nicky and Bill McIntosh took to each other because they had two things in common: British passports and Royal Air Force backgrounds. Both felt that the Thais employed by the airline were being exploited. The Scandinavians—the Swedes in particular, because of their neutrality during World War II—were apprehensive about the R.A.F. The prince firmly believed that they distrusted him because "I worked too hard for a Thai, spoke English too well, and had managed to stay in the R.A.F. for 18 years!"

Nicky Varanand's friendship with McIntosh strengthened, particularly in Zurich in 1964, where they were taking the Convair 990 simulator course together. The aircraft were owned by Swissair but were operated jointly by the Swiss national airline and S.A.S. One of them was subleased to Thai International but on the trunk route to Tokyo, via Bangkok, was flown only by Scandinavian or Swiss crews. Many of these were stationed in Bangkok, received free housing, tax-free pay (at European rates), and a car. The Thai crews of Thai International, meanwhile, were assigned only to regional routes in the Far East, south to Jakarta and Singapore and north to Tokyo.

Such an arrangement rankled with the Thai pilots, who also discovered that the legal agreement setting up their own international airline was something like those of the arrangements made between the European powers and China during the nineteenth century and now referred to by the Chinese as Unequal Treaties. Varanand admits quite frankly that he founded his own airline for purely patriotic reasons, and although its greatest achievement was to pioneer the transpacific route on behalf of Thailand, this had nothing to do with any profound foresight. "The truth only dawned ten years and $10 million later."

The contract between S.A.S. and T.A.C. (Thai Airways Corporation) was rigid. The main clauses stated that it must run for five years before any extension or cancellation could be considered, that such a change could be made only after five years' notice, that all major decisions must be unanimous, and that S.A.S. would absorb all losses but share profits during the first five years.

The board of directors of Thai Airways International comprised eleven members, of whom three were appointed or approved by S.A.S. The chairman was the commander-in-chief of the Royal Thai Air Force. On the face of it, this appeared to give the

Thai element the controlling influence in THAI's policy, but in practice, S.A.S. ran the show. They kept the books, organized the operations, and integrated the airline so that it was, except in name, a regional subsidiary.

Fortunately for Prince Nicky's aspirations to form his own airline, the minister of communications of the day, Lieutenant General Pongse Punakanta, was not too happy with the S.A.S.-T.A.C. contract, and neither were some of the other ministers. The outcome of their dissatisfaction was that they concentrated on the exact wording of the contract and perceived that S.A.S. was under the impression that, in dealing with T.A.C., it was actually dealing with the Thai government. Splitting some very fine Oriental hairs, the Thai judicial authorities determined that, even though T.A.C. was owned 100 percent by the government, this was not a government-to-government contract, for the simple reason that S.A.S. was a consortium owned by the three governments of Sweden, Norway, and Denmark.

The legal aspects of this delicate determination were not explored or debated, and the Thai government decided to encourage Prince Varanand to form his own airline. To sugar this bitter pill for S.A.S., however, the initial idea was that the newcomer should concentrate on carrying only air cargo. Thai International operated no all-cargo aircraft, so the competition would not appear to be too defiant. Even so, strong hints were cast to pilot Varanand to the effect that if he pursued this crazy idea of forming an airline, he would never make it to the left-hand seat—that is, be promoted to captain.

Nevertheless, S.A.S. did not resort to such petty vindictiveness, and Nicky Varanand was promoted in one year less than the S.A.S. statutory minimum of four years. Then, in July 1965, he received official permission to form his airline, and he handed in his resignation. For six short weeks he made the most of his flying opportunities, and he felt a sharp pang when he said goodbye to active jet flying for what turned out to be eleven long, eventful years in another capacity.

The idea of naming the airline Varanair was derived from the Canadian aircraft company, Canadair, and the suffix Siam added, not only to indicate the nationality but also to "depersonalize it a bit." Varanand's comment on the formation of Varanair was both emotional and poignant: "The official date was September 15,

1965, deliberately chosen to coincide with the 25th Anniversary of the Battle of Britain Day. Whilst the R.A.F. fought against odds in 1940, my airline was also going to fight against odds in 1965. The difference of course was that the R.A.F. survived and won its battle, whereas Air Siam lost and died at the hands of the people and country it was supposed to save."

THAI's capital at this time was 2 million baht (one baht was worth about twenty dollars) but Varanair-Siam was capitalized at 100 million baht. Only 25 percent was paid up, however, because that was all Prince Nicky could raise by mortgaging some of his landholdings. He negotiated the mortgage with the Bangkok Bank, run by an overseas Chinese management, who, it turned out, were under a false impression as to which parcel of land was involved. The choice piece that the bank expected as collateral was not yet Varanand's, and the other property was inferior. The bank was far from pleased, and this worked against Prince Nicky later on, as did his tendency to work too hard, a virtue considered by the Chinese to be unhelpful to their cause.

Prince Nicky began to put together a working airline, and it was a laborious task. Because of his British sympathies, the staff of the embryo Varanair was almost entirely British, many from the British Overseas Airways Corporation. Unfortunately, however, they were an incohesive and amateurish group, a situation that was not improved by the bankers and backers to whom the prince had had to appeal for further financial support. He insists today, in spite of the disappointments, that he too was an amateur "with very little experience in managing and directing an airline, [even though he was] the founder, chairman, and chief executive."

Against this managerial shortcoming were two massive positive factors which, given a slightly luckier roll of the dice, could have changed the entire fortunes of this bold little group of amateurs. Varanair-Siam almost bought an aircraft with which they could have made a killing in the Orient, and it did obtain an unbelievable combination of traffic rights across the Pacific Ocean.

Bill McIntosh had joined the airline in 1966, originally as director of operations, but he quickly assumed the position of executive vice president because of the severe lack of other managerial expertise. Unfortunately, he was not able to get on well with the Thais, either not recognizing the need for or refusing to adjust to the Oriental way of conducting business or, for that matter, personal relations. To put no finer point on McIntosh's position, he was not popular in Bangkok, and this was detrimental to Varanair's fortunes at a critical time.

During the latter 1960s negotiations were held with the British Aircraft Corporation for the possible purchase of the (formerly Vickers) VC-10. This was Great Britain's belated attempt to produce an airliner to challenge the Boeing 707, the Douglas DC-8, and the Convair 990 and thus retain a slender portion of the big jet airliner market. The VC-10's four engines were mounted on the rear part of the fuselage, in the manner pioneered by the French Caravelle. Although this meant that two rows of seats had to be sacrificed, the VC-10 was the quietest and smoothest long-range airliner of its day, and B.O.A.C. stressed the ample legroom and the VC-Tenderness.

For obscure reasons, B.O.A.C., which had helped to launch the aircraft with a substantial order, lost sight of the true economics of this fine aircraft, stressing only the higher unit costs as a result of the smaller number of seats. Almost criminally, the British flag carrier failed to recognize, or at least to publicize, the fact that the VC-10 pulled in substantially more revenue than did the American rivals, because of its low cabin noise and its excellent flying qualities. Indeed, it carried out a campaign of denigration which, in retrospect—as it seemed to many at the time—was appalling, not only damaging itself, but stabbing the British industry in the back.

The VC-10 would have been perfect for a new airline such as Varanair-Siam, which would have been able to promote a superior service, aided by cabin courtesy of equally superior standards, in a burgeoning market that included a large percentage of highly discriminating passengers who insisted on the best of everything. Discussions held with the British were eventually dropped, because, it was said, the VC-10 lacked range and economical performance, compared with the latest jets from the U.S. But the Super-VC-10 was just round the corner, and if the British had played their cards correctly, this might easily have made a severe dent in the American monopoly. Varanair's only problem would have been that rival airlines in the Orient would also have bought some VC-Tenderness.

In a later era the highly successful European Airbus made its breakthrough into the East Asian market in Thailand. In retrospect it appears that the VC-10 could have done the same.

The other positive factor of literally global significance was the acquisition of traffic rights on a transpacific route to Los Angeles, via Hong Kong, Tokyo, and Honolulu. These rights are jealously guarded by the fortunate countries that can exploit their territorial sovereignty with systematic, sometimes ruthless effectiveness. The trading of rights through bilateral agreements between governments, usually through the agency of designated airlines, is always conducted with meticulous attention to the protection of commercial advantage. No country ever grants rights to foreign operators unless it receives what it considers to be equal rights in exchange, except in special—normally political—conditions of expediency.

In spite of all indications to the contrary, and in an amazingly short time during 1967, Varanair-Siam, now calling itself more simply Air Siam, obtained priceless operating authority from the British in Hong Kong, the Japanese in Tokyo, the Americans for points in the Pacific, and the Thai government itself. The first success was with the United States, which possibly underestimated Air Siam as a potential intercontinental threat to Pan American and recognized also that Bangkok's strategic position in East Asia was too precious to jeopardize. The bilateral agreement, assuring Air Siam of a foothold in California, was signed on April 27, 1967.

Next was the Thai authority itself, granted on August 19, and then, within a single week, Japanese and British traffic rights covering Hong Kong and Tokyo were granted on October 26 and 31, respectively. The British were sympathetic because they were fully aware of the fact that THAI was operating into Hong Kong for and on behalf of S.A.S., simply hiding behind Thai skirts as a legal expedient. They hoped that perhaps Air Siam would be recognized as the flag carrier of Thailand and thus eventually remove the Scandinavian incursion. Japan had no objection to Air Siam, for it already permitted S.A.S. into Tokyo, both from the traditional southern Asia route and via the polar route, via Anchorage, Alaska, and THAI operated into Osaka.

The implications of these combined traffic rights were breathtaking in scope. Not only could Air Siam operate a Bangkok–Tokyo–Honolulu–Los Angeles route—as prestigious and as lucrative an itinerary as any in the world—but the nations had also granted to Varanand's airline the full Fifth Freedom rights. These, under mutual understandings reached by all members of the International Civil Aviation Organization (ICAO), permitted airlines not only to operate to and from foreign points, but also to operate, with full traffic and commercial privileges, *between* foreign points. Thus Air Siam could pick up passengers and freight from Hong Kong and fly to Tokyo, or could pick up in Tokyo and fly to the United States, or over any combination of these segments, in both directions. On the face of it, it seemed almost like the Ultimate Freedom, the right to print your own money, and needless to state, it constituted a major victory for the so far inoperative airline over S.A.S. and Thai International.

While Air Siam could proudly display its precious operating certificates as attractive and impressive wall decorations, it had to face the real world. The VC-10 negotiations having fallen through and a leasing arrangement with the Flying Tiger Line also having failed to materialize, Air Siam had to settle for a more modest vehicle with which to enter the tough world of air transport. In February 1970 Prince Nicky and Bill McIntosh went to Australia and bought a Douglas DC-4 from Trans-Australia Airlines. The prince reported, "Thanks to the King of Thailand's sister, who was my wife at that time, the arrival at Bangkok's Don Muang Airport was quite a posh affair. Some days later, we had a maiden flight to Hong Kong, carrying 12 kilograms of freight for Swissair! It was only symbolic, but Air Siam was officially airborne." The following month, on the basis of three round trips a week to Hong Kong, Air Siam became the 105th member of the International Air Transport Association (IATA).

After it had jogged along quietly in an operation which, to put it bluntly, was not quite up to the stature of most IATA members, there were rumors at the end of 1970 that Air Siam was finally going to get under way. Overseas National Airlines (ONA), a U.S. Supplemental (nonscheduled) airline, wet-leased to Air Siam a long-range Douglas DC-8-63, at first fitted with seats for fifty-seven passengers, with the remainder of the cabin allocated to thirteen cargo pallets. "The Princess Sister and I went to Hong Kong to fly in our DC-8 on her maiden flight to Bangkok. This time, the arrival was greeted by no less a person than the Princess Mother, the King of Thailand's mother. Thus the Thai flag went intercontinental for the first time on March 31, 1971, beating Thai International, which opened service to Australia, by two days."

Air Siam sensibly subcontracted its handling, maintenance, and passenger service on its new transpacific operation with the best airlines—Cathay Pacific, for example, at Hong Kong, and

United Air Lines, including catering, at Los Angeles and Honolulu. But this was expensive. And so was the ONA leasing charge. This was reported to be at $1,750 per block hour, and with the initial cabin configuration the aircraft had to be 90 percent full to break even. On July 28 Prince Varanand announced that seating would be increased to 152, including 12 first class, as well as the cargo load, and that plans were in hand to increase frequency across the Pacific from two to four a week. An agreement was signed with All Nippon Airways, the big Japanese domestic operator, to coordinate interline bookings and to combine in charter flights from Japan to the United States, but this was to no avail. Air Siam was losing money heavily and consistently. Prince Nicky recalled "throughout our trans-Pacific operation, only one week in which revenue was greater than expenditure."

In desperation, he tried to allot more land as collateral for further cash from the banks, but they would not take the slightest risk, insisting on the enterprise yielding a profit every day from Day One onward. Had this criterion been applied to Thai International, S.A.S. would never have established its foothold. Instead, the Scandinavians had absorbed initial losses until the airline learned its lessons and got onto a sound financial footing.

By the end of 1971 the crisis point had been reached. Air Siam was believed to owe about $2 million to ONA in leasing charges, yet to compete effectively the airline really needed to increase frequency, and this was quite impossible with an inadequate fleet. The transpacific service was suspended on January 11, 1972.

In a further desperate attempt to survive, McIntosh persuaded Virachai Vannukul, a senior executive of Thai International with a reputation for sharp business acumen, to join Air Siam, as a consultant in March 1972. Virachai's reasons for leaving THAI were never disclosed, but apparently few tears were shed at his departure, and the atmosphere should have been a warning to Nicky and others who were trying to save Air Siam.

One of Virachai's first acts was to turn to the Chinese business community in Bangkok in an effort to raise money in exchange for Air Siam stock. Failing on home territory, he then turned to the Chinese in Singapore, where he found a millionaire, Mr. Robin Loh, who had been a taxi driver before finding a magic touch for big business in southeast Asia. He owned a sizable fleet of ships and flew a B.A.C. One-Eleven as a private aircraft. He was prepared to lease this to Air Siam in exchange for stock.

Ostensibly, this was a solution. It provided the beleaguered airline with a modern jet to replace the old DC-4 on the Hong Kong route, and service was resumed on May 25 to Hong Kong. This was later extended to Tokyo, at a frequency of three round trips a week. Air Siam was recapitalized by a consortium of Thai businessmen, who acquired 55 percent of the capital. Prince Varanand and his sister, Princess Suda Siri Sotha, retained 40 percent, the Shell Oil Company of Thailand took 4 percent, and the remainder went to a small group of individual stockholders. The ONA debt was settled by the American airline's acceptance of a valuable plot of land in Bangkok owned by Prince Varanand.

Virachai Vannukul exuded confidence during this trying period, showing little concern for the way in which he was manipulating other people's money. Ebullient, ambitious, conceited, and often devious, he made it quite clear that he would challenge Thai International head-on, especially on the Hong Kong route, which was one of the most important traffic arteries between a pair of cities in southeast Asia. This contravened the spirit and indeed the the idealistic promise that Prince Varanand had made to the minister of communications, that he would operate as a supplement to but not as a challenge to THAI.

The differences in philosophy between Varanand and Virachai deteriorated into serious differences of opinion and a personality clash. Idealism against pragmatism, patriotism against expediency, oil against water, such ingredients never mix. As he became more isolated, despairing of the trend of events when Virachai arranged for the lease of a Boeing 707 to operate to Tokyo, blatantly discounting fares and openly announcing his opposition to IATA, Prince Varanand resigned from Air Siam in June 1973. Virachai also fired McIntosh, but the prince's sister remained as the titular chairman.

In one sense, Virachai was right about one thing, the membership in IATA. Very few of the airlines in East and Southeast Asia believed in the cartel-motivated price-fixing of that organization. Aggressive airlines such as Cathay Pacific, Malaysian Airline System, Singapore Airlines, China Airlines, and Korean Air Lines believed in open competition with high-quality service, charged fares according to what the market would bear, and thrived on the system. Air Siam had nothing to gain by remaining aloof from such opponents in a ruthlessly cutthroat operating environment.

The new team in Air Siam, brashly led by Virachai, blamed the whole financial mess on the founder, Prince Varanand, who paid dearly for his commercial naïveté. But the company did not, at least at that time, go into voluntary liquidation, for this would have been considered bad for Thailand, disastrous for the dream of creating a truly Thai airline, and humiliating for the royal family.

The subsequent story of Air Siam, although out of Prince Nicky's control, is worth a brief outline—not that he could have saved the airline from forces that were gathering to polarize the issue of route authority and the right to operate as a Thai airline. Virachai plunged ahead with an aircraft-procurement policy that defied all the laws of airline economics and bewildered the airline world. Air Siam started a Boeing 747 service to Tokyo and Honolulu on September 1, 1973, with an aircraft leased from Irish International, and intensified the service to Hong Kong with a European Airbus (A-300B) on October 21, 1974. A contract was also signed with the German charter company Atlantis to lease a Douglas DC-10-30. This should have begun the transpacific service, Bangkok–Tokyo–Honolulu–Los Angeles on November 30, 1974, but this never got completely under way.

At the beginning of 1975, Air Siam could boast a fleet of four different jet airliners: a 387-seat Boeing 747 (now leased from K.L.M., the Dutch airline), a 328-seat DC-10, a 230-seat A-300, and a 170-seat Boeing 707. Four types, one of each, all leased, not a single one owned. The assets, in fact, consisted of little more than the transpacific route certificates that Prince Nicky and Bill McIntosh had patiently and effectively put together back in 1967.

Virachai continued trying to persuade the Thai government that Air Siam was the airline of the royal family and therefore untouchable, pointing out that Prince Varanand was both the king's cousin and his brother-in-law. Varanand explained to the minister of communications that he had had nothing to do with Air Siam since mid 1973 and suggested a solution: that Thai International should carry passengers and Air Siam should carry freight, each one exclusively. This was hardly a practical solution and predictably did not appeal to either party. The alternative, he suggested, was to ground Air Siam, which clearly had no future and was simply being bled dry by the investors.

Gradually, Air Siam's position went from bad to worse, but, in what has been described as Thailand's byzantine politics, it was propped up by two influential members of the government who were actually on the board of Thai International. Niels Lumholdt, who was practically running THAI and was keeping his head when others about him were losing theirs, commented, "We had the incredible situation where Thai International was being actively undermined by its own shareholders on behalf of a private company."

Virachai added salt to THAI's wounds, real or imagined, by applying for a network of routes to Europe, openly challenging the incumbent airline and playing the nationalist patriotic game for all it was worth. The possibility of a merger was put forward to confuse the issue still further. As the danger of the ministers conceding to Air Siam's demands increased, the employees of Thai International called a strike—illegal under Thai law—on August 3, 1976, and demanded the dismissal of the two ministers who were firmly believed to be about to stab them in the back.

The following month was, to put it mildly, hectic. Although the prime minister nominated a commission of inquiry, Undersecretary of State Gun Nagamati, one of the conspirators, called for the immediate arrest of leading figures in Thai International. But then the government collapsed. To quote the magazine *Insight*, "One week later, Dr. Gun was ignominiously dismissed from the Thai Civil Service by Admiral Sa-naged Chaloryu's military-backed regime and most of his pro-Air Siam cohorts were flushed out of the ministry. Meanwhile, Virachai fled the country after bouncing a cheque for 8 million baht—allegedly countersigned by Budget Bureau deputy director general Metta Poomchusri" (one of the Air Siam shareholders).

For the remaining three months of its life, Air Siam was taken over by Paul Sithi-Amnuai's group—one of the its principal creditors—until its eventual collapse on January 12, 1977, when all Air Siam services were terminated. On February 4, the minister of communications revoked all the Air Siam route licenses and in September the company was declared bankrupt.

Undoubtedly Thai International was mightily relieved to see the back of Air Siam, and not only because it was rumored that a hired assassin was patrolling the streets of Bangkok, seeking out leading members of the Thai International hierarchy. Although Air Siam's objectives, after the departure of Varanand, had not justified the methods used to obtain them, their validity was condoned by a great many people in Thailand who were not necessarily involved in the unimaginable corruption that can only happen in Thailand. Air Siam's stand, and Prince Nicky's cavalier patriotism, had struck many a sympathetic chord. While the S.A.S. element of Thai International would eventually have worked out a gradual plan to hand over ownership and control to Thailand, Air Siam's snapping at their heels accelerated the process and made the ultimate transfer of power more certain. By March 31, 1977—only a month after Air Siam had gone bankrupt—S.A.S. withdrew its financial stake in THAI completely, although it continued to provide advice and assistance in marketing, technical, and other fields of activity.

Furthermore, Air Siam opened Thai International's eyes to the enormous potential of the transpacific market. S.A.S. had, during the 1960s, never shown the slightest interest in it and was cynically not concerned with Thailand's position as one of the great tourist destinations for American tourists. For the managements in Stockholm and Copenhagen, the transpacific route was simply not worth the effort. But after Air Siam's demise, THAI was almost honor-bound to resume service to the United States—which it did, to Seattle and Dallas, in 1980. Niels Lumholdt generously acknowledges the debt to Air Siam for having, however clumsily, paved the way.

Disliking the idea of being unemployed, Prince Nicky Varanand eventually went to work as an aviation adviser to the Ministry of Agriculture. To his disillusionment, he was hired not for his flying knowledge, but because he was the king's brother-in-law. This was less of a case of nepotism than it would appear at first sight to be. Certain self-proclaimed experts were accustomed to using the king's name too freely to support their pet schemes and Prince Nicky was able to curb these excesses. As the aviation adviser, the prince was able to travel abroad, to Australia, the United States, and England. He was popular among the lower ranks of the department, particularly in the field, where his friendly, democratic approach was in striking contrast to the caste system which had been customary.

By 1976—at about the same time that the squabble between Air Siam and Thai International had reached detonation point— Prince Varanand was missing the life of a pilot, and the higher pay that went with it, so much that he negotiated his way back to Thai International, a delicate process that must have demanded much heart-searching on all sides, not least by the prince himself, for whom a certain amount of pride had to be dispensed with. Also, the practical aspects of his return were odd, a little reminiscent of his earlier induction into the S.A.S.-THAI flying ranks.

In conditions of near secrecy, he had to take an aptitude test in Stockholm. The Swedish professors declared him to be in the top 4 percent of all applicants, and he returned to Bangkok to collect the four rings on his uniform and to qualify for DC-10 duties. He served for a short while as a systems operator before being promoted to the rank of copilot, but he was never again given a command "because of age and remaining time before retirement."

His last years with Thai International were uneasy. As someone who had previously been head of his own airline, his position was somewhat unusual, especially since he was the king's brother-in-law. He was also an active member of the pilots' union, apt to ask awkward questions about possible discrimination between Scandinavian and Thai employees.

And so His Highness the Prince Varanand of Siam served out the remainder of his working life until a fateful night in 1982, when he suffered a stroke, just before reporting for duty to take a Thai International flight to Amsterdam. This put an abrupt end to his restlessness and ambitions and simultaneously put an end to his difficult marriage with the sister of the king of Thailand. He retired to California, after convincing the social security people that *His* and *Highness* were not simply unusual first names. Echoing a famous television commercial, they almost literally asked whether they could call him Nicky.

He sometimes reminisces about his eventful life and the draining of his substantial personal fortune, which kept his dream of a genuinely Thai (or Siamese) airline alive until the resources ran out. By selling pieces of property to keep priming the financial pump, he was a postwar exponent of the method used by the early British airline promoter, Eric Gandar Dower. Like his predecessor, he had to succumb to political forces and financial realities beyond his power to control or influence.

Prince Varanand has estimated that the value of his property and other resources which evaporated through myriad channels during the period of his struggle to keep Air Siam alive would be worth about $50 million today. His experience should at least qualify for inclusion in the *Guinness Book of World Records*.

▶▶▶▶▶▶▶▶▶▶▶▶▶▶▶▶▶▶

Australia

▶▶▶▶▶▶▶▶▶▶▶▶▶◀▶▶▶▶▶

Ray Parer

The Battler from Bulolo

Two of the greatest qualities of a man, in Australian eyes, surpassing mere intellect or talent, or physical prowess, are determination and perseverance. These were the qualities in which Sir Reginald Ansett took great pride and held in esteem beyond all others. Such a man, in Australian parlance, is a battler, and Ray Parer was a textbook example of the type, although the term is not known to figure in the normal classifications of personality. The general description does not necessarily imply, however, that to be a battler is the only virtue needed for success in life. Whereas Sir Reginald became a millionaire, Ray Parer ended up in modest, if not humble circumstances. Unlike Ansett, Ray Parer was accident-prone—though his accidents were often brought about by his own carelessness—and he was also the victim of the most abominable luck.

Such was his erratic career in aviation that any writer or biographer would be hard pressed to avoid the temptation to end every sentence or so with an exclamation point. No sooner is one adventure ended when Battling Parer seems to be up to his neck in another, invariably ending in disaster. Nevertheless, in his happy hunting ground of the formidable mountains of New Guinea, where the gold rush generated a need for airplanes and pilots, Ray Parer was the only one who was in at the beginning and was still there at the end.

Of course, there were interruptions, and these were on such a scale of improbability that, even without his achievements in New Guinea, the name of Ray Parer will always be remembered by Australians, who saw in him the epitome of one of their own aspira-

383

The smaller figure in this picture is Ray Parer, an Australian pilot who, with his companion, John McIntosh, entered the competition set by the Australian government in 1919 to fly from England to Australia. They took 208 days to complete the journey, itself a minor miracle of obstinate survival. The episode earned Parer the nickname, respected throughout his country, as the "Battler." The aircraft was a de Havilland D.H. 9.

tions, the quality of resilience and the ability to come up smiling, no matter how disastrous the circumstances.

Ray Parer was born just before the turn of the century. Even as a boy he was enthralled by aviation. He learned to fly as soon as he could, early in World War I, at Point Cook, Melbourne. Soon after the end of the conflict, in 1919, Alcock and Brown made their acclaimed flight across the North Atlantic, and the Australian government, seized with enthusiasm for the benefits of air transport, offered a prize of £10,000 to the first Australian crew to fly from England to Australia.

This was the kind of challenge that appealed enormously to

the young Ray Parer. He teamed up with a fellow adventurer, John McIntosh, and entered the race. They made an interesting pair. John Cove McIntosh was a tall, handsome Scot. Ray Parer, a typically rugged-looking Australian, was of a stature politely described as diminutive. Together they set off for England, where they obtained a de Havilland D.H. 9 ex-bomber, which cost them £900, a sum generously provided by Peter Dawson, a Scottish whisky millionaire. His only stipulation was that they should hand-deliver a bottle of the finest vintage scotch to the popular Australian prime minister, Billy Hughes.

The war-surplus D.H. 9 was not exactly the best machine for the mission, even had it been perfectly maintained and cared for. But Parer and McIntosh's aircraft was in such poor condition that weeks were to elapse before they could make it airworthy. By the time they were ready, Keith and Ross Smith, two members of the Royal Flying Corps, had already arrived in Australia, in twenty-nine days, in a Vickers Vimy twin-engined bomber.

Whether or not Parer and McIntosh thought that there might be a second prize is not known. But on January 8, 1920, the last of the competitors to start, they set off on what turned out to be a most improbable journey. Their story could have been taken out of a fictional serial, in which the author strove to punctuate each episode with an adventure. The de Havilland kept breaking down—a characteristic habit that later seemed to befall almost any aircraft Ray Parer laid hands on—and this did not help, because spare parts for ex-bombers were not exactly over-the-counter items in the bazaars of the Middle East or the emporiums of southeast Asia.

Forced down in the Arabian desert, they were saved from attack by bandits only by—as one writer neatly put it—"a hand grenade which McIntosh had thoughtfully brought along." They had to scrounge parts and earn their keep by hiring out the D.H. 9 as a flying billboard. In Burma, after a forced landing, they had to persuade the local residents of a riverside village to improvise a landing strip in the jungle. They had to repair the aircraft after some hard landings or simply because of normal wear and tear, literally, of the fabric-covered wings and to put out fires that erupted in flight.

The two pilots managed to coach their reluctant aircraft across the Timor Sea to arrive in Darwin, Northern Territories, on August 2, 208 days after leaving England. This was hardly worth

This picture shows Battling Ray Parer's Bristol F2b ex-fighter at Parer's headquarters in New Guinea during the 1930s. With primitive aircraft such as this, and even more primitive ground equipment, installations, and airstrips, Parer epitomized the determination of an adventurous group of airmen to provide air service to some of the least accessible communities in the world.

entering in the record books, but they were pleasantly surprised to find themselves national heroes, and as the D.H. 9 drew to a halt—because it had used its last drop of fuel—they were surrounded by cheering crowds. To them this was a demonstration of the battler spirit, defying the odds and winning through. The time might just as well have been 208 hours. They were guests of honor at a dinner at the Grand Hotel, Melbourne, and the Commonwealth government awarded them £500 each for their achievement. Sadly, McIntosh did not live to enjoy his fame very long, for he was killed in an air crash on Easter Sunday, 1921.

Ray Parer bought an FE-2B pusher biplane to go barnstorming around Australia. This type of aircraft was obsolete before the end of World War I, but it was typical of Ray Parer that he should compound any risk he undertook. At all events, when flying at Kalgoorlie, Western Australia, he had an altercation with a telegraph wire and crashed into a butcher's wagon, and that was the end of his flying career for a while. He gave up aviation temporarily and moved to King Island, off the northern coast of Tasmania, where he ran a small garage for a time, doubtless improving his capacity for improvisation in the process.

In 1922 a legendary prospector called Shark-Eye Park had discovered gold in Koranga Creek, a tributary of the Bulolo River, forty miles from the northeast coast of New Guinea. By 1924 a gold rush was well under way, and at the beginning of 1926, a phenomenal deposit of free alluvial gold was discovered at nearby Edie Creek. As with so many gold discoveries, however, there was a big transport problem. The Bulolo River and its tributaries were tucked behind a large fold of the Owen Stanley mountain range, and the trek from the coast took between eight and ten days and cost £30 per porter, each of whom could carry fifty pounds of supplies. The journey was not made any easier by the presence, often the resistance, of hostile New Guinea tribesmen.

Several people had the vision to realize that air transport was the solution. One was Cecil J. Levien, a local administrator who quickly perceived the realities of the situation and systematically set about exploiting it, first by forming, with a group of investors in Adelaide, the Guinea Gold No Liability company, in May 1926, and then, after purchasing a small syndicate that had acquired a de Havilland D.H. 37 biplane, the Guinea Gold Air Service, in January 1927. Levien hired A. E. Mustard, a World War Camel Corps and Australian Flying Corps veteran, as pilot.

Another visionary was Ray Parer, who, in partnership with Eric Gallet, formed the Bulolo Goldfields Aeroplane Service (B.G.A.S.), in November 1926. They purchased a de Havilland D.H. 4 ex-bomber biplane and made arrangements to ship it from Sydney to Rabaul, the capital of the New Guinea Mandated Territory. Parer soon found himself in another race, as usual with built-in handicaps. At first, the B.G.A.S. partnership thought they had the advantage, having booked the only available deck space on the good ship *Melusia*. Typically, however, they did not have the money to pay for it, and were obliged to surrender it to Pard Mustar—he had dropped the last letter of his name—who gleefully substituted his D.H. 37, still in the crate in which it had arrived from England.

Having raised the cash for the shipment, Parer followed by the next boat, the *Marsina*, and arrived in Rabaul on March 27,

Papua New Guinea. *Even compared with those of Central and South America, the natural barriers that handicapped the development of surface transport in New Guinea were so formidable as to be totally defeating. Air transport was the answer, to the extent that during several years of the early 1930s more air freight was carried in this territory than in the entire United States.*

1927, by which time the rival D.H. 37 had already been assembled and flown to Lae, on the New Guinea mainland, forty miles from the Bulolo River goldfield. As if this was not disappointment enough, Parer then found that the D.H.4's tires, exposed to wind and weather during the voyage, had been ruined. The spare tires arrived from Sydney the day after Guinea Gold had made its maiden test flight with the D.H. 37. To cap the chapter of accidents, Parer and Gallet then capsized the D.H.4 on its maiden flight at Rabaul, and Gallet was injured to the extent that Battling Ray Parer lost a partner, for Gallet went back home.

On June 23, 1927, Ray Parer flew the D.H.4, now repaired, to Lae, and during the next four weeks he made seven flights to and from Wau, an airfield close to the Bulolo gold workings. To describe the Wau site as an airfield is perhaps an exaggeration. The strip was 800 yards long, 400 yards wide at one end and 75 yards wide at the other. The two ends should perhaps be described as top and bottom for the gradient of the cleared area was and is still a sharp 1 in 12, an alarming prospect for all but the most seasoned pilots.

By this time, C. J. Levien's Guinea Gold Air Service was operating regularly, charging £25 per passenger one way, and one shilling per pound of freight. Though expensive, this was good value, measured against the time taken on the surface route, not to mention the ravages of disease and cannibals. Levien wisely hired a second pilot, so that more trips could be made, and bought another aircraft. Parer responded by obtaining finance from several of the miners and prospectors, among whom he was a popular figure. In November 1927 he used his newfound wealth to purchase a D.H.9, which was hardly practical as a freight carrier, and a Bristol F-2b ex-fighter, which was hardly practical for anything. Meanwhile, Levien and his associates had formed Guinea Airways, with a share capital of £20,000, to go into commercial aviation in a substantial way.

Nevertheless, Parer did, for a while, manage to compete on a nearly equal footing with Guinea, whose best aircraft was a D.H. 60, because the traffic depended as much on instant availability of an aircraft or pilot, or even on his personal standing, as it did on corporate strength. But the writing was on the wall for Parer when, on April 14, 1927, the first of four handsome metal-built Junkers W-34s arrived for Guinea Airways.

Parer did not exactly help himself. First, one of his pilots crashed the Bristol Fighter. W. P. Wiltshire arrived to fly the D.H. 9—he refused to fly the D.H.4, leaving that doubtful privilege to Parer—and Parer then returned to Australia for a break. Unfortunately, he forgot to pay Wiltshire, who promptly left to join another small outfit, one of several that had joined in the aviation fray on the Lae-Wau shuttle.

For all his shortcomings of organization and business acumen, Ray Parer possessed an intuition which, if properly used, could have brought him much success. As early as the summer of 1928 he was thinking about flying directly from the goldfields to Port Moresby, and thence to the Australian mainland. He made several flights from Lae to Port Moresby and planned a route along the southwest coast of New Guinea, across the Torres Strait at its narrowest point, thence to Thursday Island and Normanton, which was halfway toward civilization. But Parer had allowed his pilot's license to lapse and was in trouble with the authorities. After he apologized and promised not to do it again, the threatened prosecution was dropped. Parer's irresponsibility was exceeded only by his charm.

Truth to tell, the authorities at this time could afford to be lenient, for they were hardly setting impeccable standards themselves. For many years, until the mid 1930s, there was no proper supervision of airfield or aircraft standards or of flying and maintenance qualifications throughout New Guinea. This was just as well, because the imposition of even the most lenient regulations would have grounded almost the entire air fleet when it was most needed. As it was, a diary of operations around the goldfields area would have shown an aircraft crash or accident of some kind every few entries. Every now and then one of these would be recorded as a write-off, but the powers of improvization in repairing and recovering the aircraft casualties were little short of miraculous, as was the low fatality rate, considering some of the spectacular incidents.

Ray Parer's Bulolo Goldfields Aeroplane Service ceased operating toward the end of 1928, to be superseded by a partnership with P. J. Macdonald under the name of Morlae Airlines, which, as its name suggests was intended to provide a service from Port Moresby to Lae. The new company got off to a reasonable start with the purchase of a D.H. 9C. It was unable to obtain a subsidy, although the request was reasonable: £4,000 a year for three years to provide a saving of seven days over the quickest surface route. Consequently, the fare was high—£20 per flying hour—but so great was the need that the airline seemed to be succeeding.

Then the Parer luck took a hand. Ray was confident enough to offer to take the lieutenant-governor of Papua, Sir Hubert Murray, for a flight over Port Moresby. With a record of dashed hopes already firmly established, it was almost inevitable that the D.H. 9C should crash on this prestigious flight, and the fact that Sir Hubert was not at all displeased—he thought that taxying at full speed into trees was some kind of stunt laid on for his benefit—it was one more item in Parer's growing list of incidents that might have been carried out with greater aplomb.

Not that the news was always bad. On June 28, 1929, for instance, Ray Parer flew six round trips between Lae and Wau, spending eight hours in the air, a record that was to stand for several years, until more reliable aircraft came along. And, much to the disgust of the larger Guinea Airways, Parer made the first landing on the newly constructed airstrip at Bulolo, in territory that Guinea tended to regard as its exclusive domain.

The latter airline, well financed from the Australian mainland, well organized, and well staffed, exemplified a complete success story. Its operation, specializing in the transport of heavy freight, was unique in its day. It was closely associated with Bulolo Gold Dredging, registered in Canada with capital of $4 million, which owned two of the aircraft operated by Guinea Airways. After careful evaluation of the aircraft and its own experience of the sturdy Junkers construction, Guinea Airways made a number of Junkers-G 31 three-engined craft, specially equipped with a large access door in the top so that large items could be loaded by crane, the mainstays of its fleet.

With the G 31s, Guinea Airways' most remarkable achievement was to transport the parts and the construction equipment needed to build on site several enormous gold dredges, mainly for the Bulolo Gold Dredging company, of which it was a partner. Having already carried, in pieces, a crushing mill for the Day Dawn company, including two items weighing 1,000 pounds each, in the Junkers-W 34s, and having set world records in so doing, Guinea now proceeded to beat its own records by an impressive margin. During the early 1930s the G 31s transported four Bulolo dredges, each weighing about 1,100 tons, with at least as much again in other equipment. The biggest item was a 6,870-pound tumbler shaft, and the tumbler itself weighed almost as much. Guinea also flew in a small British car for the local doctor and a specially designed truck with a narrow wheelbase for one of the companies in the goldfields. This was probably the first time that any airline had carried a motor vehicle anywhere in the world.

The published statistics of Guinea Airways were as impressive as the bizarre sight of the engineering colossus deep in the heart of the New Guinea jungle. During the fiscal year 1931–32, the airline carried about 4,000 tons of freight, almost as much as the whole of Europe combined and eight times as much as all the airlines of the United States put together.

Against such a star performance, the other little companies, operating mostly small biplanes of the de Havilland series, with the occasional Fokker or other larger (but usually obsolescent) type, had only walk-on parts. But they were a happy band of battlers, cheerfully vying with each other for the available traffic, and always willing to cooperate with each other—by lending pilots or helping to salvage wrecked aircraft—in a united effort to compete with what threatened to be a Guinea Airways monopoly.

The Junkers operator was an intriguing reflection of the attitudes of the former Prussian landowning gentry whose name was carried by the demonstrably superior aircraft, and it acted in a monopolistic manner. It charged as high a tariff as the market would bear, and for the miners and gold panners it was a Hobson's choice. They either paid the high tariffs, to bring supplies or to fly themselves, or they went by foot. The road between the coast and the Bulolo River was not built until after World War II.

This might have been tolerated with a great deal more understanding—for the enterprise of Guinea Airways in its vision and investment was freely acknowledged—had it not been for the knowledge that the directors in Adelaide regularly paid out handsome dividends to its shareholders. The smaller prospectors and miners felt that profits were being made out of their pockets, so they instinctively gave their business to the likes of Ray Parer when they could. Such was Guinea's reputation that the initials were said to have stood for God Almighty.

For his part, Ray Parer was clearly one of the mates, identifying himself with the narrow borderline between modest prosperity and dismal poverty that seemed to be the lot of that special band of adventurers consumed with gold fever. Whereas the Guinea Airways accountants would pester the independent prospectors with written demands for overdue payments, Ray was more inclined to do everything by word of mouth and a "That's all right, mate, pay me when you can" attitude. The miners knew full well that he and the other small operators needed the money badly for their underfinanced concerns and played their part in keeping them alive.

This is not to say that Ray Parer was necessarily a saint. His irresponsibility was self-evident, and although he had a reputation of flying anything as long as the propeller would turn, he was also inclined to act spontaneously, without consultation, often with unfortunate consequences. Thus, Morlae Airlines came to an end because Parer and McDonald had a disagreement that ended up in litigation, and Ray Parer turned to the formation of another enterprise.

Pacific Aerial Transport (P.A.T.) seems to have been promoted by a group of independent operators, instigated by Ray Parer, who felt that, united, they could at least hold their own against the dominant Guinea Airways, whereas each individual, on his own, was certain to fail. In this assertion he was probably right. Thus the various goldfield flyers joined together and got themselves a half-decent aircraft. This was a Fokker F-III, formerly owned by the Dutch airline, K.L.M., and now purchased for £300, with an additional £400 for spare parts, transport, and assembly. A further £1,000 went toward the cost of two Bristol Jupiter engines, salvaged from an old Handley Page Hampstead owned by New Guinea Goldfields.

On March 14, 1931, Ray Parer proudly demonstrated the Fokker to a group of leading commercial representatives at Salamaua, a coastal settlement that had come to supplement Lae as a base for the Bulolo goldfields routes. One of these figures was none other than J. R. Carpenter, of W. R. Carpenter and Co., the biggest trading company in the southwest Pacific, and P.A.T. had high hopes of obtaining a good contract.

Four days later Ray Parer crashed the F-III on takeoff at Salamaua. And now he was repaid for his past generosity and lenient attitudes in the matter of unpaid debts by many who felt that he was their one hope against the feared Guinea Airways monopoly. They literally passed the hat and put up the money for P.A.T. to buy a replacement aircraft. One of the benefactors was Flora Stewart, owner of the Pub at Wau, and she, along with others, became a shareholder in the airline.

Parer's crash may have been a blessing in disguise, for the replacement was a single-engined Fokker F-VII, of later design, formerly used by the Belgian airline, SABENA, and able to carry nine people. Not that the comparatively elegant Fokker was used exclusively for passengers. Far from it. On one occasion, in a noble effort to provide the miners with a source of fresh milk, Parer and his friends managed to cram a cow on board, and on another journey someone brought a wild boar with him. On both flights, the Fokker was somewhat the worse for wear on arrival.

In emergencies, Ray Parer used an unfailing method to ascertain whether the apparent landing strip was firm enough to land. He dropped a bottle of beer and if it burst, spewing out the white froth, clearly visible from the air, he knew he was "cleared to land." If the bottle survived intact, the ground was too soft.

The special breed of pilots, of whom Ray Parer was only one, risked their lives daily while crossing the jungles and mountains in weather that was so unpredictable and could change in such a short time that, by bitter experience, they all adopted a strict "no see, no fly" rule. Occasionally a pilot broke this unwritten law, with tragic results. The pilots were not exactly helped by the customers. Carrying gelignite was risky enough, but one miner sent a cargo of detonators in a box presumed to contain a pair of boots. Cartons of Japanese matches were not of the safety variety and were inclined to demonstrate their incendiary properties if dropped. The little aircraft sometimes carried solid gold—1,500 pounds in a single load—as well as whisky, medicine, tools, batteries, false teeth, and panama hats. New Guinea pilots would carry anything.

Their maintenance procedures were not to be found in any textbook. A roll of six-inch sticking plaster was essential equipment for the pilots of the old aircraft the wings and fuselage of which had fabric covering, which had a dreadful habit of splitting from time to time. There was an instance when Parer was stuck in an inaccessible spot with a broken fuel line, which he repaired by using a piece of bamboo of the exact diameter.

In the early years, this did not raise too many eyebrows. Such procedures were accepted as normal. But by about 1933, the authorities stepped in where bureaucracy had feared to tread, and P.A.T. suffered the indignity of being haled up before the District Court of Salamaua for breaches of the Air Navigation Regulations—

that is, flying a Fokker and a D.H. Moth without registration. P.A.T. was fined £125, and no doubt the hat was passed round again.

Parer's luck continued. The Fokker F-VII was badly damaged in November 1933, when it was undergoing repair at Wau. Guinea Airways, of all companies, had allowed P.A.T. to use its crane to lift the wing from its attachment points, and at a critical moment, the crane jib collapsed, putting the aircraft out of action for several weeks. It could only happen to Battling Parer.

Ever restless, Parer felt the wanderlust again and became interested in the idea of flying in another England–Australia Air Race. This was the famous MacRobertson race, sponsored by Sir McPherson Robertson, the Australian confectionery magnate, which, incidentally, demonstrated beyond all shadow of doubt that the days of wooden-built aircraft were over, at least for commercial purposes. On June 13, 1934—the date should have warned them—a group of Parer's friends, with infinite faith, formed the New Guinea Centenary Flight Syndicate, to sponsor and finance his entry for the race.

Geoff Hemsworth, another P.A.T. pilot, joined Ray Parer, and the two went to England, where they bought a battered Fairey Fox that needed a complete overhaul. The syndicate raised £1,400 to cover the cost, of which the purchase price was only £200—about as much as Ray Parer would ever permit himself to pay for an airplane. This venture left P.A.T. short-handed—three pilots, including one newly hired, to fly three assorted aircraft.

History repeated itself, although at least Parer and Hemsworth had left England by the time the race-winning Comet and the headline-stealing Douglas DC-2 had reached Melbourne. They were, in fact, in Paris, with engine trouble. The New Guinea Centenary Flight Syndicate entry reached Melbourne on February 13, 1935, 116 days after leaving Mildenhall, England. This was only about half the time Parer had taken on his first attempt, in 1919, but on this occasion there was no consolation prize.

Whether or not Ray Parer had become disenchanted with the new routine life of flying the Salamaua-Lae–Wau-Bulolo routes is not clear. Possibly the other partners in P.A.T. had become disenchanted with Parer. At all events, by 1935 he was seeking new worlds to conquer. He had already relinquished control of the airline, although he retained a small financial interest, and his brother Kevin took over as manager. He went north with the Fairey Fox and another small Fairey aircraft he had obtained and began to operate in the Sepik River district, rather cheekily under the name of the New Guinea Centenary Flight Syndicate.

True to form, both aircraft had lost their certificates of airworthiness by 1937, and he replaced them with a de Havilland D.H. 83 Fox Moth. This crashed in the summer of 1938, was repaired, and was finally destroyed in the Bitoi Valley in November 1939. By this time, Ray Parer had already flown to Melbourne to collect an old Boeing B-40, formerly owned by New Zealand National Airways, and had written this off within four months. Ever battling on, he collected a second Boeing and put it into service in August 1940. This one, not withdrawn until November 1941, came close to setting a record for any airplane's length of service while in Ray Parer's tender care.

For once Parer's timing was excellent. One month later, the Japanese attacked Pearl Harbor and moved swiftly to occupy the western Pacific. They landed at Rabaul on January 23, and at Salamaua on March 8, 1942. All the various airline aircraft that survived strafing attacks on the airfields were flown to Port Moresby and requisitioned by the Royal Australian Air Force. Commercial aviation in New Guinea ceased abruptly, and indeed all commercial activity of any kind came to an end.

Ray Parer joined the Australian Air Force but was humiliated at being offered a desk job, under the not unreasonable ruling that, as he was nearing fifty years of age, he was too old for flying. Possibly some of the selection board had witnessed or had heard about some of his more hair-raising exploits in New Guinea. For whatever cause, he resigned from the Air Force and took a job as an engineer on a small coastal steamer, which, under the direction of the U.S. Navy, carried out clandestine operations along the northeastern coast of New Guinea, an area with which Ray Parer was familiar.

One night a Japanese soldier scrambled aboard, wielding a knife, while the ship was at anchor in a sheltered inlet. Parer killed the assailant in hand-to-hand combat, on this occasion possibly having picked on somebody his own size. Ray Parer was also known to have gone duck shooting on the Japanese-occupied coast, but rumors that he was planning to start an airline in the area at the time were never confirmed.

After his life in New Guinea, almost anything that Ray Parer did after World War II was bound to be an anticlimax, and little more was heard of his prowess in touching the hem of the garment of success but never quite putting it on. He settled in Queensland, and from known reports led an uneventful life until he died of natural causes, as they say, in 1967. That Ray should have died of natural causes was quite against his form, and the prospect of this happening would have been regarded with sheer disbelief by his associates back in the 1930s in New Guinea.

By a remarkable chain of events, he and Reg Ansett, who became a millionaire and was knighted for his efforts, were eventually to become distantly connected through a complex genealogical progression. For Ray Parer was the inspiration behind Pacific Air Transport, which merged with the W. R. Carpenter interests in 1936 to form Mandated Airlines, which, in turn, was taken over by Ansett in 1961. Completely impartial to the intricacies of New Guinea airline politics, Ansett had already engulfed what was left of Guinea Airways, which confined its activities to South Australia after World War II.

While both Ansett and Parer epitomized the classic Australian battler, they were poles apart. Measured by materialistic standards, Ansett was a complete success, Parer a complete failure. But by other standards by which that elusive quality, the enjoyment of life and a contented existence, is assessed, Parer was a success. Certainly he had fewer enemies, for in his drive to the top Sir Reginald had left a few casualties in his wake. Ray Parer left behind an indelible memory of an indomitable spirit and an endearing image in the hearts and minds of his peers. As the supreme rebel among a hard-bitten group who were themselves rebels, Ray Parer was unique and immortal.

▶▶▶▶▶▶▶▶▶▶▶▶▶▶▶▶▶▶▶▶▶▶▶ ◀

Sir Reginald Ansett

"R.M."

Few men in aviation, or, for that matter, in almost any other kind of business undertaking, have been so feared by their competitors—in his case, usually the Australian government—yet have at the same time, albeit grudgingly, won so much respect. In Australia, where officialdom is cordially disliked and thumbing the nose at bureaucracy is regarded almost as a passport to paradise, Reginald Myles Ansett's lifelong adversary relation with the law and its regulators made him a national hero. His success in building a transport empire out of airline operations made his name not simply a household word in his time, but carved it in Australian history far more incisively than that of any politician, industrialist, or even cultural figure.

To begin with, he has always looked the part of the backwoods Australian, beloved of folklore and legend. Described precisely as a man 5 feet 11½ inches tall, and weighing 11 stone (154 pounds), lean and limber, with an easy gait, he has also been characterized generally as well-lined and sand-blasted, with a craggy look, and as a flinty, hard-driving businessman with a bear-trap mind. Most people who have had any dealings with Reg Ansett, or R.M., as he was always known to his close associates, would consider such references understatements. He was ruthless in his efforts to gain his ends, and although he never broke the law, he would go to ingenious lengths to evade it or circumvent it and, when necessary, challenge it. That in some instances the law was changed according to Ansett's wishes is some measure of his strength, determination, and effectiveness.

His start in life was modest enough. He was born on February 13, 1909, at Inglewood, near Bendigo, one of the middle-sized towns that grew during the Victorian gold rush and have survived as commercial centers to this day. He was the second youngest of a family of five children, and when, in 1915, his father joined the armed forces and went overseas, his mother moved to Melbourne, where Reg went to state schools and to Swinburne Technical College. At the age of fourteen he went to work for his parents in a small knitting factory, where within a few years he became qualified as a mechanic on the knitting machines. In 1929, when a small life assurance policy matured, he used the money to learn to fly and obtained Australian Pilot's License no. 419.

Uncertain yet as to his future vocation, he took a ship to Darwin, in the Northern Territory of Australia, with an idea of growing some kind of cash crop, such as peanuts, but on the voyage he met a man who persuaded him to join a survey party. He worked as an axeman—and an expert one at that—and lived in the bush for eighteen months.

Early in 1930, while swinging his axe, he saw the English aviatrix Amy Johnson being escorted by three other aircraft on her historic flight from England to Australia, and this may have influenced him somewhat. More material factors, such as the realization that in the Northern Territory he would be completely isolated, led him to abandon thoughts of farming, and he went back to Victoria. The sense of isolation had, however, sharpened his awareness of the need for transport and the vital part it played in people's lives and in modern society, as necessary as food and shelter.

His first venture was a limousine service between Maryborough and Ballarat, two other Victorian towns northwest of Melbourne that had survived the decline of the gold rush. Reg Ansett's "fleet" consisted of one second-hand Studebaker, which he bought for £70. He was his own driver, mechanic, business manager, office boy, and salesman. But although he worked all hours of the day, and sometimes of the night, during the year 1931, he found he was losing money.

This did not deter him. He analyzed the situation correctly as being one of geography. Maryborough and Ballarat were too well

A young Reg Ansett stands in front of his Tiger Moth, with his chief pilot, Vern Cerche (in flying togs). Starting with a single air route in Victoria in 1936, Ansett built up an airline empire, was knighted by the Queen, and became one of the most powerful men in Australia.

established on railway routes and main roads to provide a newcomer with enough traffic. Accordingly, he moved his base to Hamilton, another town farther to the west, the hub of a regional road network, connected to Melbourne only by somewhat circuitous rail lines. He spent his last remaining capital, £50, on a new car and started again on December 7, 1931. Covering the whole of the western district of Victoria, the new road service showed enough promise to encourage him to extend the Hamilton–Ballarat route to Melbourne. Unfortunately, this move coincided with a new law passed by the Victorian government in 1933, the Transport Regulation Act. This, in effect, ordained that road operators should not be allowed to ply their trade on routes which were directly competitive with those of the cherished Victorian State Railways.

There is an apocryphal story that at the time the law was passed the Ansett Road Service carried passengers without charge, but that, as a condition of carriage, each occupant of a seat had to purchase a very expensive apple. True or not, this would not have been practicable, however attractive the idea might have been to his clientèle. Reg Ansett acted more practically and decisively, by switching his attention to commercial flying. He already owned a two-seater Gipsy Moth, purchased in September 1934, and he flew it to Sydney on Boxing Day (December 26) of that year to buy a seven-seater Fokker Universal for £1,000. On February 17, 1936, he started a scheduled air service from Hamilton to Melbourne, making daily round trips from Monday to Friday. On May 25 he received a contract from the postal authorities to carry the mail.

Success did not come easily. At the weekends, the Fokker was used to give joyrides, at 15 shillings (£0.75) each, and Reg Ansett himself would give an adventurous passenger the thrill of looping the loop in the Gipsy Moth. One of the mechanics was even persuaded to give parachute jumping displays, and Ansett admits to helping the "volunteer" to overcome his fears on his first jump by "putting my foot in the small of his back and giving him a hard push. After that he was all right."

A useful addition to the bank account was the £500 that Ansett won, in a dimunitive two-seat Porterfield, in the handicap section of the 1936 Air Race from Brisbane to Adelaide. With such supplementary aviation exploits, Ansett's fortunes improved sufficiently to enable him to obtain an Airspeed Envoy. This British airplane had eight comfortable seats and was much faster than the Fokker. With the two aircraft, Reg Ansett and his chief pilot, Vern Cerche, were able to increase the frequency of the Hamilton–Melbourne service to twice daily, beginning on February 8, 1937.

Shortly afterward, on April 14, Ansett Airways was incorporated as a public company, with an issued capital of £8,303. It then expanded immediately by issuing £25,000 in ordinary shares to its own shareholders and £110,000 worth to the public. It ordered three Lockheed L.10 Electras—fast, modern ten-seaters—at £16,000 each and proceeded to add more routes to the network. These made Ansett an interstate airline and moreover linked Melbourne with Sydney and Adelaide, state capitals of New South Wales and South Australia, respectively. The first new route, long-haul by Ansett standards, was actually to Broken Hill, the important mining city of western New South Wales. This service opened on September 6, 1937, and was quickly followed by Melbourne–Sydney, on October 4, and Sydney–Adelaide, on November 29. The important triangular pattern included essential stopping points at Mildura and Narrandera, because even the Electras did not have sufficient range.

At that time, the largest airline in Australia was Australian National Airways Pty. (A.N.A.). It was rightly named. A descendant of Tasmanian Aerial Services, founded in 1932 by Captain V. C. Holyman with a single de Havilland Fox Moth, it had grown

This is the single-engined Fokker Universal with which Reg Ansett started his first scheduled air service from Hamilton to Melbourne, Victoria. From this small beginning, Ansett continually challenged the authorities to gain a dominant position, not only in the airways, but also in trucking, buses, and a host of activities connected with the travel industry as a whole.

lustily by doing a roaring trade across the Bass Straits to Tasmania. By acquisitions and mergers, A.N.A. had built up a network that linked all the big cities of Australia and in 1937 had put into service a fleet of fourteen-seat Douglas DC-2s, the most modern airliners in Australia.

Reg Ansett was thus faced with some very serious competition, and indeed, most people in his shoes would probably never have dared to enter what appeared to be captive markets. Even when Ansett Airways lost £30,000 in its first year and his own chairman of the board wanted to sell the airline to A.N.A., he held on, in typical fashion, to the extent that the company soon had a new chairman.

When Australia went to war, as part of the British Commonwealth, in 1939, all commercial air services were severely curtailed, and in 1940 Ansett Airways suspended its scheduled services to the public. Two Electras were transferred to a paramilitary function, operating a service between Melbourne and Townsville, Queensland, in support of the American forces in the southwest Pacific theater. The two Electras, in fact, constituted Ansett's total fleet at this time. In February 1939, a fire at the company's hangar at Essendon Airport, Melbourne, had destroyed Ansett's five other aircraft.

Reg Ansett's relations with the government waxed and waned. He must have been encouraged when, on July 4, 1939, after the government had set up a separate Department of Civil Aviation, the minister approved a program of subsidies that included £45,000 a year for Ansett Airways. Then, on May 14, 1944, the airline began to operate under a contract with the Australian government, suggesting that the fledgling airline was gaining official blessing.

Such a sense of security was quickly dashed when, at the end of 1944, the new Commonwealth Labour government adopted a policy of nationalization of certain key industries, including commercial aviation. The contract was terminated on January 21, 1945. Undeterred, Ansett began operations on two revised scheduled routes, Melbourne–Adelaide via Mt. Gambier, and Melbourne–Canberra, the capital of the Commonwealth, via Wagga Wagga, on February 5.

This episode was one of the early clashes with the government from which Reg Ansett emerged slightly scarred but victorious. When at first he was refused licenses to operate his routes, he fought the issue so strenuously and received so much support, including sympathetic pressure from many members of Parliament, that the director-general of civil aviation is reported to have pleaded, "Please don't carry the matter any further. We will find you the routes somehow."

The Labour government, bent on starting its own airline, passed the Australian Airlines Act on August 16, 1945, Ansett and Holyman having joined forces in opposing a threatened takeover of their airlines by challenging the constitutionality of a proposed nationalization scheme. The Australian National Airlines Commission was appointed on February 12, 1946, and the name Trans-Australia Airlines (T.A.A.) was adopted on August 1, 1946, to avoid confusion with Holyman's Australian National Airlines. T.A.A. began scheduled service, with converted Douglas DC-3s, on October 7 of the same year.

Meanwhile, Ansett had extended its route system modestly, also with DC-3s, to Sydney, in June, and to Hobart, in December, 1946. At the end of 1947, he introduced a second-class fare level and in March 1948 cut all fares by 20 percent. The government was perturbed by this attempt to bring the pleasures of air transport to a wider section of the public, while the two large airlines, A.N.A. and T.A.A., were both trying to meet rising costs, caused partly by top-heavy staffs. The government actually threatened to ban Ansett from all Commonwealth airports if he refused to fall in line. Reg Ansett fought the case and won. A Sydney newspaper cartoon depicted a frenzied minister searching a statute book to find "a law against being more efficient than the government."

During the early 1950s, there were thus two large domestic airlines in Australia—T.A.A., representing government interests, and A.N.A., the standard-bearer of private enterprise, backed by shipping interests. Ansett was still on the fringe of a national airline network, as were other regional companies, such as Guinea Airways, MacRobertson Miller, and Butler. Late in 1952 A.N.A. consolidated its position through the Airlines Agreement Act. This gave it equal rights with T.A.A., which had enjoyed many advantages, such as mail contracts and interest-free loans. Ansett, a minor leaguer, was still seeking outlets for expansion beyond the southeast quadrant of Australia, but his purchase of Barrier Reef Airways in 1952 and Trans Oceanic Airways in 1953 did not raise too many eyebrows, even though the flying boats of the two acquisitions served Queensland, Tasmania, and Lord Howe Island. Shrewd observers, however, may have noticed that Reg Ansett purchased Hayman Island, in Queensland, with the declared intention of turning it into a holiday resort.

The government's policy of aiming to preserve two large airlines was basically sound, if it is true that the benefits and virtues of competition can normally be conferred by the existence of only two rival parties. This principle can be challenged in situations in which the market is so large that both theoretical competitors tend to become complacent in practice, and such was the case in Australia, although A.N.A. was the chief offender. It had ambitions to operate internationally, by involvement in overseas airlines such as B.C.P.A. and Air Ceylon, and this may have affected its decision to buy four-engined DC-6Bs in 1955. But within Australia, these were competitive neither with T.A.A.'s turboprop Viscounts nor with Ansett's twin-engined Convair 340s, which continued to nibble at the heels of both big airlines.

The year 1957 witnessed an astonishing turn of events in the

Australian airline world. Having just announced, in March 1957, expansion plans that included the purchase of Convairliners, Viscounts, and new Lockheed L.188 Electras, Reg Ansett made a dramatic takeover bid for A.N.A. in June of the same year. A.N.A.'s financial situation had deteriorated, its management was unable to cope with the problem, and the government suddenly found that, in its two-airline policy, it may have backed the wrong horse.

Ansett offered A£3,000,000 for A.N.A., and his offer was accepted on August 28, 1957. The terms included the transfer of all the benefits that A.N.A. had gained under the 1952 act. The formal purchase of Holyman's pioneer airline was completed on October 4, and by the end of that month the schedules of both airlines had been integrated and an order placed for four of the four-engined turboprop Electras. Within a matter of months, the balance of power in the Australian airline world had been transformed. The traditional name of A.N.A. disappeared, being relegated to second place in the hyphenation of the two airline names, and a new star was seen to be in the ascendant: Reginald Ansett.

The entire Ansett organization then went into top gear, as it consolidated its position throughout Australia by taking over the regional airlines, thus moving into territory where T.A.A. had formerly reigned supreme. The first victim—and that was the correct word—was Butler Air Transport, in which A.N.A. had held a 52 percent shareholding. Butler had been founded in April 1934 to operate routes to connect with QANTAS's service from England. It had taken over some small airlines of its own, including Queensland Airlines, and had a substantial network throughout New South Wales and Queensland. In 1957 it had begun to operate the attractive de Havilland-Airspeed Ambassador airliners and was a well-respected operator.

Butler's shareholders never knew what hit them. Reg Ansett had been quietly buying as many shares as he could on the market and had farmed these out to his employees. At the critical meeting at Sydney, when it was confidently expected that an Ansett offer would be turned down, several airplane loads of "shareholders"—Ansett's

Growth of the Ansett Empire. *This genealogical chart shows how almost every airline in Australia, except those owned or controlled by the Commonwealth government, fell sooner or later into Reg Ansett's grasp. He created a private airline monopoly to compete with a state-owned one.*

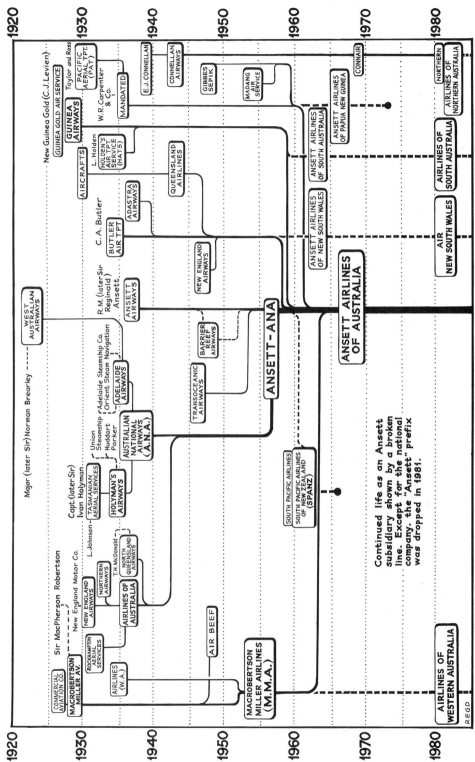

proxy voters—arrived. Ansett instructed them "When I raise my right hand, you raise yours." They did, and Butler passed to Ansett.

By this time, Ansett Airways was only a part of the developing Ansett transport empire, formed under the name of Ansett Transport Industries (A.T.I.) on May 31, 1946. This holding company controlled the fate and—inevitably—the good fortunes of a myriad of activities, all related to transport. These included, as well as the airline, interests in bus and truck lines, bus and truck manufacturing, hotel chains, holiday resorts, and ticketing and travel agents everywhere.

The next subsidiary to be added to A.T.I.'s list was Guinea Airways, an airline with a romantic past of pioneering in the mountainous jungles of New Guinea and Papua, which had transferred its base to Adelaide. In an effort at self-protection, it had, on February 28, 1957, formed Guinea Holdings as a holding company and, on June 30, 1958, transformed an A.N.A. operating agreement to Ansett's archrival, T.A.A. Guinea didn't have a chance. A.T.I. took control of Guinea Holdings in 1959.

By this time the ninety-eight–seat Lockheed Electra had been introduced on the trunk routes linking the four large cities of south-eastern Australia, on March 18, 1959, and the routes of a small post-war airline, Southern Airlines, absorbed on November 1, 1958. Ansett had no qualms about the fine definition of turboprop, or propjet, power being dependent on propellers. The Electras were described as Golden Jets.

The policy of entering the regional airline field was uncompromisably declared when, on December 17, 1959, the name of Butler Air Transport was changed to Airlines of New South Wales, and Guinea Airways became Airlines of South Australia. The country speculated as to where the Ansett tentacles would stretch next. The answer was soon forthcoming. Wisely avoiding rash involvement in Queensland, where T.A.A. held sway, Ansett nevertheless joined with the government's domestic airline in taking over the direct air route from Sydney to Port Moresby, New Guinea, starting service on July 9, 1960. Then another confrontation evolved.

On September 1, 1960, displaying a commendable willingness to play Ansett at his own game, T.A.A. took over the New Guinea local services, together with all the aircraft and ground installations from the Australian overseas flag carrier, QANTAS, which wished to concentrate on long-haul routes. Ansett replied by taking over, in January 1961, the independent airline of New Guinea, Mandated Airlines, sweeping up in the process the bush operators, Gibbes Sepik and Madang Air Services. T.A.A. protested that, by purchasing Mandated and obtaining a license to add other New Guinea internal routes, Ansett had gained an unfair advantage. But once Reg Ansett gained a foothold, he was hard to dislodge.

As if to prove that even the omnipotent R.M. could occasionally slip up, another venture conducted at this time was a failure. Looking across the Tasman Sea, where New Zealand enjoyed—or perhaps tolerated—a nationalized airline, N.Z.N.A.C., Ansett tried to set up a rival company, South Pacific Airlines of New Zealand (SPANZ). Some DC-3s were transferred across the water, but, possibly to the surprise of many airline observers in the area, the project died a natural death, and Ansett cut his losses by shutting down SPANZ before it could lose too much money.

Nevertheless, the inexorable progress of the Ansett empire could only be delayed, not halted. Having run true to form by renaming his most northerly branch as Airlines of Papua New Guinea—which continued until all air activities there became Air Niugini, when that country gained its independence—Reg Ansett cast his eyes to the only part of the Australian map where neither T.A.A., A.N.A., nor Ansett had ever gained even a toehold. Western Australia was the domain of MacRobertson-Miller Airlines, which traced its history back to 1921, at the dawn of commercial aviation in the Commonwealth. Isolated, as it were, from the remainder of Australia by distance and time, Western Australia was vigorously independent from the east, resenting incursions from Sydney or Melbourne in much the same way that Californians are suspicious of New Yorkers or New Englanders on principle.

Such considerations were almost irrelevant. When Reg Ansett wanted something, he usually got it, through sheer persistence. Many thought that this was one recognizably state-supported regional airline which would never fall. But it eventually became part of the A.T.I. conglomerate in April 1963, and, predictably, its name was changed in due course to Airlines of Western Australia.

Geographically the airline empire was complete. The two-airline policy was now honed to a well-defined two-equal-airlines policy, for Ansett was at least as strong as T.A.A., and the share of the Australian domestic air traffic market varied little one side or the other from the 50 percent mark, because both state and private enterprises consolidated between them one of the most efficient transport systems in the world. Under the policy, fares, frequencies, and, to a certain extent, choice of equipment were strictly regulated and controlled, to the extent that only an Australian would be sensitive to the competitive issues.

Instead of watching other world airlines and following their lead, as in days gone by, Ansett was now one of the leaders of the industry in aircraft analysis and selection and among the early customers for new types. Manufacturers listed Melbourne, where Ansett's and T.A.A.'s headquarters were little more than a stone's throw from each other, as one of the first places to visit with the latest brochures and estimates of operating costs. Ansett-A.N.A. put the first trijet Boeing 727-100 into service on November 2, 1964, and it was followed by the smaller Douglas DC-9-10 in January 1967.

The year 1969 was in many ways a watershed year for Ansett. The name of the airline was changed to what every Australian regarded as the inevitable—Ansett Airlines of Australia. The very name had a triumphant ring about it. R. M. Ansett, the man who thirty-three years earlier had skimped and scraped to put a single well-worn old aircraft into service, could now proudly point to a handsome fleet of the most modern jet airliners in the world. He had progressed from a single route from a small provincial town— and had had to fight tooth and nail to retain that—to become part of the Establishment. His transport empire reached into every community, his services were used by almost every citizen in the land, and if he chose to stop operating, half of Australia would come to a grinding halt.

Almost symbolically, R.M. accepted a knighthood from Queen Elizabeth in that same year, 1969. There were those who claimed that there must have been some kind of deal and that Reg must have negotiated his own terms. But Sir Reginald Ansett had mellowed a little. He had once declared that he would retire at the age of thirty-five, and by now even this human dynamo was taking things a little easier. He gradually stopped driving the forty miles from downtown Melbourne to his country estate and took a helicopter—one belonging to Ansett Industries, of course. He lived the life of the country gentleman, breeding horses, cattle, and sheep and enjoying fishing, yachting, and horse-racing. He was generous in his patronage of the local Mornington Race Club. But he was still R. M. to his intimate friends, and he still found time to drop into the local to have a beer with the boys.

Ansett Transport Industries was eventually to pass under the control of two other giant Australian companies, Rupert Murdoch's News Ltd. and Sir Peter Abeles's T.N.T. Murdoch and Abeles became joint managing directors, and Sir Reginald continued as chairman until he died on December 23, 1981.

He was survived by his widow, Lady Joan, and three daughters. He was also survived by two sons from a previous marriage. At the time of his death, the former one-man business employed almost 15,000 people, with assets of A$659 million and revenues of A$789 million.

He left behind a name that is an institution in Australia, much in the same way as Messrs Sears and Roebuck have left an indelible legacy in the United States, and Messrs Marks and Spenser have similarly impregnated British life. In the entire world of air transport, Ansett is one of the few airlines that perpetuates the name of its founder. Respected names such as Wien (of Alaska) have disappeared; Wideroe and Braathens (of Norway) and Faucett (of Peru) are regional, rather than national, airlines and are hardly of world status, while the former U.S. trunk and international carrier, Braniff, has declined to the status of a regional airline.

Reg Ansett achieved this unique position through determination, an acute competitive instinct, and a belligerent dislike of bureaucracy. But he also accepted certain limitations and always stopped short of rashly overreaching himself, either in investment or in challenging authority to the point of illegality. He said himself, "One thing I hate is government enterprise. But, mind you, I don't think private enterprise should be allowed to go mad—some government control is necessary."

Outside his office there was a plaque which expressed his philosophy of life, and the words of wisdom serve both as Ansett's epitaph and as a fitting closure to this profile:

> Nothing in the world can take the place of persistence.
> Talent will not; nothing is more common than
> unsuccessful men with talent.

Genius will not; unrewarded genius is almost a proverb. Education will not; the world is full of educated derelicts. Persistence and determination alone are omnipotent. The slogan "press on" has solved, and always will solve, the problems of the human race.

▶▶▶▶▶▶▶▶▶▶▶▶▶▶▶▶▶▶▶▶▶▶▶▶▶

Bibliography

While I was writing this book, I discovered that the availability of other published works was a case of feast or famine. There was a glut of material about well-known persons such as Howard Hughes and Sir Freddie Laker, and the problem was to separate the wheat from the chaff. Of others, such as Stan Weiss, Edward Hillman, and Marcel Bouilloux-Lafont, the absence of biographies comes close to being a miscarriage of justice.

Stan Weiss's audacious campaign should already have been more widely recognized for its vision and foresight. Hillman was the Laker of his day, but he died too soon and was quickly forgotten. Bouilloux-Lafont's story was the aviation equivalent of the Dreyfus Affair, but the great efforts he made on behalf of his country have been deliberately suppressed for half a century.

Other, more recent careers, such as those of Ed Daly, Frank Lorenzo, Max Ward, and Sir Adam Thomson, will undoubtedly be the subjects of notable life stories when the time is right for their publication. One colorful episode in Ed Daly's career has, in fact, already been written and lavishly produced, but *World Airways in Southeast Asia* became Daly's epitaph rather than a contemporary tribute and was never published. A precious copy is housed in the Ramsey Room, the sanctum sanctorum of the National Air and Space Museum, where it is available for joyous browsing.

I have thus been delighted to realize that this book sometimes breaks new ground, and the absence of references to primary source materials is simply because the subjects have often escaped attention or have preferred privacy and kept their own counsels. I am particularly gratified to have been able to set down the remarkable achievements of such men for the first time in book form.

With these reservations, then, I recommend the following books for further reading:

The United States

Ralph O'Neill. *A Dream of Eagles.* Boston: Houghton Mifflin Company, 1973.

413

Charles Baptie. *Capital*. Annandale, Virginia: Charles Baptie, 1985.

Robert Sterling. *Maverick*. New York: Doubleday, 1974.

———. *Howard Hughes' Airline: An Informal History of TWA*. New York: St Martin's Press / Marek, 1983.

John J. McDonald. *Howard Hughes and His Hercules*. Shrewsbury, England: Airlife, 1981.

Noah Dietrich. *Howard: The Amazing Mr. Hughes*. Greenwich, Connecticut: Fawcett, 1972.

The United Kingdom

John Stroud. *Annals of British and Commonwealth Air Transport*. London: Putnam, 1962.

Captain E. E. Fresson. *Air Road to the Isles*. London: David Rendel, 1963.

C. Martin Sharp. *D. H.: An Outline of de Havilland History*. London: Faber and Faber, 1960.

Howard Banks. *The Rise and Fall of Freddie Laker*. London: Faber and Faber, 1982.

Roger Eglin. *Fly Me, I'm Freddie!* New York: Rawson, Wade, 1980.

Harald Penrose. *British Aviation: Widening Horizons, 1930–1934*. London: Her Majesty's Stationery Office, 1979.

Europe

Jean-Gérard Fleury. *La Ligne*. Paris: Gallimard, 1944.

Paul Vachet. *Avant les jets*. Paris: Hachette, 1964.

Canada

Ronald Keith. *Bush Pilot with a Briefcase*. Toronto: Doubleday Canada, 1972.

Latin America

David Yerex. *Yerex of TACA: A Kiwi Conquistador*. Carterton, New Zealand: Ampersand, 1985.

Philip Schleit. *Shelton's Barefoot Airlines*. Annapolis: Fishergate, 1982.

Australia

James Sinclair. *Wings of Gold*. Sydney, Australia: Pacific Publications, 1978.

Out of the thirty years of research that provided much of the background and perspective for *Rebels and Reformers of the Airways* came also the following books of mine for wider general reference:

A History of the World's Airlines. London: Oxford University Press, 1964; reprinted, New York: AMC Press, 1983.

Airlines of the United States since 1914. London: Putnam, 1972; reprinted, with revisions, Washington, D.C.: Smithsonian Institution Press, 1982.

Airlines of Latin America since 1919. London: Putnam, 1984; Washington, D.C.: Smithsonian Institution Press, 1984.

Continental Airlines: the First Fifty Years. Houston: Pioneer Publications, 1984.

Supplementing these books are numerous official documents, such as the dockets of the late Civil Aeronautics Board and the comprehensive reports published by the British Air Ministry before World War II. In some instances annual reports and other publications of airlines such as Continental, British Caledonian, Canadian Pacific, and Ansett proved to be valuable sources of documented information. The magazine *Fortune* can be relied upon for immaculate analyses of airline crises and unusual developments, while the contemporary recording of events is well covered by such periodicals as *Aviation Week* and *Air Transport World* in the United States and *Air Pictorial* and *Flight International* in the United Kingdom. The U.S. *American Aviation* and the British *Aeroplane* are no longer published but are available in many libraries.

Index

A.A.J.C. (Associated Airways Joint Committee: Fresson's association, 226; Allied Airways excluded, 237

A.B.C. (Advanced Booking Charter): tariff (Wardair), 196; Canadian domestic, 198; British Caledonian, 271

Abeles, Sir Peter, 411

Aberdeen Airways, 232–36

Adami, Angel S. (Uruguayan air pioneer), 284

Adelaide Airways, genealogy, 407

Advanced Booking Charter. *See* A.B.C.

Advanced Purchase Excursion fares. *See* APEX

AEMCO, Transocean engineering base, 110

Aerolíneas Peruanas. *See* APSA

Aeroposta Argentina, 289

Aéropostale: competes with NYRBA, 17; history, 286–93

Aerovias Brasil: founded by Yerex, 329; purchased by REAL, 352

Aerovias Centrales (Pan American affiliate), 12

Affinity Charter rules, by Max Ward, 194

Aguardiente (Honduran beverage), 335

Air Ceylon, linked with A.N.A., 405

Air Charter, formed by Laker, 244

Air Djibouti, 107 (map), 110

Air Ferries, San Francisco air service, 8

Air France: formation, 293; Laker contract, 247

Air Line Pilots' Association. *See* ALPA

Air Mail Scandal: effect on Varney, 12; effect on railroad ownership, 52; summary, 68

Air Micronesia, Continental control, 41

Air Navigation Regulations (Australia), broken by P.A.T., 394–95

Air Niugini, ancestry, 409

Air Orient, 293

Air Shuttle, New York–Washington, 142

Air Siam, 372–78

Air Traffic Controllers' strike, 159

Air Transport Advisory Council. *See* A.T.A.C.

Air Transport Association. *See* A.T.A.

Air Transport Auxiliary. *See* A.T.A.

Air Transport Committee of Canadian Transport Commission, 198

Air Union (French airline), 291, 293

Air West, 62

Airbus A-300: Laker order, 251–52, 256; Fontana order, 355; Air Siam, 326

Airline Deregulation Act: foreshadowed, 91; signed and passed, 117, 134, 143, 155

Airlines Agreement Act (Australia), 405

Airlines of Australia, genealogy, 407

Airspeed Ambassador, with Butler, 406

Airspeed Envoy, with Ansett, 402

Airspeed Ferry, rival to D.H. Dragon, 209

Airways Interests (Thomson), 268

Airwork: purchases Laker, 244; merges with British United, 269

Akureyri Airline Company, 302

Alaska Highway, C.P.A. involvement, 181

Alexandra, Princess, with Gandar Dower, 231

Alger, Horatio, Award, to Carmichael, 81

All-American Air Meet, 1934, Hughes wins, 50

All-Nippon Airways, association with Air Siam, 374

Allied Airways (Gandar Dower), name changed from Aberdeen Airways, 236

Allied British Airways, 222

Aloha Airlines, interest in UMDA, 41

ALPA (Airline Pilots' Association): Orvis Nelson, vice president, 102; confrontation with Lorenzo, 145–48

Amazonia Suite (composition by Fontana), 360

American Airlines: interchange with Continental, 36; abandons Pacific' route, 43; Hughes as copilot, 49

American Export Lines, challenges Pan Am, 326

Amtorg (Soviet trading agency), flying rights, 179

A.N.A. (Australian National Airways), 402–7

Ansett, Sir Reginald: connection with Parer, 397; complete profile, 399–412

Ansett Airways, 402–10

Ansett Transport Industries, 408

APEX fares, 271

APSA (Aerolíneas Peruanas), 338, 341

Arbuthnott, Viscount, 232

Arc-en-Ciel (Couzinet aircraft), 296

Armstrong-Whitworth biplane, flown by Fresson, 215

Arrowsmith Holidays, purchased by Laker, 247

Associated Airways Joint Committee. *See* A.A.J.C.

A.T.A. (Air Transport Association), supports C.A.B. rulings, 91

A.T.A. (Air Transport Auxiliary), Laker service, 242

A.T.A.C. (Air Transport Advisory Council), U.K., advises independents, 245

A.T.L.A. (Air Transport Licensing Authority) (U.K.), 237

A.T.L.A. (Air Transport Licensing Authority) (Hong Kong), Laker route application, 253

A.T.L.B. (Air Transport Licensing Board) (U.K.): replaces A.T.A.C., 245; Laker Skytrain, 249–50; Caledonian application, 265

ATL 90 Accountant, 244

ATL 98 Carvair (car-ferrying operation), 246

Atlantic Ferry Service, by C.P.A., 181

Atlas Corporation, acquires Transocean, 114–16

Austin, Jim (president of Northeast), 79

Australian Airlines Act (1945), 404

Australian National Airlines Commission, 404

Australian Natural Airways. *See* A.N.A.

Aviation Traders (Engineering), formed by Laker, 243

Avro 504K: flown by Fresson, 217; Flugfelag, 302

Avro Tudor, operated by Air Charter, 244

Avro York, operated by Air Charter, 244

"Baby Electra" (Lockheed 12), with Continental, 32

B.A.C. One-Eleven: ordered by Laker, 246; B.U.A. intercity service, 272; purchased by Fontana, 354; Air Siam lease, 375

Baker, Major General David H. (president of Capital Airlines), 79

Ball, Clifford, wins air mail contract, 68

Bamberg, Harold, British Eagle, 263

Bank of China, funds Shelton, 337

Barefoot passengers, by Shelton, 339

Barkley-Grow floatplanes, McConachie's, 178

Barrier Reef Airways, purchase of, by Ansett, 405, 407

Barry, Gordon (pilot for C.A.T.), 319

Battle of Britain Day, 370

"Battler" (Ray Parer), 383–84

B.C.P.A. (British Commonwealth and

Pacific Airlines), A.N.A. involvement with, 405

Bebchick, Leonard (lawyer for British Caledonian), 264, 268

Beckman, Robert (Laker's lawyer), 256

Beech 18, operated by TACA, 323

Beech 99, operated by Texas International, 141

Bellanca aircraft: Yerex personal, 318; with TACA, 323

Bellanca Skyrocket (Yellowknife Airways), 190

Bennett, Donald (Air Vice Marshal), sells Fairflight to Laker, 244

Berkoviche Steamship Company, buys World Airways flying boats, 120

Berkshire Aviation Tours (Fresson), 217

Berlin airlift (Transocean), 107, 110

Bermuda Two Air Agreement, effect on British Caledonian, 273

Berta, Rubem (president of VARIG), approached by Fontana, 350

Bez, Nick (head of West Coast Airlines), 62

Blackburn Bluebird, flown by Gandar Dower, 231

Blériot (French aircraft manufacturer), 291

Blue Cars (later Blue Sky) (British Caledonian travel agency), 272

Blue Skyway, Continental routes, 35

B.O.A.C. (British Overseas Airways Corporation): introduces Bristol Britannia, 59; sells aircraft to Laker, 243; abandons South American routes, 270–71; receives letter from Yerex, 328; Varanair staff, 370; operates VC-10, 371

Boeing Airplane Company: O'Neill as Latin American agent, 16; controls United Air Lines, 54

Boeing B-40, operated by Parer, 396

Boeing F2B, demonstrated by O'Neill, 16

Boeing P-12, modified by Hughes, 50

Boeing 40B-4, used by Varney, 7

Boeing 247 (and 247-D): Pennsylvania Airlines, 69; first modern airliner, 53; sold only to United, 54

Boeing 307 Stratoliner: ordered by T.W.A., 53; supplied to military, 56; first four-engined U.S. service, 72; flown by Shelton, 336

Boeing 314, with World Airways, 119–20

Boeing 707: Continental Airlines, 38; bomb explosion, 39; T.W.A. order, 59; World Airways, 125; Wardair, 195; Laker, 248; Caledonian, 265, 271; I.A.B., 310; Transbrasil, 359; Air Siam, 376

Boeing 727: World Airways, 127; World Danang incident, 132–33; PEOPLExpress, 162; Wardair, 194; Transbrasil, 356; Ansett-A.N.A., 410

Boeing 737, PEOPLExpress, 157–62

Boeing 747: Continental, 42; World, 127, 131; PEOPLExpress, 161–63; Wardair, 196; Air Siam, 376

Boeing 767, Transbrasil, 358

Boeing 2707 supersonic airliner: World Airways order, 126; McConachie order, 185

Bol-Inca Mining Corporation, founded by O'Neill, 28

Bonanza Airlines, merges into Air West, 62

Borman, Frank, fights to save Eastern, 150

Bouilloux-Lafont, André (son of Marcel), involved in scandal, 292

Bouilloux-Lafont, Marcel, complete profile, 283–98

Braathens S.A.F.E., aircraft lease to Loftleidir, 305

Braniff, Paul (pilot for C.A.T.), 319

Braniff International Airways, acquires PANAGRA, 343

Brazilian air shuttle service: begins, 250; participation by Sadia, 354

Brazilian Mail and Telegraph Company, association with Transbrasil, 356

Brearley, Sir Norman (founder of West Australian Airways), 407

Breese aircraft, used by Varney, 6

Breguet (French aircraft manufacturer), 291

Brintnell, Leigh, influence in Canadian airline, 180

Bristol Aeroplane Company, Hughes test flight of Britannia, 50

Bristol F2b, 386

Bristol 170, Wayfarer or Freighter: Wardair, 192; Air Charter, 244; flown by Thomson, 261

Bristol 175 Britannia: flown by Hughes, 50; Hughes consideration, 59; flown by Carmichael, 78; service with C.P.A., 184, 194; purchased by Laker, 247; Caledonian, 265; Canadair CL-44 conversion, 309

Bristol Jupiter engines, bought by P.A.T., 393

Britavia Group: merges with B.U.A., 246, 269; Adam Thomson as pilot, 261; troop contracts, 261

British Aircraft Corporation, Laker order, 246

British Airways (1935): takes over Hillman, 212; formation, 212; changes name from Allied, 222

British Airways (postwar): indebtedness, 256; Laker lawsuit, 257–58; inefficiency, 276; privatization policy, 279

British and Commonwealth Shipping, shareholder of B.U.A., 270

British Caledonian Airways: awarded Hong Kong route, 253; sends nastigrams, 257; succeeds Caledonian and B.U.A., 271; abandons Atlantic market, 272

British Commonwealth Air Training Plan, 181

British European Airways (B.E.A.): launches Viscount, 77; absorbs Highland Airways, 220; absorbs Allied, 239; orders Trident, 246; employs Thomson, 260

British Overseas Airways Corporation. See B.O.A.C.

British United Airways. See B.U.A.

British West Indian Airways. See B.W.I.A.

Britt Airways, purchased by PEOPLExpress, 165

Brizendine, John (president of McDonnell Douglas), 257

Brooks, Miguel (Shelton's partner), 337

Brown, Gilbert, charters Soviet ship for Caledonian, 265

Brown, Walter Folger (U.S. postmaster general): manipulates mail contracts, 12; favors Chosen Instrument, 20

Brunning, Miss (C.B.) (companion to Gandar Dower), 233

Bryan, Charles (head of I.A.M. union), confronts Frank Borman, 151

B.U.A.: formation, 245, 269; merges with Britavia, 246; Edwards Report, 269; Gatwick facilities, 270; purchased by Caledonian, 271

Buckner, Harold (Varney pilot), 6

Bucyrus mechanical shovel, transported by TACA, 324

Bulolo Gold Dredging, association with Guinea Airways, 391

Bulolo Goldfields Aeroplane Service (B.G.A.S.), 387–90

Burnett, J. G. (M.P.) (guest on Aberdeen Airways), 232

Burr, Donald C., complete profile, 153–68

Bush pilots, Max Ward's qualifications, 190

Butler, C. A., founder of Butler airline, 407

Butler Air Transport, 406–8

B.W.I.A. (British West Indian Airways), founded by Yerex, 328, 330

C.A.A. (British). See Civil Aviation Authority

C.A.B. See Civil Aeronautics Board

Cadman Committee, advocates formation of B.O.A.C., 269

Caledonian Airways, 262–71

Caledonian Case, C.A.B. ruling in, 264

California Gas and Electric Co., employs Robert Six, 32

Cambodian airlift (World Airways), 131

Canadair CL-44, Loftleidir and Cargolux, 309–10

Canadian Airways: controlled by C.P.R., 171, 180; promotes Prairie Air Mail, 173

Canadian Car and Foundry, provides aircraft to McConachie, 178

Canadian National Railways, founding stockholder of T.C.A., 171, 180

Canadian Pacific Airlines (C.P.A.): formation and history, 180–85; leases aircraft to Wardair, 193

Canadian Pacific Railway (C.P.R.): early airline interest, 171; mops up small airlines to form C.P.A., 179–80

Canadian-U.S. Joint Defence Board, modernizes route to Alaska, 179

Capital Airlines, 65–81

Capital Airlines Association, 81

Caravelle (French airliner): flown by Carmichael, 78; pioneers twin-engined jet, 246; in Brazil, 354

Cargolux Airlines, 310

Carías, Andino (president of Honduras), hires Yerex, 319

Carmichael, James H., complete profile, 65–82

Carney, Robert J., association with Lorenzo, 139, 142

Carpenter, J. R., attends Parer demonstration, 393

Carpenter, W. R. & Co.: P.A.T. attempts association with, 393; P.A.T. merger, 397; Ansett genealogy, 407

Carter, Jimmy: approves Continental Pacific route, 43; signs Airline Deregulation Act, 117, 251

C.A.S. (Continental Air Services), subsidiary of Continental Airlines, 41

C.A.T. airline, employs Yerex, 318–19

Cathay Pacific Airways: awarded Hong Kong route, 253; subcontractor for Air Siam, 373; aggressive marketing, 375

Cavaillès, Louis (Aéropostale flight engineer), 296

Cayser family (Anthony, Nicholas), discuss Caledonian-B.U.A. merger, 270

C.E.A. (Ecuadorian airline), 338, 341

Central Airlines: outbids Pennsylvania Airlines for mail contract, 68; merges to form P.C.A., 69

Cerche, Vern (pilot for Ansett), 401–2

Cessna T50 Crane, flown by Max Ward, 189

C.G.E.A. (French airline), formed by Latécoère, 285

Chaloryu, Admiral Sa-naged, dismisses Dr. Gun, 377

Chandler, June (Mrs. Ed Daly), 122

Channel Air Bridge (car-ferrying operation), 244

Chapter 11 (bankruptcy code): invoked by Lorenzo, 145–52; comparison with *liquidation judiciaire*, 291

Chase Manhattan Bank, seeks assistance in Texas airline problem, 140

Checker Air Service, formed by Varney, 3–4

Chiang Kai-shek, Mme, befriends Shelton, 336

Chickenfeed fares (Continental), 43

Chiffley, Ben (Australian prime minister), negotiates with McConachie, 182

China Airlines, aggressive marketing by, 375

Chulalonghorn, Rama V (king of Siam) (grandfather of Prince Varanand), 363

Churchill, Winston, directs continuation of airlines during war, 227

Chutatuj Taradilok, Gromadhun Petchabune Interachai, Prince (father of Prince Varanand), 363

CIDNA (French airline), 291, 293

Civil Aeronautics Board (C.A.B.): rigid control, 35; "grandfather certificates," 70; restrictions on P.C.A.; 73; aboard Constellation flight, 54; belated Capital route award, 79; frustrates Hughes, 57; T.W.A. legal battles, 61; approves Hughes control of Air West, 62; sustained legal confrontation with North American Airlines, 83–100; restricts Transocean airline activities, 113–17 relations with World Airways, 126; widens Supplemental airline role, 127; rejects World application, 128; ponderous machinery reviewed, 155; denies Laker permit, 250; Caledonian Case, 264; complaint against transatlantic carriers, 268; American Export certificate, 326; disapproves Am Ex bid to purchase TACA, 327; T.W.A. permit, 342

Civil Aviation Authority (C.A.A.) (British): considers Laker application, 250; rejects Laker Hong Kong bid, 253

Civil Aviation Review (British): re-evaluates airline policy; Thomson case, 278

Club Coach, Continental Airlines service, 38

Clydesdale Bank, appoints receivers for Laker Airways, 255

C.M.A. (Compañía Mexicana de Aviación), purchased by Pan Am, 20

Coach-class service, Capital's first in world, 75

Cobb, Sir Cyril, recognizes Gandar Dower's bravery, 230

Cohen, General Morris ("Two-Gun"), grants rights to Wop May and McConachie, 183

Coleman, D. C., president of C.P.R., 181

Collier Trophy, won by Hughes, 47, 51

Companie Générale d'Enterprises Aéronautiques. See C.G.E.A.

Comte de la Vaulx (aircraft flown by Mermoz), 290

Concorde (Franco-British airliner), ordered by Six, 40

Concórdia, S.A. Industria e Comércio, formed, 346

Condor Syndikat, obtains Brazilian air rights, 287

Consolidated Aircraft Corporation, builds flying boats for NYRBA, 18

Consolidated Commodore, 21–23

Consolidated Fleetster, used by NYRBA, 24

Consolidated PBY-5A Catalina: Trust Territory operation, 112; Flugfelag Islands, 302

Consolidated Liberator (Flugfelag), 302

Continental Air Services. See C.A.S.

Continental Airlines (and Air Lines): map (1937), 9; established, 13; under Robert Six, 31–46, 143; possible merger with Capital, 79; under Lorenzo, 144–52

Convair 240 (Continental), 35

Convair 340 (A.N.A.), 405–6

Convair 440 (Ed Daly's personal aircraft), 129

Convair 880 (Capital), 79

Convair 990: with APSA, 341; flown by Prince Varanand, 368

Coolidge, Calvin, meets with O'Neill, 18

Coote, Ginger (and Ginger Coote Airways), merges with United Air Transport, 178

Coronation (L.N.E.R. train), connects with Allied Airways, 237

COTAC (Brazilian commission), approves Fontana plan, 358

Coulter, John and Richard, own Central Airlines, 68

Council of British Societies promotes V.F.R. travel clubs, 267

Courtnay, Bill (associate of Hillman), 208

Couzinet 70 (French aircraft), 296

C.P.R. See Canadian Pacific Railway

Crawford, Frederick R., buys Clifford Ball airline, 68

Cruzeiro do Sul: airline approached by Fontana, 350; financial difficulties and sale, 356

Cuddeback, Leon (Varney pilot), 4–5

Curtiss engine, used by Varney, 6

Curtiss C-46: Transocean transpacific ferry, 109; leased by Marvin Stadden, 120, DEW-line contract, 122–23; TAN, 339; competes with four-engined aircraft, 341; VARIG, 350

Curtiss Condor (TACA), 323

Daly, Edward, complete profile, 119–36

Damm, Alexander (president of Continental Airlines), 44

Damon, Ralph (president of T.W.A.), 58

Danang, World Airways incident, 132–33

Daurat, Didier, administers C.G.E.A., 286

Dawson, Peter, lends money to Parer, 385

Day Dawn company, patronizes Guinea Airways, 391

Deep-discount fares (Texas International), 141

De Havilland Aircraft company, negotiates with Edward Hillman, 207–8

De Havilland Gipsy Moth: with Fresson, 217; with Ansett, 401–2

De Havilland Tiger Moth, 401

De Havilland D.H.4: used by O'Neill, 16; purchased by B.G.A.S., 387

De Havilland D.H.9: obtained by Parer, 385: by Morlae Airlines, 390

De Havilland D.H.37, Guinea Gold Air Service, 387

De Havilland D.H.80A Puss Moth: owned by Prince Galizine, 174; flown by Hillman, 206–7

De Havilland D.H.83 Fox Moth: Max Ward's favorite aircraft, 189; flown by Parer, 396; Tasmanian Aerial Services, 402

De Havilland D.H.84 Dragon: produced by de Havilland, 209; Highland Airways, 216, 219; resilience, 225; Aberdeen Airways, 233

De Havilland D.H.86B Express, Allied Airways, 236

De Havilland D.H.88 Comet, wins MacRobertson Trophy, 395

De Havilland D.H.89A Rapide: with Hillman, 210; with Fresson, 222; with Aberdeen Airways, 236; with Flugfelag Islands, 302

De Havilland D.H.104 Dove, flown by Thomson, 261

De Havilland D.H.106 Comet: Capital Airlines order, 78–79; Canadian Pacific Airlines, 184–85

De Havilland D.H.121 Trident, ordered by B.E.A., 246

De Havilland FE-2B, bought by Parer, 386

De Havilland Canada DHC-2 Beaver, with Wardair, 191–92

De Havilland Canada DHC-6 Twin Otter, Wardair, 198

De Havilland Canada Dash Seven, Wardair, 198

De la Haye, John, with Caledonian, 261–63

Denby, Alfred, employed by Pan American, 326

Denver Service Case: Continental route application, 37–38; heard by C.A.B., 90

D'Erlanger, Gerard (managing director of B.E.A.), 226

Deutsche Lufthansa (prewar): South Atlantic service, 288; gains rights to Azores, 296

DEW-line (Distant Early Warning) contract, World Airways, 122

Diamond Head Lounge (Continental Airlines), 42

Dickens, Punch: Canadian airline pioneer, 180; influence on Max Ward, 187–88

Dien Bien Phu incident, 123

Dietrich, Noah (associate of Howard Hughes), 49, 55–57

Diplomat (Capital Airlines Viscount service), 77

Dirty Tom's map of gold mine, 174

Dixon Speas Associates, advises Eliasson, 309

Dollar, R. Stanley, finance agreement with Transocean, 114

Donaldson shipping company, provides capital for Caledonian, 267

Douglas aircraft, competition with Lockheed, 58

Douglas B-18 bomber, with TAN, 339

Douglas C-47. *See* Douglas DC-3

Douglas C-54. *See* Douglas DC-4

Douglas DC-1, inspired by Jack Frye, 53

Douglas DC-2: with T.W.A., 53; Aerovías de Guatemala, 326; competes in MacRobertson Trophy Race, 395; A.N.A., 403

Douglas DC-3 (and C-47): with Continental, 34; sponsored by American, 53; with P.C.A., 70; Fireball Air Express, 85; Trans Texas, 140; Pionair conversion, 260; Flugfelag glacier rescue, 301–4; TAN, 337; leased by Sadia, 348; with REAL, 352; with T.A.A. and Ansett, 404; with SPANZ, 409

Douglas DC-3 Replacement, ATL 90, 244

Douglas DC-4 (and C-54): under development, 53; competes with Constellation, 54; first service, 72; purchased by Nelson, 104; by Ed Daly, 122; conversion to ATL 98 Carvair, 246; with Loftleidir, 303–5; leased by Air Siam, 373

Douglas DC-6 and DC-6B: Capital lease from Pan Am, 80; North American Airlines, 91; leased by North American to Eastern, 97; World Airways lease, 125; Wardair, 193–94; Caledonian, 264;

Loftleidir, 306; APSA, 341; A.N.A., 405

Douglas DC-7, DC-7B, and DC-7C: Continental Airlines, 38; Caledonian Airways, 262, 264; Cameroon crash, 263

Douglas DC-8: World Airways, 129; Canadian Pacific, 185; I.A.B., 310; Icelandair, 314; Air Siam, 373

Douglas DC-9: Texas International, 141; Ansett-A.N.A., 410

Douglas DC-10. See McDonnell Douglas DC-10

Dream of Eagles, A (O'Neill), 28

Drinkwater, Terry (acting president of Continental), 34

Dulles International Airport, prospects reviewed, 160

Eagle Airways, transatlantic charters, 263

Eagle Nest flight school (T.W.A.), at Albuquerque, 56

Earhart, Amelia, her aircraft flown by Carmichael, 67

Eastern Air Lines: Sells DC-4s to North American, 89; leases DC-6Bs from North American, 97; Air Shuttle route challenged, 142

Ecuatoriana, Compañía de Aviación (C.E.A.), 338, 341

Edinburgh, Duke of, comment on Laker, 250

Edmonton Aero Club, instructs McConachie, 172

Edwards Report (Sir Ronald Edwards): implications for Caledonian, 269; effect on British Airways, 277

Eliasson, Alfred, complete profile, 299–316

Elizabeth II (queen of England), confers knighthood on Ansett, 410

Embraer EMB-110B Bandeirante, first service, 355

Empresa Dean (Honduran transport company), 321, 334

Empresa Nacional de Transportes Aéreos. See ENTA

England-Australia Air Race, Parer enters, 395

ENTA (Costa Rican airline), 323, 334

Equitable Life, holds T.W.A. debentures, 59–60

Erlanger (banking house), 211

Essair (early name for Pioneer), 36

Ethiopian Airways, T.W.A. assists, 330

Exempt Charter Service, British Caledonian, 271

Expreso Diferido, TACA service, 321

F.A.A.: Carmichael association, 81; rejects ALPA campaign, 148; grounds DC-10, 252

Fairchild FC2W2, acquired by McConachie, 176

Fairchild Aircraft Corporation, association with Carmichael, 80–81

Fairey Fox, purchased by Parer, 395

Fairflight, purchased by Laker, 244

Fantasia del Aire (composition by Fontana), 360

Farley, James A. (postmaster general), opens air mail bids, 12

Farman (French airline), 291

Farquhar, Admiral, guest on Aberdeen Airways inaugural flight, 232

Federal Aviation Administration. See F.A.A.

F.E.E.C., formed and sold by Shelton, 337, 340

Feldman, Al (president of Continental), 44, 143

Fireball Air Express, founded by Weiss and Sherman, 85

First Western Bank and Trust Company, purchased by Daly, 128

Fischgrund, James (partner in Standard Airlines), 86

Fishermen's Airlift by Transocean, 107, 109

Fitzgerald, R. A., condemns North American Airlines, 92

Five Freedoms of the Air: discussion of, 306–7; Loftleidir, 311; granted to Air Siam, 372

Fleet, Reuben, builds Consolidated flying boats, 18

Fleet biplanes, evaluated by McConachie, 178

Flight Aid. See Flughjalp

Flight Engineering and Equipment Corp. See F.E.E.C.

Flugfelag Akureyrar: formed, 302; merges with Loftleidir, 311

Flughjalp, Icelandic relief work, 310

Flugleider, formed, 311

Flying Scotsman (train), competes with airline, 236

Flying Tigers (airline): low bidder for transpacific contract, 105; lease arrangement with Air Siam, 373

Fokker aircraft, operated by ENTA, 334

Fokker Universal: aircraft owned by McConachie, 173, 175; photograph, 170, 403; purchased by Ansett, 402

Fokker F-III, acquired by P.A.T., 393

Fokker F-VII, acquired by P.A.T., 394

Fontana, Atillio (father of Omar), founds company, 345–46

Fontana, Denilda (wife of Omar): 347; active in airline, 351

Fontana, Marise (daughter of Omar), heads Transbrasil, Inc., 358

Fontana, Omar, complete profile, 345–62

Ford Motor Company: first air mail contract, 5–6; interest in NYRBA, 19

Ford Tri-Motor: 5–AT, used by NYRBA, 19; flown by Hughes under alias, 49; Central Airlines, 68; spectacular forced landing, 69; purchased by McConachie, 175; starts United Air Transport service, 177; serves TACA as workhorse, 323–24

Forsblade, Robert C.: influences Shelton, 333; partner in Honduras, 337; quoted on beef airlift, 339; reactions on Shelton's death, 343

Franklin, James B. (vice-president of Capital Airlines), 75

Fresson, Captain Edmund E.: complete profile, 215–28; competes with Gandar Dower, 234

Friedkin Aeronautics, becomes P.S.A., 89

Frohboese, Edith (Mrs. Orvis Nelson), 104

Frontier Airlines: bid to purchase by Lorenzo, 150; purchased by PEOPLExpress, 164

Fröysaa, Einar, represents Braathens, 306

Frye, Jack: discusses T.W.A. purchase with Hughes, 52; inspires Douglas airliners, 53; delivers Constellation, 54; leaves T.W.A., 57; involved with TACA, 329; heads T.W.A. during TACA period, 336

Funston, Keith, influences Donald Burr, 155

Galizine, Prince (partner of McConachie), 174

Gallet, Eric (partner of Parer), 387

Gambia Airways (British Caledonian association), 272

Gandar Dower, Eric L.: leases aircraft to Hillman, 211; builds airfield at Aberdeen, 219; complete profile, 229–40; compared to Varanand, 379

Gates Flying Circus, Lowell Yerex as member, 318

Gatty, Harold, flies into Edmonton, 173

Gibbes Sepik, taken over by Ansett, 407, 409

Gibson, Marshal, invests in British Caledonian, 262

Gilpin Airlines, connects with Varney, 10

Gnôme et Rhône (French engine manufacturer): accused of wrongdoing, 292; forms SPELA, 294

Gold Book, by British Caledonian, 277

Gold Carpet Service (Continental Airlines), 36, 38

Gold Rush, Transocean operation, 111; map, 107

Golden Jet (Continental Airlines service), 38

Golden Jets (Ansett's Electras), 408

Gomes, Linneu (head of REAL), 352

Gorst, Vern: San Francisco Bay service, 8; Air Ferries Ltd., 10

Grace, W. R., Corporation, forms PANAGRA, 20–21

Graf Zeppelin: survey flights, 288–90; regular service, 297

"Grandfather certificates," issued by C.A.B., 70

Great Universal Stores, provides capital for Caledonian, 267

Greene, Judge Harold H., presides over Laker lawsuit, 257

Greet, Ben (Sir Philip), promotes Shakespearean touring company, 230

Gross, Robert: offers to buy Varney stock, 8; offers Varney Lockheed job, 13; Constellation development, 53–54

Grosvenor, Gilbert H. (publisher of *National Geographic*), 27

Grumman Goose, in Iceland, 301–2

Grumman Gulfstream, used by Wardair, 198

Guatemala, Aerovías de, founded by Pan American, 326

Guinea Airways: history, 389–97; genealogy, 407; name change, 408

Guinea Gold Air Service: formed and operated, 387–89; genealogy, 407

Guinea Gold No Liability Company, 387

Guinea Holdings, 408

Gunnarsson, Gunnar, represents Loftleidir, 306

Hagg, Arthur (designer of de Havilland Dragon), 209

Hajj pilgrimage flights: by Transocean, 107, 110–11; by Wardair, 198; by British Caledonian, 272

Halifax, Lord, receives comments on Yerex, 327

Hambrecht & Quist, backs Donald Burr, 160

Handley Page Dart Herald, operated by Sadia, Transbrasil, 353–54

Handley Page Halifax, conversions by Laker, 243

Handley Page Halton, purchased by Laker, 243

Handley Page Hampstead, P.A.T. cannibalizes for parts, 393

Handley Page Hermes, flown by Thomson, 261

Hann, George R.: buys Clifford Ball airline, 68; chairman of Capital executive committee, 79

Harmon Trophy, won by Hughes, 47, 51

Hart, Ross R. (founder of Viking Air Lines), 87

Haueter, Ted (Continental chief of operations), 34

Hawaiian Airlines, stock purchased by T.W.A., 330

Hawker Hurricane fighter aircraft, destroys Ford Tri-Motor, 178

Hawker Siddeley 748, resemblance to ATL 90, 244

Hayman Island, purchased by Ansett, 405

Healy, Ken (World Airways pilot at Danang), 133–34

Helgason, Sigurdur (elder), 312–13

Helgason, Sigurdur (younger), succeeds father, 314

Hell's Angels (Hughes film), 50

Hemisphere Air Transport (part of North American agency), 87

Hempstead, Florence (Mrs. C. N. Shelton), 335

Hemsworth, Geoff (partner of Parer), 395

Henshaw, employs Yerex, 319

Herlihy, Jack (vice-president of United), requests subcontract from Nelson, 104

Herod, Gerry, Caledonian marketing efforts, 268

Hertz, John, association with T.W.A., 52–53

Hibbard, Hal (Constellation designer), 53

Highland Airways: opening service and establishment, 216–17, taken over, merges into Scottish Airways, 222–23

Highland Show, uses Aberdeen airfield, 221

Hillman, Edward, complete profile, 205–14; leases aircraft to Aberdeen Airways, 233

Hillman's Airways, 207–13, 221–22

Hogarth (shipping company), provides capital for British Caledonian, 267

Holmes, F. J. V., (operator of Berkshire Aviation Tours), 217

Holyman, Captain V. C. (founder of Tasmanian Aerial Services), 402

Holyman's Airways, genealogy, 407

Homecoming contract (World Airways), 129

Hoover, Mrs. Herbert, christens Commodore flying boat, 22

Howard, Charles (alias of Howard Hughes), 49

Howe, C. C. (Canadian prime minister), lays down conditions for McConachie, 181–82

Hub-and-spoke airline route system, 155–56

Hudson bomber program, Varney as copilot, 13

Hughes, Billy (Australian prime minister), 385

Hughes, Howard: complete profile, 47–64; meets Yerex, 329; directs T.W.A., 336

Hughes, Howard, Sr., designs oil drill, 48–49

Hughes Air West, formed 62; offers to buy Texas International, 140

Hughes Aircraft Company: association with Hughes, 47; founding, 50; continued survival, 56

Hughes H-1 Racer: photograph, 48; breaks records, 51; inspiration for XF-11, 56

Hughes Hercules flying boat, 50, 55

Hughes, Howard, Medical Institute, owns Hughes aircraft, 59

Hughes steam car, failure, 49

Hughes Tool Company (Toolco): association with T.W.A., 47–61; with Airwest, 62

Hughes XF-11, development and crash, 56

Hull, Theodore (founder of C.A.T.), 319

Hungarian airlift (World Airways), 124

Hunting-Clan Group, merges into British United, 245, 269

Hurlingham Country Club, home of Yerex, 331

I.A.B. *See* International Air Bahama

I.A.M. *See* International Association of Machinists

IATA: discusses sandwich ingredients, 85; charter regulations, 249, 263; fares compared with Loftleidir's, 305; Flugfelag membership, 307; South American fare schedule, 339; Air Siam joins, 373

Icahn, Carl, outbids Lorenzo to buy T.W.A., 150

ICAO: Five Freedoms of the Air, 306–7, 372; Loftleidir Fifth Freedom, 311; Loftleidir Sixth Freedom, 308–9; Shelton's plan to exploit freedoms, 340; TAN challenges, 342

Icelandic Airlines, 306

Immigration and Naturalization Department, attempts to fine World Airways, 134

Imperial Oil Company (Canada), backs McConachie, 177–78

Independence (Capital Airlines Viscount service), 77

Independent Airways (McConachie), 173

Industrial Commercial Finance Corporation: provides capital for Caledonian, 267–68; arranges Caledonian-B.U.A. merger, 270–71

Inn of the Sixth Freedom, fanciful name for Loftleidir hotel, 309

Insight (magazine), quoted on demise of Air Siam, 377

Insurance Company of North America, almost sold to Daly, 129

Inter-American Airways Agency, incorporated by T.W.A. and Yerex, 329

International Air Bahama, acquired by Loftleidir, 310

International Air Transport Association. *See* IATA

International Association of Machinists: Continental strike, 144–47; conflict with Frank Borman, 151

International Civil Aviation Organization. *See* ICAO

International Founders, interest in NYRBA, 19

International Motor Trucks Company, services *Spirit of St Louis*, 318

International Refugee Organization, Transocean contract, 106–7

International Vacations Ltd., Wardair travel agency, 196

Iranian Airways, stock purchased by T.W.A., 330

Iraqi Air Force, busy de Havilland Dragon, 209

Irigoyen, Hipolito (president of Argentina), discusses mail contract with O'Neill, 18

I.R.O. *See* International Refugee Organization

Irving Trust: interest in NYRBA, 19; T.W.A. finance plan, 60

Japanese Air Lines (and Japan Air Lines) (J.A.L.), formed by Transocean, 113

Jersey Airways, taken over by Whitehall Securities, 222

Jet Capital Corporation, association with Texas International, 139–41

Jewish immigrant airlift (Transocean), 107, 110–11

Jimmie the Greek, involved in Hughes case, 63

Johannesson's Flying School, teaches Eliasson, 300

Johnson, Amy: christens aircraft for Hillman, 209; influence on Ansett, 400

Johnson, Senator Edwin, chairman of hearings on nonscheduled carriers, 90

Johnson, Kelly: designs Constellation, 53–4; leads "Skunk Works," 58

Johnson, Orn O. (Flugfelag board member), 312

Jolly Green Giant (Daly's personal aircraft), 130

Junkers company, intercedes in China, 216

Junkers monoplane, hired by McConachie, 174

Junkers-F 13: metal construction suited for South America, 285; Icelandic Aircraft Company, 302

Junkers-G 31, with Guinea Airways, 391

Junkers-W 33, Icelandic Aircraft Company, 302

Junkers-W 34: with Guinea Airways, 389; transports crushing mill, 391

Kaiser, Henry J., plans giant flying boat, 54–55

Kelly Air Mail Act, 4

Kennedy, John F., ratifies Caledonian Case, 264

Keys North American Group, investment in Varney, 7

Keystone-Loening Air Yacht, used by Air Ferries, 10

Kleinwort Benson, arranges merger of Caledonian and B.U.A., 270

Klemetsen, R., negotiates with Loftleidir, 306

Kluge, John (executive aircraft owner), 67

Knights of Columba, Caledonian group charter, 263

Korean Air Lines, aggresive marketing, 375

Korean airlift, by Transocean, 107, 112

Kristjansson, K. J., represents Loftleidir, 306

Kung Lin-Kai (Shelton's silent partner), buys shares, 337, 340

Laker, Sir Freddie: collapse of Skytrain, 161; Edward Hillman the prototype, 213; complete profile, 241–58; succeeds British Caledonian on North Atlantic, 273; claim as first cheap fare reviewed, 299; Icelandair competes, 313

Laker Airways, 247–58

La Ligne (Ligne Latécoère), founded, 285

La Luz mine, equipped by TACA, 324

Lancaster bomber, used by T.C.A., 171

Lane, W. Lloyd, president of Texas International, 141

LANEP (Nicaraguan airline), purchased by Yerex, 323

Large Irregular Carriers, 121

Latécoère, Pierre-Georges (French airline pioneer), 285

Latécoère 28, aircraft used by Mermoz on epic flight, 290

Latécoère 38, bizarre episode, 289–97

Latécoère 300, French flying boat, 295, 296

Latécoère 521, French flying boat, 295

Laurent-Eynac, Victor (French air minister), agreement with Bouilloux-Lafont, 291, 295

Lawrence, Harding, Pioneer Airlines vice-president, 37

Leche, John H. (British envoy in Gua-

temala), supports Yerex cause,
327–28

Lehman Brothers, association with
T.W.A., 52

Leslie, Eric (stage name of Eric
Gandar Dower), 230

Levien, Cecil J.: recognizes importance of air transport, 387; Ansett
genealogy, 407

Lewin, Jack B. (founder of Viking Air
Lines), 87

L.I.A. (Italian airline), stock purchased by T.W.A., 330

Ligne Latécoère, founded, 285

Lindbergh, Charles A.: Pan American
technical director, 25; T.A.T. technical adviser, 52; comparison with
Hughes, 56

Líneas Aéreas de Nicaragua Empresa
Palacios. *See* LANEP

Líneas Aéreas Occidentales. *See*
L.A.O.

Lloyd's Bank, purchases First Western from Daly, 128

Lockheed Vega: L.A.O. (Varney), 11;
Varney Southwestern Division, 13;
Earhart's airplane, flown by Carmi-
chael, 67; operated by C.A.T., 319

Lockheed Orion (Model 9): Varney
Speed Lines, 8; crash at Hayward,
Calif., 11, L.A.O. (Varney), 11

Lockheed L-10 Electra: with T.C.A.,
171; TACA, 323; B.W.I.A., 328;
Ansett, 402, 404

Lockheed L-12: purchased by Continental, 33; TACA, 323

Lockheed L-14: Hughes flies around
the world, 51; called Flying Laboratory, 56; T.C.A., 171; TACA, 323

Lockheed L-18 Lodestar: with Continental, 34; Yukon Southern, 179;
TACA, 323

Lockheed L-049 Constellation: association with Hughes, 51; specifications, 53; Capital Airlines, 76; later
development, 58

Lockheed L-1049 Super Constellation: development, 58; World Airways, 125

Lockheed L-1649A Starliner: development and service, 58–59; World Airways, 125

Lockheed L-188 Electra: ordered by

Capital, 80; operated by A.N.A.,
406; Ansett, 408

Loening, Grover, approves Hughes
Hercules, 55

Loening amphibian aircraft, owned
by John Kluge, 67

Loftleidir, Icelandic airline: offers
low fares across Atlantic, 96; history, 300–311

Loftleidir-Braathens partnership, 306

Loftleidir Hotel, 309

LOGAIR (Logistics Air Lift) Contract,
World Airways, 124, 128–29

Loganair, comparison with Highland
Airways, 220

Loh, Robin, leases aircraft to Air
Siam, 374

London Aero Motor Service, employs
Laker, 242

London and North Eastern Railway
(L.N.E.R.), transports aircraft
parts, 224; competes with airlines,
236

London, Midland and Scottish Railway (L.M.S.): owns half of Scottish
Airways, 223; employs Thomson's
father, 260

Lord Brothers, purchased by Laker,
247

Lorenzo, Frank: acquires Continental
Airlines, 44; complete profile, 137–
52; meets Donald Burr, 155; buys
PEOPLExpress, 166

Lozano, Julio (Shelton shareholder),
337

Ludington Airlines, J. H. Carmichael
as pilot, 67

Lufthansa (or Luft Hansa), Deutsche
(prewar): inaugurates South American air service, 288; dispute in Iceland, 302

Lufthansa (postwar): sells Boeing
737s to Burr, 157; sends
nastigrams, 257

Luis, Washington (president of Brazil), meets O'Neill, 17

Lumholdt, Niels, acknowledges debt
to Air Siam, 378

Lyle (shipping company), provides
capital for Caledonian, 267

MAC (Military Airlift Command), Continental contract, 41

McAndrews, Edward, forms Twentieth Century Airlines, 87

MacArthur, General Douglas, grants permit to McConachie, 183

McBain, Major Willie, associated with Fresson, 215

McBrayne, David, associated with L.M.S. Railway, 223

McConachie, Grant, complete profile, 169–86

McCracken, William (chairman of NYRBA), 24

McDonald, John J. (author), on Howard Hughes, 50

Macdonald, P. J. (partner of Parer), 390

McDonnell Douglas Corporation: relationship with Laker, 254; receives nastigrams, 257

McDonnell Douglas DC-10: with Continental, 42; World, 135; Chicago crash, 135, 251–52, 274, 312; Wardair, 197; Laker Skytrain, 242, 250; photographed, 245, 349; with British Caledonian, 273–74; Icelandair, 312; Air Siam, 376

McDonnell Douglas MD-11, British Caledonian order, 280

McDonnell Douglas MD-80, purchased by Continental, 147

McIntosh, John Cove (associate of Parer), 384–85

McIntosh, Captain William (associate of Prince Varanand), 367–70

Mackenzie Air Service: operates in northern Canada, 179; influence on Max Ward, 187

Mackey, Bill, Laker receivership, 255

McLaren, Black Mike, strikes gold, 174

Maclay, Hardy (counsel for Stan Weiss), 95

McLean, Dan (Canadian Air Transport Board member), admonishes Ward, 190

McLean, Margaret (Mrs. Grant McConachie), 176

Macrae and Dick, Inverness motor vehicle dealers, 217

MacRobertson-Miller Airlines, 407, 409

MacRobertson Trophy Race, Parer participates in, 395

McWilliam, James, invests in Caledonian Airways, 262

Madang Air Services, 407, 409

Malaysian Airline System, aggressive marketing, 395

Mali airlift (World Airways), 136

Mandated Airlines: formation, 397; taken over by Ansett, 407, 409

Martin, Augustine, hired by World Airways, 122

Martin 2-0-2, operated by Pioneer Air Lines, 37

MATS (Military Air Transport Service): Transocean contract, 107; World Airways, 123, 124, 126

May, Wop: Canadian airline pioneer, 180; visits Orient with McConachie, 183; influence on Max Ward, 187–88

Mayo, W. B. (Ford Motor Company) (NYRBA director), 19

Meadows, Audrey (third Mrs. Robert Six), 40

Merman, Ethel (second Mrs. Robert Six), 37

Mermoz, Jean (French airman), 284, 290

Michael, Prince, supports Laker, 255

Mid-Continent Airlines, employs Shelton, 335

Midland and Scottish Air Ferries (and Airways), absorbed by Whitehall Securities, 222

Military Airlift Command. See MAC

Military Air Transport Service. See MATS

Mills, Ernie, teaches aircraft maintenance to Ward, 189

Minnesota Enterprises, buys Texas airline, 140

Moare, Jack (associate of Max Ward), 189

Moffett, Admiral William A., cooperates with O'Neill, 18

Moloney, Guy (Irish adventurer), associate of Yerex, 320

Moltrop, Merle (veteran airline pilot), 67

Monospar ST 4, aircraft flown by Highland Airways, 217

Monro, C. Bedell, association with P.C.A. airline, 68–73

"Montenegro, Battle of," NYRBA–Pan American dispute, 23

Morlae Airlines, 390, 393

Mornington Race Club, patronized by Ansett, 411

Morris, Christopher (Laker liquidator), 257

Mountbatten, Earl, guest aboard British Caledonian inaugural flight, 271

Mueller, Louis H.: advises Varney, 7; finances Varney airline, 13, 32

Munson, Frank C. (director of NYRBA), 19

Munson Steamship Line, interest in NYRBA, 19

Murchison, Charles (chairman of Capital Airlines committee), 79

Murdoch News, Ltd., controls Ansett corporation, 411

Murray, Sir Hubert, flies with Parer, 391

Muse Air, competes with Continental Airlines, 43

Mustard, A. E. (pilot for Guinea Gold), 387

Nagamati, Gun, conspires in Thai strike, 377

Nastigrams sent to McDonnell Douglas, 257

National Aeronautics Association, names Hughes aviator of the year, 51

National Air Carrier Association, rejects Laker fares, 254

National Airlines: interchange agreement with Capital, 76; purchased by Pan American, 142

National Aviation Corporation, joined by Burr, 155

National Geographic (magazine), publishes article on NYRBA, 27

Neal, W. M. (Canadian Pacific Railway executive), 180–81

Nelson, Orvis: Trust Territory operations, 41; complete profile, 101–18

New Guinea Centenary Flight Syndicate, 395

New South Wales, Airlines of, Ansett subsidiary, 407–8

New York Air: formed, 142; competition from PEOPLExpress, 160

New York, Rio and Buenos Aires Airline. *See* NYRBA

Newark Air Service, J. H. Carmichael as instructor, 66

Newark Airport, examined and selected by Burr, 156

Nicaragua, Líneas Aéreas de, Empresa Palacios. *See* LANEP

Nicholson, George, forms Northern and Scottish Airways, 223

Nighthawk (Capital Airlines), 75

Nixon, Richard M.: approves control of Air West by Hughes, 62; denies Laker route award, 251

Noorduyn Norseman, with Flugfelag, 302

Nordeste (Brazilian airline), founded by Fontana, 356

North American Airlines, 83–99

North Eastern Airways, connects with Aberdeen Airways, 235

North Star aircraft, Canadian-built DC-4s, 182

Northeast Airlines: Hughes gains control of, 61; buys P.C.A. aircraft and discusses merger, 73

Northern Airways, buys McConachie's Ford, 176

Northern and Scottish Airways, merges into Scottish Airways, 223

Northern Exploration, sells aircraft to McConachie, 175

Northrop, Jessie (Mrs. J. H. Carmichael), 66

Northrop Gamma, transcontinental speed record, 51

Northwest Airlines (Northwest Orient): T.W.A. association, 57; proposed merger with Capital, 76; association with Transocean, 107; with Thai Airways, 366

NYRBA, 15–29

NYRBA do Brasil: formed, 22; changes name to Panair do Brasil, 25

N.Z.N.A.C. (New Zealand airline), 409

Oakes, Doc, remembered by Max Ward, 187

Oakes, Harry, sells Ford Tri-Motor to McConachie, 175

O'Carroll, Scotty, employs Ed Daly, 121

Occidentales, Líneas Aéreas. *See* L.A.O.

Odlum, Floyd, acquires Transocean stock, 114–16

Olafsson, Sigurdur (founder of Loftleidir), 300

Olason, O., represents Loftleidir, 306

"Old Santa Fe Trail" (Continental Airlines promotion), 33

Olsen, Kristian (founder of Loftleidir), 300

O.N.A., leases aircraft to Air Siam, 373

ONAT (Orvis Nelson Air Transport), 104

O'Neill, Ralph, complete profile, 15–30

Ontario Securities Commission, irritant to Wardair, 199

OPEC (Organization of Petroleum Exporting Countries), effect on airlines, 272

Orient Airways, buys P.I.A. aircraft, 108

Orkney and Shetland Steam Navigation Company, supports Fresson, 217

Orvis Nelson Air Transport. *See* ONAT

Outlaw, The (Hughes film), 50

Overseas National Airlines. *See* O.N.A.

Overseas Visitors Club, associated with Caledonian, 262

Pacific Air Transport, founded by Vern Gorst, 8

Pacific Airlines, merges into Air West, 62

Pacific Alaska Airways, developed by Pan American, 179

Pacific Overseas Airways, transpacific contract, 104

Pacific Southwest Airlines. *See* P.S.A.

Pakistan International Airlines. *See* P.I.A.

P.A.L.: association with Transocean, 105–7; with T.W.A., 330

PANAGRA: competes with NYRBA, 19; formation, 20–21; fares policy, 339; protests TAN permit, 342; acquired by Braniff, 343

Pan American Airways: competes with Varney, 11–12; Trippe leadership, 15; formed by Trippe, 18; purchases NYRBA, 25; Robert Six as employee, 32; Trust Territory operations, 41; Constellation purchase, 56–57; dominance challenged by T.W.A., 57; orders jets, 59; sabotages Transocean installations, 108; purchases National Airlines, 142; develops Pacific Alaska Airlines, 179; competes with Laker, 254; financial difficulties, 256; named in Laker lawsuit, 257; objects to Caledonian Case award, 264; reacts to formation of TACA, 326; fares policy in South America, 339; protests TAN permit, 342; alliance with Thai Airways, 366; Air Siam as threat, 372

Pan American-Grace Airways. *See* PANAGRA

Panair do Brasil: name changed from NYRBA do Brasil, 25; Fontana as copilot, 347

Pangborn, Clyde (colleague of Yerex), 318

Papua New Guinea, operating environment (map), 388

Papua New Guinea, Airlines of, Ansett subsidiary, 407–9

Parer, Ray, complete profile, 383–98

Pareti, Harold: launches PEOPLExpress service to London, 161; president, 166; founds Pesidential Airways, 166

P.A.T. (Pacific Aerial Transport): history, 393–97; Ansett genealogy, 407

P.B.A., purchased by PEOPLExpress, 164–65

P.C.A.: created by merger, 69; name changed to Capital, 75

"Path of the Eagle" (Clifford Ball airline), 68

Patterson, William (president of United Air Lines): underestimates Atlantic air market, 58; declines opportunity to enter Pacific, 103; gives CV440 to Arthur Godfrey, 130

Peanuts Fares, Texas International promotion, 141

Pearson, Clive (head of B.O.A.C.), receives letter from Yerex, 328
"Pelo Ar par seu Lar" (Sadia slogan), 348
Pennsylvania Airlines (and Transport Co.) (ancestor of Capital Airlines), 67–69
Pennsylvania-Central Airlines. *See* P.C.A.
Pennsylvania Railroad, association with T.W.A., 52
People's bus service, absorbed by London Transport, 207
PEOPLExpress: history, 153–66; comparison with Laker Airways, 258
Percival Prentice, aircraft converted by Laker, 244
Peruanas, Aerolíneas (APSA), Shelton airline, 338, 341
Philippine Air Lines. *See* P.A.L.
Phillips, Barney, hires McConachie, 174
P.I.A., association with Transocean, 107–8
Pierson, Lewis (NYRBA director), 19
Pigeon, George, forms Yellowknife Airways with Ward, 190
Pilgrim aircraft, operated by TACA, 323
Pioneer Air Lines, acquired by Continental, 36
Pittsburgh Airways, ancestor of P.C.A./Capital, 67
Playboy Bunnies employed by Continental Airlines, 37
Poincaré, Raymond (president of France), 295
Polaris Charter Company, formed by Ward, 189
Polynesian Pub (Continental Airlines service), 42
Pongse Punakanta, Lieut. General (Thai Minister), 369
Ponte Aerea. *See* Brazilian air shuttle
Poomchusri, Metta (Thai International shareholder), 377
Porterfield aircraft, flown by Ansett, 402
Post, Wiley: record broken by Hughes, 51; flies into Edmonton, 173; flies with C.A.T., 319
Potez (French aircraft manufacturer), 291

Potez 25, aircraft used by Aéropostale, 288
Pounds, Dr. T. C., operates airline in Honduras, 319
Prairie Air Mail, 173
Pratt & Whitney Aircraft Company, O'Neill as Latin American agent, 16
Prescott, Robert W. (founder of Flying Tigers), leases aircraft to Stan Weiss, 87; low bidder for transpacific contract, 105
President (Capital Airlines Viscount service), 77
"Proud Bird with the Golden Tail" (Continental slogan), 42
Provincetown-Boston Airlines. *See* P.B.A.
P.S.A.: competes with Continental Airlines, 43; formed by Ken Friedkin, 89

QANTAS: connects with Butler, 406; hands over New Guinea routes to T.A.A., 408
Queensland Airlines, 407

R. & R. (Rest and Rehabilitation) flights (World), 128
Raad, J., negotiates with Loftleidir, 306
Rama VII (king of Siam) (uncle of Prince Varanand), 364–65
Rand, James (president of corporation), backs O'Neill, 18
R.A.S. (Railway Air Services): challenged by Hillman, 210; association with A.A.J.C., 238
Reagan, Ronald: declines offer of CV440, 130; intervenes in Laker lawsuit, 257
REAL (Brazilian airline), 352–53
Rede Integração Nacional. *See* RIN
Remington Rand Corporation, backs O'Neill, 18
Reynolds, James E. (NYRBA director), 19
Richter, Paul, discusses T.W.A. purchase with Hughes, 52
Rickenbacker, Eddie, relations with Stan Weiss, 89
Ridley, Nicholas (U.K. transport secretary), supports Thomson, 278

Riggins, John, compared with Lorenzo, 138
RIN (Brazilian airline system), 353
Ritchie, Ian, Thomson's marketing director, 265
Rizley, Ross (chairman of C.A.B.), in N.A.A. case, 95
Roberts, T. Glover (U.S. bankruptcy judge), disallows union claims, 148
Robertson, Sir McPherson: sponsors air race, 395; Ansett connection, 407
Rockne, Knute, killed in crash, 10–11
Rodgie, Jean, meets Thomson, 261
Roedean School for Girls, site of Gandar Dower's fist airplane flight, 229
Rolls-Royce car: owned by Hillman, 210; by Laker, 243; promised to Fontana, 347
Rolls Royce 400, name for Canadair CL-44, 309
Rolls-Royce Dart engine: powers Viscount, 76; promotional value, 77; powers ATL90, 244
Rolls-Royce Tyne engine, in Canadair CL-44, 309
Roosevelt, Franklin D.: cancels air mail contracts, 12; presents Collier Trophy to Hughes, 51
Rose, Franklin (Varney pilot and partner), 8
Rowland, Roland, plan to revive Laker Airways, 255
Royal Aeronautical Service (Siam), 366
Royal Air Force, Prince Veranand's career in, 365–66
Royal Australian Air Force, requisitions Parer aircraft, 396
Royal Flying Corps, Lowell Yerex as pilot, 317
Royal Humane Society, presents award to Gandar Dower, 230
Royal Swan Service (Transbrasil), 355
Royal Thai Air Force, association with T.A.C., 368
Rupner, Brigit (Mrs. Donald Burr), 155
Ryan Brougham, operated by C.A.T., 319

SABENA (Belgian airline): sends nastigrams, 257; leases aircraft to Caledonian, 262; sells aircraft to P.A.T., 394
Saber Air, joint service with British Caledonian, 271
Sadia (acronym for Brazilian company), 346
Sadia, S.A.–Transportes Aereos, 351–55
St. Exupéry, Antoine de (French pilot), 286, 290
St. George the Second (nickname of Fresson pilot), 226
Salvador, Transportes Aéreos (T.A.S.), acquired by Fontana, 353
Sanderson, Bobby, employs Laker, 242
S.A.S. (Scandinavian airline): sends nastigrams, 257; competes with Loftleidir, 304; protests Loftleidir activity, 311; association with Thai Airways, 366–68; withdraws from Thai association, 378
Saudi Arabian Airlines, technical assistance from T.W.A., 330
SCADTA (Colombo-German airline), 290
Scarface (Hughes film), 50
SCELA (Société Centrale), forms Air France, 293
Schleit, Philip: comments on Yerex, 326; quoted on aguardiente, 335
Schoenfeldt, Bill: sells ENTA to Yerex, 323; founding of ENTA by, 334
Scotsman, The (newspaper delivered by Highland Airways), 218
Scottish Airways, association with Fresson, 223–26
Scottish Aviation, leases aircraft to Flugfelag, 302
Scottish Motor Traction Company, associated with John Sword, 223
Seaboard World Airlines, leases Super Constellations from Weiss, 97
Second Force airline (U.K.): recommended by Edwards Report, 269; as British Caledonian, 277
Senate Aviation Subcommittee, Robert Six's testimony, 44
Senate Interstate and Foreign Com-

merce Committee, hearings on non-scheduled carriers, 90

Senate Select Committee on Small Business, reviews nonscheduled carriers, 90–91

"Seven Planes That Stayed Home" (P.C.A. wartime fleet), 71

S.G.T.A. (French airline, component of Air France), 291, 293

Sharp, Walter, association with Howard Hughes, Sr., 48–49

Shatto, Stan (chief of Continental maintenance), 34

Shell Oil Company of Thailand (Air Siam shareholder), 375

Shelton, C. N.: succeeds Yerex, 330; complete profile, 333–344

Sherman, Colonel Charles (airline entrepreneur), 85

Shore, Peter (U.K. Trade Secretary), issues C.A.A. guidelines, 251

Short Brothers, employ Laker as teaboy, 241

Short Scion (Aberdeen Airways), 232

Sierra Leone Airways, associated with British Caledonian, 272

Sikorsky S-38, with NYRBA, 18–23

Sikorsky S-39, used by Air Ferries, Ltd., 10

Silver City Airways: competes with Laker, 244; Adam Thomson as pilot, 261

Simmons, George, buys McConachie's Ford, 176

Sithi-Amnuai, Paul, takes over Air Siam, 377

Six, Henriette (first Mrs. Robert Six), 37

Six, Robert: purchases interest in Varney, 13; complete profile, 31–46; discusses merger with Capital, 79; under siege, 144–45

Six-Guns (Continental team), 37

Sixth Freedom of the Air: Loftleidir, 308–9; Shelton's plan, 340; TAN challenges, 342

"Sky Trails" (Loftleidir), 300

Skycoach (Capital Airlines), 75

Skystreamer, Continental DC-3, 35

Skytrain, history, 249–55; competition from Icelandair, 313

Slusser, W. Peter, influences Donald Burr, 155

Smith, Adam (Highland Airways pilot), 225

Smith, Keith, arrives in Australia, 385

Smith, Robert Cowell, influences Gandar Dower, 231

Smith, Ross, arrives in Australia, 385

Sociedade Portuguesa de Estudos e Linhas Aereas. *See* SPELA.

Société Centrale pour l'Exploitation de Lignes Aériennes. *See* SCELA.

Somaliland airlift (World Airways), 136

Soriano, Colonel Andres, charters aircraft from Transocean, 105

South Australia, Airlines of (Guinea Airways), 407–8

South Pacific Airlines of New Zealand. *See* SPANZ

Southern Airlines, absorbed by Ansett, 408

Southwest (airline), competes with Continental, 43

Sowapa, Queen (grandmother of Prince Varanand), 363

SPANZ (Ansett subsidiary), 407, 409

Sparkman, John (senator) (chairman of hearings on nonscheduled carriers), 90

Spartan Airlines, merges to form British Airways, 212, 222

SPELA (Sociedade Portuguesa de Estados e Linhas Aereas): formed by French interests, 294–96

Spirit of St Louis, serviced by Yerex, 318

Sportsman's Trophy, won by Hughes, 50

"Spruce Goose" (Hughes Hercules), 55

Stadden, Marvin, acquires irregular carrier certificate, 120

Standard Air Lines, 86

Starling, Eric: comments on Hillman, 207; on Fresson, 222; on Scottish flying, 224, 226; early career, 232–33

Stearman C3B (and other type): with Varney, 6; TACA, 323

Stewart, Flora (shareholder in P.A.T.), 393

Stinson aircraft, TACA's first, 319

Stinson Model A, with Central, 69

Stinson Reliant, with Loftleidir, 301
Stinson Station Wagon, flown by
    Max Ward, 190
Stinson trimotor, with Ludington
    and Pittsburgh, 67
Stroud, John, comments on
    Monospar, 225
Struthers, Major (guest on Aberdeen
    Airways inaugural), 232
Studebaker car, Ansett limousine ser-
    vice, 400
Suaqui Grande Mining and Milling
    Company, purchased by Varney, 13
Suda Siri Sotha, Princess (Air Siam
    stockholder), 375
Summa Corporation, pays Air West
    shareholders, 63
Super Starliners (Trans Texas Air-
    ways' DC-3s), 140
Supermarine Stranraer, with
    Wardair, 192
Supermarine Walrus, purchased by
    Thomson, 260
Supplemental carriers: Transocean
    the first, 107, 115; C.A.B. authority,
    122–23; World certificate, 124;
    clarification of status, 126
Surrey Flying Services, merges into
    Air Charter, 244
Swallow aircraft, with Varney, 3–5
Swidler, Mauri, forms Trans-
    American, 87
Swinging London Weekend (Caledo-
    nian marketing effort), 268
Swissair: sends nastigrams, 257; uses
    Air Siam, 373
Sword, John (Scottish airline opera-
    tor), 222–23

T.A.A.: Air Siam lease, 373; name
    adopted, 404; New Guinea service,
    408
T.A.C. (Thai airline), contract with
    S.A.S., 368
TACA: association with T.W.A., 57;
    formed and operated by Yerex,
    319–31
T.A.E. (Greek airline), purchased by
    T.W.A., 330
T.A.L. See Transocean Air Lines
Taloa Academy of Aeronautics, trains
    P.I.A. pilots, 108

TAN (Honduran airline): succeeds
    TACA, 330; operations, 337–38
Tarifa Economica Noturna. See TEN
Tarifas Diferenciadas (Brazilian air
    fares), 357
T.A.S. (Brazilian airline), acquired by
    Fontana, 353
Tasmanian Aerial Services (Ansett
    connection), 402, 407
Taves, Oscar and Roberto (founders
    of Aerovias Brasil), 329
T.C.A. See Trans Canada Airlines
Tebbitt, Norman (U.K. trade secre-
    tary), supports British Airways
    against Thomson, 278
TEN (Brazilian air tariff), 357
Texas Air Corporation: formed, 142;
    buys PEOPLExpress, 165
Texas International Airlines (TXI): ac-
    quires control of Continental, 44;
    name changed from Trans Texas
    Airways, 140
Thai Airways, 366
Thai Airways International (THAI):
    begins service, 367; strike by em-
    ployees of, 377
Thatcher, Margaret (British prime
    minister), supports Laker, 253, 255
Thomas, Charlie (president of
    T.W.A.), 60
Thompson, Bruce (federal judge),
    rules on Hughes Air West, 63
Thomson, Sir Adam: complete pro-
    file, 259–82; review of claim for
    first cheap fares, 299
3 and 8 Rule: established by C.A.B.,
    87; criticized, 91
Thurgood, W. L. (operator of People's
    bus service), 222
T.I.A., as supplemental airline, 116
"Tin Goose" (Ford Tri-Motor), 323
Tinker Toy Airways (Trans Texas Air-
    ways), 140
T.M.A. (Lebanese airline), supported
    by T.W.A., 330
Toolco (Hughes Tool Company): asso-
    ciation with T.W.A., 47–61; associa-
    tion with Air West, 62
Touche, Ross, and Company, files
    antitrust suit on behalf of Laker,
    257
"Trail of the Conquistadores" (promo-
    tional name of Varney), 13

Trans American Airlines, name changed from North American, 96

Trans-American Airways, 87

Trans-Australia Airlines. *See* T.A.A.

Trans-Canada Air Lines: contract with Transocean, 106–7; founding, 171; reluctance to fly Pacific route, 182; withdraws from South America, 183–84; operates Vanguard, 194

Trans International Airlines. *See* T.I.A.

Trans-National Airlines, 87

Trans Oceanic Airways (Ansett subsidiary), 405, 407

Trans Texas Airways, purchased by Jet Capital Corp., 140

Trans World Airlines. *See* T.W.A.

Transafricaine, Compagnie (Bouilloux-Lafont), 290

Transbrasil Airlines (U.S.A.), 358

Transbrasil Foundation, 356

Transbrasil (Brazilian airline), 355

Transcontinental Air Transport (T.A.T.), merges to form T.W.A., 51

Transcontinental and Western Air. *See* T.W.A.

Transocean Air Lines (T.A.L.): Trust Territory operations, 41; history, 104–16

Transpacific Route Case, 116

Transport Regulation Act (Australia), effect on Ansett, 401

Transportes Aéreos Centro-Americanos. *See* TACA

Transportes Aéreos Nacionales. *See* TAN

Travelair aircraft, operated by TACA, 323

Travellers International (Caledonian marketing effort), 268

Trimotor Safety Airways (name used by NYRBA), 17

Trippe, Juan: Pan American leadership, 15; upstages O'Neill, 23; challenged by American Export, 326

Trust Territory of the Pacific, airline operation: by Continental, 41; by Transocean, 112

T.T.A. *See* Texas International Airways

Tulio Gonzales, Marco, arranges TAN permits, 340–41

Turner, Roscoe, steals Carmichael's business, 66

T.W.A. (Transcontinental and Western Air, later Trans World Airlines): association with Howard Hughes, 47–62; name change, 57; bid to purchase, by Lorenzo, 149; competes with Laker, 254; named in Laker lawsuit, 257; objects to Caledonian Case award, 264; invests in TACA, 329; Shelton as pilot, 335

Twentieth Century Aircraft, 97

Twentieth Century Airlines (North American Airlines agency), 87; carries military personnel, 98

TXI. *See* Texas International Airlines

Ubico, General (dictator of Guatemala), 326

U.M.D.A., formed by Continental, 41

United Air Lines: controlled by Boeing, 54; offered Atlantic routes, 58; merger with Capital, 80; hires Nelson as copilot, 102; Transocean contract, 104–5, 107; leases from World, 128; subcontractor for Air Siam, 374

United Air Transport (Canada), 175–78

United Aircraft Corporation, buys Varney, 7

United Airways (U.K.), 212, 221–22

United Micronesia Development Association. *See* U.M.D.A.

United Service Organizations (U.S.O.), World contract, 129

United States Overseas Airlines, takes over Transocean routes, 116

Unwin, L. B. (first president of C.P.A.), 180

U.S. Army Air Transport Command, joined by Robert Six, 34

U.S. Navy, Transocean contract, 107, 109

U.S.O. *See* United Service Organizations

U.S.O.A. *See* United States Overseas Airlines

U.T.A. (French airline), sends nastigrams, 257

Vachet, Paul (Aéropostale pilot), 288

Vachon, Romeo (Canadian Air Transport Board member), admonishes Max Ward, 190
Valley Flying Service, founded by Six, 32
Van Arsdale, John (founder of P.B.A.), 165
Van Dusen, Bill (O'Neill's publicity specialist), 22
Vannukul, Virachai (consultant to Air Siam), 374–77
Varanair-Siam, 369–72
Varanand, Prince, complete profile, 363–82
VARIG: approached by Fontana, 350; buys REAL, 352–53; owns Cruzeiro do Sul, 356; monopoly of routes, 359
Varney, Ella (Walter's mother), 3, 5
Varney, Thomas (Walter's father), 3
Varney, Walter T.: complete profile, 3–14; founds Continental, 32
Varney Air Ferries, 9
Varney Air Lines, 4–9
Varney Air Transport, 9, 13, 32
Varney Speed Lanes, 8
Varney Speed Lines: and Air Service, 8–11; Southwest Division, 9, 12
VASP, Brazilian airline, competes with Fontana, 354
"VC-Tenderness" (B.O.A.C. slogan), 371
V.F.R. See Visiting Friends
Vickers Vanguard, operated by T.C.A., 194
Vickers Viscount: with Continental, 38; Capital, 67, 76–80; T.A.A., 405–6
Vickers VC-10: ordered by Laker, 246; with B.U.A., 270; Varanair's assessment of, 371
Victorian State Railways, competition eliminated, 401
Vidockler, Murray (investor in Caledonian), 262
Vié-Klaze, Marie-Paule (French author), comments on aircraft, 296
Vietnam War, World Airways involvement in, 123
Viking Air Lines, competes with Standard, 86–87
Virgin Atlantic, compared to Laker, 258

Visiting Friends and Relatives (V.F.R.) air traffic category: early growth, 262; price, 266

Waco aircraft: TACA operation, 323; Shelton barnstorming, 333
Wall Street Crash: effect on NYRBA, 23; on Bouilloux-Lafont, 291
War Production Board, approves Hughes Hercules, 55
Ward, Maxwell, complete profile, 187–204
Wardair (and associated companies), 192–201
Warren, Felix (stage coach driver), 5
Washington National Airport, problems of, 160–61
"We Really Move our Tail for You" (Continental slogan), 42
Weiller, Paul-Louis (head of Gnôme et Rhône): accused of wrongdoing, 292; forms SPELA, 294
Weiss, Stanley D., complete profile, 83–100
West African Airways Corporation, employs Thomson, 260
West Australian Airways, Ansett connection, 407
West Coast Airlines, merges into Air West, 62
West Indian Aerial Express, bought by Trippe, 20
Western Air Express, merges with T.A.T. to form T.W.A., 51
Western Australia, Airlines of, Ansett subsidiary, 407, 409
Western Canada Airways: pioneers Prairie Air Mail, 173; influence on Max Ward, 187
Wheatcroft, Stephen, reviews Canadian air routes, 184
Wheeler, Herb (head of Whitepass company), confronts McConachie, 177
Wheless, Judge R. F., Jr., denies union motions in Continental Chapter 11 Case, 146–47
"Whispering Giant": Bristol Britannia nickname, 184; Canadair CL-44, 309
White Russians, airlift of (Transocean), 107, 109
Whitehall Securities (British finan-

cial group): divides U.K. domestic air routes, 212; forms United Airways, 221; takes over small operators, 222

Whitepass company, confronts McConachie, 177

Williams, Captain Bill (Caledonian pilot), 263–64

Wilson, Max (shareholder in Caledonian), 262

Wiltshire, W. P. (Parer pilot), 390

Winnie Mae (Post and Gatty aircraft), influence on McConachie, 173

Woods, Harold (Hillman pilot), 209

World Airways: supplemental function, 116; history, 119–36

Worldamerica Investors Corp., formed by Daly, 128

Wright Whirlwind engine, used by Varney, 6

Wyatt, Miles (chairman of B.U.A.), dispute with Laker, 245–47

Wyoming Air Service, purchased by Continental, 33

Yellow Cabs, association with T.W.A., 52

Yellowknife Airways, formed by Max Ward, 190

Yerex, Antonietta (Mrs. Lowell Yerex), 321, 330–31

Yerex, David (nephew and biographer of Lowell Yerex), 331

Yerex, Lowell, complete profile, 317–332; employs Shelton, 335

Youth Argosy, Transocean contract, 107, 112

Yukon Southern Air Transport, formed by McConachie, 179

The photographs in this book were sometimes provided by the profiled subjects themselves, notably the Prince Varanand, Sir Adam Thomson, Sir Freddie Laker, and Omar Fontana; by their widows: Jessie Carmichael, Jane O'Neill, June Daly, and Edith Nelson; by Allan Weiss (son of Stan Weiss) and Guillemette de Bure (granddaughter of Marcel Bouilloux-Lafont); also by their good friends, Eric Starling (Eric Gandar Dower), John Stroud (Edmund Fresson), Mike Ramsden (Edward Hillman), Charlie Mathews (Lowell Yerex), Philip Schleit (C. N. Shelton) and Terry Gwynn-Jones (Ray Parer). Other pictures were selected from the files of the National Air and Space Museum, which, in turn, is indebted to many airlines for the strength and depth of its collection. The maps and chart are by the author.